THE CAMBRIDGE COMPANION TO OCKHAM

Each volume of this series of companions to major philosophers contains specially commissioned essays by an international team of scholars, together with a substantial bibliography, and will serve as a reference work for students and nonspecialists. One aim of the series is to dispel the intimidation such readers often feel when faced with the work of a difficult and challenging thinker.

The Franciscan William of Ockham (c. 1288–1347) was an English medieval philosopher, theologian, and political theorist. Along with Thomas Aquinas and John Duns Scotus, he is regarded as one of the three main figures in medieval philosophy after around 1150. Ockham is important not only in the history of philosophy and theology but also in the development of early modern science and of modern notions of property rights and church-state relations.

This volume offers a full discussion of all significant aspects of Ockham's thought: logic, philosophy of language, metaphysics and natural philosophy, epistemology, ethics, action theory, political thought, and theology. It is the first study of Ockham in any language to make full use of the new critical editions of his works and to consider recent discoveries concerning his life, education, and influences.

New readers will find this the most convenient and accessible guide to Ockham currently available. Advanced students and specialists will find a conspectus of recent developments in the interpretation of Ockham.

Paul Vincent Spade is Professor of Philosophy at Indiana University.

D0322242

CAMBRIDGE COMPANIONS TO PHILOSOPHY

The Cambridge Companion to
OCKHAM

Edited by

Paul Vincent Spade
Indiana University

CAMBRIDGE
UNIVERSITY PRESS

PUBLISHED BY THE PRESS SYNDICATE OF THE UNIVERSITY OF CAMBRIDGE
The Pitt Building, Trumpington Street, Cambridge, United Kingdom

CAMBRIDGE UNIVERSITY PRESS
The Edinburgh Building, Cambridge CB2 2RU, UK   www.cup.cam.ac.uk
40 West 20th Street, New York, NY 10011-4211, USA   www.cup.org
10 Stamford Road, Oakleigh, Melbourne 3166, Australia
Ruiz de Alarcón 13, 28014 Madrid, Spain

First published 1999

Printed in the United States of America

Typeface Trump Medieval 10/13 pt.   *System* LATEX 2$_\varepsilon$ [TB]

*A catalog record for this book is available from
the British Library.*

Library of Congress Cataloging-in-Publication Data

The Cambridge companion to Ockham / edited by Paul Vincent Spade.
     p.   cm.
    Includes bibliographical references (p.   ) and index.
    ISBN 0-521-58244-X
    1. William, of Ockham, ca. 1285-ca. 1349.   2. Philosophy, Medieval.
I. Spade, Paul Vincent.
    B765.O34C36   1999
    189'.4 – DC21   98-38076
                                                            CIP

ISBN 0 521 58244 x hardback
ISBN 0 521 58790 5 paperback

In Memory of Gedeon Gál

CONTENTS

ix

CONTRIBUTORS

MARILYN MCCORD ADAMS is professor of historical theology at the Yale Divinity School and of religious studies at Yale University. She is cotranslator of *William Ockham: Predestination, God's Fore-knowledge, and Future Contingents* and author of the study *William Ockham* as well as of other publications on Ockham, medieval philosophy, and philosophy of religion.

DAVID CHALMERS is professor of philosophy and associate director of the Center for Consciousness Studies at the University of Arizona and a former member of the Philosophy Board, Humanities Division, at the University of California, Santa Cruz. He is author of *The Conscious Mind: In Search of a Fundamental Theory* and of other publications in the philosophy of consciousness.

WILLIAM J. COURTENAY is Charles Homer Haskins professor of history at the University of Wisconsin, Madison. His publications on medieval intellectual history include *Adam Wodeham: An Introduction to His Life and Thought* and *Schools and Scholars on Fourteenth-Century England*.

ALFRED J. FREDDOSO is professor of philosophy at the University of Notre Dame. He is cotranslator of *Ockham's Theory of Propositions: Part II of the Summa logicae* and of *William of Ockham: Quodlibetal Questions* as well as author of papers on medieval philosophy and philosophy of religion.

ANDRÉ GODDU is associate professor of philosophy at Stonehill College, where he has also served as director of the Program in History and Philosophy of Science. He is author of *The Physics of William of Ockham* and other writings in the history and philosophy of science.

xi

ELIZABETH KARGER is affiliated with the Centre Nationale de la Recherche Scientifique in Paris. She is author of "Mental Sentences According to Burley and to the Early Ockham" and other articles on Ockham's metaphysics, logic, and semantics as well as on late medieval philosophy.

JOHN KILCULLEN is professor in the School of History, Philosophy, and Politics at Macquarie University. He is translator of Ockham's *A Short Discourse on Tyrannical Government* and *A Letter to the Friars Minor*, coeditor and translator of Ockham's *Dialogue*, and author of other publications in the history of political thought.

PETER KING is associate professor of philosophy at the Ohio State University. He is translator of *John Buridan's Logic: The Treatise on Supposition, The Treatise on Consequences* and of *Augustine: Against the Academicians and The Teacher* and author of other publications on medieval philosophy.

GYULA KLIMA is a member of the Institute of Philosophy, Budapest; and has been a member of the Departments of Philosophy at Yale University and the University of Notre Dame. He is author of *Ars Artium: Essays in Philosophical Semantics, Medieval and Modern* and other publications in medieval metaphysics and semantics.

A. S. MCGRADE is professor emeritus of philosophy at the University of Connecticut. His publications include *The Political Thought of William of Ockham* and other writings on Ockham.

CALVIN G. NORMORE is professor of philosophy at the University of Toronto and the University of California, Los Angeles. His publications include "Ockham on Mental Language" and Chapter 18 ("Future Contingents") in *The Cambridge History of Later Medieval Philosophy*.

CLAUDE PANACCIO is professor of philosophy at the Université du Québec à Troi-Rivières. His publications include *Les mots, les concepts et les choses: La sémantique de Guillaume d'Occam et le nominalisme d'aujourdhui* and other writings on Ockham and medieval philosophy.

PAUL VINCENT SPADE is professor of philosophy at Indiana University. He is translator of *Five Texts on the Mediaeval Problem of*

Universals and of *Peter Abelard: Ethical Writings* and author of other publications on medieval philosophy, logic, and semantics.

ELEONORE STUMP is Robert J. Henle professor of philosophy at Saint Louis University. She is coeditor of *The Cambridge Companion to Aquinas* and author of several books and articles in medieval philosophy and philosophy of religion, including *Dialectic and Its Place in the Development of Medieval Logic*.

REGA WOOD is senior research scholar in the Department of Philosophy, Yale University, and adjunct professor of the Yale Divinity School. She is coeditor of two volumes of Ockham's *Opera theologica*, principal editor of Adam Wodeham's *Lectura secunda in I Sententiarum*, translator of Ockham's *De connexione virtutum* (under the title *Ockham on the Virtues*), and author of other publications on medieval philosophy and theology.

ABBREVIATIONS AND METHOD
OF CITATION

Primary sources are cited in as abbreviated a form as will allow readers to locate passages readily in the Latin texts and English translations. In many instances, references are only by standard internal divisions. Where a more precise location is needed, page numbers in the Latin editions are included in parentheses. (For the critical editions of Ockham, the series and volume numbers are omitted in such references. They are listed in Section II of the Introduction.) References to translations are normally given only when references to the Latin are not enough. (For a list of translations keyed to the editions, see the Introduction, Section II.) A dagger (†) in a reference to the Latin indicates that, although the question or section referred to has been translated in part, the particular passage being cited is not translated. Other references in the notes are in abbreviated form, by author and date. For full publication information, see the Bibliography.

'Resp.' in a reference refers to an author's response to a question, and 'ad' to the reply to an objection.

The following abbreviations refer to individual writings and collections cited in the chapter notes. (For the political writings, the abbreviations conform to the list in OPol IV.xiii–xviii.) Numbers in parentheses following the abbreviations refer to items listed in the Introduction, Section II.

OCKHAM'S WRITINGS

OPh = *Opera philosophica*, in Ockham 1967–88.
OPol = *Opera politica*, in Ockham 1956–97.
OTh = *Opera theologica*, in Ockham 1967–88.

(The editors' introduction to volumes of OPh and OTh have page numbers marked by asterisks.)

Act. virt. = *Utrum voluntas possit habere actum virtuosum respectu alicuius obiecti respectu cuius est error in intellectu.* (19)

AP = *An princeps pro suo succursu, scilicet guerrae, possit recipere bona ecclesiarum, etiam invito papa.* (40) Cited by chapter.

Brev. = *Breviloquium.* (47) Cited by book and chapter.

Brev. Phys. = *Brevis summa libri Phyiscorum.* (30) Cited by book and chapter.

CB = *Tractatus contra Benedictum.* (45) Cited by book and chapter.

Centil. = *Centiloquium* (spurious). (37) Cited by thesis.

Connex. = *De connexione virtutum.* (18) Cited by article and line.

De fine = *De causalitate finis.* (5)

Dial. = *Dialogus.* (49) Cited by part, book, and chapter. Part III is divided into two tracts, cited as III-1 and III-2, and then into books and chapters.

Epist. = *Epistola ad fratres minores.* (43)

Expos. Elench. = *Expositio super libros Elenchorum.* (28)

Expos. Perih. = *Expositio in librum Perihermenias Aristotelis.* (26)

Expos. Phys. = *Expositio in libros Physicorum Aristotelis.* (29) Cited by book, chapter, and section.

Expos.Praed. = *Expositio in librum Praedicamentorum Aristotelis.* (25) Cited by chapter and section.

IPP = *De imperatorum et pontificum potestate.* (48)

OND = *Opus nonaginta dierum.* (42) Cited by chapter and, where necessary, line numbers. Line numbers restart with each chapter.

OQ = *Octo quaestiones de potestate papae.* (39) Cited by question, chapter and, where appropriate, line numbers.

Phil. nat. = *Summula philosophiae naturalis.* (31) Cited by book and chapter.

Praedest. = *Tractatus de praedestinatione et de praescientia dei respectu futurorum contingentium.* (27) Cited by question.

Proom. et Porph. = *Expositio in libros artis logicae, prooemium et expositio in librum Porphyrii de Praedicabilibus.* (24)

Qq. Phys. = *Quaestiones in libros Physicorum Aristotelis.* (32) Cited by question.

Quant. = *Tractatus de quantitate.* (21)

Quodl. = *Quodlibeta septem.* (20) Cited by quodlibet and question.

Sent. = *In libros Sententiarum.* (1) The abbreviation '*Sent.*' is used here for both the *Scriptum* (on Book I) and the *Reportatio* (on Books II–IV). References are to book and then, for the *Scriptum*, to the Prologue or distinction and question numbers; for the *Reportatio*, to book and question. When a distinction in the *Scriptum* has a single question, the question number is sometimes omitted in references.

SL = *Summa logicae.* (23) Cited by part and chapter number. Part III has four subparts, III-1 through III-4.

OTHER

PL = Migne 1844–64.

SCG = Thomas Aquinas, *Summa contra gentiles.* Cited by book and chapter.

Sch. = Anselm 1946–61 (= Schmitt edition). Cited by volume and page.

ST = Thomas Aquinas, *Summa theologiae.* Cited by part, question, and article. IaIIae = first part of the second part; IIaIIae = second part of the second part.

Introduction

Standard histories have long recognized that the three most important figures in the philosophy of the High Middle Ages were Thomas Aquinas (1224/5–74), John Duns Scotus (c. 1266–1308), and William of Ockham (c. 1288–1347).[1] Of the three, Aquinas is comparatively well known to modern readers, whereas Scotus and Ockham largely remain mere names.

Even Aquinas, however, is more foreign to students than Plato and Aristotle are, much less Descartes or Hume. Indeed, as Kretzmann and Stump have observed in *The Cambridge Companion to Aquinas*,[2] such unfamiliarity is characteristic of all medieval philosophy.[3] This sad fact is partly due to the scarcity of translations but more fundamentally to the lack of reliable modern editions of primary texts and thus of good critical analyses and studies of them in the secondary literature.

The situation does not arise from any lack of raw materials but instead, it might be argued, from just the opposite. There are many early printed editions from the late fifteenth and early sixteenth centuries and an enormous number of surviving manuscripts of medieval philosophy and theology. But the early editions are often unreliable, whereas the manuscripts frequently present wildly different versions of the same work. They are written in a highly compressed and arcane system of abbreviation, a kind of shorthand that requires special training to read; early printed editions often retain the same system. Frequently the manuscripts are incompletely cataloged or not cataloged at all, and thus their contents are discovered only by chance.

In such circumstances, it is a complicated and painstaking business to produce a reliable, modern edition of a philosophical text, and without such editions there can of course be no useful translations or

I

critical studies. It is no wonder, therefore, that even a major philosopher like Ockham remains largely unknown to modern readers.

Nevertheless, the situation has improved dramatically in recent decades. New and excellent editions of many works and authors have appeared. Ockham in particular has benefited, and we are now in a position to begin to appreciate and assess more confidently his true place in the history of philosophy. This development was made possible by the publication, between 1967 and 1988, of the first modern critical editions of all Ockham's philosophical and theological writings. The speedy completion of this enormous task by Gedeon Gál and his colleagues at the Franciscan Institute is one of the most impressive achievements of modern textual scholarship.[4] Ockham's political writings, which occupied him almost without pause from 1328 until his death in 1347, have likewise now all been critically edited with the exception of *Dial.*, which is in progress.[5]

With these editions, new and reliable translations have begun to appear. Although a much smaller portion of Ockham's work has been translated than, say, Aquinas's, a surprising amount is available in English, including several works in their entirety.[6] Likewise, there is now enough good secondary literature that curious readers can get a thorough grounding in all aspects of Ockham's thought. The most important secondary literature may be found by consulting the chapter notes and the Bibliography at the end of this volume, but the following sources in particular deserve special mention:

(1) For Ockham's philosophy and theology, with the exception of ethics and political theory, the indispensable starting point is Adams 1987a. There is no other work that studies a single medieval philosopher in such breadth and depth. Much briefer, but extremely clear and useful, is Chapter 3 of the introduction to Wood 1997. That chapter includes a discussion of Ockham's ethics as well. Indeed, it offers readers of the present volume an excellent orientation to Ockham's thought generally.

(2) For Ockham's ethics, Freppert 1988 is a good starting point, as is Adams 1986. The translation and commentary in Wood 1997 are superb.

(3) For Ockham's political philosophy, the best single study is undoubtedly McGrade 1974b.

Ockham's life was full of controversy. Although his philosophical and theological views were not in themselves especially radical, they generated considerable opposition even while he was still in his thirties.[7] In 1324 he was summoned to the papal court, then in Avignon, to answer charges of heresy. The pope then, John XXII, was engaged in controversy with the Franciscan order, to which Ockham belonged, over the notion of "apostolic poverty" – that is, over whether Jesus and the apostles owned property and had property rights, and therefore over whether the Franciscans' renunciation of all property could be regarded as an "imitation of Christ." On instructions from Michael of Cesena, the Franciscans' minister general, Ockham reviewed the situation and concluded that the pope was in heresy and so had ipso facto renounced his office.[8] In 1328 Ockham fled Avignon with the minister general and ended up in Munich, living out the rest of his life under the protection of Louis of Bavaria, the Holy Roman Emperor. It was during this time that Ockham composed most of his political writings, challenging the claims of John XXII and his successor, Benedict XII. Ockham died, excommunicated, in 1347.[9] So effective was he as a polemicist that at one point the pope threatened to burn down the city of Tournai if it failed to capture him and turn him over![10]

After such a contentious life, it is little wonder that the Franciscans failed to champion his cause, as they did for their confrere John Duns Scotus, or as the Dominicans did for their own Thomas Aquinas. There was never an Ockhamist "school" of philosophy as there was a Thomist or a Scotist school.[11] Indeed, well into this century, Ockham's name continued to carry the faint odor of disreputability and scandal in certain quarters.

Not surprisingly, this reputation sometimes led to Ockham's being cast, depending on a particular writer's sympathies, either in the role of the great destroyer of the medieval worldview or in the role of a herald of the new, modern era. David Knowles has summarized the situation aptly as follows:

Neglected in his turn for centuries, save as a bogy to scare young Thomists, he was re-discovered as an historical figure by the students of medieval thought who, followers as they were of Thomas or Duns, regarded him as Apollyon, the grand deceiver and destroyer who ruined the fabric of the golden age of medieval thought. Others again, in more recent years, have seen in him one of the great creators, one of that group of contemporaries in whose writings Cartesian philosophy, anti-papal reform, modern science and the secular state can be seen in embryonic form.[12]

Fortunately, recent scholarship permits a more realistic assessment of Ockham's position in medieval thought. Although it is true that he contributed to, and was part of, the intellectual and social transformations taking place in fourteenth-century Europe, he did not originate them, cannot bear sole responsibility for them (whether credit or blame), and did not even approve of all of them. In fact, the true situation is far more complex, as the essays in this volume show.

Beginning in the 1970s, English-speaking philosophers of a broadly "analytic" training came to regard Ockham as a kindred spirit. This development was prompted by the realization that Ockham and certain other medieval thinkers were not only sophisticated logicians and philosophers of language but had also – like twentieth-century analytic philosophy – applied their logical techniques and skills to a wide variety of philosophical problems.[13] Medieval philosophy, or at least certain parts of it, had suddenly become "legitimate."

No doubt much of Ockham's thinking is genuinely similar to recent analytic philosophical work; it would be foolish to deny it.[14] But it is equally foolish to view Ockham, or any past philosopher, *solely* through a present-day lens.[15] That approach, by filtering out what is unfamiliar, guarantees in advance that we never really learn anything new from the history of philosophy. Ideally, what should happen is that readers will use what seems already familiar in Ockham as a pathway to probe more deeply into his thought and into medieval thought generally, thereby encountering and coming to appreciate problems, techniques, and perspectives that had perhaps never occurred to them previously or that they had never found reason to take seriously before.

II. A CONSPECTUS OF OCKHAM'S WRITINGS

Ockham's writings are conventionally divided into two groups: academic and political works. Except for items 33–4 listed in Section II.1.3, this corresponds to a chronological division into works written

before Ockham fled Avignon in 1328 and those written afterwards. I
here list all Ockham's works, with the best Latin editions and English
translations. (The translations are not always based on the most recent editions.) Earlier translations of some items are listed in Beckmann 1992. For each item, the Latin title (and, where appropriate,
the abbreviation used in this volume) is followed by a translation of
that title. Works are listed in the order in which they are printed in
the critical editions.[16]

II.1. *Academic Writings*

The academic writings are published in a modern critical Latin edition, Ockham 1967–88, in two series: *Opera theologica* (OTh, 10
vols., 1967–86) and *Opera philosophica* (OPh, 7 vols., 1974–88).

II.1.1. THEOLOGICAL WORKS

1. *In libros Sententiarum* = *Sent.* (*Commentary on the Sentences*).
   Book I (*Scriptum*, completed shortly after July 1318). Books II–
   IV (*Reportatio*, 1317–18). Students progressing toward a degree
   in theology were required to lecture on the four books of Peter
   Lombard's *Sentences*, a standard textbook of the time. Ockham's
   lectures survive in two versions. For Book I we possess an *ordinatio* or *scriptum* – a text corrected, revised, and approved
   for dissemination by the author himself. For Books II–IV, we
   have only a *reportatio*. Unlike a *scriptum*, a *reportatio* is a tran-
   script of actual lectures, taken down by a "reporter." Such *re-
   portationes* are more reliable than modern-day students' "lecture notes" but have not had the benefit of the lecturer's careful revisions and corrections.[17] Ockham's *Scriptum* is divided
   into several "questions" on Lombard's Prologue and on each of
   the "distinctions" into which Book I of Lombard's *Sentences* is
   divided. The three books of the *Reportatio* dispense with "distinctions" (although Lombard has them) and are divided directly
   into "questions." The edition is distributed over OTh I–VII as
   follows: OTh I (I. Prol.–1.6); OTh II (I.2.1–3.10); OTh III (I.4.
   1–18.1); OTh IV (I.19.1–48.1); OTh V (II); OTh VI (III); OTh VII
   (IV). Translations: Boehner 1990, 18–25 (from I.Prol.1); Bosley
   and Tweedale 1997, 335–8, 419–25 (from I.2.3); Spade 1994,

114–231 (I.2.4–8, complete); Boehner 1990, 102–6 (from I.2.9); MacDonald and Pasnau forthcoming (I.27.3); Hyman and Walsh 1983, 679–86 (from I.30.1); Boehner 1990, 133–5 (from I.38), reprinted in Schoedinger 1996, 218–19; Adams and Kretzmann 1983, 80–95 (I.38–9, complete), I.38 reprinted in Bosley and Tweedale 1997, 301–7; Bosley and Tweedale 1997, 78–83 (from I.42), 83–9 (from I.43.1–2); Wippel and Wolter 1969, 447–54 (I.43.2, complete); Bosley and Tweedale 1997, 89–91 (from I.44); Hyman and Walsh 1983, 670–9 (from II.12–13),[18] 689 (from III.4).[19] The passage in Hyman and Walsh 1983, 693–700, described as from III.12, is in fact from item 18 listed in this section.

Two questions (dates unknown) that may be extracts or adaptations of parts of the lost *Reportatio* on Book I of the *Sentences*:

2. *De necessitate caritatis* (*On the Need for Charity*), OTh VIII. 3–27.
3. *Utrum anima sit subiectum scientiae* (*Is the Soul the Subject of Science?*), OTh VIII.28–55.

Three disputed questions, dates unknown:

4. *De aeternitate mundi* (*On the Eternity of the World*), OTh VIII. 59–97. Translation: Bosley and Tweedale 1997, 231–44.
5. *De causalitate finis* = *De fine* (*On Final Causality*), OTh VIII. 98–154.
6. *De intellectu agente* (*On the Agent Intellect*), OTh VIII.155–91.

Miscellaneous notes, discussions of doubtful points, statements of views (dates unknown except as noted):

7. *De locutione angelorum* (*On the Speech of Angels*), OTh VIII. 195–206. Dated after the *Reportatio*.
8. *Quid totum addit super partes* (*What a Whole Adds to the Parts*), OTh VIII.207–19.
9. *Discursus de peccato originali* (*Discourse on Original Sin*), OTh VIII.220–4. Consists of three brief notes, "*De peccato originali*" ("*On Original Sin*"), "*De necessitate absoluta gratiae*" ("*On the Absolute Need for Grace*"), and "*De speculo et obiecto*" ("*On the Mirror and Its Object*").
10. *De peccato originali in Beata Virgine* (*On Original Sin in the Blessed Virgin*), OTh VIII.224–7.
11. *De nugatione* (*On Nugation*), OTh VIII.228–33.

12. *De univocatione entis* (*On the Univocation of Being*), OTh VIII.
    233–7.
13. *De intellectu possibili secundum Averroem* (*On the Possible Intellect According to Averroes*), OTh VIII.237–43. Before *Reportatio* IV.4.
14. *De donis spiritus sancti* (*On the Gifts of the Holy Spirit*), OTh VIII.243–50.
15. *Circa delectationes et dolores* (*On Pleasures and Pains*), OTh VIII.251–72. After the *Reportatio* but before item 18.
16. *Circa virtutes et vitia* (*On Virtues and Vices*), OTh VIII.272–86. After the *Reportatio* but before item 18.
17. *Dubitationes addititiae* (*Additional Doubtful Points*), OTh VIII. 286–320. Five discussions: "*Utrum caritas habeat aliquam causalitatem respectu actus meritorii*" ("Does Charity Have Any Causality with Respect to a Meritorious Act?"), "*Quomodo de potentia dei absoluta aliquis ex puris naturalibus posset esse acceptus deo sine aliquo absoluto*" ("How, by God's Absolute Power, Could Someone on the Basis of His Purely Natural [Powers] Be Accepted by God Without Anything Absolute [Added]?"), "*In quo consistit perfecta delectatio et quietatio potentiae beatae*" ("What Do the Perfect Delight and Repose of a Blessed Power Consist in?"), "*An dilectio et delectatio distinguantur*" ("Are Love and Delight Distinguished?"), "*Utrum actus exterior habeat propriam bonitatem*" ("Does an Exterior Act Have Its Own Goodness?"). Probably after item 18.
18. *De connexione virtutum* = *Connex.* (On the Connection of the Virtues), OTh VIII.323–407. Dated 1319.[20] Translation: Wood 1997. The translation preserves the line numbers of the edition.
19. *Utrum voluntas possit habere actum virtuosum respectu alicuius obiecti respectu cuius est error in intellectu* = *Act. virt.* (Can the Will Have a Virtuous Act with Respect to Some Object About Which There Is Error in the Intellect?), OTh VIII.409–50.

Other theological writings:

20. *Quodlibeta septem* = *Quodl.* (*Seven Quodlibets*), OTh IX. Probably based on disputations held in London 1322–24, but revised and edited in Avignon 1324–25. Translations: Freddoso and Kelly 1991 (complete);[21] Bosley and Tweedale 1997, 425–7 (from IV.35), 427–30 (from V.10), 430–3 (from V.12–13), 433–5 (from V.23), 125–36 (VII.11 [with parts of III.1], VII.15, VII.17).

21. *Tractatus de quantitate = Quant.* (*Treatise on Quantity*), OTh X.3–85. Probably 1323–24.
22. *De corpore Christi* (*On the Body of Christ*), OTh X.89–234. Probably 1323–24.

Items 21–2 are sometimes (wrongly) treated as constituting a single work, *De sacramento altaris* (*On the Sacrament of the Altar*). In this form they are translated in Birch 1930.

II.1.2. PHILOSOPHICAL WORKS

23. *Summa logicae = SL* (*Summa of Logic*), OPh I. Dated c. 1323. Divided into three parts, the third with four subparts. Translations: Loux 1974 (I, complete); Spade 1995 (Wodeham's Prologue, Ockham's Preface and I.1–5, 6, 8–13, 26–8, 30–1, 33, 63–6, 70, 72); Bosley and Tweedale 1997, 235–6 (from I.70); Freddoso and Schuurman 1980 (II, complete); Boehner 1990, 83–4 (from III-1.1), 92–5 (III-2.27); Kretzmann and Stump 1988, 314–36 (III-3.10–6); Adams and Kretzmann 1983, 110–14 (from III-3.30); Boehner 1990, 84–8 (III-3.38).[22]
24. *Expositio in libros artis logicae, prooemium et expositio in librum Porphyrii de Praedicabilibus = Prooem. et Porph.* (*Exposition of the Books of the Art of Logic: Prologue, and Exposition of Porphyry's Isagoge*), OPh II.3–131. Translation: Kluge 1973–74 (*Exposition of Porphyry* only).
25. *Expositio in librum Praedicamentorum Aristotelis = Expos. Praed.* (*Exposition of Aristotle's Categories*), OPh II.135–339.
26. *Expositio in librum Perihermenias Aristotelis = Expos. Perih.* (*Exposition of Aristotle's On Interpretation*), OPh II.345–504. Translations: Boehner 1990, 43–5 (from I.Prol.6); Adams and Kretzmann 1983, 96–109 (I.6.7–15, on *On Interpretation* 9).
27. *Tractatus de praedestinatione et de praescientia dei respectu futurorum contingentium = Praedest.* (*Treatise on Predestination and God's Foreknowledge with Respect to Future Contingents*), OPh II.507–39. Translation: Adams and Kretzmann 1983.

Items 24–7 were published together under the title *Summa aurea* (*Golden Summa*) in Ockham 1496. Dated 1321–24.

28. *Expositio super libros Elenchorum = Expos. Elench.* (*Exposition of the Sophistic Refutations*), OPh III. After items 24–6, before item 29.

29. *Expositio in libros Physicorum Aristotelis = Expos. Phys.* (*Exposition of Aristotle's Physics*), OPh IV (Books I–III); OPh V (Books IV–VIII). Incomplete. Dated 1322–24. Translation: Boehner 1990, 2–16 (Prol. only).

Parts of item 29 were loosely excerpted by an early scribe and combined into a separate work known as the *Tractatus de successivis* (*Treatise on Successive [Entities]*). Only in this indirect sense is the latter "authentically" Ockham's. It is edited, Boehner 1944. Partial translations: Grant 1974, 229–34 (from III.2.4–6); Hyman and Walsh 1983, 686–8 (from III.2.6).

30. *Brevis summa libri Physicorum = Brev. Phys.* (*Brief Summa of the Physics*), OPh VI.2–134. Dated 1322–23. Translation: Davies 1989.
31. *Summula philosophiae naturalis = Phil. nat.* (*Little Summa of Natural Philosophy*), OPh VI.137–94. Incomplete. Dated 1319–21.
32. *Quaestiones in libros Physicorum Aristotelis = Qq. Phys.* (*Questions on Aristotle's Books of the Physics*), OPh VI.397–813. Before 1324. Translation: Boehner 1990, 115–25 (from qq. 132–6).

II.1.3. DOUBTFUL AND SPURIOUS WORKS

33. *Tractatus minor logicae* (*Lesser Treatise on Logic*), OPh VII.3–57.
34. *Elementarium logicae* (*Primer of Logic*), OPh VII.61–304.

The authenticity of items 33–4 is suspect; recent opinion leans toward accepting them.[23] Both probably from 1340–7.

35. *Tractatus de praedicamentis* (*Treatise on Categories*), OPh VII. 307–32. Probably inauthentic. If authentic, probably before 1323.
36. *Quaestio de relatione* (*Question on Relation*), OPh VII.335–69. Spurious.
37. *Centiloquium = Centil.* (*One Hundred Theses*), OPh VII.373–505. Spurious.
38. *Tractatus de principiis theologiae* (*Treatise on the Principles of Theology*), OPh VII.507–639. Spurious. Dated 1328–50.

II.2. *Political Writings*

With the exception of items 49–50, Ockham's political writings are published in critical Latin editions in Ockham 1956–97. Item 53 is a "special case."

39. *Octo quaestiones de potestate papae = OQ (Eight Questions on the Power of the Pope)*, OPol I.13–217. Fall 1340–summer 1341. Translations: Fairweather 1956, 437–42 (II.1, 7); McGrade and Kilcullen 1995, 303–33 (III).

40. *An princeps pro suo succursu, scilicet guerrae, possit recipere bona ecclesiarum, etiam invito papa = AP (Can the Ruler Take the Churches' Goods to Aid Him in War, Even If the Pope Is Unwilling?)*, OPol I.230–71. Incomplete. August 1338–end of 1339.

41. *Consultatio de causa matrimoniali (Advice about a Marriage Case)*, OPol. I.278–86. Late 1341–February 1342.

42. *Opus nonaginta dierum = OND (The Work of Ninety Days)*, OPol I.292–368 (Chapters 1–6), OPol II (Chapters 7–124). Between 1332–34. Translation: McGrade and Kilcullen 1995, 19–115 (Chapters 2, 26–8, 65, 88, 93); William of Ockham 1998 (complete).

43. *Epistola ad fratres minores = Epist. (Letter to the Friars Minor)*, OPol III.6–17. Spring 1334. Translation: McGrade and Kilcullen 1995, 3–15.

44. *Tractatus contra Ioannem (Treatise Against [Pope] John [XXII])*, OPol III.29–156. Dated 1335.

45. *Tractatus contra Benedictum = CB (Treatise Against [Pope] Benedict [XII])*, OPol III.165–322. Dated 1337–early 1338.

46. *Compendium errorum Iohannis papae XXII (Compendium of the Errors of Pope John XXII)*, OPol IV.14–77. Late 1337–early 1338. Probably authentic, although there is some doubt.

47. *Breviloquium = Brev. (Short Discourse)*, OPol IV.97–260. Translation: McGrade and Kilcullen 1992. Between 1341 and 1342.

48. *De imperatorum et pontificum potestate = IPP (On the Power of Emperors and Pontiffs)*, OPol IV.279–355. Dated 1346–47.

49. *Dialogus = Dial. (Dialogue)*, Goldast 1614, 398–957; the last portion, lacking in Goldast, published in Scholz 1911–44, II.392–5. An "on-line" critical Latin edition and complete translation are being prepared in Ockham forthcoming; portions of the project are being posted on the Internet as they are completed. *Dial.* has three parts. Part I (seven books, subdivided into chapters) was completed before 1335. What now survives as Part II was not part of the *Dial.* but instead is item 50. Part III (two tracts, each in several books, subdivided into chapters) is variously dated

1338–46. Translations also in Lewis 1954, II.398–402 (from I.vi.84); McGrade and Kilcullen 1995, 121–207 (III-1.ii complete), 207–19 (III-1.iii.8–11), 219–26 (III-1.iv.8–11), 226–9 (III-1.iv.22), 235–81 (III-2.Prol., i.1–17); Lewis 1954, I.302–10 (from III-2.ii.20, 23, 26–8); Lerner and Mahdi 1963, 494–9 (III-2.ii.26–8); McGrade and Kilcullen 1995, 281–98 (III-2.iii.5–7); Lerner and Mahdi 1963, 499–505 (III-2.iii.6).

50. *De dogmatibus Johannis XXII* (*On the Teachings of* [*Pope*] *John XXII*), Goldast 1614, 740–770. Dated 1334. Treated as Part II of item 49.

II.2.2. DOUBTFUL WORKS

51. *Allegationes de potestate imperiali* (*Dispatches on Imperial Power*), by Ockham and others. OPol IV.367–444. Dated 1338.

52. *De electione Caroli quarti* (*On the Election of Charles IV*), OPol IV.464–86. Probably spurious.

53. *Allegationes religiosorum virorum* (*Dispatches from Religious Men*), Eubel 1898, 388–96. By Ockham and others, 1329. "This work explicitly names Ockham among its authors, . . . But it has proved quite impossible to enucleate Ockham's specific contribution to this collaborative production."[24]

III. THE ESSAYS IN THIS VOLUME

The essays below touch on all main aspects of Ockham's life and thought.

In Chapter 1, William J. Courtenay describes the major events and influences in Ockham's career as an academic and as a political polemicist. It should be emphasized that much of what Courtenay reports has only recently been uncovered, particularly the details of the fourteenth-century Franciscan educational system and the persons interacting with Ockham. Courtenay also discusses Ockham's influence into the fifteenth century, both in England and on the Continent.

In Chapter 2, Calvin Normore surveys the main outlines of Ockham's logic. He inventories the explicitly logical works, as well as the nonlogical writings in which the working out of logical issues is a prominent component. After describing the scope of what Ockham regards as logic, Normore turns to an account of Ockham's views: his semantics, including signification and supposition; the theory of truth conditions for simple and more complex propositions, including their tensed and modal variants; the theory of consequence; his reworking of the theory of topical "middles"; and his sophisticated treatment of categorical and modal syllogistic.

In Chapter 3, Claude Panaccio further describes Ockham's semantics and the role "mental language" plays in it. He explains Ockham's account of signification, connotation, supposition, truth conditions, and "exponible" propositions. He then describes how Ockham uses this machinery in arguing against universals and other entities his contemporaries favored and concludes that it serves a primarily metaphysical role for Ockham and should not be thought of as formulating an ideal "deep structure" of thought, as many scholars have supposed.

In Chapter 4, David Chalmers takes up the "standard" view that Ockham rejected synonymy in mental language. He notes that Ockham's texts are ambiguous and offers an array of theoretical arguments that Ockham *ought* to have allowed mental synonymy, even if he did not. It is striking to find Chalmers, in a paper drafted in 1991, pushing on largely philosophical grounds toward a view Panaccio and others have recently reinterpreted Ockham as actually having held, that there *is* mental synonymy after all and that synonymy is forbidden only between *simple* mental terms.[25]

In Chapter 5 I set out some main themes of Ockham's nominalist metaphysics, concentrating on his so-called "Razor" and his attempt to reduce ontological commitment by "paraphrasing" away certain entities. I argue that he remains committed to more than is usually thought. I claim too that his arguments against universals are not decisive, although they do weaken the case for realism.

In Chapter 6, Gyula Klima takes up Ockham's criticism of "old way" (via antiqua) semantics that he thinks leads to "multiplying entities according to the multiplication of terms." Ockham's alternative semantics avoids such a commitment and allows him to reduce the number of ontological categories. But Klima argues that Ockham's criticisms are misdirected. *Via antiqua* semantics is quite capable of avoiding the ontological commitment Ockham objects to. This suggests that what motivated Ockham was not so much ontological parsimony as it was his semantic project of simplifying the conceptual basis of all the theoretical sciences.

In Chapter 7, André Goddu surveys Ockham's natural philosophy. He shows that, although Ockham was an Aristotelian here, his Aristotelianism serves his own agenda. For instance, Ockham's views on matter and form are in some respects compatible with atomism. Again, he was uncomfortable with Aristotle's theory of final causality. Goddu goes on to outline Ockham's views on motion, infinity, place, void, time, eternity, continuity, and other physical notions.

In Chapter 8, Eleonore Stump examines some important features of Ockham's epistemology, using Aquinas's theory for comparison. She asks why Ockham felt compelled to reject the theory of sensible and intelligible "species" in cognition and suggests that the development of the notion of "intuitive" and "abstractive" cognition after Aquinas may have been in part a response to a lingering puzzle for the species theory. She explores Ockham's own account of intuitive and abstractive cognition in this context. Finally, she suggests that Ockham's epistemology may not have all the theoretical economy he claims for it.

In her discussion of Ockham's theory of intuitive and abstractive cognition, Stump puts what has become the "standard" reading of that theory into a historical context, providing what may be part of the motivation for the theory. It is all the more important, therefore, that in Chapter 9, Elizabeth Karger argues that the "standard" reading is a mistake based on a misunderstanding of key texts. She traces the origins of this reading through the modern secondary literature and argues that the texts in fact support a quite different understanding of Ockham's theory, according to which abstractive cognition is not by nature capable of causing false judgments, intuitive cognitions are not by nature incapable of causing false judgments, and there is no privileged connection between intuition and evidence.

The opposing views in Chapters 8 and 9 provide a perfect example of a current lively debate in Ockham scholarship. Readers are invited to study these chapters carefully and to form their own conclusions.

In Chapter 10, Peter King sets out the main features of Ockham's ethics. He shows how Ockham combines normative principles from Christian revelation with a conceptual apparatus derived from Aristotle. King also discusses Ockham's views on the moral neutrality of exterior acts, the claim that the only intrinsically virtuous act is loving God, Ockham's theory of five levels or stages of moral action, the role of "right reason" and divine commands, the sense in which humans are obliged to subordinate their will to God's, and Ockham's theory of the virtues.

In Chapter 11, Marilyn McCord Adams examines Ockham's controversial doctrine of "liberty of indifference": that even if it is aware of decisive reasons for an action, the will can choose to do it, not to do it – or even to do the opposite! This is the basis for the criticism that Ockham cuts morality off from nature, reducing ethics to obeying an arbitrary God whose choices can be as irrational as ours can. She defends Ockham against this charge, and along the way compares his views with those of his predecessors' – particularly Anselm's, Aquinas's and Scotus's.

In Chapter 12, A. S. McGrade combines the ethics in Ockham's academic writings with the politics in his later works. The question prompting his essay is how to reconcile the emphasis in the former on obeying God's will, who can command anything whatever, with the appeal to reason and natural law in the political writings. McGrade concludes that the shift of emphasis is not a change of mind and that the two are parts of one unified view.

In Chapter 13, John Kilcullen discusses the political issues and writings that occupied Ockham's last twenty years. He explains the facts and questions surrounding the controversy over "poverty" that was the kernel of Ockham's dispute with Pope John XXII. Kilcullen also surveys Ockham's views on property, legal and natural rights, heresy and heretics, the authority of the pope and the Holy Roman Emperor, the limits on that authority, and the role of women.

In Chapter 14, Alfred J. Freddoso takes up Ockham's views on faith and reason, contrasting them with those of his predecessors – particularly Aquinas. Freddoso argues that, although Ockham had a great admiration for natural reason, especially as represented by Aristotle, he did not – unlike Aquinas – regard Christian faith as fulfilling classical pagan metaphysics and ethics according to intellectual standards accepted by the pagan philosophers themselves. Accordingly, Freddoso concludes, Ockham was much more willing than Aquinas to allow irresoluble conflicts between faith and reason.

In Chapter 15, Rega Wood defends Ockham against the frequent charge that his theology of salvation is in effect a version of the ancient heresy known as Pelagianism, which denies the doctrine of original sin and holds that humans can reach salvation without any special divine grace. She argues that Ockham affirmed the necessity of grace for salvation, merit, and divine acceptance but *not* for virtue; unlike Saint Augustine, Ockham allowed for genuinely virtuous pagans. Wood further argues that, although Ockham maintained that an act of human free will is needed for merit and salvation, he is not thereby committed even to the more attenuated heresy of semi-pelagianism, which regards grace as necessary for salvation but questions the Augustinian doctrine of predestination by holding that the human will can take the initiative and thereby "control" God's grace. For Wood, Ockham's theology is orthodox here as well.

NOTES

All references are given by author and date. Full particulars may be found in the Bibliography.

1 Copleston 1947–75, for example, devotes eleven chapters to Aquinas, six to Scotus, and seven to Ockham and Ockhmism. Each is more than is devoted to any other late-medieval thinker, although Bonaventure with five chapters is a contender.

2 Kretzmann and Stump 1993, 2–3. Sections II–V of their introduction (ibid., 2–10) contain much background information useful to readers of the present volume as well.

3 This is true even though the medieval period is the longest in the history of Western philosophy. If we include Saint Augustine (354–430), as we must in any serious account of medieval philosophy, it lasted for more than a thousand years.

4 The story is told in Gál and Wood 1991. By contrast, the first volume of the Scotus Commission's critical edition of John Duns Scotus (Scotus 1950–) appeared almost fifty years ago and, although the project is arguably more complicated than the Ockham edition, it is still very incomplete. The critial "Leonine Edition" of Thomas Aquinas (Aquinas 1882–) is far from complete after more than a century.

5 See Section II.2.1, item 49.

6 See Section II.

7 Courtenay in Chapter 1. For insightful speculation on why Ockham's views generated such resistance, see Wood 1997, 12–13.

8 On the issues and personalities involved, see Kilcullen in Chapter 13.

9 Courtenay in Chapter 1. On Ockham's death, see Gál 1982.

10 Wood 1997, 6.

11 Boehner 1990, li. This needs to be stated carefully. Boehner explains (ibid.), "Ockham's philosophy had an enormous influence. But it seems that he had few disciples. It is difficult to find an 'Ockhamist' school in the same sense as we encounter a Thomist or Scotist school. Ockham's teachings had, rather, a stimulating effect. They awakened many somewhat independent thinkers who were united at least against the realism of the older scholastics. The 'Nominales' (in the mediaeval sense) constituted the *via moderna*, which was not so much a school as a trend of thought." See also Courtenay in Chapter 1, Section V.

12 Knowles, 1962, 318–19.

13 Moody 1935 had already called attention to Ockham's logical accomplishments and some of their applications, as had Boehner 1952, Moody 1953, Bocheński 1961, and Kneale and Kneale 1962 (although the Kneales were far from sympathetic to Ockham). Real interest among analytic philosophers in medieval logic and semantics did not emerge, however, until the publication of Kretzmann 1966 and 1968, and Scott 1966.

14 For a good example of the fruitfulness of reflection from a modern point of view on issues raised by Ockham, see Chalmers in Chapter 4.

15 Freddoso stresses this point in Chapter 14.

16 Some of the chapters in this volume give dates other than those given here. I have taken my own dating from discussions in the critical editions, but these matters are not yet fully settled.

17 Wood 1997, x–xi.

18 Described in Hyman and Walsh as II.15.

19 Described ibid. as II.26.

20 See Wood 1997, x, "Ockham's *Connex.* was his *Quaestio Biblica*, a formal academic exercise that a met a degree requirement in theology for a public lecture or lectures on a biblical topic."

21 The translation includes page references to the Latin edition.

22 Listed as III-3.36 in Boehner 1990.

23 See the introduction to Wood 1997, 10–11, n. 22.

24 OPol IV.x.

25 Since I have been party to this dispute, I should report that I do not find the textual support for this as compelling as Panaccio and others do, although I agree with both Panaccio and Chalmers that it makes the best overall sense out of the evidence.

1 The Academic and Intellectual Worlds of Ockham

William of Ockham has long been considered one of the foremost fig-ures in the history of medieval philosophy and theology. As such his thought is often contrasted with that of the other seminal thinkers of High Scholasticism: Thomas Aquinas, Henry of Ghent, Giles of Rome, and John Duns Scotus, as if those were the appropriate and sufficient voices of debate within which Ockham's thought was de-veloped. The completion of the critical edition of Ockham's philo-sophical and theological writings has, on one level, confirmed that picture and revealed Scotus as the single most important figure on Ockham's intellectual horizon. The editors, however, along with scholars working on lesser-known figures in the early fourteenth century, have at the same time uncovered a more complex picture of intellectual exchange in which Ockham's immediate contempo-raries – those active between 1305 and 1325 – exercised a profound impact on his thought, and he on theirs.

Other contributions of recent scholarship that change or at least refine the way Ockham is viewed today are a more extensive know-ledge of the lives of those with whom he interacted, the educational system of the Franciscan order that determined the physical settings in which Ockham was active, and the structure and intellectual ac-tivity at universities and other *studia* in England and on the Conti-nent. These allow a fresh examination – a more nuanced picture – of Ockham's intellectual heritage and the influence his thought had on subsequent generations.

17

I. THE FORMATIVE YEARS, 1305–16

William of Ockham was born around 1288 at the rural village of Ockham in Surrey, a day's ride southwest of London. Nothing is known of his family or social background and thus whether his native language was French or Middle English. Having joined or, more likely, been given to the Franciscan order as a young boy before the age of fourteen, Latin quickly became his language of conversation and writing. When he later went to Avignon, visited Italy, and lived the last twenty years of his life in Germany, it was probably through Latin that he communicated with those among whom he lived.

No Franciscan convent existed in the region of Ockham's birth, although the Dominicans maintained a convent at the nearby town of Guildford. Ockham's earliest education before entering the Franciscan order was more likely obtained through the local parish priest or perhaps at the house of Austin Canons at Newark.[1] His grammatical and philosophical training, however, was received from the Franciscans in the opening years of the fourteenth century, probably at Greyfriars[2] in London, which may also have been his "home" convent.

The London convent was the principal teaching center for the London custody, one of the seven administrative units into which the English province of the order was divided. Alongside Oxford, London had the largest Franciscan convent in England, which was situated on the northwest edge of the old city at Newgate with around 100 friars usually in residence.[3] Its size was needed to facilitate its mission to the largest city in England and to take advantage of proximity to the royal court and episcopal residences that lay along the Thames between the city and Westminster. London Greyfriars was also the principal residence of the Franciscan provincial minister for England when he was not abroad on business of the order.

In addition to lectors appointed for instruction in logic, natural philosophy, and theology, the London convent profited intellectually from a flow of students, masters, and officials moving between Oxford and Paris. Throughout the English phase of Ockham's life, that is, before he left England for Avignon in 1324 never to return, English secular and mendicant students crossed the Channel to Paris for study in arts and theology, bringing back with them ideas and texts, just as Oxford learning through the same connections migrated across to the classrooms and libraries of Paris. Thus, in looking at the intellectual environment that Ockham experienced at the London convent, one must look not only at the personnel and resources of the convent itself but at the influences of Oxford and Paris that passed through it in the first two decades of the fourteenth century.

What those influences were depends very much on knowing the years in which Ockham was probably resident in London. We know that he was in London in February 1306, when he was ordained subdeacon at Southwark by Robert Winchelsey, archbishop of Canterbury.[4] Because there is no indication that he received a dispensation for being younger than the minimum canonical age for that minor order, nor any reason to believe his superiors would have delayed his first ordination much beyond the canonical minimum, it has been assumed he was eighteen at the time, from which the approximate date of his birth is conjectured.[5] According to that reasoning, he would have been twenty-nine when he began reading the *Sentences* in 1317–18, approximately the normal age for that academic exercise.

How much earlier than the academic year 1305–06 Ockham was at the London convent is unknown. He was already in the order before 1302 and probably also at London by that date, as training in logic and natural philosophy usually began around fourteen years of age, and it is the most likely convent for his reception into the order. He would have completed his training in philosophy between 1308 and 1310 and then advanced to the study of theology either at London or Oxford.

No information has survived on who might have been lecturing in philosophy at London during these years. Henry de Sutton was Guardian (that is, principal administrative officer) of the convent from 1303 to 1309.[6] Adam of Lincoln, Oxford D.Th. (c. 1293) and provincial minister for England from 1303 to 1310, would have been at the convent frequently. John Duns Scotus might have resided there or at Oxford during his exile from Paris between June 1303 and April 1304. In fact, at one time or another most of the leading English Franciscan theologians of this period would have visited London on business of the order.

By 1310 Ockham had advanced to the study of theology. Because there was no strict sequence of courses that marked the stages of the internal Franciscan educational program before the baccalaureate, young friars probably availed themselves of whatever lectures were being given so long as there were places in the classroom and the student had sufficient training to understand the material and analysis. Ockham would have begun his studies in theology either at the custodial school in London or at the provincial *studium generale* with which the London custody was affiliated, namely Oxford.

The decision regarding the *studium* to which Ockham was sent lay with the provincial minister and the provincial chapter. They were also the ones who chose from among the many students who had completed two or three years of theological study those few (approximately six to eight per decade) who would be sent to Paris for the second half (another four or five years) of the theological training necessary for being appointed a lector in a convent or custodial school. The opportunity for Parisian study was reserved for those who were thought capable ultimately of advancing to the baccalaureate at one of the three universities with a faculty of theology: Paris, Oxford, or Cambridge. The order supported two students at Paris from each province, and the province could send an additional student at its own expense, which the English province usually did. Selection depended on merit, as determined by the provincial leadership and on the timing of vacancies opened by students returning to England. Roger Marston, John Crombe, William of Alnwick, and probably John Duns Scotus were among those who had been chosen for the lectorate program at Paris. A few English students of Ockham's academic generation would also have been sent. Was Ockham among those few?

We have no evidence that links Ockham to Paris during the years in which he would have been eligible for consideration, approximately 1312–16. Ockham's *Reportatio* on the *Sentences* does not reflect any first-hand knowledge of theologians active at Paris at that time. His familiarity with some of Peter Auriol's views, presented at Paris in 1316–17, was apparently acquired through reports or notes of others. Although it is unlikely that Ockham had any direct personal contact with Parisian classrooms, he certainly had access to texts and accounts that came back to England.

The selection of Ockham for advancement to the baccalaureate at Oxford would have been at the direction of Richard Conington, provincial minister in England from 1310 to 1316, with the agreement or consent of the provincial chapter. Conington was himself a former regent master in theology at Oxford whose opinions, as expressed in his first *Quodlibet*, were discussed by Ockham in his *Sent.* I.Prol.5. Conington belonged to that generation of English Franciscans who were more influenced by Henry of Ghent than by Scotus. Yet Conington remained one of the important contemporary theologians whose ideas were discussed into the 1340s.[7]

The Oxford to which Ockham was sent for the baccalaureate provided an exciting intellectual environment for the young Franciscan. Henry of Harclay, a secular theologian who had studied at Paris before returning to Oxford, was elected chancellor of the university in 1312. In the previous decade at Paris, Harclay had been deeply influenced by Scotus and had participated in the editing of Scotus's work and in the discussions that created the first generation of Scotists at Paris.[8] With his return to Oxford, however, Harclay moved in a different direction and, alongside Richard Campsall, began to criticize assumptions of Scotus in metaphysics and natural philosophy. Harclay formulated positions on the question of universals and the Aristotelian categories that anticipated elements in Ockham's thought as expressed a few years later in the latter's Oxford lectures on the *Sentences*.[9]

Others active at Oxford between 1310 and 1316 were the secular theologians Robert of Kykeley (Kigheley), from whom we have a series of quodlibetal questions, Antony Bek (future chancellor of Lincoln and later bishop of Norwich), Simon of Mepham (future archbishop of Canterbury), and Richard Campsall. Of these Campsall was by far the most important. He was a fellow of Merton College and a master of arts by 1308, at which time he was probably beginning his studies in theology. He was a bachelor of theology by July 1317, probably having read the *Sentences* in the previous academic year. Although in many ways a more traditional mind than his near contemporary Ockham, Campsall applied terminist logic, particularly supposition theory, to the analysis of theological problems – a method that can also be found in Ockham.

After a dispute with the university over the theological curriculum, the Dominicans resumed teaching at Oxford in 1314–15 with Nicholas Trevet as regent master in theology. Although Trevet has been described as a Thomist, strict support of Aquinas's thought was already on the wane among younger Dominicans at Oxford and Paris by 1310.[10] By contrast, before 1314 Scotism had not established firm roots among the Franciscans at Oxford. Robert Cowton, who lectured on the *Sentences* at Oxford sometime between 1304 and 1311 and who may have remained in residence at Greyfriars, favored Henry of Ghent, as did Richard Conington. The same may be true for the less-studied William of Nottingham, who lectured on the *Sentences* at Oxford shortly before Cowton and who succeeded Conington as provincial minister in 1316. Thus Ockham's presentential training in theology coincided with a time of weakening interest in Aquinas among English Dominicans, little evidence of supporters of Giles of Rome among English Austin Friars, and only modest support for Scotus among Franciscans.

That began to change by 1314, but only in regard to Scotus. The anonymous Franciscan *sententiarius* at Oxford in 1314–15 was not only influenced by Scotus but carried Scotus's theory of "priorities" (*signa*) in the Godhead into a discussion of whether God the Father could have produced creatures before begetting the Son – a discussion that led to the condemnation of eight of his propositions in February 1315.[11] John of Reading, who was the Franciscan *sententiarius* at Oxford in 1315–16 or 1316–17, was a thoroughgoing Scotist and was later described by Ockham's *socius*, Adam Wodeham, as Scotus's "disciple and most noted follower."[12] Reading probably remained at Greyfriars until 1322 and was appointed lector at that convent around 1320. Ockham cited Reading in his Sent.I.Prol.3, and, when Reading revised his lectures on the *Sentences*, he entered into a detailed critique of Ockham's lectures, relying first on Ockham's initial version (his *Reportatio*) and then on the revised version (Ockham's *Ordinatio*). Finally, William of Alnwick, the disciple and redactor of Duns Scotus, returned to Oxford and became regent master (lector) of the convent – probably in 1316. Although Alnwick's regency lasted only a year, he probably remained in England, most likely at Oxford, until he went as a delegate to the general chapter of the order at Assisi in June 1322 and stayed in Italy and southern France until his death in March 1333. Thus, Scotism was well established at Oxford Greyfriars on the eve of Ockham's advancement to the baccalaureate.

II. OXFORD AND LONDON, 1317–24

In the autumn term of 1317, Ockham began his lectures on the *Sentences* at Oxford, which occupied his attention across the biennium 1317–19.[13] Only his *Reportatio* on Books II–IV and the citations by

John of Reading from the first three distinctions of Ockham's lectures on Book I remain from what he presented there. If there is some uncertainty as to whether he only read at Oxford or read first at London (1317–18) and then at Oxford (1318–19 or 1318–20), there is no room for dispute regarding the dates. Ockham's *Reportatio* shows he knew William of Alnwick's *Quodlibeta* (1316–17) and Peter Auriol's Parisian *Scriptum* I (1316–17) but was not yet aware that Auriol had incepted as a master of theology (by October 1318).[14]

Ockham was principally concerned with the leading minds of the previous academic generation: Henry of Ghent, Giles of Rome, and John Duns Scotus. Yet Ockham also cited his immediate contemporaries, John of Reading, who read the *Sentences* at Oxford a year or two earlier, William of Alnwick, who may still have been lector at Oxford in the autumn of 1317, and Peter Auriol, who read the *Sentences* at Paris in 1316–18. Knowledge of the latter would have come back to London and Oxford through English Franciscans returning from the Paris convent.

Around 1321 Ockham was appointed lecturer in philosophy at one of the Franciscan schools in England, probably at the London convent.[15] By this time he was a "formed bachelor" awaiting an opportunity to be selected to proceed to the doctorate at Oxford. At the same convent Ockham lived in the company of Walter Chatton, who was lecturer in theology, and Adam Wodeham, a student in theology who also acted as Ockham's *socius* or assistant. This was the most productive writing period of Ockham's career. Between 1321 and 1324 Ockham produced his commentaries on the beginning books of logic, namely his expositions of Porphyry and Aristotle's *Categories, On Interpretation,* and *Sophistical Refutations.* In the same period Ockham wrote his textbook on logic (*Summa logicae*), his commentary and questions on Aristotle's *Physics,* his treatise on predestination and future contingents, the first five groups of his quodlibetal disputations, and probably his treatises on the Eucharist (*Tractatus de quantitate* and *De corpore Christi*).

It was also in this period that some of Ockham's opinions came under attack. John of Reading, who was regent master at Oxford Greyfriars around 1320–21, frequently attacked Ockham in the redaction of his own lectures on the *Sentences* that was revised between 1318 and 1322. Similarly, Walter Chatton, who was lecturing on the *Sentences* in the same convent as Ockham between 1321 and 1323, attacked Ockham on many points, including the status of universals (leading Ockham to alter his opinion), the relation of grace to justification, the status of quantity and relation, and Eucharistic doctrine. In fact, the writings of Ockham and Chatton in this period show a surprising degree of interdependence and dialogue.[16] Similarly, a work on logic written in England in this period and incorrectly attributed to Richard Campsall also attacked Ockham's views on supposition, universals, and the Aristotelian categories.[17] Among the numerous points of debate between Ockham and his contemporaries in this period, the principal ones that were emerging were Ockham's position on universals, his belief that only _____ qualities are real ent _____ Aristotelian categori _____ cognition of a nonex _____ acceptation in the doctrine of grace and justification, and _____ pretation of transubstantiation.

issues of attack

It was probably a result of this mounting criticism that Ockham was asked to explain his position on relation and the other Aristotelian categories at a provincial chapter of the order in England in 1323.[18] No information regarding his response or any action taken by the chapter has survived. Within that same year, however, someone, possibly John of Reading, who went to Avignon in 1322, brought charges at the papal court against Ockham for false and heretical teaching.[19] Around May 1324, Ockham left England for Avignon, where he took up residence at the Franciscan convent for the next four years.

III. AVIGNON, 1324–28

The normal route from London to Avignon would have taken Ockham through Paris, which was probably his first direct contact with that university city and convent. Parisian theologians were also very much in evidence at Avignon, which was the center of Church life. Although subsequent events shifted Ockham's attention away from philosophy and theology, Avignon was his first exposure to an international community of scholars, many of whom had been trained in the more diverse intellectual environment of Paris. The time that was not taken up with responding to his inquisitors, which must have occupied very little of his four years at Avignon, allowed him access to disputations, sermons, and discussions with other scholars, secular and mendicant. Among the Franciscans who visited or resided at Avignon during these years were John of Reading, Francis Mayronis, Francis of Marchia, Guiral Ot, Elias of Nabinali, William of Rubione, Pastor de Serrescuderio, and of course Michael of Cesena, who, in addition to earlier visits, was in residence from December 1327 until May 1328.

All of those appointed to serve on the commission to examine Ockham's orthodoxy were, save one, Parisian doctors of theology. Two of them were Dominicans whose training dated to a period in which Thomism was obligatory in that order: Raymond Béguin, Patriarch of Jerusalem, and Dominique Grenier, lector at the Sacred Palace and bishop elect of Pamiers. Thomism was also the preferred doctrine of the only non-Parisian theologian on the commission: John Lutterell, former chancellor of Oxford. Two others belonged to the Augustinian Hermits and presumably had been schooled in the thought of Giles of Rome: Gregory of Lucca, bishop of Belluno-Feltre, and John Paignote, a more recent doctor of Paris. The only member of the commission who was not wedded to late thirteenth-century realism and who was somewhat sympathetic to Scotistic theology was Durand of St. Pourçain, a Dominican theologian and bishop of Meaux whose un-Thomistic views had earlier brought him into conflict with theologians in his order. With the exception of Durand, the commission favored the views of Thomas and Giles of Rome. At the same time, all were doctors of theology from Paris or Oxford and were thus familiar with the types of discourse or scholastic analysis of university classrooms.[20]

The only works of Ockham that were under review at Avignon were his lectures on the *Sentences*, specifically his *Ordinatio* on Book I and the Reportatio on Books II–IV. Even before the appointment of the commission, Lutterell was assigned the task of going through the text of Ockham's questions on the *Sentences* that the latter had brought with him and presented to the pope. In all probability Lutterell's antagonism toward Ockham began at Avignon and was not among the issues that led to Lutterell's dismissal as chancellor nor the reason for his departure from England to Avignon. Ockham was only a bachelor of theology at the beginning of Lutterell's tenure as chancellor, and Ockham never came up for examination or licensing and was probably not resident at Oxford after 1321. Lutterell's conflict with the regent masters in arts and theology at Oxford was personal and probably had to do with the way he exercised the powers of his office. And his move to Avignon was for career advancement, as the letter of invitation from Stephen Kettelbergh shows.[21] His *libellus* against Ockham, written at Avignon, was both the sincere reaction of a committed Thomist and a means of proving himself useful to the papal curia.[22]

Although the list of propositions initially identified by Lutterell as censurable contained philosophical as well as theological statements, the commission restricted the investigation to theological propositions and a reduced number of philosophical statements that had implications for theology. Most of the propositions were taken from the beginning part of the *Ordinatio* and from Books III and IV of the *Reportatio*. Many of the propositions extracted were not concerned with statements about the way the orders of nature and grace actually work but were taken from statements made *de potentia absoluta*, that is, whether a relationship or combination of qualities, such as the relationship of merit and reward, grace and justification, Christ's human nature and the inability to sin, are absolutely necessary or only contingently necessary, and whether their counterparts are absolutely impossible or only because God so ordained.

IV. MUNICH, 1329–47

On the night of 26 May 1328 Ockham fled Avignon in the company of Michael of Cesena, Bonagratia of Bergamo, and Francis of Marchia, going first to Italy, where they joined the court of Louis of Bavaria, and then to Munich, where Ockham remained for the rest of his life. Apart from the attraction of the imperial court, which brought some scholars to Munich on diplomatic service, or the presence of the group of dissidents resident there, such as the Franciscans who had fled Avignon or the secular master Marsilius of Padua, Munich was not a center of learning for any of the mendicant orders. Without some knowledge of German, which we have no reason to believe he possessed, Ockham was more isolated than he had been at Avignon. Latin remained his language of communication both in writing and conversation, but the religious and scholarly community to which it was limited was small. Ockham probably did not spend all his time in Munich. He may well have attended provincial chapters of the southern German (Strasbourg) province of the order, such as were held at Basel in 1340, where he may have renewed contact with John of Rodington and Adam Wodeham.[23]

These years of exile in southern Germany (1329–47) were dedicated to writing political treatises against John XXII and Benedict XII because of Ockham's conviction that they had fallen into heresy on the issue of apostolic poverty and, in the case of Pope John, on the doctrine of the beatific vision. Among the most important of the books and treatises he wrote in this period were *OND* and *Dial*. In these writings Ockham examined the meanings of lordship (*dominium*), the relationship of ownership and use, and the ideas of legal and natural rights. He also addressed the question of authority within the Church: the role of the pope, scripture and tradition, a general council, and the place of secular monarchs in ecclesiastical affairs. Although Ockham's political writings have often been associated with Marsilius of Padua's *Defensor pacis* (1324), some of Ockham's argumentation on the authority of a council and on the authority of the pope was aimed against Marsilius. Ockham remained a stronger believer in papal authority in the Church and in the determination of doctrine even while acknowledging the possibility (for him a reality) of a pope's falling into error.[24]

V. OCKHAM'S HERITAGE

Although Ockham's political writings played an important role in discussions of the relation of Church and state alongside Marsilius of Padua's *Defensor pacis* from Ockham's century until today, the most influential parts of his thought from the fourteenth to sixteenth centuries were his philosophy and theology. The traditional picture of Ockham's influence claimed him to be the initiator, the "venerable inceptor," of a new school of thought in late medieval Europe: nominalism. It supposedly dominated intellectual life at Oxford for almost a half century, until the advent of John Wyclif. Similarly at Paris; after an initial reaction against Ockham's thought in 1339 and 1340, he has been credited with carrying Paris into a nominalistic current that had no serious competitors until challenged by Thomism and Albertism in the early fifteenth century.

That picture has undergone considerable revision in recent decades. In England Ockham was among a group of fourteenth-century authors who continued to be cited until the end of that century, yet even his closest followers, such as Adam Wodeham, were critical of Ockham on several issues – particularly in the area of epistemology. Ockham's removal of sensible and intelligible species in his explanation of the acquisition of knowledge was rejected by most of his English contemporaries, as was his definition of the object of knowledge.[25] Ockham is better seen not as the leader or center of a movement but as one of many contemporary authors whose opinions were widely discussed, sometimes accepted, and sometimes rejected. He became less influential at Oxford in the 1340s because of two countercurrents. One of these was Augustinianism as espoused by Thomas Bradwardine, who attacked Ockham's views on grace and justification as being Pelagian.[26] The other current was realism, which reappeared at Oxford in the late 1340s. Ockham was still admired by some, such as an anonymous Oxford author writing around 1350 who took Ockham's *Sentences* commentary as the model for his own.[27] Yet many of Ockham's presuppositions in logic, natural philosophy, and theology were discarded or opposed by such figures as Ralph Strode, Richard Brinkley, Nicholas Aston, and John Wyclif.[28]

The situation at Paris was somewhat different. Ockham's philosophical writings, principally *SL*, were known at Paris in the late 1320s, and by the mid-1330s Ockham's natural philosophy had attracted a following in the arts faculty. After a relatively brief attempt to suppress Ockham's writings and thought at Paris between 1339 and 1342, opposition weakened in the face of a large influx of English philosophical and theological texts that came into Paris in the early 1340s. Ockham's natural philosophy was generally adopted by the Augustinian theologians Gregory of Rimini and Hugolino of Orvieto in the 1340s, although they were critical of Ockham in other areas. By the mid-fourteenth century Ockham was an important source for Parisian scholars, and his influence can be seen in Henry Totting of Oyta (directly and by way of Adam Wodeham), and more especially in Pierre d'Ailly. Much depended on the specific issue, and most Scholastics of this period chose their positions and arguments without attention to one school of thought. Despite similarities in the thought of Ockham and Jean Buridan, the latter represents a different form of terminist logic that was influential on Albert of Saxony and Marsilius of Inghen.[29]

The situation changed in the fifteenth century with the reemergence of schools of thought and the division in faculties of arts between a philosophical preparation based on the Aristotelian commentaries of Albert, Thomas, and Giles on the one side (the *via antiqua*) and a preparation based on the commentaries of Ockham, Buridan, Marsilius of Inghen, and other fourteenth-century authors (the *via moderna*). Ockham became textually wedded to the "modern" approach and an important authority for the *Nominalistae* at Paris and universities in Germany. By the end of the fifteenth century Ockham's name had become identified with a school of thought, and "Ockhamist" took its place alongside "Thomist," "Albertist," and "Scotist."[30]

The Middle Ages ended with Ockhamism as one school of thought more or less on a par with others. Its reception in more recent times is the topic for another study.

NOTES

1 On the possibility of Ockham's contact with Newark Abbey, see Brampton 1963.
2 "Greyfriars" was a common term for the Franciscans.
3 Kingsford 1915, 62.
4 Graham 1952, 981.
5 On the assumption that the minimum age for ordination to the subdiaconate was twenty-one, Ockham's approximate date of birth was traditionally given as 1285. The Clementine Constitutions from the Council of Vienne in 1311 probably codify contemporary practice. Friedberg 1879–81, II.1140 (= Clem. I.vi.3).
6 Kingsford 1915, 55.
7 On Conington, see Doucet 1937; Brown 1966; Cova 1993.
8 Balić 1956 and 1959.
9 Pelster 1924; Gál 1971.
10 Roensch 1964; Courtenay 1987b, 175–82.
11 Etzkorn 1987; Courtenay 1991a.
12 Adam Wodeham, *Lectura Oxon.* I.1.12 (MS Vat. lat. 955, fol. 70ᵛ). On Reading, see Courtenay 1978, 62–3; Longpré 1924.
13 Gedeon Gál has argued that Ockham lectured on the *Sentences* at London (1317–18) before lecturing a second time at Oxford (1318–19) (OTh VII.14*–18*). Although possible, there is no firm evidence that the requirement of reading the *Sentences* at a lesser *studium* before doing so at a university, codified by Benedict XII in 1336, was already practiced two decades earlier. In this period the mendicant orders at Oxford lectured on the *Sentences* across a two-year period, and we know that Ockham was in residence at the Oxford convent by June 1318, when he

was licensed to hear confessions in the diocese of Lincoln (Emden 1957–59, 1384). Had he lectured at London in 1317–18, it is unlikely that he would have gone to Oxford before September 1318.

14 John XXII instructed the chancellor at Paris, Thomas de Bailly, on July 14, 1318 to grant the license to Auriol, and we know Auriol was regent at Paris in 1318–19 (Denifle and Chatelain 1889–97, II.225 [= §772], 227 [= §776]). Licensing and inception therefore took place between late July and the beginning of the autumn term. For the dating of Ockham's lectures on the *Sentences*, see OTh I.34*–36*.

15 Although the original reason for assuming that Chatton and Ockham were not resident at Oxford at this time has been called into question, the references in Ockham's *SL* to London suggest, as Gedeon Gál argued, that London was the place of composition and therefore residence (OPh I.47*–56*; Courtenay 1990). Ockham also determined quodlibetal disputations during this period, which at Oxford were permitted only to regent masters.

16 Brown 1985. See also Gál's introduction to OPh I, and Wey's introduction of OTh IX.

17 Campsall 1982.

18 Etzkorn 1990.

19 No summons has survived, but in his letter to the Franciscans gathered at the general chapter of the order at Assisi in 1334 (= *Epist.*) Ockham said he remained at Avignon for almost four years until he fled in May 1328. George Knysh has argued that Ockham went to Avignon for nonjudicial reasons and only later came under suspicion while resident there (Knysh 1986 and 1994). The weight of scholarly opinion, however, supports the traditional view. See Miethke 1994.

20 Brampton 1964.

21 Salter 1924, 303–4.

22 Hoffmann 1959.

23 On Wodeham's and Rodington's visits to Basel, see Glassberger 1887–97, II.177–8, III.637.

24 Tierney 1954; 1988, 205–38. McGrade 1974b; McGrade and Kilcullen 1995; Miethke 1992.

25 Tachau 1988.

26 Leff 1957; Oberman 1957; Genest 1979 and 1992; Dolnikowski 1995. For a defense of Ockham against the charge of Pelagianism, see Wood in Chapter 15.

27 Etzkorn 1987.

28 For further discussion, see Courtenay 1987a; Courtenay 1987b, 193–355.

29 For a more extensive discussion of the early stages of the introduction of Ockham's thought into Paris, see Courtenay 1984 and 1997.

30 Kałuża 1988; Hoenen 1993.

2   Some Aspects of Ockham's Logic

Medieval logic begins for most purposes with the work of Boethius, who attempted a Latin rendering of the standard late-antique Greek logic course. As the Boethian treatises began to be more widely studied in the ninth and tenth centuries, an indigenous Latin tradition in logic developed that reached its zenith during the twelfth century in the work of figures like Peter Abelard. It was within this indigenous tradition that the major developments in the medieval theory of inference took place and that the foundations of later pictures of meaning were laid. As the work of the Byzantine grammarian Priscian became known in Western Europe, the grammatical and semantic theory embodied in it fused with the indigenous tradition. The resulting picture was then transformed by a flood of new translations of texts of Aristotle, of Greek commentaries, and of Islamic commentaries and treatises. The thirteenth and fourteenth centuries saw the digestion of this material and its integration into the already existing tradition. Some consequences of this were new theories of the semantic properties of terms (including theories of the analysis of sentences), the development of propositional logic more or less as we know it today, the working out of the theory of the categorical syllogism (including its modal extensions), the flowering of modal logic generally, and the development of a general theory of inference. By the mid-fourteenth century these developments were more or less complete. William Ockham is one of the greatest of the figures who completed them. He is in some ways an idiosyncratic logician, but his importance can hardly be overestimated.

31

I. WORKS

Ockham's explicitly logical writings consist of two distinct bodies of work. The first is a cycle of commentaries on parts of the standard logic curriculum of his time. This includes commentaries on Porphyry's *Isagoge* and Aristotle's *Categories, On Interpretation,* and *Sophistic Refutations.* It was probably written in this order probably between 1319 and 1322 while he was lecturing on the material at one of the Franciscan houses of study. The second consists of a single large work, *Summa of Logic* (*SL*). It is now widely thought that this work was made available in parts and that it was completed around 1323, though none of this is very certain. Given the short period in which all of this work was done, it is not surprising that Ockham seems to have revised his views significantly in only a few areas between the commentary cycle and *SL* and between parts of the latter. In several of Ockham's theological and quasi-theological works, logical issues also figure prominently. Some of his *Quodlibets* deal with logical and semantic issues, and his *On Predestination* has a number of important arguments that turn on issues in tense and modal logic.

II. THE SCOPE OF LOGIC

We can glean the scope of what Ockham is prepared to call logic from the structure of *SL*. The work is divided into three parts. Part I deals with terms, Part II with sentences, and Part III with arguments of various kinds. Part I begins with a division of language into written, spoken, and mental and proceeds to lay out a theory of terms, including a theory of signification. A discussion of the major topics in Porphyry's *Isagoge* and in Aristotle's *Categories* follows with consideration of how these are to be handled semantically. The last chapters of Part I develop the theory of supposition of terms in both subject and predicate position.

Part II begins with an account of truth conditions: first for assertoric categorical sentences and then for modal and tensed categorical sentences and more complex categorical forms as well as for molecular (hypothetical) sentences.

Part III is itself divided into four parts. The first of these is a treatise on syllogisms in the sense of Aristotle's *Prior Analytics.* The assertoric categorical syllogism was well understood by Ockham's time, and he treats it deftly, completely, and fairly briefly. The bulk of his discussion of the syllogism is devoted to the modal syllogism. He works out the complete theory of the categorical modal syllogism for all the combinations of premises and conclusions that are modal in the divided or the composite sense or are assertoric. This seems to be novel; the (inauthentic) *Questions on the Prior Analytics* attributed to Scotus[1] works out the modal syllogism for combinations of assertoric and divided sense modal sentences but does not treat the composite sense.

The second part of Part III is a treatise on demonstrative syllogisms covering some of the ground of Aristotle's *Posterior Analytics*.

The structure of the third part of Part III is quite complex. Ockham begins with what he calls the general rules governing consequences. Governing such consequences are metalinguistic rules laying out the patterns of acceptable inference. Many of these are formal, like the rules of the truth functional propositional calculus (which Ockham states), but others are rules that depend on nonformal semantic relations among terms like the rule that what holds of every member of a genus will hold of every member of a species of that genus. Ockham considers these as rules governing the use of terms taken in personal supposition. He then turns to rules governing the use of terms taken in simple and material supposition – notably the predicables treated by Porphyry, but in the unusual order of accident, genus, and *proprium* followed by a discussion of definition and then treatment of species and differentia. This is in turn followed by a treatise on induction in the Aristotelian sense, a discussion of the "art" of *obligatio*, and finally a short chapter on the Liar Paradox.

The fourth part of Part III is a treatise on fallacies and corresponds to Aristotle's *Sophistic Refutations*.

I now turn to the exposition of Ockham's picture of some of the central parts of logic. In so doing I will not follow his order of presentation nor lay emphasis where I think he would have laid it. My aim is to give some sense of his logical achievement.

III. OCKHAM'S SEMANTICS IN THE
TWINKLING OF AN EYE

In Ockham's view logic is a *scientia sermocinalis*, a science concerned with discourse,[2] and one especially concerned with syllogisms, broadly understood to include arguments of all sorts, and their parts. The immediate parts of syllogisms are sentences (*propositiones*), and these are resolved into what Ockham in the first chapter of *SL* calls "terms." Terms, broadly speaking, come in two sorts: categorematic and syncategorematic. A categorematic term is one that has signification. A syncategorematic term has no signification by itself. Ockham says that a syncategorematic term is one that alters the signification of, or "exercises some other function with respect to" categorematic terms,[3] but that account is narrower than his practice, which is to admit that syncategorematic terms can not only combine with other terms but combine sentences (as do 'and,' 'or,' 'because,' and the like) and affect other syncategorematic terms (as 'not' affects words like 'all'). Syncategorematic terms seem to be "logical words" in a sense akin to, but broader than, the current notion of logical constant.

Categorematic terms have a "fixed and definite signification."[4] Ockham explains that, in the narrow sense, a term signifies whatever it is "verified" of. A term is verified of a thing if it can be truly predicated of a proper name or demonstrative pronoun picking out that thing in a singular affirmative categorical sentence with the present tense and unmodified copula 'is' (*est*). Thus 'human' signifies, in the narrow sense, Socrates if and only if 'Socrates is human' is true. This is not a definition of signification, and 'signification' is not a term Ockham attempts to define. Indeed he gives the truth conditions for singular sentences in ways that rely on signification. In *SL* I.33, Ockham presents another, "wider" sense of signification in which a term signifies a thing if it can be truly predicated of a proper name or demonstrative pronoun picking out that thing in an affirmative singular sentence with the copula 'can be' (*potest*). In this wide sense the term 'green' can be said to signify even the White House if that building can be green. It is often suggested that, in introducing this wider sense of signification, Ockham commits himself to an ontology of *possibilia*.[5] It should be remembered, though, that Ockham does not regard signification as a real relation. (Indeed it is not clear that he thinks of it as a relation, properly speaking, at all). Moreover, Ockham is very reluctant to use present-tensed assertoric sentences to talk about significates in the wide sense. These significates *will be, were,* or *can be*. Ockham does not attempt to reduce tensed and modal talk to present-tensed assertoric talk about a wider range of entities as twentieth-century modal and tense logicians typically do, and it is far from clear that he would take such tensed and modal talk as ontologically committing.

The signification relation connects language to the world, and Ockham suggests that the signification of mental categorematic terms is natural. We encounter objects in the world, and these encounters produce (absolute and, if there are any, simple connotative) mental terms. Thus we acquire these terms but do not learn them in any sense requiring that we have already represented the world. But the signification relation does not enter directly into the truth conditions for sentences. For that we need another relation – that of supposition.

Supposition is a relation a term has to things when that term is a term strictly speaking, that is, when it is the subject or predicate of a sentence. Ockham's official doctrine is that only whole subjects or predicates have supposition, but in practice he often assigns supposition to parts of subjects or predicates. Ockham distinguishes three basic kinds of supposition: personal, simple, and material. A term has personal supposition when it stands in a sentence for what it signifies. Personal supposition is in many ways the default supposition for Ockham; for example, predicates (as contrasted with subjects) always have personal supposition. A term has simple supposition when it stands in a sentence for the mental term to which it is subordinated. Ockham thinks genera and species are mental terms, and thus he thinks that in a sentence like '(The) Donkey is a species,' 'donkey' stands for the concept of donkey. A term has material supposition when it stands in a sentence for itself or a related term. The device of quotation was just being invented in Ockham's time, and material supposition does much of the same work. There are differences though; for example, it is the same term (and not a name of that term) that has material supposition as has personal, and there is no way of iterating material supposition as there is of iterating quotation marks.

If we take signification as a primitive relation in Ockham's semantics we could, perhaps, define supposition using no other semantic relation. Personal supposition can be defined in terms of signification, but simple and material cannot be directly so defined. When a term supposits simply or materially it supposits for something but does not signify it. We might say, however, that a term supposits simply when it stands for that to which it is subordinated – and then define subordination in terms of signification – and we might say that a term supposits materially when it stands for itself or a suitably grammatically related form.

Whereas Ockham does not distinguish types of simple or material supposition, he provides a complex and slightly idiosyncratic account of the ways a term may supposit personally. Some categorematic terms, namely the discrete terms, when used as subject or predicate of a sentence supposit discretely – that is, so that as a semantic matter they supposit for exactly one thing. Other categorematic terms are common terms and supposit commonly. A term suppositing commonly may happen to supposit for just one thing (even as a matter of the nature of the thing, as medievals thought 'phoenix' did), but there is nothing about the semantic features of the term that guarantees that. There are several ways in which a term may supposit commonly, and in which way it does depends on the sentential context in which the term appears. The simplest categorical sentences consist of two categorematic terms joined by a copula (e.g., 'Socrates is human,' 'Possums are found in Australia'). The predicates of such sentences always have common supposition. Among sentences of this form there are examples in which the subjects have any of simple, material, discrete personal, or common personal supposition. If we restrict ourselves to the case in which the subject too has common personal supposition (as in 'Humans are [not] animals'), Ockham claims that both subject and predicate have determinate supposition.

Among many writers in an earlier period (and perhaps among some writers in Ockham's time), a term with determinate supposition stood for just one thing. (Consider the temptation to think that 'a horse' stands for just one horse in 'There is a horse in the paddock; bring *it* to me.')

Ockham rejects this picture. In his view any term with common personal supposition stands for everything it signifies. What distinguishes determinate supposition from other kinds is the type of *descent* and *ascent* it supports. Ockham claims that if a term has determinate supposition one can infer from the sentence containing it to a disjunction of sentences otherwise the same (allowing for slight variation to preserve grammaticality) in each of which that term is replaced by a name of, or demonstrative pronoun picking out, one of the things the terms stands for. Thus, if Alfie, Bruce, and Corinne are all the possums, we can infer from 'Possums are found in Australia' to 'Either Alfie is found in Australia, or Bruce is found in Australia, or Corinne is found in Australia.' Moreover, Ockham claims, we can infer from any one of these disjuncts to 'Possums are found in Australia.' The combination of these descent and ascent conditions characterizes determinate supposition. Terms have determinate supposition in categorical sentences with no syncategorematic terms other than a copula and also, for example, in categorical sentences in which the subject or the predicate term is prefixed by 'some' (*aliquis*). If a common term standing personally does not have determinate supposition it has confused supposition. This in turn comes in two flavors characterized by ascent and descent conditions.

If one can descend under a term in the way described in the preceding paragraphs from a sentence to a conjunction of instances but cannot ascend from any one conjunct, the term is said to have confused and distributive supposition. Thus, in 'All humans are animals,' 'human' has confused and distributive supposition because, if Alfie, Bruce, and Corinne are all the humans, one can infer 'Alfie is an animal, and Bruce is an animal, and Corinne is an animal,' but one cannot infer 'All humans are animals' from any one of those conjuncts. If a term has confused supposition but not confused and distributive supposition, Ockham will say it has merely confused (*confuse tantum*) supposition.

Although (or because?) the theory of the types or *modes* of personal supposition has probably received more attention from twentieth-century scholars than any other part of Ockham's logic, it is one of the most mysterious parts of his logic. For one thing, what phenomenon it is a theory of and what, if anything, it is for remain unclear. It has been proposed that this theory is an analogue of quantification theory and more recently that it describes a phenomenon that modern logic parcels out between quantifiers and scope indicators. Some commentators have suggested that the function of Ockham's theory of the modes of personal supposition is to describe how sentences containing quantifier expressions (like 'all' and 'some') are related to singular sentences. More recently, it has been proposed that the theory serves to classify inferences and provide tools for detecting fallacies. None of these proposals is unproblematic.

The view that the modes of personal supposition "cash out" quantified sentences in terms of singulars has to be reconciled with the fact that in some cases the collection of sentences to which Ockham permits descent from a given sentence is not equivalent to the original sentence. (Consider 'Some human is not an animal'). Either Ockham (and several figures who followed him) simply made an elementary logical mistake or the process of ascent and descent was never meant to provide equivalences. On the other hand, not only does Ockham not make any systematic use of the theory of modes in his account of fallacies, but had he done so it is very hard to see how the theory could have helped in any but the most elementary cases. The mystery remains.

IV. THE THEORY OF TRUTH CONDITIONS

Whatever the theory of the modes of personal supposition may be for, the term "supposition" itself figures prominently in Ockham's account of truth conditions for sentences. Ockham's fundamental division of sentences is into categorical and molecular (*hypothetica*). In *SL* II.1, he explains that a categorical sentence is one that "has a subject and a predicate and a copula and does not include more than one such [categorical] sentence." A molecular sentence is one composed of more than one categorical sentence. Ockham's remark that a categorical sentence has a subject, a predicate, and a copula suggests that he thinks of a sentence as having at least three fundamental parts, and his practice is to act as though this is so. But he sometimes speaks as if he thinks of a sentence as always consisting of a name and a verb. Quite possibly this reflects a tension between Aristotle's explicit description of a sentence in *On Interpretation* and the demands of syllogistic, which requires that every sentence have two categorematic terms and a copula around which these terms may be converted. If so, it is a tension Ockham never explicitly addresses.

The simplest categorical sentence has a discrete term as subject, a common term as predicate, and 'is' as copula. Ockham says that such a sentence is true if "the subject and predicate supposit for (a) same thing." That is, the sentence is true if the predicate supposits (inter alia) for the thing the subject supposits for. This model is extended to the other types of simple categorical sentences that appear in syllogisms. Thus, particular affirmative sentences (e.g., 'Some human is an animal') are true if the subject and predicate have at least one suppositum in common, and universal affirmative sentences ('Every human is an animal') are true if the predicate supposits for everything for which the subject does.

Ockham does not treat negation as a sentential operator. Rather he distinguishes two kinds of copulas – affirmative and negative – which he treats as equally fundamental logically. Sentences formed with an affirmative copula are false if their subject terms have no supposita, and sentences formed with a negative copula are true if the subject term has no supposita. The truth conditions given in the preceding paragraph are stated affirmatively and so "build in" this existential requirement. Particular negative sentences like 'Some humans are not Inuit' are true if the subject and predicate have no supposita in common – and this is automatically satisfied if one of them has no supposita at all. Universal negative sentences are true if the predicate does not supposit for everything for which the subject supposits – and this is automatically satisfied if either has no supposita. Taking affirmative sentences to have existential import, and negatives not to, preserves the traditional square of opposition without restricting the theory to nonempty terms.

Not all categorical sentences are as simple as these. Some, like those that include *qua*-clauses (e.g., 'Socrates, insofar as he is human, is an animal') or exceptives ('Every human except Socrates is asleep') are categorical in grammatical structure but semantically equivalent to molecular sentences and so have the truth conditions the corresponding molecular sentences have. Others, particularly explicitly tensed or modal sentences, require extensions of the basic semantic picture.

Like most of his contemporaries, Ockham thought that most explicitly tensed sentences and sentences with a modal copula (sentences like 'Some white thing will be black' or 'Some white thing can be black') are ambiguous "in the third way." A sentence like 'Some white thing will be black' has two readings. In both readings the supposition of the predicate term 'black' is displaced so that it stands not for the things that are now black (which is what it signifies in the narrow sense) but for the things that will be at any future time black. In one (I shall call it the "default" reading), the subject term is treated as outside the scope of the tense indicator and continues to supposit for its (narrow) significates – that is, for the things that are now white. In the other (I shall call it the "displaced" reading), the supposition of the subject term is also altered so that it stands not for what is now white but for what will be at any future time white. This "displacement" causes the term to supposit for what it does not signify in the narrow sense but leaves it suppositing for things it signifies in the wide sense Ockham discussed in *SL* I.33. Ockham's understanding of this displaced reading seems somewhat idiosyncratic. His contemporaries, like Jean Buridan and Buridan's followers, thought an explicitly tensed or modal copula could ampliate the supposition of the subject term so that it would stand, in the example, for both what is now white and what will be white. Ockham does not have this ampliated reading.

There is one exceptional kind of sentence for which Ockham thinks there are not two readings. It is a sentence with a tensed or modal copula and a discrete subject term – a subject term that is a proper name or demonstrative pronoun used alone. Because such terms are semantically fitted to signify exactly one thing (or in the case of the demonstrative just one thing on each occasion of use), even in the wide sense, Ockham thinks the mode of the copula can have no effect on their supposition. As we shall see, such sentences provide him with a tool for exploring the relations among other sentences.

Once we take into account the effect the tense or modal auxiliary in the copula has on the supposition of the terms in the sentence, there is nothing unusual about the way truth conditions for sentences with such copulas are given. Just as in the basic cases, a particular affirmative sentence is true just in case its subject and predicate terms have at least one suppositum in common; a universal negative is true just in case its terms have no supposita in common, and so on. Thus modal and tensed copulas affect the suppositions of terms but not the relations among sentences. We shall see that this simplifies a significant part of Ockham's modal syllogistic.

So far I have discussed explicitly tensed sentences and what Ockham calls modal sentences without a *dictum* (i.e., without the analogue of an English 'that' clause). He contrasts these modal sentences with modal sentences with a *dictum* – sentences of the form 'It is possible (necessary, contingent, etc.) that *p*' or 'That *p* is possible (necessary, contingent, etc.),' where 'that *p*' is a *dictum* formed from an assertoric sentence.

One might wonder why Ockham thinks sentences like this are categorical rather than molecular. The answer is that they do not, strictly speaking, contain an embedded sentence. Latin has two natural ways of forming a *dictum*. One is structurally just as in English, namely with '*quod*' (= 'that') followed by what looks just like a sentence. The other is by a construction that puts the subject of the clause in the accusative case and uses an infinitive form of the verb. This accusative-infinitive construction (as in the English 'I believe *her to be a great leader*') is the more common in Latin, does not look much like a sentence, and seems to have influenced theorists to avoid the thought that the '*quod*' clause contained an embedded sentence. Thus *dicta* were not considered sentences.

Ockham thinks sentences with a *dictum* have two senses. In the "sense of division" they are equivalent to the corresponding sentence without a *dictum*. Thus, 'It is possible that some white things be black,' read in the sense of division, is equivalent to 'Some white things can be black,' and can be treated in exactly the same way. For this reason medieval writers and modern commentators often indifferently describe both sentences without a *dictum* and sentences with a *dictum* but read in the divided sense simply as sentences in the divided sense. There is an alternative terminology that calls them "sentences *de re*."

The other sense in which sentences with a *dictum* can be read Ockham and the tradition call "the composite sense" (the alternative terminology speaks of "sentences *de dicto*"). Some writers in Ockham's time (Walter Burley, for example) refuse to consider such sentences as properly modal at all on the grounds that, from a logical standpoint, they are just assertoric singular sentences with a *dictum* as one term and a modal predicate as the other. Ockham is aware of these views but takes a different tack. He, following Aristotle he says,[6] classifies modal sentences in the composite sense as singular, particular, or indefinite on the basis of the structure of the embedded *dictum*.

Ockham does not admit tensed sentences in the composite sense. Modal sentences read in the composite sense are true, says he, when the sentence picked out by the embedded *dictum* is as the modal predicate would have it – that is, is "necessary or contingent, or true, or impossible or known or unknown or believed and so on"[7] – a list that shows his readiness to consider epistemic as well as alethic modalities. Unfortunately he has almost nothing to say in detail explicitly about these truth conditions.

He does say that for a claim like 'That God exists is necessary' to be true, it is not required that the sentence 'God exists' be itself necessary. A sentence with a *dictum* does not contain an embedded sentence, but Burley is right to think that if we treated the *dictum* as a term it would have to supposit for a sentence. Because a typical modal sentence with a *dictum* is affirmative, this raises issues of existential import about sentences. Ockham treats the issue by suggesting that for a necessity claim in the composite sense to be true it is not required that the sentence picked out by the *dictum* be a necessary object, or even that it always exist, but only that it be true whenever it does exist. This leaves his account vulnerable to the problems Buridan raises at the beginning of his *Sophismata*, Chapter VIII. The sentence 'No sentence is negative' is false whenever formed. Yet it seems possible that no sentence be negative – indeed that no sentence be at all!

Ockham is also interested in the relations between universal and particular modal sentences taken in the composite sense and their instances – that is, the sentences involved in the descent or ascent conditions for the supposition of their terms. This issue interacts for him with the logic of future contingents. Although Ockham himself is resolutely committed to bivalence, he thinks that Aristotle held that singular contingent sentences about the future are neither true nor false. He also thinks that Aristotle made no such exception for general sentences about the future. Thus, he thinks, Aristotle is committed to the view that a general sentence about the future may be true (or false) even though not one of its instances has a truth value. This issue has a shadow in Ockham's own logic in the question of the relation between a sentence like (1) 'That every true future contingent is true is necessary' and its instances. Ockham thinks (1) is true even though (1') 'That this is true is necessary,' pointing to some future contingent sentence, is simply false. Of course all this would be grist for the mill of someone, like Burley, who wanted to deny that sentences like (1) are really universal at all.

One way to approach the truth conditions for molecular sentences is through the question of whether we find in Ockham the truth functional sentential calculus so central to twentieth-century logics. I have already suggested Ockham does not think of negation in general as a sentential operator. He does have the notion of the contradictory of a sentence and seems to think the contradictory of an affirmative sentence will be a negative sentence and vice versa. Moreover, the contradictory of a singular affirmative sentence is formed simply by replacing the affirmative copula with a negative copula. But the contradictory of the negative singular sentence is formed not by adding another negation but by replacing the negative copula with the affirmative. Thus, although Ockham's negation is truth functional in that the contradictory of a sentence is in some sense its negation and is true just when that sentence is false, it behaves syntactically a little differently from our own.

Ockham does have the familiar truth functional accounts of conjunction and disjunction, and he does state principles like "the contradictory opposite of a conjunction is a disjunction formed of the contradictories of the parts of the conjunction."[8] So although he does not quite discuss the sentential calculus in the twentieth-century sense, he does seem to have the fragment of it that does not require iterated negations. This fragment of the sentential calculus is only a fragment of his language of molecular sentences, however. He also discusses the truth conditions for molecular sentences joined by causal particles (like 'because'), temporal particles (like 'while'), and 'spatial' particles (like 'where') and takes up the issue of conditionals but postpones it on the ground that the truth conditions for a conditional are the same as the validity conditions for the corresponding argument (consequentia) and so are better discussed there. It is there that I too now turn.

V. CONSEQUENCES

Ockham postpones treatment of the truth conditions for conditional sentences with the remark that because a given conditional is true just in case the corresponding argument or consequence is valid, the topic is best taken up in discussion of consequences. This remark by itself shows both that Ockham does not simply assimilate conditionals and consequences and that he accepts a version of what is now called the Deduction Theorem. Both points are worth noting, the first because there has been some debate in the scholarly literature about whether consequences are themselves sentences that have a truth value, and the second because his acceptance marks him off from some earlier figures, like Abelard, who denied the Deduction Theorem.

Next to the theory of supposition, it is probably on the characterization of his consequence relation that most of the twentieth-century ink devoted to Ockham's logic has been spilt. Ockham begins his discussion of consequences in general in *SL* by dividing them into those that are good as of now (*ut nunc*) and those that are good simply (*simpliciter*). He uses both temporal and modal language in characterizing both. A consequence is good as of now, he says, if it is not possible as of now for its antecedent to be true without its consequent being true, but it will be possible. A consequence is good simply if it never was, is, nor will be possible for its antecedent to be true without its consequent being true.

We can make sense of these remarks if we take modality to be tensed. What is possible changes over time. Ockham accepts the necessity of the present and the thesis that if something is really a given way and can be otherwise then it can change from the first way to the second. Thus, he has the conceptual resources to distinguish between what is possible, holding constant the way things now are, and what was, is, or will be possible at any time.

There has been (and is) much discussion of whether Ockham's as-of-now consequences are good just in case the corresponding material conditional (in the twentieth-century sense) is true. This discussion has been fueled by interest in whether Ockham has a conception of material implication, and that in turn by interest in how much of our own "classical" sentential calculus he accepts. It is uncontroversial that Ockham thinks valid consequence preserves truth – there are no acceptable consequences whose antecedents are true and consequents not true – but, I suggest, this necessary condition is not a sufficient condition even for valid consequence as of now. Ockham's language in dealing with all types of consequence is invariably modal, and if we attend to it we can find cases in which even the as-of-now consequences would be false while material conditionals in the twentieth-century sense would be true. Counterexamples would come from situations in which, although a sentence is true as of now, it can be false as of now. Future contingent sentences provide such cases. Consider the consequence 'Mother Teresa has died; therefore, the Antichrist will come.' The antecedent is true and so, if the usual interpretations of Christian scripture are to be believed, is the consequent. Hence, the material conditional formed from them is true. But the antecedent is really (*secundum rem*) about the present or past and so is necessary as of now. The consequent, however, is really about the future and so, although true, is contingent as of now. If Ockham means the modalities in his account of as-of-now consequence, one would expect him to reject consequences like my example on the ground that even as of now it is possible for the antecedent to be true and the consequent false.

For Ockham, a consequence is simply valid if at no time will it be possible for its antecedent to be true and its consequent false. One might understand this to be a loose way of saying an inference is simply valid if it neither was, is, nor will be possible for its antecedent to be true without its consequent being true. But Ockham's explicit use of the future tense in his explanation of simple consequence is backed up by his acceptance (in *SL* III-3.6) as simply valid of inferences in which the antecedent never could have been false but the consequent could have been false, though it no longer can be or become false. These strongly suggest that Ockham thinks an inference simply valid if it is now impossible for its consequent to be or become false while its antecedent remains true.

Ockham takes true sentences really about the (actual) present and the past to express what is necessary in his strongest and most basic sense. But there is a distinction between the immutability of what now makes a sentence true and the immutable truth of that sentence. The same sentence may describe different situations at different times and, if some of the situations it comes to describe do not obtain as it describes them to obtain, then the sentence may become false even though what it described earlier may have been and be immutably so. Consider, for example, 'The Antichrist has not existed.' This is a true sentence about the past and what it now claims is now unpreventable. But after the Antichrist comes to be, that sentence will be false. Of course it will not be that what the sentence now claims will have ceased to be so but rather that the sentence will then make a different claim that includes more time, and that stronger claim will be false. Ockham, I suggest, would admit 'God exists; therefore, the Antichrist has not existed' as a good consequence as of now because what the consequent claims is as of now just as necessary as God's existence. But whereas the sentence 'God exists' will be necessarily true whenever it is formed, the sentence 'The Antichrist has not existed' will not. Hence the inference is not simply valid.

Among simply valid consequences Ockham distinguishes between those that are formally valid and those that are materially valid.

These are valid in the same sense of 'valid,' and the very existence of materially valid inferences in that sense shows that Ockham's logic is not (merely?) a formal logic. Nevertheless formally valid inferences are by far the most important class of simply valid inferences from a logician's perspective. The distinction between the form and the matter of sentences was a traditional one by Ockham's time. The matter of a sentence is its categorematic terms; the form is the matrix of syncategoremata (including the copula) in which these terms are embedded. Traditionally, a consequence would be formally valid if its validity could be determined from the forms of its sentences no matter what categorematic terms were involved. It would be materially valid if its validity depended upon semantic relationships among the terms that were not indicated in the formal structure of the sentences. This is, for example how we find the distinction in figures like Buridan and Albert of Saxony. In Ockham, however, matters are complicated by what in the current state of our knowledge seems to be one of his more idiosyncratic logical projects: his reworking of the theory of topical "middles" (*media*).

Ockham divides consequences into those that hold through extrinsic middles and those that hold through intrinsic middles. As I understand his cryptic remarks in *SL* III-3.1, he is claiming that material consequences hold because of features of the categorematic terms of the individual sentences involved that give those sentences the truth values and the modal status they have. Ockham's examples of material consequences are always cases in which the antecedent is impossible or the consequent necessary, and in *SL* III-3.38 he explicitly says that the rules 'From the impossible anything follows' and 'The necessary follows from anything' yield consequences that are not formal. Formal consequences, on the other hand, hold immediately or mediately through a general rule. They hold mediately through a general rule if they hold because of some implicit relationship among the terms that has to be made explicit in order for a general rule to apply. Ockham's favorite example is 'Socrates does not run; therefore, a human does not run.' What needs to be made explicit here is that Socrates is a human. Once that is made explicit, we have an expository syllogism governed by the general rules of the expository syllogism.

Formal consequences that hold immediately through a general rule are as perfect as inferences get. Ockham suggests[9] all syllogisms hold through such general rules. There was a continuing debate among medieval logicians about whether syllogisms require justification by some rule. In Ockham's own time, Richard Campsall held that they do not and Walter Burley seems to have held that they do. Ockham, I think, implicitly sides with Burley.

Ockham insists that when the subject of a modal sentence is a discrete term, the divided-sense reading and the composite-sense reading of the sentence are equivalent. He uses this basic fact to establish other relationships. For example, he argues that from an indefinite sentence *de possibili* (that is, with 'can be' as the copula) in the composite sense to the corresponding indefinite sentence in the divided sense is a valid consequence if the subject of the divided-sense sentence has displaced supposition.[10] His procedure is to take as an arbitrary example the sentence 'This is possible: a white thing is sweet.' He then claims that if this is true, then so are 'This is possible: That is a white thing' and 'This is possible: That is a sweet thing' where 'that' picks out the same thing in both cases. But then so are these true: 'That can be white' and 'That can be sweet' where 'that' picks out the same thing in both cases. But from these it follows 'A white thing can be sweet.' We have to read the subject of this last sentence with displaced supposition because there is no guarantee that what is picked out by 'that' in the intermediate singular sentences is something that actually exists.

Ockham's syllogistic for modal sentences in the composite sense is generated by applying general rules of modal consequence to assertoric syllogisms, and it is in the context of modal syllogistic that he states the basic rules he needs as follows:

(1) If the premises of a valid argument are necessary, so is the conclusion.[11]

(2) If the premises of a valid argument are possible and compossible, then the conclusion is possible.[12]

(3) If the premises of a valid argument are contingent and compossible, then the conclusion is contingent.[13]

In his discussion of modal consequences more generally he also states the crucial 'weakening' rules for modalities as follows:

(4) A necessary sentence, whether in the composite or the divided sense, always entails the corresponding assertoric sentence.[14]

(5) An assertoric sentence entails the corresponding possible sentence.[15]

He explicitly combines these rules to conclude that a necessary sentence entails the corresponding possible sentence.[16]

VI. SYLLOGISMS

By far the most important class of formally valid inferences in Ockham's eyes are the syllogistic inferences. In making syllogisms central to his account of formally valid inference, he is distinguished from, for example, Walter Burley. In *SL*, Ockham spends on general nonsyllogistic inference about as much space as Burley spends in his *On the Purity of the Art of Logic* (probably written in reply) on syllogistic inference; Burley spends twelve lines.

The logic of the assertoric syllogism was well understood by Ockham's time and, although his presentation is not always standard, I know of nothing important he adds to it. Modal syllogistic was, however, still a subject under rapid development, and Ockham advances it considerably.

As we saw in Section IV, Ockham distinguishes sharply between modal sentences in the composite and in the divided sense. Some authors in his own time and some earlier had argued that only one of these was properly speaking the province of modal logic, but Ockham thinks otherwise. He classifies and examines the entire set of syllogisms that can be formed when premises and conclusion are all taken in one of the two ways and a collection of mixed syllogisms in which one premise or neither is taken in the same sense as the conclusion.

The number of such syllogisms is staggering, and although Ockham does consider a large number of cases his analysis seems to rest on a relatively small number of central ideas. It is on these I will focus here.

As we saw in Section IV, a modal sentence in the divided sense is equivocal. It has one reading in which its subject term stands for whatever it would stand for if the copula were not modal, and another reading in which the subject term is affected by the mode of the copula so that if *a* is the subject term and *m* the modality involved in the copula, the subject terms stands for what is *m*-ly *a*. The predicate term is always affected by the mode of the copula in this way. Now there are formal relations among modally affected terms. All things that are necessarily *a* are *a* and all *a* are possibly *a*. All things that are contingently *a* are *a*. The converses do not hold. Again all things that are contingently *a* are contingently non-*a*, and the converse does hold.

If I understand correctly Ockham's analysis of the syllogistic with all sentences in the divided sense, it can be obtained by treating '*a*,' 'things that are necessarily *a*,' 'things that are contingently *a*,' and 'things that are possibly *a*' as distinct terms related by the logical relations just cataloged and treating a modal sentence in the divided sense as an assertoric sentence with the appropriately modal predicate term and the appropriate subject term. Once the sentences have been transformed in this way, the entire modal syllogistic in the divided sense reduces to the ordinary assertoric syllogistic using these special terms and drawing such immediate inferences as the relations among these terms allow.

The logic of the uniform composite sense modal syllogistic is similarly straightforward. It is obtained by taking the standard assertoric syllogistic and applying to each of its valid syllogisms the general rules of modal consequence sketched at the end of Section V.

The theory of modal syllogisms with one premise taken in each sense, or with a conclusion taken in a different sense from the premises, is more complex. Ockham relies on two basic techniques. One is to see if the syllogism in question can be obtained by strengthening a premise or weakening the conclusion of a uniform syllogism and using one of the rules relating modal sentences in the two senses. The other is to analyze the truth conditions of the sentences in terms of singulars and determine validity in the way illustrated in Section V.

There has been considerable twentieth-century debate about which modal system comes closest to capturing the structure of Ockham's modal theory. We saw that Ockham accepts the principle that if the premises of a valid argument are necessary so is the conclusion, and the principle that if a sentence is necessary, then it is true. He also accepts the view that the principles of nonmodal logic are themselves necessarily true. If we suppose that he has a full sentential calculus, we have then attributed to him all that is required for the modern system *T*.

Ockham's modal syllogistic is a remarkable accomplishment. But modal syllogistic is only a first degree fragment of a modal logic in the twentieth-century sense. Ockham does not consider cases in which modalities are embedded inside others, nor cases in which copulas

are both tensed and modal. Consideration of his explicit theory of modal inference thus leaves unanswered some of the basic questions about his conception of modality. To answer these we must look at the interaction between time and modality in Ockham's picture.

Ockham thinks the past necessary.[17] Moreover, he thinks that having in its consequent a claim about the past (and so necessary in the way the past is necessary) makes a consequence simply valid.[18] Thus, the kind of necessity the past has is the kind involved in the account of simple consequence. What is past changes over time. Hence, what is necessary in the way the past is necessary changes over time. The past changes by addition. What was past remains past, but new items become past. Thus, as time passes, there are new necessities and the foreclosure of old possibilities. Hence, the fact that something is possible does not guarantee that it will continue to be possible. We cannot attribute to Ockham the view that if something is possible it is necessarily possible, the characteristic axiom of the modal system $S5$. What of the principle that what is necessary is necessarily necessary? Once a singular or particular affirmative sentence about the past has been true, it stays true (though the subject of the particular may have to be understood with its displaced rather than its default supposition). Its negation becomes and stays impossible. The same is not true for universal sentences. If something which was, was white, then nothing can undo that. But even if nothing was white, the next thing may be, and if it is, then forever after that something will have been white. Thus, we cannot attribute the principle that if a sentence is necessarily true it is necessarily necessarily true to Ockham in an unrestricted way. But the difference here between Ockham and the modern advocates of $S4$ has nothing much to do with their views on modality. It is because Ockham's basic categorical sentences are tensed and can take different truth values at different times that Ockham cannot accept the usual statement of the necessary necessity of the necessary. I suggest that Ockham's modal conception is in the $S4$ family but think much more work will be required to spell it out with any precision.

VII. CONCLUSION

Ockham did not do his logical work in a vacuum. He was the heir to a strong tradition of thirteenth- and early fourteenth-century English logic. His great older contemporary Walter Burley peeks out from many pages of his work, and some of Ockham's discussions only make sense against the background of Burley.[19]

But Ockham was a great logician. His consistent development of his semantics, his working out of the modal conception of consequence in a tensed framework, his discussion of future contingents, and especially his development of what may be the most comprehensive modal syllogistic of the Middle Ages all manifest his acumen and skill. Ockham was a great logician but not always a careful or a clear one. The sheer volume of his technical writing between 1319 and 1324 attests to his working very quickly indeed. It is no surprise, then, that he left unresolved several problems that later writers took very seriously. Many of these concerned his semantic program, and there was much later work indebted to his discussion of basic semantic relations like supposition. Some others concerned just what it was that modal sentences in the composite sense were about. Ockham talks as though these are claims about the modal status sentences would have if they were formed. But he has no account of the conditional used in that very formulation, and it does not on the face of it seem very plausible. His successors divided into strict inscriptionalists like Buridan and those, like Adam Wodeham, who introduced unusual ways in which *dicta* signified – ways that seductively invited reification as abstract objects. Some of Ockham's other loose ends concerned the nature and structure of consequence itself. His complex overlapping divisions of the consequence relation invited restructuring, his casual development of general rules of consequence in the context of his syllogistic invited a more elegant presentation, and his emphasis on syllogistic was already beginning to seem a bit old-fashioned in his own time. Perhaps it was in part because his work combined intellectual power with a certain stylistic looseness that it was well suited to be central to a research program. And central it was. There are over sixty-five manuscripts of *SL*, and it was edited at Oxford as late at 1675. One still finds the echoes of Ockham's semantics at the beginning of Hobbes's *Leviathan*. We still have much to learn from Ockham's discussions of time and of modality and from his articulation of the view that consequence itself is wider than our formal reconstructions of it.

NOTES

1 Scotus 1639, 1.273–341.
2 *SL* I.3.

3 *SL* I.4.
4 Ibid.
5 See, for example, Panaccio in Chap. 3, Secs. I and III, and Spade in Chap. 5.
6 *SL* II.9.
7 Ibid.
8 *SL* II.32.
9 *SL* III-3.1.
10 *SL* III-3.10 (633–4).
11 *SL* III-1.20 (412–3).
12 *SL* III-1.23 (419).
13 *SL* III-1.26.
14 *SL* III-3.11.
15 Ibid.
16 *SL* III-3.12.
17 For example, *Quodl.* II.5.
18 *SL* III-3.6 (608).
19 For example, that of the Liar Paradox at *SL* III-3.46.

3 Semantics and Mental Language

At the outset of *SL*, Ockham endorses Boethius's old distinction between three sorts of discourse: written, spoken, and mental. The first two, he explains, are physically perceptible, whether by the eye or by the ear, and are made up of conventional signs. The units of mental language, by contrast, are concepts. They are internal to thinking minds, and their signification is natural rather than conventional. Being mental, they are not directly perceptible – at least not in this world – to anybody but the person who internally produces them in the course of his or her private thinking. But being originally acquired as the result of a natural process, they are nevertheless strongly similar – and identically organized – from one human being to another. Although it is not a public medium of communication, mental language is potentially common to all. Mental language is prior to, and underlies, every reasonable speech utterance and provides it with meaning. Ockham's semantical theory, as presented in *SL* and elsewhere, is primarily an explication of the various ways in which the natural conceptual signs that constitute the language of thought are linked with their external referents; and secondarily, of the ways in which conventional discourse is derived from this mental language.

The theory of signification and other semantical properties such as connotation or supposition thus turn out to be essential, in Ockham's framework, to understanding the intellectual working of the mind. They are expected to provide a detailed account of how concepts, as natural signs, can be legitimately assembled into mental propositions describing the world, which are the direct objects of belief and knowledge and the basic units of human reasoning.

In conformity with the requirements of nominalism, the theory is supposed to admit nothing but singular entities, whether in the mind

53

itself or out there in the external world. This is, actually, the most salient feature of Ockham's semantics. The main problem for a nominalist like Ockham, who wanted to avoid ontological commitment to real universals in the world, is to account in detail for generality in thought and language without accepting at any point anything but irreducibly singular beings. Ockham intended to achieve just that by founding external language on mental language and then by explaining the representational capacities of the latter exclusively in terms of various meaning relations linking certain singular entities in the mind – the concepts – with their singular referents.

I. PRIMARY SIGNIFICATION

Some of the semantical properties called upon in this endeavor are attributed by Ockham to single terms in themselves prior to their being inserted into propositions, whereas another property is said to characterize terms only when they occur as parts of propositions. The former are the basic ones: primary signification and connotation (or secondary signification), whereas the latter, called 'supposition,' is derived and context-dependent.

Signification, here, is the main notion. At variance with the terminology of most of his predecessors, Ockham does not treat signification as a relation between spoken words and the underlying concepts. Signification, for him, first and foremost, belongs to the component units of mental language: it is the relation that holds between natural signs within a particular mind and the outer things they represent for that mind. Spoken and written words receive their signification only derivatively through the following process: a certain spoken sound is conventionally associated with – "subordinated to," Ockham says – a given concept by a particular speaker or group of speakers, and as a result, it thereafter starts conventionally signifying for these speakers whatever it is the concept naturally signifies.[1] The spoken word 'horse,' for example, will not be said to signify the corresponding concept, as Aristotle had proposed in *On Interpretation* 1.16ᵃ3–4, nor, of course, a common nature, because nothing of the sort exists for Ockham, but the external singular horses themselves, just as the concept did: through being conventionally subordinated to a mental term, the spoken sound inherits the latter's significates. *Mutatis mutandis* the process is iterated from spoken to written words.

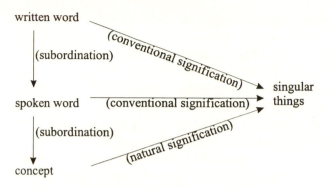

Figure 3.1. Natural and conventional signification.

Ultimately, the conventional significations of all external words are made to rest on the natural signification of conceptual tokens.

Not all mental terms, though, are endowed with signification in the proper sense. Ockham sees mental language as displaying a fine-grained grammatical structure very similar to that of spoken languages with not only names and verbs in it but also adverbs, conjunctions, and prepositions.[2] There are, in particular, mental equivalents for such words as 'every,' 'no,' 'from,' 'except,' 'insofar as,' and so forth, that do not by themselves represent any distinct reality but are used in propositional contexts to determine the modes of reference of names and verbs and the logical structure of the propositions. These purely functional units are called *syncategorematic* terms, and the others – terms like 'horse,' 'white,' 'whiteness,' 'to run,' and so on – are the *categorematic* ones, the dividing line being precisely that the latter do signify distinct things by themselves, whereas the former do not.[3]

Categorematic concepts constitute the basic blocks of mental language. What Ockham calls their primary signification simply is their relation to every distinct object they are true of. 'Horse,' for example, primarily signifies every single horse; 'white' primarily signifies every single white thing; 'whiteness' primarily signifies every single whiteness (Ockham admits singular qualities in his ontology); and the verb 'to run' primarily signifies everything that runs. In short, the primary significates of a mental categorematic term are all the singular things that this term represents in the mind in such a way that it can stand for them in a mental proposition. In the case of general terms, primary signification is a one-many relation between a certain conceptual token and several individuals in the world; it is closely akin to what modern philosophers have called "multiple denotation" or "plural reference."

Ockham further distinguishes between primary signification in the strictest sense and primary signification in a wider sense.[4] In the narrow sense, a given term is said to signify primarily only entities that actually exist at the time of utterance: only actual and presently existing horses, for example, in the case of 'horse.' In the wider sense, however, it is admissible to say the term primarily signifies past, future, and even merely possible individuals as well: 'horse' can thus be said to signify primarily in the wide sense not only presently existing horses but also all past, future, and merely possible horses. Through the acceptance of this wider relation, Ockham turns out to be committed to attributing a certain ontological status to past and future beings, and even to mere *possibilia*.[5] This does not run counter to his nominalism, though, for the extra ontological commitment still extends to nothing but individuals.

II. CONNOTATION

Among categorematic terms, some have only a primary signification, whereas others, in addition, have a secondary signification, or *connotation*.[6] The former Ockham calls *absolute terms*. They correspond, in modern philosophical terminology, to natural kind terms, such as 'man,' 'horse,' 'animal,' 'tulip,' 'flower,' and so forth. What characterizes them is that each one signifies all its significates in exactly the same way and can indifferently stand for any of them in propositions. Consider 'horse,' for example. According to Ockham, it signifies nothing but horses; and every horse it signifies equally: it can stand for any of them in propositions such as 'Every horse is a mammal,' 'Some horses are white,' or 'Bucephalus is a horse.'

A connotative term, by contrast, has at least two series of significates. Like absolute terms, it has primary significates such as red things in the case of 'red' and horsemen in the case of 'horseman'; but in addition it also refers the mind, in virtue of its very meaning, to some other singular beings in the world, for which it normally will not stand in propositions (e.g., rednesses in the case of 'red' and horses in the case of 'horseman'). Those are said to be its secondary significates or *connotata*. In mental as well as in spoken languages, the class of connotative terms is very extensive for Ockham – much more than that of absolute ones. It includes all concrete qualitative terms such as 'red,' all relational terms ('father,' for instance, primarily signifies all fathers and connotes their children), many psychological, semantical, and moral terms such as 'intellect,' 'will,' 'true,' 'good,' and so forth, all quantitative and dimensional terms such as 'figure,' 'length,' 'solid,' and so on, and generally, Ockham says, "all the expressions in the categories other than substance and quality."[7]

One salient difference between absolute and connotative terms in Ockham's view is that the former can never be completely defined, whereas the latter can. Because absolute terms refer equally to whatever it is they signify, their meaning cannot adequately be broken into ordered sequences of other terms. For any connotative term C, on the contrary, there is in the same language a unique complex expression E such that E is a complete nominal definition of C. 'White,' for example, is defined as 'something having a whiteness' and 'cause' as 'something upon the existence of which another thing follows.'[8] In such definitions, Ockham explains, the secondary significates of the defined connotative term are normally referred to by some grammatical complements; whitenesses, for example, are explicitly referred to by the term 'whiteness,' which occurs as a grammatical complement in the definition of 'white' as 'something having a whiteness.'

In view of this special feature, it has often been doubted whether connotative terms as such should be accepted in mental as well as in spoken language in Ockham's best doctrine.[9] Because there is no synonymy in Mentalese for him,[10] can it not be concluded that all connotative terms should be represented in the mind by their explicit nominal definitions? The consequences of this would be far-reaching: the only categorematic terms in the natural language of thought would be absolute, and all the rest could be considered logical constructions out of these. But this, in fact, is not what Ockham says. The distinction between absolute and connotative simple terms is registered by him among those that are present in mental as well as in conventional language,[11] and more than once does he explicitly refer to simple connotative concepts in the mind.[12] The type of synonymy Ockham wants to exclude from mental language is only synonymy between simple terms; he has no objection – quite to the contrary – to the coexistence in Mentalese of a simple connotative term with its complex nominal definition.

The philosophical role of Ockham's distinction between primary and secondary signification is to rarefy the ontology, not the mental apparatus for knowledge. Ockham's project is to explicate all semantical and epistemological features – truth values, for instance – in terms of relations between sign-tokens and singular objects of the world. Nothing prevents more than one such relation from being considered basic in the process. The duality of primary and secondary signification allows, in fact, for the admittance of a wide array of nonsynonymous concepts, while avoiding the reification of universals and other abstract entities. To borrow Quine's famous example, 'renate' (defined as 'animal with a kidney') and 'cordate' (defined as 'animal with a heart') can be admitted as two distinct, nonsynonymous simple concepts even though their primary significates are the same (supposing every renate is a cordate, and conversely); this can be done without recourse to special abstract properties of renateness or cordateness simply because the secondary significates of 'renate' and 'cordate' are not the same: 'renate' connotes kidneys; 'cordate' connotes hearts. Relational and quantitative concepts, being connotative, can be accepted in the same way without having to enrich the ontology with special entities such as relations or quantities. Because a relational term like 'father,' for example, is described as primarily signifying fathers and secondarily signifying their children, no extra entity is needed in its explication besides the *relata*. Connotation in Ockham's hands turns out to be a highly effective device in the service of ontological economy.

III. SUPPOSITION

When a categorematic term, whether absolute or connotative, is inserted in a proposition as subject or predicate, it thereby acquires a new semantical property called "supposition," which is the particular referential function it receives in the context of this proposition.[13] Ockham inherited this doctrine from the thirteenth-century terminist logicians but exploited it in his own way by entrusting it with a central role in the semantical machinery of his nominalistic system. The core intuition here is that the propositional surrounding *always* affects, in some way, the reference of the subject and predicate.

Taking as input the semantical import of the term considered in itself – its signification (primary and secondary) – the propositional context determines the exact set of referents for which the term stands in this particular proposition and the special way it stands for them. Ockham's theory of these phenomena has striking consequences for ontology and epistemology.

There are three main varieties of supposition for him, and all three are found in mental as well as in spoken and written languages.[14] The most basic one is *personal supposition*. It corresponds to the normal use of a subject or predicate term (whether simple or complex) as standing for its primary significates. Thus, 'horse' is taken in personal supposition as standing for horses and nothing but horses in propositions such as 'All horses are animals,' 'Some horses are black,' 'Some animals are horses,' 'No horse is a human,' and so on. In all such cases – even when it is accompanied by 'some' or 'no' – the categorematic term stands for the same significates but *in different ways* according to the logical form of the proposition and the place of the term in it. Various subdivisions of personal supposition (distributive, determinate, confused . . .) are thus identified, and their logical impact is described in some detail.[15] The important point here is that, all across its various modes, personal supposition remains a referential connection holding, in the context of an actual linguistic or mental occurrence, between a token of some categorematic term and the singular beings that term is true of.

It sometimes happens, however, that a term is not used significatively and does not stand for its significates at all. This is the case when the term is taken in one of the other two main varieties of supposition: material or simple. If 'Horse is an English noun' is to be accepted as true, for example, 'horse' must be taken in this proposition as standing not for real horses but for spoken or written tokens of the word 'horse.' This is *material supposition*. When the term stands nonsignificatively but for natural mental signs rather than spoken or written ones, as 'horse' in 'Horse is a concept,' it is said to be taken in *simple supposition*. In both cases, the referents are different from the significates, but they are no less singular, namely written, spoken, or mental occurrences of signs.

Supposita, then, are always irreducibly singular. This is not to say they are all actual and presently existing. If the main verb of the proposition is in the past tense, Ockham holds, the subject and predicate terms may supposit (personally or otherwise) for past individuals that do not exist anymore: in 'All horses were running,' the subject term 'horses' may, in one admissible interpretation, be taken to stand for past horses, some of which might not exist at the time of utterance.[16] The same is true, *mutatis mutandis*, of propositions with a future-tense verb (in 'All horses will run,' 'horses' can – in one admissible interpretation of the sentence – supposit for future horses), and even of propositions with a modal auxiliary such as 'can' (in 'All horses can run,' 'horses' can legitimately be interpreted as standing for all possible horses). Ontologically, it follows from this, as from Ockham's theory of signification in the wide sense, that an ontological status is attributed to past, future, and merely possible beings, for they all can be referred to in actual propositions, whether mental, spoken, or written.

As for epistemology, Ockham's theory of supposition conveys an intriguing – and far-reaching – picture of how the language of thought is supposed to work. The distinction between signification and supposition; the division of the latter into personal, simple, and material; the further subdivision of personal supposition into many branches – all of this is taken to apply to mental as well as to conventional language. It follows, in particular, that Mentalese is liable in principle to certain sorts of semantical ambiguities.[17] Ockham in effect formulates a number of precise rules for determining the supposition of terms in given propositional contexts – whether it should be personal, material, or simple, for instance, or whether the term stands for past, future, or possible individuals in a given occasion. But these rules crucially leave open some ambiguities. Ockham holds, for example, that any proposition with an ordinary nonmetalinguistic subject and a metalinguistic predicate (such as 'Horse is a name,' 'Horse is a concept,' or even 'Horse is a species') is semantically ambiguous according to whether the subject term is taken to be in personal, material, or simple supposition.[18] And a similar phenomenon touches all propositions with a past- or future-tense verb or with a modal auxiliary[19]: 'All white things were white yesterday' might mean that everything that is now white was white yesterday (which is probably false) or that everything that was white yesterday was then white (which is trivially true). One must conclude that the language of thought, for Ockham, is not by itself semantically pure. Interestingly enough, this seems to invite acknowledgement that a person may be confused, on certain occasions, as to what exactly he or she is actually thinking, but Ockham never developed the point.[20]

IV. TRUTH CONDITIONS

The main function of supposition theory within Ockham's semantical system is to provide a bridge between signification and truth value. Signification, as we have seen, is a property of terms considered in themselves. A proposition as a whole does not signify anything, properly speaking. Ockham refuses to admit special objects in the world as significates for propositions. The distinctive semantical property of propositions, instead, is that they are true or false; and truth and falsity, as Ockham endeavors to show in some detail in *SL* II, can be accounted for without enriching the ontology further. For each basic kind of elementary proposition, truth conditions are given that solely rest, for ontological import, on the supposition of their component terms. The process is then extended to complex propositions such as disjunctions, conjunctions, and so on.

Thus, a necessary and sufficient condition for the truth of a singular affirmative proposition, such as 'Bucephalus is a horse,' Ockham explains, is that its predicate supposits for what its subject supposits for.[21] Similar rules are given for elementary general propositions from the usual Aristotelian foursome: universal affirmative ('All horses run'), universal negative ('No horse runs'), particular affirmative ('Some horse runs'), and particular negative ('Some horse does not run').[22] A universal and negative proposition, for example, is counted true if and only if its predicate supposits for nothing its subject supposits for. A particular and affirmative proposition is true if and only if its predicate supposits for some of the things its subject supposits for. And so on. An interesting consequence of this set of rules, which, as a matter of fact, Ockham repeatedly acknowledges, is that if the subject or predicate supposits for nothing, the proposition is always false when affirmative, and true when negative, independently of whether it is universal, particular, or singular[23]: 'A unicorn is an animal' comes out as false in this system, and 'Santa Claus is not bearded' as true.

Formulations of this type for truth conditions obviously cannot have been intended as explications for syncategorematic terms such as negations and quantifiers ('no,' 'all,' 'some,' etc.) because these are freely used by Ockham in the metalinguistic wording of the truth conditions. Their role, instead, is to account for the systematical and compositional organization of thought and language without further *ontological* complication other than what was required for the semantical analysis of single categorematic terms.

Detailed attention is given by Ockham in this context to the truth conditions for modal propositions, two varieties of which he distinguishes according to whether they are taken in *the sense of composition* or in *the sense of division*.[24] A modal proposition, in this vocabulary, is said to be taken in the sense of composition when the modality is attributed to the proposition as a whole: 'It is necessary that *p*,' in this sense, really means 'That *p* is necessarily true.' Once it is recognized that the subject 'that *p*,' in such cases, has material or simple supposition and that it stands, therefore, for certain propositional tokens, the usual truth conditions are seen to apply to all these cases without undesirable ontological commitment. In modal sentences taken in the sense of division, on the other hand, the modality is best expressed, according to Ockham, by an adverb accompanying the copula, as in 'Horses necessarily are animals.' Such a proposition is said to be true if and only if each singular proposition of the form 'This horse is an animal' is necessarily true. Talk about modalities is ultimately reduced in this case as well as in the preceding, albeit indirectly, to metalinguistic discourse about certain propositional tokens.

As for complex propositions – which Ockham collectively calls "hypothetical" – they are subdivided into species: conditional, conjunctive, disjunctive, causal, temporal, and local, each being built out of a plurality of more elementary propositions through the use of such connectors as 'if,' 'and,' 'because,' and so forth. Their truth conditions are given metalinguistically by Ockham: conjunctions, for instance, are said to be true if and only if each one of their component parts is true.[25] We find in Ockham no attempt, though, to reduce the whole array of these complex propositions to extensional truth functions, as in today's standard propositional calculus. A conditional proposition, for instance, is said by him to be true if and only if its consequent follows from its antecedent,[26] which leaves unreduced the notion of a proposition "following from" another one. Similarly the truth conditions for causal propositions leave unreduced the notion of a causal relation itself, and those of temporal propositions leave unreduced the ideas of simultaneity and temporal priority, and so on.[27] But Ockham wanted to maintain that causality, temporality, and place are not needed as independent objects in the process for all that. Indeed, he dedicated a remarkably large number of pages, mainly in the context of his physical treatises, to showing, precisely, that none of these is a thing in itself, but that statements such as 'A caused B,' or 'A is prior to B' can nevertheless be determinately true or false.[28] The whole structure of propositional discourse is ultimately brought to rest, for its truth and falsity, upon the ways in which the various singular beings of the world are arranged with regard to each other along certain ordered series, such as the causal, the temporal, and the local ones. The orderings themselves, though, are denied any independent reality.

V. EXPONIBLE PROPOSITIONS

Special truth conditions are given – sometimes in detail – by Ockham for a certain subclass of elementary propositions: those equivalent to complex propositions (especially conjunctions) despite having the form of elementary ones (subject + copula + predicate).[29] These propositions cover a wide variety of interesting cases, including, for example, reduplicative propositions (such as 'All horses *qua* horses are animals'), exceptive propositions ('All horses run except Bucephalus'), exclusive propositions ('Only Bucephalus runs'), and propositions with some special verbs such as 'to begin,' 'to cease,' and 'to become.' Above all, this subclass of elementary propositions includes all propositions with a connotative subject or predicate, among which are counted all those that have a negative or fictitious term in them, such as 'immaterial' or 'unicorn,' and even more importantly *all relational propositions* ('A is similar to B,' 'A caused B,' 'A gave B to C,' and so forth). In all such cases, the truth conditions for the proposition under analysis are given by those of its complex equivalent.

When the complex equivalent is a conjunction – as in virtually all of Ockham's examples – the truth conditions of the original proposition come down to those of the elementary components of this conjunction. These are then said to be its '*exponentes.*' Thus, 'All horses run except Bucephalus' is broken into two *exponentes:* 'All horses other than Bucephalus run' and 'Bucephalus does not run'[30];

'A white thing runs' (where 'white thing' is a connotative term defined as 'something having a whiteness') is broken into 'Something
runs' and 'This thing has a whiteness'[31]; 'Socrates is blind' (where
'blind' is a disguised negative term) is broken into 'Socrates exists,'
'Socrates should have sight,' and 'Socrates does not have sight.'[32]
And so on. In each of these cases, the original sentence will be true
if and only if all its *exponentes* are.

What exactly was the point of such analyses is not an obvious
matter. One attractive answer is that they were meant to reveal the
true logical structure of mental discourse by contrast with that of a
spoken or written utterances. It is very tempting, indeed, for modern philosophers to view Ockham's mental language as a semantically ideal deep structure, in which, among other features, the "exponible" propositions are explicitly represented by the conjunctions
of their *exponentes*. But it was not so for the *Venerabilis Inceptor*
himself. Remember, all propositions with connotative terms in them
are counted by Ockham among those equivalent to complex ones,
and, accordingly, are broken into *exponentes*. But, as we have seen
earlier, there are simple connotative terms in Ockham's mental language, and there must be, therefore, distinct elementary propositions
featuring them as subject or predicate. Even in the internal language
of thought, these are not to be identified with the complex propositions they are equivalent to in truth conditions.

Actually, the main job of the *exponentes* in Ockham's semantics,
to be judged from the numerous examples he gives, is to render con-
spicuous the ontological import of the propositions under analysis,
whether these are mental, spoken, or written. The theory of "exponible" propositions, in his hands, is a means for ontological, not
psychological, exploration. Take 'Socrates is white,' for instance. Its
truth conditions, Ockham says, are given by 'Socrates exists' and
'Socrates has a whiteness.' The point here is not to eliminate 'white'
from the basic vocabulary of the language of thought but to provide
for a well-chosen equivalent of the sentence under analysis, an equivalent in which everything that is required to exist for this sentence
to be true is explicitly referred to by the new subject and predicate
terms: 'Socrates' and 'whiteness' in the alleged example.[33] 'All horses
run except Bucephalus,' to recall another example, is explicated into
'All horses other than Bucephalus are running' and 'Bucephalus is
not running.' Here the suppositing subjects and predicates within

the *exponentes* are 'Bucephalus,' 'running,' and the complex term 'horse other than Bucephalus'; the ontological import of the original proposition will correspond to whatever has to be supposited for by any one of these three terms in order for both *exponentes* to be true. Such truth conditions, then, are means for clarifying the ontological commitment associated with exponible propositions: this is done by looking at the supposition needed for the subjects and predicates of their *exponentes*. In the end, the operation is expected to show that no extra entities besides the singular referents of ordinary categorematic terms are required for an adequate understanding of any of these cases.

VI. UNIVERSALS

From the signification of terms to the truth conditions of propositions, the whole semantical apparatus we have described so far can be seen as a sophisticated analytical machinery for alleviating the ontological commitments of true discourse. It was so used by Ockham, in fact, in the discussion of a wide array of issues in metaphysics and philosophy of nature. What he would strive to do in these fields, characteristically, was to submit the relevant philosophical theses to close semantical scrutiny and to provide, with the help of his theory of signification and supposition, new readings of well-accepted Aristotelian or Christian dicta, readings that render them more innocuous for ontology than realist philosophers would have taken them to be.

The most salient case is the famous problem of universals, raised by Porphyry at the outset of his treatise *On the Predicables* (= *Isagoge*). Given that there are species and genera, such as man or animal, What are they? Porphyry asked. Do they exist by themselves out there in the world or are they mere creatures of the mind? Ockham's answer is unequivocal: species and genera are concepts. Which is to say they are but *natural signs* within the mind.[34] Their generality does not amount to a special ontological feature they have but to a semantical one: a general concept, after all, is simply a singular mental occurrence that *signifies* several other singular entities.

Accordingly, such sentences as 'Man is a species' or 'Animal is a genus,' which are standardly accepted as true within the Aristotelian framework, are interpreted as being about nothing but signs. With the technical help of supposition theory, they are read as metalinguistic statements about mental discourse. 'Man is a species' is true indeed, Ockham says, but only if the subject term 'man' is taken in *simple* supposition.[35] If 'man' were in personal supposition instead, it would stand for singular men; but none of these, of course, is a species, and hence the adage would turn out to be false. It is saved, however, by 'man' being given simple supposition, for the term then stands not for men themselves but for (occurrences of) the mental sign 'man.' The predicate term 'species,' on the other hand, is counted by Ockham among *names of second intention*, which he defines as names signifying mental signs.[36] What the sentence 'Man is a species' should be taken to mean is something like 'The mental sign *man* is a sortal concept.' And that is true.

This is what the American nominalist philosopher Wilfrid Sellars saw as a "major breakthrough" in philosophy due to Ockham: statements about universals were reinterpreted, thanks to semantical analysis, as metalinguistic in character.[37]

There are recalcitrant cases, of course. Ockham's opponents would typically mention the following, for example: 'Man is the most dignified creature.' Here, they would say, 'man' cannot supposit for singular men because it cannot be true of each man that he is the most dignified creature. But, on the other hand, 'man' cannot be taken metalinguistically either as suppositing for certain conceptual tokens, for it is certainly not true of any conceptual token that it is the most dignified creature in the world. The only possibility left, the objector would conclude, is that it supposits for a common nature, and common natures, therefore, should be admitted among the external referents of mental concepts. Ockham's strategy in reply is twofold.[38] First, he concedes that the sentence 'man is the most dignified creature' is literally false, for it turns out false whether the subject term is taken in personal, simple, or material supposition. But second, he proposes to save it nevertheless by seeing it as a conveniently simplified, nonliteral way of speaking: what those who use the dictum really mean – or should mean – is something more complicated and cumbersome such as 'Any man is a more dignified creature than any creature that is not a man,' the truth of which does not require the existence of anything but singular creatures.

In this example, the proposition in need of reformulation is rewritten in a more explicit way, making it clear that the information it purports to convey is about external individuals in the world and nothing else. In some other cases, though, Ockham favors a metalinguistic construal: a proposition such as 'Man is the only animal capable of laughing,' for example, is also reckoned to be literally false whether 'man' is in personal, simple, or material supposition. But what it is used to convey, according to Ockham, is a true metalinguistic assertion such as: 'The predicate *capable of laughing* is true of no animals besides men.'[39] In the end, such reformulations always bring us back either to the ordinary referential use of a general term as standing for its singular significates (personal supposition) or to a special self-referential use of the term (simple supposition). One way or the other, external universals are avoided thanks to semantical analysis.

VII. ABSTRACTIONS

Besides genera and species, some philosophers, in the line of Duns Scotus, thought it necessary to posit special abstract entities such as animality, horseness, fatherhood, or even individual abstractions such as Socrateity (which is the property that differentiates Socrates from any other human being) to account for the ontological structure of the world. But these too Ockham would strenuously reduce to singular substances and qualities through semantical considerations. His focus here was on the distinction we find in conventional languages between concrete terms, such as 'horse,' 'white,' and 'father' and their abstract counterparts.[40] It is not to be supposed, Ockham insisted, that the availability of such linguistic couples generally reveals a corresponding duality between concrete and abstract entities. First of all, the very unity of the distinction is merely verbal and hangs on superficial features of written and spoken words: a concrete term and its abstract counterpart "have the same stem, but differ in ending,"[41] as for 'horse'/'horseness,' 'father'/'fatherhood,' and the like; often, but not always, the abstract terms will have more syllables than the concrete ones, and typical endings too, such as '-ity,' '-ness,' or '-hood' in English. These superficial regularities, however, are misleading and correspond to no uniform semantical distinction. Ockham in effect identifies four different modes of relations that can be found between the signification of concrete words and that of the corresponding abstract ones.

In some cases (this is the first of the four modes) the concrete and the abstract terms do signify (primarily or secondarily) different things. 'White,' for example, primarily signifies white things, whereas 'whiteness' primarily signifies their whitenesses; and whitenesses are not themselves white. In all such cases, the significates of both terms, however distinct from one another, will never be anything but singular beings: white things are but singular substances, and whitenesses are singular qualities.

It sometimes happens, on the other hand (this is the second mode), that the concrete and the corresponding abstract terms are wholly synonymous, according to Ockham,[42] in which cases (this is Ockham's definition of synonymy) nothing is signified by one of them, primarily or secondarily, that is not signified in exactly the same way by the other one. Salient and intriguing examples of this are provided by such couples as 'horse'/'horseness' or 'animal'/'animality.' Horseness and animality, contrary to whiteness or virtue, are not accidents of substances. They are not something that a horse or an animal *has*. If they are anything at all, they are to be identified, Ockham insists, with the singular horses or animals themselves; the abstract names, therefore, should not be taken as referring to anything not referred to in the same way by their concrete counterparts. Both terms in such cases are legitimately interpredicable: sentences such as 'A horse is a horseness' or 'Horsenesses are horses,' however surprising, are thus counted true.

Ockham significantly ranges under this same mode many concrete and abstract terms from the Aristotelian categories of quantity and relation. The term 'quantity' itself, for example, is nothing in his eyes but a verbal variant in the guise of an abstract term for its concrete counterpart 'quantum.' A "quantum," in Ockham's terminology, is anything that has parts outside parts, and exactly the same is true of a quantity: a material body can indifferently be said to be a quantum or a quantity. Pairs of relational terms such as 'father'/'fatherhood' or 'cause'/'causality' are treated in the same way. Quantities and relations are thus reduced to substances and qualities.

The third mode is especially interesting. It has to do with pairs of concrete and abstract terms that, although not synonymous to one another, ultimately refer nevertheless to the very same objects.[43]

This is possible because in some cases the abstract word is but a verbal abbreviation for a complex expression incorporating the concrete name plus some syncategorematic terms or adverbial qualifications. 'Manhood,' for instance, might mean in some uses something like 'man *qua* man' or 'man necessarily.' 'Manhood runs' will then be false even if 'A man runs,' or even 'All men run' were true, simply because men do not *necessarily* run. Some differences in truth values are thus accounted for without postulating extra referents on one side or the other.

Finally, it happens that an abstract name is sometimes really a collective term capable of standing for many of the significates of its concrete counterpart taken together.[44] 'People' and 'popular' provide an example of this. Both refer to nothing but men, but although a single man might be said to be popular, none can be said to be a people by himself. In this case, as in the previous ones, the verbal distinction between concrete and abstract terms is given a semantical interpretation that requires no special abstract referents distinct from ordinary singular substances and qualities.

VIII. PSEUDONAMES

The first and fourth modes of distinction between concrete and abstract terms in conventional languages correspond to genuine distinctions in mental language: 'white' and 'whiteness,' for example, are respectively subordinated to distinct concepts, and so are 'popular' and 'people'. The second mode constitutes a merely verbal redundancy because the concrete and abstract terms, in this case, are wholly synonymous. The third mode, however, is very special with regard to the semantical correspondence between conventional and mental discourse. It instantiates, in Ockham's eyes, a more general linguistic phenomenon that deserves special attention in itself because it is frequent in the practice of ordinary languages and potentially very misleading in philosophy:

For the speakers of a language can, if they wish, use one locution in place of several. Thus, in place of the complex expression 'every man', I could use '*A*'; and in place of the complex expression 'man alone', I could use '*B*', and so on with other expressions.[45]

This is what happens when a single abstract word such as 'manhood' is used in place of a complex sequence involving an adverbial qualification such as 'man necessarily'.

In such cases, the abbreviated complex sequence does not always constitute a genuine logical unit and is not always subordinated to a single concept. The sequence 'man necessarily' is precisely a case in point: the modal adverb 'necessarily' in a sentence such as 'Man necessarily is rational' is not part of the subject at all, and the sequence 'man necessarily,' in effect, is logically adventitious. This does not prevent any given speaker or group of speakers from abbreviating it into a single word in such a sentence or in any other where it is found. But this possibility exists only for conventional discourse. In mental language, 'man' and 'necessarily' are naturally kept apart and never merge into one single concept.

This is how pseudonames are created in spoken and written languages. They are single conventional words that superficially belong to the grammatical category of nouns but are not subordinated to genuine conceptual names, whether proper or common, and which, moreover, are not even subordinated to a well-arranged conceptual sequence capable of being by itself a subject or predicate in a mental proposition. Ockham is quite explicit about such phenomena in his *Treatise on Quantity*, in which he discusses quantitative and physical terms such as 'point,' 'line,' 'surface,' 'instant,' 'change,' 'generation,' and so on.[46] None of these, he says has "the precise strength of a name." If they did, one would have to concede that there exists something they signify and which they can stand for in true propositions. But the ontological commitment is avoided in this situation by seeing that the relevant terms are mere abbreviations for complex sequences incorporating adverbs, prepositions, conjunctions, or verbs. In literal discourse, Ockham insists, these pseudonames cannot even be used as subjects or predicates of well-formed propositions. They belong, in fact, to *figurative speech*. A sentence like 'Generation occurs in an instant,' if found in some authorities, should not be understood as asserting, as it seems to, a relation between one determinate thing – a generation – and another one – an instant – but as a figurative way of saying something like "When a thing is generated, it is not generated part after part, but the whole of it is generated simultaneously."[47]

These ways of speaking are found by Ockham to be frequent not only in ordinary language but also in poetry, philosophy, and theology, where they are introduced for the sake of prosody, elegance, or brevity. They are quite legitimate, he thinks, as long as one knows what one is doing, as the ancient authorities did. When simple-minded philosophers start taking such stuff literally, however, numerous and important mistakes inevitably follow – especially with regard to what one takes to be the basic furniture of the world.

Ockham provides no explicit set of general rules for unfolding the meanings of figurative abbreviations of this sort. The interpretation must be based, in each case, on what can be gathered of the speaker's intentions and on what makes the best sense in the context. Most of the time, as his examples show, the philosophical analysis should deal with complete propositions such as 'Generation occurs in an instant' or 'Movement is in time,' rather than with isolated terms such as 'generation,' 'movement,' or 'time' precisely because such pseudonames considered in themselves have no determinate signification.[48] Unlike real connotative names, in particular, they do not have self-sufficient definitions capable of serving as subjects and predicates in literal sentences. Being but conventional abbreviations for adventitious sequences, they do not correspond to natural units of mental language.

It can be gathered from Ockham's thus relegating such pseudonames to figurative speech that in his eyes one necessary condition for speaking literally or properly is that one's external utterances should duplicate, at least approximately, the logical structure of the underlying mental propositions. 'Generation is in an instant,' or 'Man is the most dignified creature,' to recall another sort of example we have met with earlier, both belong to figurative speech precisely because, in the sense in which they are acceptable, their subjects and predicates do not correspond to those of the underlying true mental proposition. Mental language, in Ockham's doctrine, regulates the structure of proper external ways of speaking.

IX. NOMINALISM AND THE LANGUAGE OF THOUGHT

To sum up, the foundation of Ockham's whole semantical system is ontological: only singular beings are accepted as real; only they can be referred to in any way, whether by natural internal concepts or by conventional words. Through a wide variety of analytical devices,

Ockham consistently strives to highlight that only singular beings are needed for true knowledge and language.

The basic semantical relation in this approach is the natural primary signification of mental categorematic terms, which, in the case of general concepts, is a one-many relation: such a concept naturally signifies all the individuals it is true of. Some concepts, the connotative ones, have in addition a secondary signification linking them with certain singular beings they are not true of but that nevertheless they bring to mind obliquely, so to say. When a categorematic concept is inserted in a proposition as subject or predicate, it thereby acquires a determinate referential function called supposition, which in most cases directly derives from its signification and which in all cases will serve as the basis for the truth conditions of the proposition. Conventional terms are created through subordination of spoken sounds to concepts or of written marks to spoken sounds. Abbreviations and other sorts of verbal reorganizations are then possible, but they introduce deviations from the logical structure of the underlying mental discourse and thus open the door to important mistakes if interpreted literally.

In order to play its regulating role, the internal language of thought had to be endowed with a general organization very much like that of conventional languages. Ockham thought that most of the usual grammatical categories – such as nouns, verbs, adverbs, conjunctions, distinction of singular and plural, and so on – are found in mental as well as in conventional language. Mental terms, like external ones, are also divided into categorematic and syncategorematic, absolute and connotative, first intentions and second intentions. And Mentalese, like spoken discourse, works with the three main varieties of supposition (personal, simple, and material) and with the various subdivisions of personal supposition as well. Semantical theory was expected to provide a very fine-grained description of the structure and working of human thought and knowledge.

Of course, there remain some irreducible structural differences between spoken and mental discourse. Not only is the former articulated into syllables, which, of course, is not the case for Mentalese, but there are moreover certain superficial grammatical distinctions that have no relevance for the analysis of internal thought because they serve no distinct semantical function and, in Ockham's eyes, could not have been introduced in the mind in a purely natural way. This is the case, for example, with genders and declensions[49]: natural concepts are neither masculine nor feminine, and they can have no distinctive endings such as '−us,' '−a,' or '−is' in Latin. Such superficial distinctions are merely conventional. They are introduced into communicative languages for the sake of nonsemantical considerations, such as elegance or variety.

This is not to say, however, that mental language is logically ideal or maximally economical from a semantical point of view as modern philosophers often want formal languages to be. We have seen that there can be redundancies in Ockham's Mentalese, because simple connotative terms can coexist in it with their complex nominal definitions, and exponible propositions with the conjunctions of their *exponentes*; the only form of redundancy explicitly excluded is synonymy between simple terms. Moreover, there may even be certain sorts of ambiguities in Mentalese, when, for instance, the main verb of a given mental proposition is in the past or future tense or when the predicate is a metalinguistic term. Ockham, on the whole, is much more interested in nominalistic ontological economy than in the logical purity of human thought.

NOTES

1 *SL* I.1. On Ockham's theory of signification, see Moody 1935, Chap. 3; Boehner 1946a; Adams 1978, 444–59.

2 *SL* I.3.

3 Ibid., I.4.

4 See ibid., I.33, where Ockham enumerates several senses of 'to signify.' Those we are talking about now are the first two. The third one is discussed in Sec. II under the label 'connotation.' The fourth one corresponds to the loosest possible use of 'to signify.'

5 Adams 1977; Karger 1980; McGrade 1985. But see Chap. 2, Sec. III in this volume.

6 *SL* I.10.

7 Ibid. Quotations from *SL* I are taken from Loux 1974.

8 *SL* I.10.

9 Spade 1975 and 1980; Normore 1990.

10 *SL* I.3.

11 *SL* I.11: "All divisions we have considered so far apply both to terms which naturally signify and to terms which are merely conventional signs." This obviously includes the distinction between absolute and connotative simple terms discussed in *SL* I.10.

12 See for example *Sent.* I.3.2 (405): "I say that God can be known to us in a simple connotative and negative concept which is proper to him";

ibid., I.3.3 (425): "I say that of the same thing there can be several simple denominative concepts, because of the diversity of their connotata"; see also *Quodl.* V.25: "Are absolute, connotative, and relative concepts really distinct from one another?" On all this, see Panaccio 1990; Tweedale 1992; Goddu 1993.

13 *SL* I.63. On Ockham's theory of supposition, see Boehner 1946b; Swiniarski 1970; Adams 1976.

14 *SL* I.64.

15 Ibid., I.70–4. For detailed presentations of the theory of modes of personal supposition and discussions of its interpretation, see Panaccio 1983; Karger 1984; Markosian 1988.

16 *SL* I.72 ad 1.

17 Spade 1974 and 1980.

18 *SL* I.65. That all three varieties of supposition are found in mental as well as in conventional language is explicitly mentioned by Ockham (*SL* I.64).

19 *SL* I.72 ad 1. See also *SL* II.7.

20 Of course, the confusion between the different interpretations left open by the semantical rules is not *unavoidable*; but disambiguation, in such cases, would seem to require the intervention of certain nonsemantical features of the situation. Ockham, however, remains mute about this.

21 *SL* II.2.

22 Ibid., II.3–4.

23 Ibid., I.72 ad 2.

24 Ibid., II.9–10.

25 Ibid., II.32.

26 Ibid., II.31.

27 Ibid., II.34–5.

28 Goddu 1984a.

29 *SL* II.11–20.

30 Ibid., II.18.

31 Ibid., II.11.

32 Ibid., II.13.

33 'To have' in sentences such as 'Socrates has a whiteness' is treated by Ockham as a kind of copula.

34 Ibid., I.14–15. I leave aside here Ockham's elaborate critique of realism with regard to universals to concentrate on his semantical analysis. This critique is most detailed in *Sent.* I.2.3–8. On Ockham's theory of universals, see Moody 1935, Chap. 3; Adams 1987a, Chaps. 1–4.

35 *SL* I.65.

36 Ibid., I.12.

37 Sellars 1970, 62.

38 *SL* I.66 ad 1.
39 This is a slight adaptation of an example ibid., ad 2.
40 *SL* I.5–9.
41 *SL* I.5.
42 *SL* I.6.
43 *SL* I.8.
44 *SL* I.9.
45 *SL* I.8.
46 *Quant.* 1, especially 21–35 (= Birch 1930, 37–65); see Stump 1982, especially §5.
47 *Quant.* 1 (31).
48 Ibid., (30).
49 *SL* I.3.

4   Is There Synonymy in Okham's Mental Language?

William of Ockham's semantic theory was founded on the idea that thought takes place in a language not unlike the languages in which spoken and written communication occur. This mental language was held to have several features in common with everyday languages. For example, mental language has simple terms, not unlike words, out of which complex expressions can be constructed. As with words, each of these terms has some meaning, or signification; in fact Ockham held that the signification of everyday words derives precisely from the signification of mental terms. Furthermore, the meaning of a mental expression depends directly on the meaning of its constituent terms, as is the case with expressions in more familiar languages.

As one might expect, there are many important differences between mental language and everyday languages. For example, mental languages signify their objects naturally rather than conventionally. At a more concrete level, Ockham suggested that numerous features of spoken or written language – participles and pronouns, for example – might not exist in mental language.

Two ubiquitous features of everyday languages are the phenomena of equivocation and synonymy. The first of these is exemplified in English words such as 'bank', which has two entirely different meanings. The second is exemplified by pairs of terms such as 'bachelor' and 'unmarried man,' which share a common meaning. The question arises, Are these features also found in mental language? It seems to be commonly accepted that they are not. Ockham himself is not entirely clear on the matter, but Trentman and Spade have argued on the basis of both textual and theoretical considerations, that the most coherent position broadly compatible with Ockham's work is that neither synonymy nor equivocation may occur in mental language.[1] I will not discuss equivocation in this paper, for I find the arguments on that topic persuasive. However, I will argue that the case against synonymy is not as strong.

My argument for synonymy is largely theoretical, although it also has a textual element. The theoretical case has a positive and a negative part. On the positive side, I will argue that there are several reasons mental synonymy might exist and that a mental language without synonymy would be relatively clumsy, with several ad hoc features. On the negative side, I will address various arguments that have been put forward against the possibility of synonymy and will try to show they are not conclusive. Textually, I will argue that, although Ockham appears to deny the possibility of synonymy in mental language, he also makes remarks that commit him to that possibility. I do not think my arguments are entirely conclusive, but I hope to demonstrate that the possibility of mental synonymy is not as implausible as has sometimes been thought.

I. POSITIVE ARGUMENTS

1.1. Logical Equivalence

The first argument is based on the observation that once certain logical primitives are admitted into a language, it seems to follow immediately that certain complex expressions are synonymous. Consider, for example, the English expressions 'man and (cat or dog)' and '(man and cat) or (man and dog)'. The parentheses are introduced for clarity but are not strictly necessary, being straightforwardly replaceable by longer locutions (for instance, 'a man with either a cat or a dog' and 'either a man with a cat or a man with a dog'). Call the two expressions $E1$ and $E2$. It seems apparent that $E1$ and $E2$ are synonymous. It is a straightforward logical inference to go from any proposition involving $E1$ to the corresponding sentence involving $E2$ and vice versa. It is plain that the two expressions come to exactly the same thing in the matter of signification.

As it is with written language,[2] so it seems it should be with mental language – at least in this case.

Mental language presumably has among its simple terms such logical operators as 'and' and 'or'; if it does not have these, then it presumably possesses others with equivalent power, on the basis of which a similar case could be made. There is no doubt that simple expressions such as 'dog' and 'cat' exist in mental language (if not these, then any simple nouns will do). And there seems no reason why these expressions and logical operators should not be combined to form complex expressions. Thus, mental language contains the expressions 'man and (dog or cat)' and '(man and dog) or (man and cat),' or other expressions that make the same point. These expressions, it seems, must be synonymous for just the reasons given above. Therefore, there is synonymy in mental language.

There are two paths an opponent of mental synonymy might take in countering this argument. One could argue that the two expressions are not in fact synonymous, or one could argue that the two expressions are in fact identical in mental language and thus no synonymy between different expressions need be introduced. I will consider these objections in turn.

I.I.I. THE FIRST STRATEGY In *SL* I.6,[3] Ockham says that for two terms to be synonymous they must signify exactly the same things, and they must signify these *in the same way*. An opponent of mental synonymy might argue that, although the two expressions given in Section I.I signify the same things, they signify them in different ways, and so are not synonymous.

It is not entirely clear what Ockham meant by 'to signify in the same way.' Spade argues that two mental expressions signify in the same way if and only if they are syntactically equivalent – that is, if and only if they consist of exactly the same categorematic expressions in exactly the same syntactic constructions.[4] If this were the case, our two given expressions would certainly not be synonymous. However, it seems to me that this construal of synonymy buys the conclusion entirely too cheaply by defining mental synonymy out of existence, and I will argue against it in Section III.2. For now, let us consider a weaker construal of 'in the same way.' This construal captures our intuition that what is required of synonymy is not just that two terms signify the same things but that they *must* signify the same things. To be more precise, under this construal of synonymy, two terms are synonymous if their equivalence is a priori and necessary.

This yields a strong criterion for synonymy. The coextensive pair of terms 'renate' and 'cordate' fail the test, for example, because they are not necessarily coextensive. The coextensive pair of terms 'Hesperus' and 'Phosphorus' fail the test, for they are not a priori coextensive. It is difficult to know whether this criterion corresponds to Ockham's intentions, but it seems to capture a large part of our intuitions behind what is meant by 'synonymy' and in particular to capture the extra strength carried by synonymy compared with mere coextensiveness. And the logically equivalent pair of terms E_1 and E_2 clearly satisfy this criterion.

(One might also invoke a criterion according to which synonymous terms are those that are substitutable *salva veritate* even in modal contexts. I do not use this criterion here because it yields counterintuitive results when combined with the contemporary understanding of necessity: for example, 'Hesperus' and 'Phosphorus' come out synonymous. But in the medieval understanding of necessity, this criterion may yield the same results as the preceding criterion.)

An opponent might try to argue that this criterion is not strong enough: Although the logically equivalent pair of terms satisfies the criterion, the terms nevertheless signify in subtly different ways. Thus, our opponent might argue that the two terms are not intersubstitutable in certain epistemic contexts and are therefore not synonymous. For example, it might be the case that John believes that to gain admission to the party one must be accompanied by a man with either a dog or a cat, but John does not believe that to gain admission to the party one must be accompanied by either a man with a dog or a man with a cat. The reason for this, presumably, would be that John is not very capable at logic and so has not made the straightforward inference. Now, we might respond to this by arguing that in fact, if John has the first belief, he has the second belief whether he knows it or not. He believes it implicitly, one might say. But for the sake of argument let us accept that John has the first belief but not the second. If this is so, it is apparent that in this epistemic context the two terms are not intersubstitutable.

It seems to me, however, that intersubstitutability in such epistemic contexts is too strong a condition to require for synonymy.[5] If we admit this as a criterion, it would seem to follow that there are no synonyms at all. For given any pair of purported synonyms – for example, 'bachelor' and 'unmarried man' – we can construct examples like those just given. For example, John might believe that all bachelors are invited for dinner but might not believe that all unmarried men are invited for dinner – presumably because he is once again too muddled to make the required inference. (Again one might argue that if John has the first belief, he has the second whether he knows it or not. But because we disallowed this line of reasoning for the sake of argument in the preceding paragraph, we must equally disallow it here.) This conclusion shows that the suggested criterion is too strong. In fact, it seems that even Ockham himself would reject intersubstitutability in epistemic contexts as a criterion for synonymy, as the following passage demonstrates:

> Those synonyms are broadly so called ... even though not all users believe them to signify the same [thing] but rather, under a deception, they judge something to be signified by the one that is not signified by the other.[6]

It follows that this argument provides no reason to reject the synonymy of E_1 and E_2 or at least no more reason than there is for rejecting the synonymy of such terms as 'bachelor' and 'unmarried man.' Logical synonymy seems to be at least as strong as common or garden-variety conceptual synonymy. So if we want to retain the notion of synonymy at all, we had best admit the possibility of logical synonymy – at least in written language.

Once we have accepted the possibility that the two written expressions E_1 and E_2 are synonymous, it follows that either (a) they are subordinated to synonymous mental expressions, thus establishing my case, or (b) they are subordinated to identical mental expressions, thus saving the game for the opponent of mental synonymy. I will consider possibility (b) next.

I.I.2. THE SECOND STRATEGY An opponent's second strategy is to argue that only one expression in mental language is involved here: The two mental expressions we are labeling 'man and (cat or dog)' and '(man and cat) or (man and dog)' are in fact the same expression. It might be claimed that their appearing to be different expressions is an artifact of English, not mental language. The different *written* expressions E_1 and E_2 are in fact subordinated to the same *mental* expression. To get an idea of how this argument might run, consider a simpler pair of expressions: 'man and dog' and 'dog and man.' For reasons similar to those discussed earlier, these expressions seem to be synonymous. But an opponent of synonymy could very plausibly argue that these are not different expressions in mental language at all, for the only difference between them is one of word order – a feature that need not be preserved in mental language.[7] For example, it could well be argued that the term 'and' in mental language is not interpolated sequentially between two terms in a particular order but rather is bound to them both in some symmetrical fashion, such as a tree structure, or perhaps as a common ending (something like 'man-and dog-and,' where we take it that the two words are unordered). On this plausible account, the difference in the two expressions 'man and dog' and 'dog and man' would not persist into mental language.

It is difficult to see, however, how we could apply an argument like this to more complex cases such as our 'man and (dog or cat)' versus '(man and dog) or (man and cat).' These two expressions are not just superficially different; they are structurally different. One of them is a conjunction; the other is a disjunction. However we represent 'and' and 'or' in mental language, they will need to be put together hierarchically on occasion, and it seems clear that the differences in their hierarchical order must be represented in mental language.

One way out for our opponent might be to argue that logical expressions in mental language must be reduced to some common form such as disjunctive normal form. It would then be the case that any two logically equivalent terms or propositions would be represented identically. The trouble with this is that it is an ad hoc restriction that places limits on how mental terms may be combined. On the face of it, one would take it that if 'man,' 'dog,' 'cat,' 'and,' and 'or' are admissible mental terms, then 'man and (dog or cat)' would be an admissible expression in mental language; but according to the present proposal this expression would somehow be debarred from being formed for no apparent reason other than to preserve a theoretical claim. Indeed, to place such a restriction on combination of terms would seem to reduce mental language's claim to being a language in the first place, for one of the key properties of language is that complex expressions can be generated recursively and compositionally, whereas according to this proposal, although 'man' and 'dog or cat' would be valid mental expressions, 'man and (dog or cat),' their conjunction, would not be. This seems arbitrary and implausible.

It seems much more plausible for mental language to consist of a set of simple terms that can be combined and recombined without any limits other than syntactic requirements. In particular, logical operators ought to be able to combine nominal terms in any combination. But once we admit this, no matter what set of logical operators we choose, logically equivalent nonidentical expressions will be formable. We might be able to get around certain superficial differences in structure, such as that in the 'man and dog' case, by proposing certain symmetries in our operators, but there will always be propositions with different structures that turn out to be logically identical. One can see this easily by noting, for example, that although there are only four logically distinct truth functional combinations of two propositions, any compositional system will yield an infinite number of syntactically distinct complex sentences formed by combining these propositions under truth functional operators. Logical equivalence is thus endemic in any combinatorial system.

The conclusion is that, given that logical equivalence implies synonymy, it follows that synonymy will be ubiquitous in mental language unless we put highly ad hoc restrictions on the manner in which mental terms are combined.

Before passing to the next topic, I should respond to a natural objection, based on textual considerations, that may have occurred to the reader. This objection notes that, according to Ockham, synonymous written expressions are subordinated to the same mental expression,[8] and thus no matter what I have just said, the expressions $E1$ and $E2$ must be subordinated to a single expression in mental language. My response to this is of course to point out that the arguments I am giving for the existence of synonymy in mental language are equally arguments for the rejection of the claim that synonymous written expressions are subordinated to the same mental expression. If there is synonymy in mental language, a more plausible criterion is that synonymous written expressions must be subordinated to *synonymous* mental expressions. Of course, this means I am going against an explicit claim of Ockham's, but I am giving a theoretical argument, after all. I will address this issue further in Section II.

1.2. Conceptual Change

I now pass to a quite different line of argument in favor of mental synonymy. This argument stems from the observation that many terms in everyday languages, and presumably in mental language, undergo gradual changes in meaning. Many current terms do not mean exactly what they meant fifty years ago. Even within a single individual, the meaning of a term can gradually shift over time. Sometimes it may even occur that two terms that originally had quite different meanings gradually drift until they mean the same thing. Perhaps, for instance, when one was a child one used the term 'stone' only for small objects, and used the term 'rock' for big ones, but over time one's use of the term has drifted until now they are used in exactly the same way, and thus the terms are synonymous. Nothing in my argument turns on the specific example – all that is required for the argument is the *possibility* of this kind of gradual drift into synonymy taking place, and this seems indisputable.

So let us say that Y and Z are two terms that start out with different meanings but through a continuous process over time come to mean the same thing. This might even occur without the individual's within whom it is happening being conscious of the drift to synonymy. He might realize at some later point that 'stone' and 'rock' are synonymous for him, whereas they were not twenty years ago, and the drift might have occurred without his realizing it at the time. Ockham himself endorses the possibility that synonymy may go unrecognized, in *SL* I.6, quoted in Section I.1.1.

Now, as these terms gradually drift toward synonymy, what is happening in mental language? Presumably Y and Z are subordinated to mental terms Y' and Z', and Y' and Z' are also undergoing a slow drift in meaning. Now what happens on the day when Y and Z finally become synonymous? Do the terms Y' and Z' suddenly become the same term? Does one of them suddenly disappear so that for example, Y and Z are now both subordinated to Y', and Z' is gone? Neither of these possibilities is strikingly plausible. The process of change is sufficiently slow that it is hard to imagine any sudden change could be taking place in mental language. In practice, it will be very hard to locate a precise moment at which Y and Z become synonymous; there may be a long period of approximate synonymy before we can say with confidence that they are definitely synonymous. Are we to suggest that mental language has hair-trigger sensitivity to the process and thus at the exact moment when the meanings come to coincide, a jump suddenly occurs?

It seems at least as plausible to argue that as the drift takes place, the two mental terms remain distinct, gradually becoming synonymous but nevertheless oblivious, at least for a while, to each other's presence. It may well be for a long period that the subject does not make the expected inferences from propositions involving Y to those involving Z because he does not consciously realize that the two concepts have become synonymous for him. If the corresponding mental concepts had become *identical*, this inferential gap would be harder to explain. After a time, the subject may consciously realize that the concepts are synonymous – and perhaps the mental terms will then be "fused" into one – but until then there seems no reason in principle why the terms should not be distinct.

The other possibility to be considered is that as Y and Z drift in meaning, they are subordinated to a series of different terms in mental language, Y'_1, Y'_2, ..., and Z'_1, Z'_2, ... Upon every change in the meaning of Y, no matter how small, Y becomes subordinated to a new Y' in the mental language. Over time, the corresponding Y' terms gradually become more like the Z' terms until finally they become identical. This account has the virtue of avoiding the sudden change required by the previous story, but it still seems problematic. For a start, it seems to be extravagant with terms in mental language by requiring the postulation of a large number of different terms where we previously needed only two. Further, it does not solve the problem mentioned earlier of the possible inferential gap in the subject's abilities – one would think that if the corresponding concepts have become identical, any inferences from one to the other would be automatic. This seems in turn to imply that two terms cannot become synonymous without a subject's recognizing that fact, which appears to contradict Ockham's own claim in *SL* I.6.

On the balance of things it seems to me that conceptual change provides a strong argument but not a knockdown argument for mental synonymy. The opposing story just given seems feasible enough that it *could* be the case, although it does raise a serious question about compatibility with Ockham's own views on the recognition of synonymy, an issue I discuss further in Section II. However, the story I sketched of gradual drift into synonymy without identity seems equally if not more plausible, and gives another reason why mental synonymy is not an altogether unreasonable idea.

1.3. Efficiency

My final argument in favor of mental synonymy is a pragmatic one. Ockham, in his writings, gives very little idea about how mental language *functions* – how it enables one to make inferences from one proposition to another, for instance, or how mental propositions help determine the actions we take toward the world. We can imagine, however, that this functioning does not come for free but takes some work. Evidence for this can be seen in our finding it harder to make inferences from complex propositions than from simple propositions. The more complex a proposition, it seems, the harder it is for our mental system to deal with. Therefore, one might draw the conclusion that in order for our mental system to function as well as it can, mental propositions should be as simple as possible (as long as they are complex enough to express the required meaning).

Now in mental language, presumably, there are certain complex expressions that get used repeatedly.[9] In the interests of efficient functioning of the mental system, it might seem advantageous for it to introduce internal *abbreviations* for these complex expressions. Instead of having to deal with expressions like 'man who cuts cloth and makes suits,' the system would only have to deal with the simple expression 'tailor.' We certainly find this kind of abbreviation useful in our external practice; I am here suggesting it might have a role in internal functioning as well. If, as we have supposed, complex expressions are more difficult for the mind to deal with, the systematic replacement of these by simple expressions might allow a significant enhancement to our cognitive capacities.

Of course, there would have to be systematic links between a term and its abbreviation so that thoughts about 'tailor' could easily lead back to conclusions about suits and cloth when necessary. But inferences involving tailors would in general be much easier to make in this form. The only downside is that we would have introduced synonymy into mental language, but it seems to me that in this context this is only advantageous. A typical argument against mental synonymy[10] has the form Who needs it? – in other words, What is the point of mental synonymy if synonyms are truth conditionally equivalent and so have the same expressive power? Any distinction between synonyms would be a difference that makes no expressive difference and so would be unnecessary in mental language. Here, we have seen that pragmatic considerations show there might be relevant differences that are not expressive differences. Rather, they are differences that aid mental function.

This is obviously not a knockdown argument. For a start, it may be anachronistic in focusing on the way mental propositions are processed – a way of thinking that was not so common in Ockham's time. Nevertheless, all that is required to see the point is that complex mental propositions might be more cumbersome to deal with than simple ones, and this does not seem to be a particularly advanced consideration. Of course, the argument is only a plausibility argument demonstrating why mental synonymy might be a reasonable thing, and as such is a weaker argument than the two preceding arguments, but nevertheless it helps in breaking down the intuition that mental synonymy would be an entirely useless thing.

II. TEXTUAL CONSIDERATIONS

I now consider some textual issues. In particular, I must confront what seems to be the strongest argument against synonymy in Ockham's mental language: Ockham's apparent denial on at least one occasion that mental synonymy exists. This occurs in *Quodlibet* V.8:

To the principal argument, I say that everything that is an accident of a mental term is an accident of a spoken term, but not the other way around. For some [things] are accidents of spoken terms because of the necessity of signification and expression, and they belong to mental names. Others are accidents of spoken terms for the sake of the decoration of speech (like synonyms) and for the sake of well-formedness, and they do not belong to mental terms.[11]

Now, it is not entirely clear that this is a blanket denial of the possibility of mental synonymy. It might alternatively be interpreted as a denial that synonymy in spoken language is reflected in mental synonymy, leaving open the possibility of mental synonymy that arises in other ways. Or it might be interpreted as the denial that *certain* synonyms in spoken language – those that exist merely for the sake of decoration – are reflected in mental synonyms, leaving open the possibility that other (nondecorative) spoken synonyms correspond to mental synonyms. Furthermore, even if we accept this as a denial of the possibility of mental synonymy, it seems to be the only occurrence of such a denial in Ockham's writing, and thus even Spade (who argues against synonymy in mental language) concedes the textual support is not as strong as it should be.[12]

In any case, I am trying to make a theoretical argument, not a textual one, about what Ockham should have held, rather than about what he in fact did hold. In other words, insofar as Ockham can be seen to have denied the possibility of mental synonymy, my arguments should perhaps be taken more as a criticism of Ockham than as an interpretation. Of course this is a delicate matter, for if one jettisons too much of Ockham's theory one runs the risk not so much of criticizing him as of ignoring him. Nevertheless, I believe the position I am putting forward is compatible with Ockham's overall thrust and only requires the rejection of one or two specific claims. I will argue that Ockham's claims on this matter appear to be inconsistent, and thus any interpretation must reject some of them. This interpretation may thus not be worse off than any other.

The other claim of Ockham's that causes problems for mental synonymy is his statement on several occasions that synonyms in spoken or written language are subordinated to identical terms in mental language. As Spade points out,[13] it does not necessarily follow from this that mental synonyms cannot exist; all that follows is that if they do exist, they do not have associated synonyms in spoken or written language. However, this seems too weak a ground to base a defense of mental synonymy on. For a start, *if* our mental synonyms had any written or spoken terms subordinated to them, these terms would be synonyms, in violation of Ockham's claim; and on the face of it it seems reasonable that any given mental term should at least possibly have an associated written or spoken term. If we were to retain Ockham's claim and to argue for mental synonymy, we would be committed to the existence of mental terms that could not have associated spoken or written terms, and although this is not impossible it at least seems ad hoc and unmotivated. Furthermore, my best evidence for the existence of mental synonymy[14] came precisely from the consideration of synonymous spoken or written expressions that I argued had to be subordinated to different mental expressions.

For these reasons, it is best for the defender of mental synonymy to argue that Ockham's claim should be jettisoned along with his denial (insofar as it is a denial) of mental synonymy. The correct criterion for synonymy of spoken or written terms is that they should be subordinated to synonymous mental terms rather than that they be subordinated to identical mental terms. This jettisoning of Ockham's claim may reduce this account's chances of being an interpretation of Ockham, but I believe it does not reduce its overall plausibility.

I come now to the internal tension within Ockham's text. This casts further doubt on the subordination of synonymous terms to identical mental terms and indeed suggests that Ockham may be committed to the possibility of mental synonymy despite what appear to be claims to the contrary. In a passage quoted earlier, Ockham says that

> those synonyms are broadly so called ... even though not all users believe them to signify the same [thing] but rather, under a deception, they judge something to be signified by the one that is not signified by the other.[15]

Ockham goes on to point out that this is the sense of synonymy with which he is dealing for most of *SL*. According to this passage, then, it is possible that a user can judge that 'That object is an *X*' is true and at the same time judge that 'That object is a *Y*' is false even though the terms *X* and *Y* are synonymous. But this implies that *X* and *Y* cannot be subordinated to the same term of mental language! For if *X* and *Y* were subordinated to the same mental term, all mental judgments about *X's* and *Y's* would coincide. The two spoken propositions 'That object is an *X*' and 'That object is a *Y*' would be subordinated to identical propositions in mental language, and it is impossible that one could be judged to be true and the other simultaneously judged to be false. Therefore, this passage seems to contradict Ockham's claim that synonymous terms are subordinated to identical mental terms.

In fact, if we accept this passage at face value, it is hard not to draw the conclusion that the terms *X* and *Y* must be subordinated to different but synonymous mental terms (for it is surely impossible that synonymous spoken or written terms are subordinated to *nonsynonymous* mental terms), which would directly establish that synonymy exists in mental language.

It is difficult to say how we should deal with this contradiction, or how Ockham would have dealt with it, had it been pointed out to him. He might have chosen to retract the claim made in this passage; the opposing claim that synonymous terms are subordinated to identical mental terms is certainly made more often. On the other hand, he might have seen the possibility of unrecognized synonymy in spoken or written language as grounds to reject the claim about subordination of synonymous terms. In any case, the internal tension revealed here further weakens the plausibility of the claim that syn-onymous terms are subordinated to identical mental expressions and indicates the claim might be rejected without too much violence to the rest of Ockham's system.

Furthermore, insofar as Ockham's own claims are inconsistent, it follows that any consistent interpretation must reject one or more of them. So Ockham's apparent denials of mental synonymy do not provide any overwhelming reason to reject the view I have offered in favor of any other consistent interpretation. This opens the way to accepting the possibility of synonymy in Ockham's mental language.

III. OTHER NEGATIVE ARGUMENTS

The central negative argument against the possibility of mental syno-nymy is the textual argument I have just discussed. Three other negative arguments deserve consideration, however. These are (1) the argument by analogy with Ockham's treatment of grammat-ical features, (2) Spade's argument that signification "in the same way" requires syntactic identity in mental propositions,[16] and (3) the argument from the fact that concepts bear a "natural likeness" to their objects.

III.1. The Analogy with Grammatical Features

A significant argument against the existence of mental synonymy derives from Ockham's criterion for determining which grammati-cal features do and which do not persist into mental language. As Spade puts it:

Grammatical features of spoken or written language that do not serve the "needs of signification" by affecting truth conditions are not present in men-tal grammar. That this rules out all synonymy in mental language seems to be the clear intention of Ockham's whole discussion in *Quodlibet* 5, q. 8, with its repeated statement that what is in mental language is there only because of the "needs of signification," not for the sake of "decoration" or "well-formedness," and that synonymy does not serve the "needs of signification."[17]

For example, such grammatical features as gender of nouns and the different conjugations of verbs do not persist into mental language because as they are irrelevant to signification – that is, they have no effect on truth conditions. Such features would be unnecessary in mental language. If they existed there, they would have the status of mere ornaments. It seems plausible that the differences between any synonymous expressions in mental language would be equally unnecessary in mental language. Such differences would therefore not persist, implying that mental language has no synonymy.

As an initial reply, one might point out that it is not unreasonable to suppose there could be other relevant needs besides the "needs of signification." For example, I argued earlier that synonymous mental expressions might sometimes serve the needs of efficiency in mental language by providing a simpler expression for complex thoughts. This would seem to be a more relevant reason for the presence of synonyms than mere "decoration." Grammatical features such as gender and different conjugations, of course, would not serve even this purpose (in fact they would achieve the opposite by making mental expressions more complex than necessary) and so would not make it into mental language, but there are conceivably other instances of synonymy that would qualify.

As perhaps a more compelling reply, one might argue that certain instances of synonymy in mental language are not there because they serve any particular needs but rather because they must exist as a byproduct of other properties of mental language. Logical synonymy would be one example of this. If we assume mental language has a need for certain primitive logical operators and for the ability to combine any expressions according to these operators, then, as we saw above, we are forced to the conclusion that some complex expressions must be synonymous. This fact in itself does not serve any particularly useful purpose for mental language; it is a consequence of other facts about mental language.

This conclusion leads us to another line of reply to the preceding argument. We might argue that Ockham's criterion should apply to the determination of those grammatical features that persist into the *lexicon* – that is, the set of simple terms – of mental language, but that once we have determined the simple terms, complex expressions should be derived directly from these according to combinatorial principles just as English sentences are derived from words according to such principles. Thus, although no two lexical items in mental language might be synonymous, it could nevertheless be the case that certain complex expressions are synonymous. To stipulate that two apparently quite different but synonymous complex expressions should in fact be identical in mental language would require ad hoc tinkering with the structure of mental language, as we saw. By contrast, the elimination of irrelevant grammatical features from simple terms in mental language is not ad hoc at all precisely because it can be achieved by a correct specification of the elements of mental language at the basic level.

Of course, if we accept this argument against lexical synonymy, it would follow that the argument from conceptual change might have to be rejected. Although I am less convinced by the conceptual change argument than by the logical equivalence argument, I should nevertheless point out that a similar defense of it could be mounted. As with logical synonymy, the synonymy of two mental concepts that have drifted together is not in mental language to serve any need. Rather, it is there as a simple byproduct of the process of conceptual change and of the way conceptual change works. The distinction between two synonymous terms might not be immediately eliminated from mental language, as irrelevant grammatical features are, because the synonymy might not be immediately apparent. If two independent concepts have by coincidence drifted together, there might be no obvious marker of their synonymy, and thus we might expect it to take a while before mental language became sensitive to the fact of their common meaning. The existence of synonymous mental terms would not serve any purpose in mental language, and we could expect that the terms might be merged at some future time, for instance when the subject becomes aware of their synonymy. Until that time, however, the synonymous terms might both exist; their coexistence would be a byproduct of the terms' divergent histories.

III.2. Signification "In The Same Way"

As we saw earlier, Ockham's criterion for the synonymy of two terms is that they not only signify the same things; they signify those things *in the same way*. It is not clear what Ockham meant by signification "in the same way," but Spade has presented a construal of this phrase that, if correct, would destroy any possibility of synonymy in mental language.[18] It is therefore important to come to grips with this interpretation of Ockham's criterion.

Spade's suggestion is that a "way" of signifying should be interpreted syntactically as follows:

A mental expression or concept signifies a thing x in a given syntactic mode m if and only if x is signified by some constituent non-complex categorematic term occurring within that mental expression in the grammatical or syntactical construction m.[19]

If this is the case, then any two synonymous expressions must be made up of identical simple categorematic concepts in identical syntactic constructions. In other words, they must be identical. It follows that there can be no synonymy in mental language.

The ease with which this argument buys its conclusion is suspicious. It seems to *define* mental synonymy out of existence, but we have already seen plenty of cases in which the idea of mental synonymy at least seems coherent. It may be for a variety of reasons that there turns out to be no synonymy in mental language, but this does not seem on the face of it an analytic truth. The claim seems to be entirely contingent. The case we discussed earlier – of synonymous, logically equivalent but distinct propositions – seems at least a possible example, even if certain facts about the way mental language functions might indicate it is not actual. Therefore, on the face of it, it would seem unlikely that mental synonymy can be debarred definitionally.

Spade's argument for this definition is not entirely clear to me. He argues that a "way of signifying" should not be construed as one of Ockham's four "modes" of signification in *SL* I.33. He then leaps from this to the claim that a "way" should be construed purely syntactically, but the grounds for this transition are not obvious. The closest thing I can find to an argument for this conclusion is the following (in the context of a discussion of why 'blind' and 'sight' are not synonymous despite their both signifying sight):

Now, in the case of a nominal definition, or indeed of complex expressions generally, it is relatively clear what it might mean to signify a thing x "negatively." It could mean that the expression as a whole signifies x in virtue of some constituent non-complex categorematic term which signifies x and which occurs within the scope of a negation-sign in that expression. This is, in part at least, a syntactic criterion.[20]

But it does not seem to me that "negative" signification must be construed purely syntactically. It does not seem unlikely that a semantic characterization could be arrived at. For instance, there might be a characterization that exploited the fact that, although 'blind' and 'sight' signify the same *things*, expressions in which they are embedded have opposite truth values (for instance, 'James is blind' is true precisely when 'James is sighted' is not true). This might well be more along the lines of what "signifying in the same way" comes to. Indeed, it is interesting to note that on the "adverbial" theory of signification (used by Peter of Ailly, among others),[21] the same locution – signifying "in a given manner" – is used for that part of signification (of a proposition, in this case) from which truth values derive. Perhaps this is not entirely coincidental. If we are to speculate, it does not seem unlikely that Ockham might have had a similar *semantic* criterion in mind, although it is quite possible that he never formalized the criterion, leaving it at the level of intuition.

Furthermore, even if we accept Spade's argument in the quoted passage, it seems to fall far short of establishing that signification "in a given way" is a purely syntactic notion. All that is established is that "negative" signification – just a small aspect of what counts in determining a "way" of signifying – *might* have a criterion that is at least partly syntactic. This seems too weak to establish the desired broad conclusion suggested by Spade when he states that "the considerations ... above, indicate that ... the 'ways' at stake here are ... *syntactic* modes of signification."[22]

It seems to me there is something wrong with the idea that there are syntactic criteria for a notion such as synonymy, which is a deeply semantic notion. It is more plausible that synonymy ought to be characterized purely semantically in terms of the relationship between elements of language and their actual or possible referents. Looking at Ockham's criterion for synonymy, it seems to me this is what he may have been doing, although he left the crucial strengthening clause ('signify in the same way') somewhat vague. Nevertheless it seems intuitively plausible that there is an extra semantic criterion required of synonymous terms, over and above mere coincidence of signification. This can be captured by the modern idea that this coextensiveness is necessary and a priori. Ockham may not have thought about the issue in explicitly this way, but the intuitive notion is clear enough. I would therefore suggest this is what Ockham's strengthening clause in the criterion for synonymy should come to.

It seems to me that if we accept the claim that there is no synonymy in mental language, Spade's syntactic construal of the strengthening criterion will be correct in practice – but this will be precisely because synonymy does not exist, so that a syntactic check will be sufficient to ascertain identity of meaning. It seems to me further that there are no compelling grounds, other than the nonexistence of synonymy, for supposing the syntactic construal to be correct. If so, it follows that the syntactic construal cannot be used to provide support for the nonexistence of synonymy.

A further argument in favor of a semantic construal of the strengthening criterion is that it satisfies our intuition that mental expressions corresponding to 'man and (dog or cat)' and '(man and dog) or (man and cat)' are synonymous *whether or not* they are identical. For all these reasons, I believe the case for the syntactic construal of "ways" of signification is at best inconclusive and does not provide compelling evidence against the possibility of synonymy in mental language.

While on this topic, I should note that a semantic criterion for synonymy would answer another argument against mental synonymy also given by Spade:

What would equivocation or synonymy in mental language amount to? Since there is no supramental language to appeal to in the way one appeals to mental language to account for synonymy and equivocation in spoken and written language, how could it even arise in mental language?[23]

This argument seems to assume that the only real criterion for mental synonymy could be appeal to some higher language[24] – that the criterion must be a *formal criterion*. It seems to ignore the possibility of a semantic criterion, in terms for instance of referents or truth values, or both. If we have a semantic criterion for synonymy, the problem posed here by Spade is no problem at all.

III.3. *Natural Likenesses*

The final argument rests on Ockham's contention that concepts bear natural likenesses to their objects. Spade argues that it seems unlikely that two concepts could bear a natural likeness in the relevant sense to their objects but still be more than numerically distinct.[25] If this is correct, it would follow that mental synonyms could not exist.

The reply to this is simply to say it does not seem too implausible that distinct mental terms could bear natural likenesses to a common object – especially if they are complex expressions rather than simple terms. Going back to our favorite example, it seems plausible that the concepts 'man and (dog or cat)' and '(man and dog) or (man and cat)' both bear a natural likeness to their object despite the apparent difference in the expressions. These two mental expressions seems to differ in form or structure, but they are nevertheless concepts of exactly the same things. It might be difficult to imagine how two distinct *simple* terms could be the relevant likenesses simultaneously, but this difficulty vanishes in the case of complex expressions. Thus, this does not seem to be a compelling objection to mental synonymy.

IV. SIMPLE CONNOTATIVE TERMS

Before concluding, we should note the possible effect of the preceding discussion on the question of whether there exist simple connotative terms in mental language. Spade has argued that simple connotative mental terms cannot exist, for if they did, they would be synonymous with their expanded nominal definitions[26]; but of course there is no synonymy in mental language! Panaccio has pointed out another possibility: that simple connotative terms exist but in fact are not synonymous with their nominal definitions.[27]

The present discussion raises a third possibility: that simple connotative terms exist and are synonymous with their nominal definitions. Spade and Panaccio reject this possibility because of the supposed impossibility of mental synonymy, but if we accept the preceding arguments for the possibility of mental synonymy, this becomes a live option. Indeed, once we have gotten over the hurdle of mental synonymy, it may even fit certain textual evidence better than either of these claims, for Ockham certainly claimed that simple connotative terms exist, and there are strong reasons to believe connotative terms are synonymous with their definitions (although Panaccio's argument may have weakened this evidence somewhat).

The discussion I have given here even provides a reason why simple connotative terms might exist: to act as abbreviations for their nominal definitions for the sake of making mental language less cumbersome. This is perhaps the reason many connotative terms exist in everyday languages. It does not seem wholly unreasonable that they might exist in mental language for the same purpose.

Of course, I do not necessarily wish to maintain that Ockham actually held this position, for the existence of mental synonymy seems to contradict textual evidence – at least as the evidence has traditionally been interpreted. Nevertheless, I should point out that this instance of mental synonymy is less difficult to reconcile with textual evidence than the other instances we have looked at. This is because we can maintain the synonymy between simple connotative terms and their nominal definitions in mental language without giving up Ockham's claim that spoken or written synonyms are subordinated to identical mental expressions. Instead, we can hold that a spoken or written connotative term and its nominal definition are *both* subordinated to the corresponding term (the complex expression) in mental language. The simple connotative mental term is introduced entirely within the mental sphere for the purposes of abbreviation. No spoken or written term is subordinated to the simple connotative mental term because it is solely a construct introduced for mental efficiency just as connotative terms in spoken or written language are frequently introduced for efficiency.

Although this position may or may not be independently plausible, we should note that it seems to be at least as compatible with the textual evidence as Spade's and Panaccio's accounts. The only claim of Ockham's it might explicitly contradict is the passage from *Quodl.* V.8,[28] and even that passage might be interpreted in a manner compatible with the position maintained here. In any case, whether or not this position was actually held by Ockham, it seems quite attractive as a theoretical possibility.

V. CONCLUSION

I have done my best to act as an advocate for the possibility that synonymy could exist in mental language. Now is the time to pass considered judgment.

First, the question, Did Ockham believe there is synonymy in mental language? To this I believe the answer is probably no. For a start, he seems to deny it on one occasion. Furthermore, as we have seen, two of my arguments for synonymy have required overturning a claim that Ockham made several times, the claim that synonyms in spoken or written language are subordinated to identical terms in mental language. On the other hand, the third argument, from efficiency, is independent of this claim, for we can suppose that abbreviation of complex expressions could be entirely internal to the mental system; this argument also gains some additional textual support from Ockham's otherwise anomalous claims that simple connotative terms exist in mental language. Still, overall, it seems most plausible to me that Ockham was at least implicitly committed to the nonexistence of mental synonyms, although we have seen that internal tensions arise in this theory due to this commitment.

Next, the question, Should Ockham have believed that there is synonymy in mental language? To this, my answer is less clear. I believe there is a very strong argument for the possibility of mental synonymy: the argument from logical equivalence. As far as I can tell, Ockham never considered this argument. If he had, it is possible it might have caused him at least to have had some doubts about the impossibility of synonymy. Even if he had eventually come down against the possibility, he might have been required to modify his theory in some serious way or at least make several of its features more explicit. As for the second and third arguments, from conceptual change and from efficiency, I believe that neither of these is conclusive but that both provide some added plausibility for the notion of mental synonymy by demonstrating how it might come about and even perhaps serve a useful purpose. Finally, Ockham's belief that synonymy in spoken or written language can go unrecognized seems to yield the existence of synonymous terms as a natural consequence. This provides further grounds for thinking that whether or not Ockham accepted synonymy, he ought to have.

Of the negative arguments (apart from the textual considerations), I believe the argument from analogy with grammatical features has been cast into doubt by showing how certain instances of synonymy might exist without having to serve any need but rather because they are byproducts of other features of mental language. The argument from signifying "in the same way" seems to me to be quite inconclusive owing to the difficulty in ascertaining just what Ockham meant by his phrase. It does not seem too unlikely that he had a semantic criterion in mind rather than a syntactic criterion. It is possible that the final argument, from natural likenesses, could be made into a strong argument against mental synonymy with some work. I have been concerned to reply to the argument as it is given by Spade, but it is not impossible that stronger versions of the argument exist.

Still, such arguments would have to deal with the apparent existence of complex expressions that are distinct but clearly have the same meaning. If some version of natural likeness theory had the consequence that these expressions are not synonymous, it might not be unreasonable to suggest that that version of the theory should be thrown out rather than the possibility of synonymy.

Overall, I must adjudicate the case "not proven" but with some strong theoretical evidence in favor of mental synonymy that must be dealt with before a retrial. Whichever way the verdict comes down, it seems to me the possibility of mental synonymy is not as objectionable as has commonly been supposed.[29]

NOTES

1 Trentman 1970; Spade 1980.
2 For brevity, I will sometimes speak of "written" or "spoken" language only, where what I say in fact applies to both. This should cause no confusion.
3 See also Spade 1995, 17.
4 Spade 1975.
5 Contrary to what Spade 1996, 109, suggests.
6 *SL* I.6. Quotations from *SL* are taken from Spade 1995.
7 And probably is not so preserved, if one accepts the arguments of Gregory of Rimini and Peter of Ailly. See Spade 1996, 120–7.
8 *Quodl.* V.9; compare V.8, concl. 2.
9 For example, expressions corresponding to connotative terms, on Spade's account (Spade 1975).
10 See Sec. III.1.
11 Quotations from *Quodl.* are taken from Spade 1996.
12 Spade 1980, 12.
13 Ibid.
14 See Secs. I.1 and I.2.
15 *SL* I.6.
16 Spade 1975.
17 Spade 1980, 12.
18 Spade 1975 and 1980.
19 Spade 1975, 68.
20 Ibid., 67.
21 See Spade 1996, 180–2.
22 Spade 1975, 68.
23 Spade 1996, 99.

24 Spade acknowledges this, ibid.

25 Ibid., 99–100.

26 Spade 1975.

27 Panaccio 1990.

28 See Sec. II.

29 A first draft of this paper was written when I was a graduate student at Indiana University in 1991. I owe an enormous debt to Paul Vincent Spade for his insights and encouragement.

5   Ockham's Nominalist Metaphysics: Some Main Themes

The first thing one learns about William of Ockham's philosophy is usually that he was a "nominalist." But sometimes it is not explained just what Ockham's nominalism was. For medieval nominalism, like its modern namesake, took many sometimes surprising forms.[1]

At least two distinct themes in Ockham's metaphysics have been called nominalism: (1) his rejection of universals[2] and their accoutrements, like the Scotist formal distinction, and (2) his program of what can be called "ontological reduction," namely his eliminating many other kinds of putative entities, whether universal or not, and in particular his cutting the list of real ontological categories from Aristotle's ten to two: substance and quality (plus a few specimens of relation in theological contexts).[3] Although I will say something about both themes in this chapter, the emphasis will be on the second.

These two themes are independent of one another. One might deny the reality of universals, as Ockham did, yet maintain that individual entities are needed in more or fewer categories. Thus, John Buridan rejected universals as resolutely as Ockham ever did but thought there are real, irreducible entities in the category of quantity, which Ockham denied, as well as in the categories of substance and quality.[4] Conversely, one might think some of the categories in Aristotle's list can be reduced to others while insisting that universals, not just individuals, are needed in some or all the remaining categories. Thus, Ockham's contemporary Walter Burley thought the categories could be reduced to the same list of three Buridan allowed, but he was a realist about universals.[5]

Although these two strands of Ockham's thinking are independent, they are nevertheless often viewed as joint effects of a more fundamental concern: the principle of parsimony known as "Ockham's Razor." Granted, in some respects his ontology is lean and sparse compared with that of many of his contemporaries. But it would be easy to exaggerate this parsimony. For in other respects Ockham's ontology is generous. He allows individual qualities, for example; there are as many whitenesses as there are white things (although there is no *universal* whiteness). Again, he seems ontologically committed to nonexistent entities – past, future, or merely possible.[6] Also, in the early stages of his career he accepted yet another kind of nonexistent entity, "*ficta*" or thought-objects, which do not have real being but only a kind of "intentional being"; they are analogous to modern phenomenological "intentional objects."[7] Finally, and perhaps most important, I will argue that Ockham's rejection of certain kinds of entities is less sweeping than has been portrayed; there is a sense in which he remains committed to them after all.[8]

Still, there is no doubt that Ockham did devote a great deal of effort to arguing against what he regarded as his contemporaries' bloated ontological inventories. We will begin, therefore, with Ockham's Razor.

I. OCKHAM'S RAZOR

During or shortly after Ockham's life, there appeared an interesting treatise entitled *On the Principles of Theology*[9] presenting a systematic summary of his views organized around two main principles: divine omnipotence and parsimony. Although the work is not really by Ockham, it does contain only authentically Ockhamist doctrine and sometimes quotes him verbatim. Because the manuscripts do not ascribe the treatise to any other author, it is not surprising that later generations uniformly attributed it to Ockham.[10] Perhaps partly for this reason, Ockham's Razor has traditionally been regarded as a cornerstone of his thinking.

Ockham's Razor is frequently expressed in the statement "Beings are not to be multiplied beyond necessity."[11] Ockham himself never puts it that way[12] but often says equivalent things: "Plurality is not to be posited without necessity;"[13] "what can happen through fewer [principles] happens in vain through more;"[14] "when a proposition is verified of things, more [things] are superfluous if fewer suffice,"[15] and so on.[16]

These formulas are merely statements of cautious theoretical method. Confining our ontology to what is really needed, after all, guarantees it will be populated only by genuine entities. Unfortunately, this approach does not guarantee we will have gotten them all. The Razor is thus powerless for actually *denying* the existence of certain kinds of entities; all it does is prevent our positively affirming their existence.

Nevertheless, some formulations of Ockham's Razor might at first be taken to warrant a stronger conclusion. To say certain kinds of entities would be "in vain" or "superfluous" is to say there is no sufficient reason for them to exist. Thus, not only is there no positive basis for postulating them; but the "principle of sufficient reason" actually *rules them out*. "God and nature," Aristotle said, "work nothing in vain."[17] Curiously, Ockham does not cite this text, no doubt in part because he does not believe it is true – at least not the part about God.[18] Furthermore, even if one did believe an unrestricted principle of sufficient reason, these versions of the Razor would in practice be no stronger than what we have already seen. They would allow us to deny the existence of certain entities only if we were in a position to assess all possible "sufficient reasons." But we are not.

In practice, Ockham's Razor does not play any *special* role in paring down his ontology. After all, parsimony is hardly an Ockhamist innovation. Versions of it can be found throughout Aristotle[19] and Ockham's medieval predecessors.[20] Even authors whose ontologies were not as minimal as Ockham's and who proposed what has been called an "anti-Razor" to ensure that no *fewer* entities are postulated than necessary, merely shifted the emphasis.[21] *No one* advocated postulating unnecessary entities. The difference between Ockham and those he criticizes is over which entities really are necessary. The Razor by itself does not decide that; for that one needs further arguments.

II. TWO WAYS TO ELIMINATE ENTITIES

Ockham has two main lines of attack against other people's ontologies. One proceeds by arguing that the reasons others give for postulating certain entities are not good reasons, that everything that can be done with such entities can be done without them. This is the main strategy he uses, for example, to argue that real entities are not needed in most of Aristotle's ten categories. Combined with Ockham's Razor, this approach implies not only that such entities are unnecessary, but that therefore *they should not be postulated.*

As always, such reasoning is defeasible; it may well be that some apparently decisive arguments against the need for certain kinds of entities are not decisive at all; further considerations settle the matter in those entities' favor. This actually happens, according to Ockham. In several cases, as we shall see, he explicitly allows theological considerations of the Trinity, the Incarnation, and the Eucharist to override what philosophical reasoning by itself would have found the most plausible view. In another case, there is at least some basis to suspect that, were it not for the theology of the Eucharist, Ockham would have had reason to eliminate the entire category of quality as well as the other accidental Aristotelian categories.[22]

The second main line of attack is different. It argues that certain other people's ontological theories not only postulate unnecessary entities but lead to plain falsehood – either to self-contradiction or, at least, to claims that contradict established facts. This is one of the ways Ockham argues, for example, against realist theories of universals.[23] As a strategy, it may at first appear much stronger than the former; provided its arguments are correctly reasoned and not merely fallacious, it is *not* defeasible in the light of considerations from other quarters. Theology can provide additional information to decide issues left undecided by philosophy alone, but *no* considerations – theological or otherwise – are going to make falsehoods true or outright contradictions possible. But in fact, as we shall see, this strategy is not so different from the former.[24]

We begin with first strategy.

II.1. *Ontological Reduction*

Ockham is happy enough to say some things are large or small, heavy or light, round or square, long or short, hot or cold; some are related to others, some act or are acted upon, some are here or there, now or then, some are in motion, some (continuous bodies, for instance) are infinitely divisible, and so on. All these ways of speaking are legitimate and in a sense reflect the ways things are. But Ockham is not at all happy with the practice of metaphysicians who freely form abstract nominalizations out of these and other ways of speaking and then assume such nominalizations pick out new kinds of entities in the ontology. Their ontologies end up being populated not only by substances and qualities but also by quantities, relations, actions, "passions" (being acted upon), places, times, motions, points, instants, and so on. For Ockham, language is not such a simple and reliable guide to ontology – particularly not a language in which neologisms are coined with abandon.

But Ockham does not reject all abstract nominalizations; he allows, for example, that whitenesses are real things and, moreover, things really *distinct* from the white things they belong to. Again, 'humanity' signifies real humanities, although here the concrete and the abstract nouns do *not* signify distinct things; the humanities just *are* the humans themselves.[25] Such ontological questions, therefore, must be handled on a case-by-case basis.

The main vehicle Ockham uses to show we do not need distinct entities for all these abstract nominalizations is his semantic theory of connotation together with the related theory of "exposition" and "exponibles."[26] With these tools, Ockham argues that true statements containing words appearing to signify such entities are in fact equivalent, in some fairly strong meaning-based way,[27] to statements that *do not* contain such words; hence, we can say all the true things we want without committing ourselves to such entities. Strategies like this are sometimes called strategies of "ontological reduction"; talk about certain kinds of entities is "reduced" to equivalent talk about other kinds of entities, and the former (putative) entities can therefore be eliminated from the ontology.

This aspect of Ockham's thought is discussed elsewhere in this volume.[28] Nevertheless, certain observations are in order here.

II.I.I. THEOLOGICAL LIMITS ON ONTOLOGICAL REDUCTION First, Ockham allows that the supply of truths we want to maintain can come from several quarters: "For nothing ought to be posited without a reason given, unless it is self-evident or known by experience or proved by the authority of Sacred Scripture."[29] Theology, therefore, can provide evidence to answer ontological questions where unaided human reason would have inclined the other way.

In discussing the category of relation, for instance, Ockham argues that there is no good pure reasoning, self-evident principle, or experience to indicate that there exist real relations distinct from their relata. But there do. The doctrine of the Trinity, as Ockham understood it, requires us to posit such relations in God. Likewise, the Incarnation requires a real relation of union between Jesus's human nature and the Divine Word. And the Eucharist, understood according to the theory of transubstantiation, requires that the "inherence" of accidents in a substance be construed as a real relation distinct from its relata.[30]

Again, Ockham holds that for most natural-kind terms in the category of substance, and for some in the category of quality, the concrete and the abstract forms are synonymous. Thus 'dog' and 'caninity' are everywhere intersubstitutable. It follows that, despite its oddness, 'Every dog is a caninity' is true. But there is one exception, for 'man' and 'humanity.' Because the doctrine of the Incarnation holds that Jesus the man had both a human and a divine nature, it follows that *not* every man is a humanity. There is exactly one man, Jesus, who is distinct from his humanity. He *is* not his humanity; he *has* it.[31] This leads to the odd conclusion that if the number of men is n, then the number of humanities is also n, but the men and the humanities together amount to $n + 1$ distinct entities – not n, and not $2n$.[32]

These are explicit cases where, for theological reasons, Ockham departs from what he thinks unaided natural reason would find most plausible and allows certain additional entities. But there is reason to suspect that, for theological reasons, Ockham allowed a whole ontological *category* that might otherwise have been "reduced" and eliminated.

As already noted, Ockham is prepared to say things really act or are acted on, are really related to one another, and so on, but he does not think the truth of these statements requires us to postulate real entities in the categories of action, passion, or relation. Things really act, but there are no actions; things are really related without relations (except for the few exceptional cases required by theology).[33] Ockham "eliminates" all the Aristotelian categories in this way – except for substance and quality.

One wonders why he stopped there. Why is it not just as legitimate to say things are really "qualified" but there are no qualities – things are really white or red, hot or cold, although there is no whiteness or redness, no heat or cold as a distinct accidental entity in the category of quality? If other categories can be eliminated without denying any of the ways things really are, why not quality too? In that case, we would end up with a *single* ontological category: substance. Substances would be qualified, quantified, related in different ways, would variously act and be acted upon, and so on, but there would *be* only substances. None of the richness of the world would be lost, only the illusion that we need distinct entities for all the different claims we want to make about things.

In modern epistemology, there is an "adverbial" theory of perception according to which the experience of seeing something red, for example, is not to be analyzed into a mental act of awareness plus a sense-datum or mental object that is red. Rather the experience is to be thought of as a mental act of seeing "redly."[34] So too, I suggest, why should *being* red be analyzed in terms of a substance *plus* the quality of redness distinct from but inhering in it? Why should being red not be thought of simply as a substance that "exists in a certain way" – redly? Ockham already in effect does this for the other accidental categories.[35]

Ockham does not explicitly address this question, but it is tempting to suppose the answer lies in the doctrine of the Eucharist interpreted according to the theory of transubstantiation. That theory holds that at the moment of consecration the bread and wine of the sacrament cease to exist and are replaced by the body and blood of Christ. But the accidents of the bread and wine remain (without inhering in the newly present body and blood of Christ, or in any other substance). This theory of course entails that the qualities of the bread and wine are real entities distinct from their substances.

Ockham does not actually say it is the theory of transubstantiation that prevents him from "reducing" the category of quality like the other accidental categories. But the issue was raised explicitly by others later on,[36] and it is hard to see what other factors could have been involved.[37]

II.1.2. ARE THE "ELIMINATED" ENTITIES REALLY GONE? The standard interpretation of Ockham is that his ontology consists of individual substances and individual accidents in the category of quality.[38] Everything else is eliminated, as described previously and elsewhere in this volume. But there is some uncertainty whether this is really what Ockham intended and, if so, whether he succeeded.

As Adams observes, if this is Ockham's project, it "remains essentially programmatic."[39] His attempts to reduce talk about other putative entities to talk about substances and qualities are almost always incomplete; they result in propositions that do eliminate the offending terms but rarely get as far as completely reducing everything to the categories he allows.

There are several sides to this issue.[40] First, Ockham holds that categorematic terms[41] that are what he calls "absolute" (i.e., nonconnotative) ones – are acquired by "acquaintance" with corresponding objects in the world.[42] At a minimum, therefore, Ockham's program is committed to the claim that absolute terms are confined to the categories he accepts. There is no doubt Ockham did intend at least this much, and there seems little reason to doubt his success.

But by itself, this claim does not mean very much. It does nothing to relieve us of commitment to unwanted entities; all it does is ensure we are not committed to them *this* way – by means of absolute terms. Far more important are two other claims: (a) ontology includes only entities that can be signified by absolute categorematic terms[43]; and (b) all propositions containing *nonabsolute* (that is, connotative) categorematic terms, as well as all "exponible" propositions, whether they contains connotative terms or not,[44] can be fully paraphrased by the theories of connotation and exposition into nonexponible propositions containing only absolute categorematic terms plus syncategoremata.

Together, these claims make an appealing picture. Absolute terms commit us to the reality of certain kinds of entities. Claim (a) *denies* the reality of all other putative entities. Finally, claim (b) gives us a way to eliminate even the appearance of a need for additional entities.

But did Ockham hold (a) and (b)? Here there are differences of interpretation. Panaccio has argued that Ockham did not hold (b) at all.[45] Adams maintains not only that he did hold it but that, despite the incomplete reductive paraphrases Ockham typically gives, (b) can be defended.[46] I have argued elsewhere that, although Ockham probably did hold (b), the reductive analyses it promises cannot always be actually carried out; we might succeed in eliminating connotative terms in a certain category, but – short of adopting devices Ockham would likely have found unpalatable – we cannot succeed in completely eliminating everything but syncategoremata and absolute terms in the categories of substance and quality.[47]

If there is not the same disagreement about claim (a), perhaps that is because it has not yet been widely treated in the literature. I think (a) is not true of Ockham's ontology and moreover that there is little reason to suppose he thought it was.[48] As Panaccio observes, Ockham does hold that things cause one another, that they are spatially arranged, temporally ordered, and so on, even though he denies there are places, times, or relations of causality.[49] Thus, as Panaccio aptly puts it,

the whole structure of propositional discourse is ultimately brought to rest, for its truth and falsity, upon the ways in which the various singular beings of the world are arranged with regard to each other along certain ordered series, such as the causal, the temporal, and the local ones. The orderings themselves, though, are denied any independent reality.[50]

I think Panaccio is right, with one small but important revision. For in fact, it is not just the "independent" reality of such orderings that Ockham denies; he denies they are "things" at all, independent or not, distinct from "absolute" (nonrelative) things.[51] Still, Panaccio's observation illustrates a point I want to make.

Does it not sound paradoxical, even absurd, to say truth and falsehood are determined in part by the arrangements of things along various orderings and then to *deny* the reality of those same orderings? If truth is based in reality, not merely in subjective fancy, then any factor that really affects the truth values of propositions must be given *some* reality in one's ontology.[52]

What Ockham does is not to deny *all* reality to such orderings and other truth-relevant factors; instead, he merely denies they are "things." In practice, this amounts to denying only that they are factors that can be signified, and so in particular that they can be signified by absolute categorematic terms. If this is right, then Ockham's ontology turns out to be a two-tiered one. Some components of reality can be signified. They are the ones that can be referred to by the subjects or predicates of propositions; we can predicate terms of them. But other components of reality are not like that. We cannot predicate terms of them; they cannot be referred to by subjects or predicates of propositions. They cannot be signified. But they are real nonetheless – real enough to affect truth values. The difference between the two tiers, therefore, is a little like a "type distinction" in semantics.[53] Ockham does not eliminate the second tier; all he does is block our talking about it by means of nominalizations of other forms of expression.

On this interpretation, claim (a) fails. It follows that for a full appreciation of Ockham's ontological commitment, we must look at more than what he is committed to "quantifying over," or what he regards as a "property bearer."[54] These approaches *assume* claim (a).[55]

For example, Ockham denies spatial positions are a distinct kind of "thing."[56] There are no such things as "behindedness," "alongsidedness," "hereness," and "thereness." But as long as some things can truly be said to be "behind" or "alongside" others, some "here" and others "there," and as long as Ockham provides no way of fully "reducing" such statements to others that do *not* contain forms of expression from which the former nominalizations are taken, he has not completely freed himself from ontological commitment to positions. All he has done is to free himself from a commitment to their being "things."

Is this two-tiered picture Ockham's *own* picture of what he was doing? It is hard to say. Ockham probably thought of ontology as most modern interpreters do: purely in terms of "things." Certainly he says nothing to suggest otherwise. Why then attribute such a two-tiered ontology to him? Because this seems to be the way his philosophy actually works, no matter how he *thought* it worked.

Perhaps the strongest evidence here is Ockham's actual practice. He does allow that things really do cause one another, really are spatially arranged, temporally ordered, and so on. He does this even though he does *not* say, and as far as I can see does nothing to suggest, that all such talk can be paraphrased away in the way claim (a) requires. What he does suggest can be paraphrased away is all talk that would imply that causality, spaces, times, and so on, are *things*.[57] But paraphrasing the latter away is not at all the same as what claim (a) requires, even if he thought it was.

The only potential evidence I can find that Ockham did think such a paraphrase was the same thing is that he says in one passage, "the two words 'thing' and 'to be' signify the same item or items (*idem et eadem*[58]), but the one does so nominally and the other verbally."[59] One might be tempted to take this as meaning that whatever can in any way "be" (and so whatever is in the ontology) is a "thing" and therefore can be signified by an absolute categorematic term.[60] In that case, Ockham does believe claim (a) after all, but goes beyond it in practice. Yet in fact the passage makes only a weaker claim: that whatever the one word "signifies" the other does too. The passage is completely silent about whether there are ontological factors that cannot be signified by either expression.

Ockham's actual practice, however, is clear; it conflicts with (a). There is more in Ockham's ontology than "things," more than can be signified by absolute terms.

But it should not be hastily concluded that all the putative entities Ockham denies are "things" really remain anyway but are now shifted to a different logico-semantical "type." That has to be considered separately case by case.

For example, following Aristotle, *Categories* 8, medieval authors commonly distinguished four species of quality. The fourth included "qualities" like shape, curvedness, straightness, density, and thinness. Aristotle suggested that at least some of these were not really distinct qualities in their own right but had more to do with the relative position of a thing's parts.[61] With this suggestion, Ockham argues that "qualities in the fourth species ... are not things distinct from substance and the other sensible qualities" because "when some predicables can be verified succesively of the same item (and cannot be verified of the same item at once) solely because of a local motion, then those predicables do not have to signify distinct things."[62] Thus a physical body can become straight or curved, dense or thin, without requiring any new entities (Ockham thinks) but simply by rearranging the body's already existing parts. But if a physical body can come to be straight without taking on a new entity ("straightness"), then straightness can legitimately be said to be an idle hypothesis and eliminable from the ontology.

Ockham uses this kind of strategy, with its appeal to local motion without the production of any new entities, in a variety of ingenious "reductive" arguments.[63] One might doubt whether such arguments can succeed without granting some reality to places, times, and indeed to motion itself – and so to more than substances and qualities. But these arguments may very well succeed without granting any distinct reality at all – whether as "things" or otherwise – to straightness, curvedness, density, and so on. If so, straightness and the rest can perhaps be eliminated from ontology entirely, not just from the inventory of "things."

Ockham's ontology, therefore, consists, as I see it, of (1) "things" – entities that can be expressed nominally, can be signified, of which terms can be predicated. These include individual substances, individual qualities, a few theological relations, and nothing else. And (2) other factors – what cannot be expressed nominally and cannot be signified, of which terms cannot be predicated, but that cannot be fully paraphrased away and yet are real enough to affect the truth values of propositions.[64] In some of the essays in the secondary literature, in this volume and elsewhere, where one reads of Ockham's rejecting certain kinds of entities, the reader must be alert to whether they are being eliminated from (1) only or from (2) as well; the latter is the far stronger claim.

Ockham's ontology as a whole is not as sparse as sometimes portrayed. It includes much more than individual substances, qualities, and a few relations; but it still includes much less than do the ontologies of many of his predecessors and contemporaries.

II.2. The Elimination of Universals

Medieval authors had two main notions of a "universal": (1) whatever can be present in many things (a) as a whole, (b) simultaneously, and (c) in some appropriate metaphysically constitutive way;[65] and (2) whatever is "naturally apt to be predicated of many."[66] Because Ockham held that some terms of language are predicable of many things, he of course admitted "universals" in sense (2). What makes him a "nominalist" about universals is his denial that there is anything else "predicated of many," and that there is anything at all that fits (1).[67] Space allows me to treat this aspect of Ockham's doctrine only very briefly.[68]

As noted in Section II, Ockham's main strategy for arguing against universals is not the same as for reducing the number of categories. He does not hold that talk about universals can always be reduced by paraphrase to talk about singulars only. His claim is not that his opponents' theories are unnecessary in accounting for the facts but that they are outright false. Either they contradict known truths, or worse, they are internally contradictory.

Such arguments may seem decisive at first; not even God in his omnipotence can make contradictories true simultaneously.[69] But we must look closely. Ockham's actual arguments do not target the notion of a universal as such; in every case they are directed against particular theories held by his contemporaries. Often they rest on peculiar claims in those theories, and thus one wonders whether suitably revised theories might escape Ockham's criticisms.[70]

In his longest sustained treatment of the topic,[71] Ockham considers several realist views in sequence, from "most" realist[72] to "least."[73] He rejects them all concluding that "no thing outside the soul is universal, either through itself or through anything real or rational added on, no matter how it is considered or understood."[74] This apparently tight logical progression of views may give the impression Ockham has covered all possible ways universals might be taken to exist. But it is not clear that he has.

Furthermore, as Adams observes, even if Ockham does consider all possibilities, many of his arguments simply fail to show any contradiction or outright falsehood in the views he discusses; at best they show only striking and surprising consequences.[75]

It appears, therefore, that Ockham's "refutation" of realism is not an unqualified success. This is not to deny the sophistication and acuteness of individual arguments – only their cumulative effect. Even if it is true that a realist theory of universals can be formulated that escapes Ockham's attacks, and even if positive reasons can be found other than those Ockham considers for believing such a theory, the fact remains that, until such a theory and such reasons are found, Ockham has probably succeeded in weakening the case for realism. His nominalism appears a viable alternative. And as long as that is true, Ockham's Razor at least warrants his refraining from any commitment to universals.

III. CONCLUSION

This brief treatment has done no more than scratch the surface of a few parts of Ockham's metaphysical views. No short essay will prepare readers fully for all the arguments encountered in Ockham's actual texts, even though there is a wealth of secondary literature in this volume and elsewhere that will help enormously with particular doctrines and arguments.[76] Still, I hope this essay provides readers with an orientation toward some of the main themes in Ockham's metaphysics.

1 See Normore 1987; Courtenay 1991b and 1992. Note that Ockham never describes himself as a "nominalist."

2 Some authors want to say Ockham is not a "nominalist" in this sense but a "conceptualist." They reserve the word 'nominalism' for doctrines denying general or universal concepts as well as general or universal entities and confining "universals" to general spoken or written terms. See Boehner 1946c.

3 On this second strand in Ockham's nominalism, see Chaps. 6 and 7. For the relations required by theology, see Sec.II.1.1 in this chapter.

4 Normore 1985.

5 Conti 1990.

6 On both points, see Panaccio in Chap. 3, Sec. I. On the latter, see also Normore in Chap. 2, Sec. III.

7 On *ficta*, see Adams 1977 and Adams 1987a, 73–105. Ockham later abandoned the theory, apparently in part because of arguments by his confrere Walter Chatton that such *ficta* are theoretically unnecessary. See Adams 1982, 436–9.

8 See Sec. II.1.2.

9 The editors date the work 1328–50 (26*).

10 OPh VII.23*, 26*.

11 Adams 1995b. In this form, it was referred to as "Ockham's Razor" at least as early as Sir William Hamilton in 1836–37 (Hamilton 1853, 616, 629). Almost a century earlier (1746), Condillac had referred to it as "*le rasior des nominaux*" but did not link it to Ockham (Condillac 1788, I.180 n. 1). For both references, see Brampton 1964 and Maurer 1978.

12 The formulation appears to be postmedieval. See Maurer 1984, 464 n. 3.

13 † *Sent.* I. Prol.1 (74), I.30.2 (322); *Quodl.* VI.10.

14 *Sent.* I.17.3, I.26.1 (157), I.26.2 (176), II.12–13 (268).

15 *Quodl.* VII.8. In medieval parlance, to "verify" a proposition is to "make it true," not to *check* whether it is true; it is a semantic notion, not an epistemological one.

16 On various formulations of the "Razor," see also Adams 1987a, 156–61.

17 *On the Heavens* I.4.271^{a}33.

18 *Sent.* I.17.3. See also Wood in Chap. 15, Sec. II.4.

19 For example, *Posterior Analytics* I.25.86^{a}33–5; *Physics* I.4.188^{a}17–18. Compare *Physics* VIII.6.259^{a}8–12.

20 Maurer 1978, 427–8; Maurer 1984, 463 n. 3.

21 Thus Walter Chatton, "Wherever an affirmative proposition is apt to be verified of actually existing things, if two things, however present in situation (*situs*) and duration, are not able to suffice without another thing, [then] one has to posit another thing; and if three [things], however

present in situation and duration, are not able to suffice without another thing, [then] one has to posit a fourth thing, and so on." Quoted in Maurer 1984, 464 n. 7 (my translation). On the "anti-Razor," see Maurer 1978 and 1984.

22 For all these points, see Sec. II.1.1.

23 He also sometimes uses it to eliminate some of the Aristotelian categories. See Klima in Chap. 6, Sec. IV.

24 See Sec. II.2.

25 With one exception; see Sec. II.1.1.

26 For the relation between connotation and exposition, see Spade 1990, 608–12.

27 I have claimed this equivalence is actually *synonymy* (Spade 1975 and 1980), although this claim has been vigorously criticized in Panaccio 1990 (and Chap. 3 of this volume) and Tweedale 1992. I have replied in Spade 1996, 230–9.

28 See Chaps. 3, 6, and 7.

29 †*Sent.* I.30.1 (290). The words "without a reason given" indicate that sound reasoning from the sources named can be an additional basis for positing entities. See also *Sent.* III.9 (281), IV.3–5 (51–2); *Quant.* 3 (70) (= Birch 1930,127).

30 For details of these intricate arguments, see Adams 1987a, Chap. 7, especially 267–76. Adams goes on to argue that the reality of "inherence" relations cannot be confined to theologically "exceptional" cases but must be generalized to apply to the inherence of *all* accidents in their substances and of substantial forms in matter as well. Ockham himself seems to resist this conclusion. See ibid., 275–6.

31 *SL* I.6–7; *Quodl.* V.9–10.

32 Odd though it is, this conclusion is no basis for an objection to Ockham's position. The doctrine of the Incarnation *presupposes* that Jesus is an exceptional case; it is not surprising to find odd and striking consequences of it.

33 I will omit the theological qualification henceforth; readers should take it as tacit.

34 See Dretske 1995, 571.

35 Maier 1958, 330, cites an anonymous fourteenth-century *Physics* commentary that holds exactly the view I suggest about quality (quoted in Adams 1987a, 278). As pointed out ibid., such a view was condemned at Paris in 1347 surely, in part, because of the theory of transubstantiation.

36 Adams 1987a, 278.

37 Adams 1987a, 279–85, assesses the situation differently. She points out that elsewhere Ockham does not hesitate to say where he is departing from ontological parsimony for theological reasons (for instance, on real

relations in the Trinity). In her view, that Ockham does *not* do so here suggests he is not being especially motivated by theological considerations in this instance. She goes on to suggest other, purely philosophical reasons Ockham might have had instead. But the fact remains he does not explicitly give those reasons, or *any* reasons, for this aspect of his doctrine. In my view, the theological reason is perhaps still the most likely explanation.

38 For example, Adams 1987a, 143. The view is by no means original with her.

39 Ibid., 313.

40 See Spade 1998b.

41 That is, terms that can serve as subjects or predicates in standard subject-copula-predicate propositions.

42 See Spade 1990, 600. See also the important caveat ibid., 601 n. 16.

43 See Spade 1998b for a discussion of these claims. I say "can be signified" rather than "are signified" because the supply of absolute terms is determined in part by the limits of one's experience (the things one is "acquainted" with).

44 On the theory of exposition, see Panaccio in Chap. 3, Sec. V.

45 Panaccio 1990. That paper is motivated largely by worries about relational concepts. I think those worries are effectively answered in Tweedale 1992.

46 Adams 1987a, 287–313.

47 See Spade 1990, 602–6, and Spade 1998b.

48 The former point is made in Spade 1990, 607–8. Both are argued in Spade 1998b.

49 Chap. 3, Sec. V.

50 Ibid.

51 On the distinction between "absolute" and "relative things" or "respects," see Adams 1987a, 145–6. For Ockham's denials, see *Quodl.* VI.12; *SL* I.59–60.

52 For this criterion of "ontological commitment," see Spade 1990 and Spade 1998b.

53 Compare Spade 1990, 608. The analogy is heuristic and should *not* be asked to bear more theoretical weight than that.

54 Adams 1987a, 306–10, defends the success of Ockham's ontological program by measuring its commitments according to these two criteria. I agree that, measured by these criteria, Ockham's commitments do not go beyond individual substances, qualities, and a few relations. What Adams and I disagree about is whether these are *good* criteria for measuring Ockham's ontological commitment. See also Adams 1985.

55 In particular, I think the notion of a "property bearer" is not a good way to approach the question and only confuses matters. What, after all, does it

mean to be a "property bearer"? If the phrase is taken at face value, what are the "properties" so borne? If such "properties" bear further properties of their own, we are apparently committed to (an infinite regress of?) higher-order properties (accidents of accidents?) in a way nothing in Ockham's writing suggests. If they do *not* bear further properties of their own, then – on this criterion – they cannot be entities in their own right and so cannot be said in any real sense to be "borne" by other entities. On the other hand, if the expression "property bearer" is interpreted as merely "whatever we can say something about," "property bearers" turn out to be just "subjects of predication" – in short, "things," and we are back to claim (a).

56 *SL* I.61.

57 This is just claim (b). As indicated earlier, I do not think he can succeed even at this lesser claim.

58 I cannot translate this "the same thing or things" because 'thing' is a reserved word in this context.

59 *SL* III-2.27.

60 See n. 43.

61 *Categories* 8.10ᵃ16–24.

62 *Quodl.* VII.2. See also *SL* I.55; *Expos. Praed.* 14.10.

63 See Adams 1987a, Chaps. 5–8. Not all Ockham's reductive arguments proceed like this; each must be considered separately.

64 By calling them "other factors" (in subject position), I run the risk of trying to say what according to Ockham's own ontology cannot be said – in particular of trying to "signify" what cannot be signified. This might be construed as a problem for someone trying to state Ockham's ontology while committed to *accepting* it; I am not so committed. It should be pointed out that, historically, there have been many other ontological theories (notably, Wittgenstein's in the *Tractatus*) that run into similar problems of expressibility. (I am not committed to those theories either.)

65 This comes from Boethius's *Second Commentary on Porphyry's Isagoge*. See Boethius 1906, 162–3. The exact specification of (c) was a controversial matter.

66 This comes from Aristotle's *On Interpretation* 7.17ᵃ39–40.

67 In what follows I will use the word 'universal' not for the terms Ockham allows but for the entities he denies.

68 For fuller treatments, see Adams 1982 and Adams 1987a, 13–69.

69 Pseudo-Ockham's *De principiis theologiae* expresses divine omnipotence by the principle "God can do everything the doing of which does not include a contradiction" (507). Compare *Sent.* I.42; *Quodl.* VI.6.

70 The arguments are extremely subtle and in some cases hard to assess. See the detailed account in Adams 1987a, 13–69.

71 *Sent.* I.2.4–8.

72 Walter Burley's view that universals are really distinct from but really in the individuals that share them. Ibid., I.2.4.

73 Henry of Harclay's view that the same thing (*res*) is both individual and universal, depending on which concept it is conceived under. Ibid., I.2.7.

74 *Sent.* I.2.7 (248–9) (= Spade 1994, 204).

75 For example., Adams 1987a, 31–3. About Ockham's arguments against Burley, for instance, Adams remarks, "His arguments serve more to articulate the contrasting conceptions of the metaphysical structure of particulars than to refute his opponents." (Ibid., 59.)

76 The most comprehensive account by far is Adams 1987a.

6 Ockham's Semantics and Ontology of the Categories

Ockham's treatment of the ten Aristotelian categories[1] plays a crucial role in his innovative nominalist program. One of his main complaints against "the moderns," as he is wont to call his opponents,[2] is that they treat the categories as comprising ten mutually exclusive classes of distinct entities. Indeed, the unknown author of a work written against Ockham's logic (characteristically entitled "A very useful and realist logic of Campsall the Englishman against Ockham"), writes:

To such most general genera[3] there are subjected individuals that are really distinct from the individuals of another most general genus, [and] of which [this genus] is properly and directly predicated; for example, we can truly assert 'This is [a] when'[4] pointing to the relation which is caused by the motion of the first movable in the inferior things,[5] so that, if that individual had a distinct proper name imposed on it, one could just as truly respond to the question 'What is it?' by saying: '[A] when,' as one can reply to the question 'What is it?' asked about a man, by saying: 'A substance.'[6]

As should be clear even from this brief passage, the disagreement between Ockham and his realist opponent here *does not concern universals*. On the contrary, regardless of whether there are universal entities other than universal terms (be they written, spoken, or mental terms), the question here is whether we have to admit distinct particulars falling under our universal terms in each of the ten categories.

However, Ockham's disagreement with this position is not simply a matter of his espousing a different ontology. For Ockham thinks this ontological position is the consequence of an even more fundamental error in his opponents' semantic theory: a radically mistaken conception of how our words and the concepts that render them meaningful are related to the things they represent. In general, according to Ockham, this conception would entail that "a column is to the right by to-the-rightness, God is creating by creation, is good by goodness, just by justice, mighty by might, an accident inheres by inherence, a subject is subjected by subjection, the apt is apt by aptitude, a chimera is nothing by nothingness, someone blind is blind by blindness, a body is mobile by mobility, and so on for other, innumerable cases."[7] And this is nothing but "to multiply beings according to the multiplicity of terms ... which, however, is erroneous and leads far away from the truth."[8]

As we shall see, Ockham's complaints are not entirely justified. Yet they might appear as an entirely credible motivation for advancing his radically new approach to some basic issues in semantics and ontology. To see exactly what is and what is not justified in Ockham's complaints, we have to start by considering at least a sketch of the semantic conception to which Ockham objects. Then we will have to examine whether this semantic conception does indeed have the ontological commitments Ockham claims it does, and if – as I claim – not entirely, then to what extent, and why. These considerations will then provide us with a solid basis for the analysis and brief evaluation of Ockham's alternative approach.

I. *VIA ANTIQUA* SEMANTICS[9]

The semantic conception Ockham finds fault with can be characterized at least by the following principles:

(1) Common terms ultimately signify whatever the concepts to which these terms are subordinated directly represent.

(2) Common terms as the subject terms of categorical propositions supposit personally for the things that are actual in respect of their ultimate significata. (Henceforth, by 'significata' of a common term without further qualification I will mean its ultimate significata, and by 'supposita' of a common term without further qualification I will mean its personal supposita.)

(3) The significata and supposita of the abstract counterparts of concrete common terms are the same as the significata of the concrete terms.

(4) Affirmative categorical propositions in the present tense are true if and only if the supposita of their subjects are actual in respect of the significata of their predicates (as required by the quantity of the proposition).[10]

As indicated, this "minimalist" characterization of the semantic theory in question does not have the ontological commitment Ockham claims his opponents' theory has. Indeed, I provided this "minimalist" characterization precisely because in this way it will be easier for us to see exactly what further assumptions would need to be added to these principles to yield the ontological commitment Ockham is talking about. But before discussing the issue of their ontological commitment, we need a brief clarification of these principles themselves.

1.1. The Semantic Triangle

The first of these principles, being basically a reformulation of Aristotle's "semantic triangle" from the beginning of *On Interpretation*,[11] is also accepted by Ockham. Indeed, among medieval authors it was generally agreed that all our words are meaningful only in virtue of their being subordinated to our concepts. Obviously, the utterance or the inscription *'arbor'* is meaningful in Latin only because it is subordinated to the concept by which we conceive trees in general, but since it is not thus subordinated to this concept in English, it is not meaningful in English. And since the utterance or inscription *'biltrix'* is not subordinated to any concept in either English or Latin, it is not meaningful in either of these two languages.[12] To be sure, there were serious differences of opinion among medieval authors as to what concepts are, what kinds of concepts there are, and how the several kinds are related to what they represent. Nevertheless, since from our present point of view concepts are relevant only in their semantic function, we do not have to go into these questions at this point. Therefore, it is sufficient here to distinguish between the immediate and the ultimate significata of common terms by saying that the immediate significata of (written or spoken) common terms are the concepts of human minds (whatever entities concepts are in themselves), and the ultimate significata of the same are whatever these concepts directly represent (whatever sort of entities the things thus represented are in themselves).

1.2. Supposition of Common Terms

Supposition is the referring function of terms, which, according to most authors, they have only in propositional contexts.[13] To stick with our previous example, the term 'arbor' has signification in Latin, because in Latin it is subordinated to the concept of trees whether it is used in the context of a proposition or considered outside a propositional context – say, in a dictionary. But when we use this term in the context of a proposition, its function is to stand for or to refer to[14] things somehow related to this concept. According to the most commonly accepted main divisions of the kinds of supposition a term may have, depending on how the concept is related to the things thus referred to, a spoken or written term was said to have *material*, *simple*, or *personal* supposition. A term has material supposition if it refers to itself or to any other similar term subordinated to its concept. For example, in 'Arbor est nomen' ('"tree" is a noun'), the subject term stands for itself and for any other occurrence of a similar inscription or utterance subordinated to the concept of trees. The same term has simple supposition if it stands for what it immediately signifies, that is, the concept to which it is subordinated.[15] For example, in 'Arbor est genus plantarum' ('Tree is a genus of plants'), it stands for the concept of trees.[16] Finally, the same term has personal supposition if it refers to any of the things that are actual (relative to the time and modality of the proposition)[17] in respect of what the concept it is subordinated to directly represents, and thus the term ultimately signifies, namely when it refers to the things that actually fall under the concept. For example, in 'Omnis arbor est planta' ('Every tree is a plant')[18] the subject refers to actual trees because it is actual trees that are actual in respect of what the concept of trees directly represents, whether what is thus represented is said to be one universal nature (whether numerically or merely formally one) common to all individual trees, or is numerically distinct "treenesses" inhering in, but still distinct from, individual trees, or is nothing but the individual trees themselves.[19]

Given our present interest, we need not delve into the further complexities of medieval supposition theory. What we need here is only the semantic distinction between the ultimate significata and personal supposita of common terms and the understanding that this semantic distinction may, but need not, reflect any ontological distinction even within the framework of "*via antiqua* semantics."[20]

1.3. Supposition of Concrete Versus Abstract Common Terms

Another common feature of *via antiqua* semantics is to treat abstract terms as agreeing in their signification with their concrete counterparts (that is, whatever the concrete terms signify, the abstract terms also signify) but differing from them in their *mode of signification*.[21] The upshot of this difference was held to be that abstract terms could be used to refer to what their concrete counterparts ultimately signified. Therefore, whenever reference needs to be made to the ultimate significata of a concrete common term (as opposed to the supposita of it, which can be referred to by the concrete term itself), the reference is supplied by the corresponding abstract term, even in cases when the vernacular does not have such a corresponding abstract term. It is this systematic need of this semantic framework for abstract terms that explains the proliferation of the "barbaric" coinages of the technical Latin of "the schools," the constant target of mockery in postmedieval authors, who no longer shared this need with their medieval predecessors. But Ockham's complaints were certainly not motivated by such humanistic squeamishness; his concern was not so much the proliferation of these terms but the apparent proliferation of the alleged corresponding entities.

1.4. The Inherence Theory of Predication

The impression of the necessary proliferation of the corresponding entities should be reinforced by the last of the preceding principles of *via antiqua* semantics, which briefly summarizes the theory of predication often referred to in the secondary literature as the "inherence theory."[22] For if an abstract term refers to what its concrete counterpart ultimately signifies, then according to this theory the concrete term is true of a thing if and only if what its abstract counterpart refers to actually exists. According to this theory, Socrates is a man if and only if he is actual in respect of humanity, which is another way of saying that Socrates is a man if and only if his humanity exists. But then it is indeed true that he is a man by his humanity, and by the same token it is true that he is tall by his tallness, that he is white by his whiteness, he is similar to Plato by his similarity to Plato, he is walking by his walking, he is somewhere by his somewhereness, and so forth, which indeed does appear to involve us in multiplying entities according to the multiplicity of terms, as Ockham claimed.

II. THE ONTOLOGICAL COMMITMENT OF
VIA ANTIQUA SEMANTICS

Despite the apparent plausibility of Ockham's charge, commitment to the preceding semantic principles does not entail commitment to any entities other than those Ockham himself would endorse. The reason is the simple fact that these principles in themselves just as much allow the identification of the semantic values of abstract and concrete terms in diverse categories as Ockham's alternative principles do. This is precisely why Domingo Soto, who describes himself as someone "born among nominalists and raised by realists,"[23] could make the declaration:

It does not escape our attention how difficult it is to ascertain that all the ten categories are really distinct in such a manner as many realists seem to contend, namely, that all of them are distinct from one another, just as whiteness is distinct from substance, which we certainly believe to exist without substance in the sacrament of the altar. However, I shall never be persuaded that relation and the last six categories are distinct in this way from substance.[24]

Clearly, if the entities in the categories of substance, quantity, and quality are not distinct from the entities in the other categories, then the charge of multiplying entities with the multiplicity of terms is unjustified. However, it may not be quite clear how anyone who endorses the preceding semantic principles can maintain this position. After all, according to these principles, if the proposition 'Socrates is white' is true, then Socrates is actual in respect of the whiteness signified by the predicate, which is another way of saying that Socrates' whiteness exists. But Socrates' whiteness cannot be identified with Socrates. For it is certainly possible for Socrates to exist while his whiteness does not exist, namely when Socrates gets a tan and his whiteness ceases to exist. But if Socrates were identical with his whiteness, then, by substituting identicals, we would have to admit it is possible for Socrates to exist while his whiteness, that is, he himself, does not exist, which is a contradiction. Therefore, Socrates cannot be identical with his whiteness.

Apparently, the same type of reasoning can be applied to any term in any of the nine categories of accidents, for according to Porphyry's commonly endorsed definition, an accident is something that may or may not belong to a subject without the destruction of the subject. Thus, whatever is signified by any accidental predicate may or may not exist, while the subject may still stay in existence. For example, in accordance with the preceding principles, if the proposition 'Socrates is a father' is true, then an entity in the category of relation, Socrates' fatherhood, exists. But it is certainly possible for Socrates to exist while his fatherhood does not exist (for in fact he existed before he became a father, and he could have existed without ever becoming a father). But if Socrates were identical with his fatherhood, then this would mean it would be possible for the same thing, Socrates, who is supposed to be identical with his fatherhood, to exist and not to exist at the same time, which is an explicit contradiction. Therefore, Socrates cannot be identical with his fatherhood either. The same goes for all other accidents.

However, we should notice here that in these arguments we exploited a hidden assumption that is crucial concerning the distinction of the categories. To make this assumption explicit, let us consider a similar argument. Apparently Socrates cannot be identified with a father, for it is certainly possible for Socrates to exist while he is not a father. Therefore, identifying Socrates with a father would entail the contradiction that it is possible for the same thing, namely Socrates who is supposed to be identical with a father, to exist and not to exist, which is an explicit contradiction. However, something is obviously wrong with this argument. For the assumption that Socrates is identical with a father should entail no impossibility, because when Socrates is a father, which is possible, he is identical with a father.

Clearly, what accounts for the invalidity of this argument is that Socrates can be identical or nonidentical with a father while continuing to exist. That is to say, the term 'father' refers only accidentally, not essentially, to Socrates. For in accordance with Porphyry's definition it is an accidental predicate of Socrates.[25] Therefore, no contradiction is entailed by the claim that it is possible for the thing that is actually a father to exist without being a father, for the thing that is actually a father may be in existence while it is not a father.

But then the previous argument concerning the alleged impossibility of the identification of Socrates with his fatherhood may equally easily be invalidated. All we have to do is remove the implicit assumption that the term 'fatherhood' refers essentially to an entity in the category of relation, that is, the assumption that 'fatherhood' is an essential predicate of whatever it is true of. For if this assumption is removed, then no impossibility arises from identifying the entity in the category of relation referred to by this term with an entity in the category of substance, for then it is clearly possible for this same entity once to be referred to and then not to be referred to by the same term while the entity continues to exist. The same goes for the other categories.

Accordingly, we can conclude that the preceding principles of *via antiqua* semantics yield the ontological commitment Ockham claims his opponents' theory does only if we add to them the further assumption that abstract terms in the nine categories of accidents are essential predicates of their particulars. Therefore, whoever holds at least these principles and also maintains this assumption is indeed necessarily committed to the overpopulated ontology Ockham objects to, which is clearly the path taken by pseudo-Campsall.

But whoever abandons this assumption clearly *can* hold these principles *without* such an ontological commitment, and this is precisely what Soto did.

Indeed, the previous arguments should make it clear that the assumption in question need not even be coupled with *all* the preceding semantic principles to yield the ontological commitment Ockham refuses to accept. For what we needed to exploit in these arguments besides the assumption that an abstract term in one of the categories of accidents is an essential predicate of its supposita was merely the quite generally acceptable semantic intuition that a concrete term in one of the accidental categories is true of a subject if and only if a suppositum of the corresponding abstract term exists (which is of course entailed by these principles, but the converse entailment does not hold). Therefore, whoever wants to get rid of this ontological commitment, while maintaining this semantic intuition (regardless of whether he holds the preceding semantic principles), has to reject this assumption. This precisely is what Ockham did.

In *SL*, in the passage corresponding to the one quoted from pseudo-Campsall in the opening of this chapter,[26] Ockham writes the following:

All authors posit ten categories, but it seems to me that many moderns disagree with the ancients in the way they posit them. For many moderns hold that in every category there are several items that can be ordered as superior and inferior, so that the superior ones are predicated essentially (*per se primo modo*)[27] and in the nominative case of any inferior one, by means of a predication such as this: 'Every a is b.' Therefore, in order to have such predication, they make up abstract names from adverbs, as for example from 'when,' which is an adverb, they make up the abstract name 'when-ness,' and from 'where,' the name 'where-ness,' and so on.[28]

To discredit the "moderns," he appeals to the authority of the "ancients" to claim it is not necessary to assume such abstract terms are essential predicates of their supposita in every category:

But it seems to me that the ancients did not posit such an order in every category. And so they used the name 'category,' and similarly the names 'genus,' 'species' and their likes more broadly than many moderns do. Therefore, when they said that the superior is always predicated of the inferior, and that any category has under itself species, they extended [the notion of] predication to verbs, in accordance with the way in which we say that 'walks' is predicated of man, in uttering 'A man walks,' and the same goes for 'He is shod' and 'He is armed.' And they also extended [the notion of] predication to the predication of adverbs and to prepositions together with the nouns they require in the appropriate cases, as we perform [the acts of predication] in propositions such as 'This is today,' 'This was yesterday,' 'This is in the house,' 'This is in the city.' And in this way there are such predications in any category. But it is not necessary that we should always have here predication in the strict sense, [predicating] a [term in the] nominative [case] of a [term in the] nominative [case]. Therefore, not every order between a superior [term] and an inferior [term] is in accordance with predication, taking predication in the strict sense, but some [order] is in accordance with entailment and predication, taking predication in a broad sense.[29, 30]

After this rejection of the critical assumption, Ockham goes on to show that this was in fact what the "ancients" meant, by analyzing two passages, one from Aristotle and another from Saint John Damascene. Naturally, in the corresponding passage pseudo-Campsall is outraged and tries to show why these passages cannot be understood according to the "perverted" interpretation provided by Ockham.[31] However, we need not go into the details of this philological disagreement. For, despite his appeal to authority here, Ockham had much more profound reasons to claim that abstract terms in accidental categories need not be essential predicates of their supposita.

III. OCKHAM'S ALTERNATIVE SEMANTICS

As we could see, the explicit rejection of the critical assumption concerning abstract terms in the accidental categories would have been sufficient to neutralize the apparent ontological commitment of *via antiqua* semantics, much along the lines we have noted in Soto. However, for Ockham this rejection was tightly connected with his alternative semantic theory, which "automatically" eliminated all unwanted commitments from his ontology.

To facilitate the comparison with the previously sketched *via antiqua* semantics, here is a parallel summary of the relevant principles of Ockham's semantics:

(1) Common terms ultimately signify whatever the concepts to which these terms are subordinated in any way represent.

(2) Common terms, whether the subject terms or the predicate terms of categorical propositions, supposit personally for their actual ultimate significata if the term is absolute, or for the things actually related to their connotata in the manner required by the term's connotation if the term is connotative.

(3) The significata and supposita of abstract common terms are the same either as the ultimate significata, or as the connotata of their concrete counterpart, or the same as several of these significata or connotata taken together.

(4) An affirmative categorical proposition the subject of which supposits personally is true if its predicate supposits for some or all the same things as its predicate, depending on the quantity of the proposition.

III.1. Ockham's Semantic Triangle

Ockham's "semantic triangle," as noted earlier, is the same in outline as that of the *via antiqua*. However, according to Ockham, the concepts to which categorematic written or spoken terms are subordinated fall into two classes: they are either absolute or connotative. Because these terms are meaningful only insofar as they are subordinated to such concepts, the terms themselves are also to be classified as either absolute or connotative.

The precise characterization of this distinction is a disputed question in contemporary secondary literature. For present purposes, the following characterization will certainly be sufficient. A connotative term is one that signifies any of its (ultimate) significata in respect of something, whereas an absolute term, *ex opposito*, is one that signifies any of its significata absolutely, that is, not in respect of anything.[32] The major difference here from the *via antiqua* conception is that *via antiqua* authors would not accept Ockham's conception of absolute terms as ones that signify the things Ockham takes to be their ultimate significata directly and not in respect of anything. Rather, they would say the things Ockham takes to be their ultimate significata are not the ultimate significata of these terms (rather they are their personal supposita), and even if they can be said to be signified by these terms somehow (as Soto would say, *materially*, or as Burley and pseudo-Campsall would say, *secondarily*), they should be said to be signified in respect of the direct ultimate significata of these terms (for Soto, their *formal* significata, or for Burley and pseudo-Campsall, their *primary* significata).[33]

Consider again the example of the concept of trees, and the Latin term '*arbor*' subordinated to it. According to the *via antiqua* conception, the universal concept of trees directly represents the nature of trees in general in abstraction from individual trees. However, individual trees are trees only because they are actual in respect of this nature, whereas, for example, a cat is not a tree precisely because it is not actual in respect of this nature. Now, whatever it is on account of which an individual tree is a tree (and, say, not a cat), whether it is taken to be distinct from the tree itself or not, is called the nature of this tree. The tree itself is represented by this concept only with respect to this nature, which is directly represented by the concept. Therefore, what the term '*arbor*' ultimately signifies in respect of this tree is the nature of this tree (again, regardless of whether the nature of this tree is taken to be distinct from this tree or not). But of course the term represents the tree universally, in abstraction from this tree or from that tree (that is, not as the treeness of this tree but as treeness in general).[34] Therefore, the immediate significate of the term 'arbor' is the concept of trees, whereas the ultimate significate of it in respect of this tree is the nature of this tree insofar as it is on account of this nature that the tree is a tree. But the tree itself, insofar as it is something actual in respect of this nature, is not what is directly (*formally* or *primarily*) signified by this term; rather it is something that can be said to be signified only indirectly (*materially* or *secondarily*) and that therefore can be supposited for by this term by personal supposition in the context of a proposition.

As can be seen, whether universals were regarded as real entities having numerical unity or as existing only in their individualized instances having some lesser-than-numerical unity that had to be recognized by the abstractive activity of the intellect, in their semantic function they were always conceived as the entities in respect of which the concepts of the mind represented the particulars falling under them, and hence as the entities in respect of which universal terms were related to these particulars as to their personal supposita. But then Ockham's uncompromising rejection of universals even in this semantic function inevitably led to his doctrine of absolute concepts and the corresponding absolute terms, which represent particulars not in respect of anything. Consequently, all universal absolute terms directly signify only particulars.[35] And thus any other term that signifies particulars not absolutely but in some respect can be construed as signifying these particulars only with the connotation of some other (or occasionally the same) particulars, which again can be signified directly by absolute terms. Therefore, as far as Ockham is concerned, the term 'arbor' signifies all trees (including past, present, and merely possible ones) directly and not in respect of anything because the concept of trees equally directly (*primarily*) represents them. On the other hand, connotative terms in general always signify particular things in respect of some things, which are said to be their connotata.

III.2. Common Personal Supposition of Absolute Versus Connotative Terms

In view of these considerations, the personal supposition of absolute terms is unproblematic for Ockham. Absolute terms signify what their concepts directly represent, namely, the particular things falling under these concepts. Thus, these terms supposit for these same particulars in a propositional context if these particulars are actual (relative to the tense and modality of the proposition). Connotative terms, on the other hand, signify particulars in respect of their connotata. Therefore, they will supposit for their significata only if these connotata are also actual, provided they are connoted positively, or, if these connotata are nonactual, when they are connoted negatively. For instance, the term 'sighted' signifies animals with respect to their sight. But obviously this term will supposit for an animal only if the animal in question actually has sight (relative to the tense and modality of the proposition). For example, in the proposition 'Socrates was sighted' the predicate term supposits for Socrates (among all animals that were sighted in the past) because Socrates actually had sight in the past. On the other hand, the term 'blind,' which signifies animals while negatively connoting their sight will only supposit for an animal if the animal actually does not have sight. For example, in the proposition 'Homer was blind' the predicate term negatively connotes Homer's sight and thus supposits for Homer (among all animals that lacked sight in the past) precisely because, since he lacked sight, Homer's sight was not actual.[36]

III.3. Common Supposition of Abstract Versus Concrete Terms

Because concrete absolute terms for Ockham ultimately signify only the particulars falling under them, the abstract terms corresponding to them will signify and supposit for the same things. Accordingly, for example, the term 'arboreitas' ('treeness') will signify and supposit for individual trees just as the term 'arbor' ('tree') does.[37]

Abstract connotative terms, on the other hand, should be judged on a case-by-case basis according to Ockham. Some such terms signify and supposit for the same things that their concrete counterparts supposit for. Say the term 'fatherhood' supposits for the same persons that the term 'father' does, and the term 'blindness' supposits for the same blind animals that the term 'blind' does. Other such terms signify and supposit for the connotata of their concrete counterparts. For example, the term 'whiteness' supposits for the connotata of the term 'white,' namely the individual whitenesses of individual white things. Yet other such terms are taken to signify and stand for several connotata of the corresponding concrete terms. For example, 'similarity,' at least in one plausible analysis according to Ockham, can supposit for the individualized qualities of those individuals that are similar to one another in respect of that quality, say the whiteness of Plato and the whiteness of Socrates together, in the same way as collective names such as 'army' stand for several individuals taken together.[38]

III.4. The Two-Name Theory of Predication[39]

Ockham's theory of predication is clearly intended to eliminate the systematic need for the inherent entities seemingly required by the "inherence theory" of the *via antiqua*. As he writes:

Therefore, if in the proposition 'This is an angel' the subject and the predicate supposit for the same thing, the proposition will be true. And so it is not denoted that this has angelity, or that there is angelity in this, or something like this, but what is denoted is that this is truly an angel; but not that he is that predicate, but that he is that for which the predicate supposits.[40]

Ockham was not the first to propose analyzing the truth conditions of categorical propositions in terms of the identity of the supposita of their terms. For example, Aquinas explicitly uses this type of analysis side by side with the inherence theory although he remarks that the inherence analysis is the more "proper" of the two.[41] Ockham's innovation here is rather the systematic application of this analysis to eliminate the need for the inherent entities apparently required by the inherence analysis. Indeed, together with Ockham's rules of supposition and his account of the signification of absolute and connotative terms, this approach "automatically" eliminates the apparent ontological commitments of the *via antiqua*.

IV. OCKHAM'S "REDUCTIONIST ONTOLOGY" OF THE CATEGORIES

With these semantic rules at hand, it is easy to see that, according to Ockham's theory, all terms connoting something other than what they supposit for in a proposition are nonessential predicates of their supposita. For such a term supposits for one of its ultimate significata only if the thing in question is actually related to another thing (or some other things) connoted by the term in the manner required by this connotation. Because this significatum and this connotatum (or these connotata) are supposed to be distinct entities, it is at least logically possible for them to exist or not to exist independently of one another (and hence this is always possible by God's absolute power). Thus, it is always possible for the same term once to supposit and then not to supposit for the same thing on account of the existence (or non existence) of this connotatum (or at least one of these connotata). This is precisely what it means for the term to be an accidental predicate of this suppositum.

But as we have seen, what was required for the ontological commitment to ten distinct entities under the ten categories was the assumption that the abstract terms in the nine accidental categories were essential predicates of their supposita, yielding together with substance the "ten distinct, tiny things, according to the imagination of the moderns, which imagination is false and impossible."[42] Thus, to get rid of the unwanted commitment to the "ten distinct, tiny things," all Ockham needs to do is show these abstract terms are connotative rather than absolute. But how can we decide whether a term is connotative or absolute? Because this is a question concerning the signification of terms (an absolute term is one that signifies things absolutely, whereas a connotative term is one that signifies things in relation to some thing or things), we can answer it by considering the significations of terms. If, as a result of this consideration, we are able to come up with a nominal definition of the term we are considering, then according to Ockham we can be sure the term is connotative, for this is precisely what such an analysis of its signification shows. But if the term is absolute, no such analysis is available. As Ockham writes:

In fact, properly speaking, such names do not have a definition expressing what the name means. For, properly speaking, for a name that has a definition expressing what the name means, there is [only] one definition explicating what the name means – that is, in such a way that for such a name there are not several expressions expressing what the name means [and] having distinct parts, one of which signifies something that is not conveyed in the same way by some part of the other expression. Instead, such names, insofar as what they mean is concerned, can be explicated after a fashion by several expressions that do not signify the same things by their parts. And so none of those [expressions] is properly a definition expressing what the name means.

For example, 'angel' is a merely absolute name (at least if it is not the name of a job, but of the substance only). For this name there is not some one definition expressing what the name means. For one [person] explains what this name means by saying "I understand by an angel a substance abstracted from matter," another [person] by "An angel is an intellectual and incorruptible substance," and [yet] another [person] by "An angel is a simple substance that does not enter into composition with [anything] else." The one [person] explains what the name means just as well as the other [person] does. Nevertheless, some term occurring in the one expression signifies something that is not signified in the same way by [any] term of the other expression. Therefore, none of them is properly a definition expressing what the name means.[43]

As a consequence, because any categorematic term is either absolute or connotative, to show a term is connotative it is sufficient to show it has a nominal definition. Ockham observes the following on this point:

But a connotative name is one that signifies something primarily and something secondarily. Such a name does properly have a definition expressing what the name means. And often you have to put one [term] of that definition in the nominative and another [term] in an oblique case. This happens for the name 'white.' For 'white' has a definition expressing what the name means, in which one word is put in the nominative and another one in an oblique case. Thus, if you ask what the name 'white' signifies, you will say that [it signifies] the same as [does] the whole expression 'something informed by a whiteness' or 'something having a whiteness.' It is clear that one part of this expression is put in the nominative and another [part] in an oblique case.[44]

Accordingly, to eliminate unwanted ontological commitment in any of the accidental categories, all Ockham has to do is show the abstract terms in that category are connotative, and to show this, all he has to do is provide a nominal definition of the terms. Indeed, this is precisely how he treats abstract terms in the category of quantity:

Such [connotative] names also include all names pertaining to the category of quantity, according to those who maintain that quantity is not another thing than substance and quality. For example, 'body,' according to them, should be held [to be] a connotative name. Thus, according to them, it should be said that a body is nothing but "some thing having [one] part distant from [another] part according to length, breadth and depth." And continuous and permanent quantity is nothing but "a thing having [one] part distant from [another] part," in such a way that this is the definition expressing what the name means.[45]

This analysis immediately allows him to treat in a similar manner even some terms in the category of quality, namely, those belonging to the species of shape (*figura*):

These [people] also have to maintain that 'figure,' 'curvedness,' 'rightness,' 'length,' 'breadth' and the like are connotative names. Indeed, those who maintain that every thing is [either] a substance or a quality have to hold that all the contents in categories other than substance and quality are connotative names. Even certain [names] in the category of quality are connotative, as will be shown below.[46]

In the passage he apparently refers to, Ockham argues that

such predicables as 'curved' and 'straight' could be successively true of the same thing because of locomotion alone. For when something is straight, if the parts are brought closer together, so that they are less distant than before, by locomotion without any other thing coming to it, it is called 'curved.' For this reason, 'curvature' and 'straightness' do not signify things (*res*) other than the straight or curved things. Likewise for 'figure,' since by the mere locomotion of some of its parts a thing can come to have different figures.[47]

In fact, this passage provides us with a typical example of Ockham's general "eliminative" strategy. The apparent need for positing a distinct straightness in accounting for something straight becoming nonstraight is eliminated here by analyzing the concept of straightness in terms of the distance of the parts of the thing connoted by the term. Perhaps an explicit nominal definition of the term for Ockham could be 'a thing whose parts are maximally distant along its length,' or something like this. (Because in his merely programmatic and illustrative analyses Ockham does not care much about particular details, neither should I.) Thus, the analysis shows that the term 'straightness' need not be an essential predicate of whatever it supposits for. But then 'straightness' can clearly become false of something it supposited for without the destruction of this suppositum merely on account of the change in what it connoted, namely the distance of the parts of the thing, by locomotion. Thus, this term did not have to supposit for anything distinct from the thing whose parts were maximally distant along its length when it was straight and whose parts are not maximally distant now when it is curved.

In fact, it is easy to see that precisely this type of analysis accounts for Ockham's general rule:

It is convenient to use this method for knowing when a quality should be assumed to be a thing other than a substance and when not: when some predicables can be truly asserted of the same thing successively but not simultaneously because of locomotion alone, it is not necessary for these predicables to signify distinct things.[48]

For what changes by locomotion is merely the relative positions of quantitative parts of bodies, which Ockham has already "analyzed away" by analyzing quantity terms as denoting bodies with the connotation of the relative positions of their parts.[49]

However, strictly speaking, all these considerations can achieve is the elimination of the apparent ontological commitment of the theory of the categories by removing the critical assumption of the essentiality of abstract terms in the accidental categories. That is, all these considerations show is that the doctrine of the categories alone need not entail commitment to ten mutually exclusive classes of entities. But the preceding considerations do not show in themselves that there are in fact no distinct entities corresponding to the categories. To be sure, applying his famed "Razor,"[50] Ockham could get rid of any unwanted entities already on the basis of not having to posit them. But this still does not prove they do not exist. To prove this, Ockham needs further arguments to show that the opposite position would entail all sorts of absurdities. Ockham's arguments to this effect can be classified as concluding various sorts of logical, metaphysical, physical, and theological absurdities running through the whole range of the categories of accidents. For the sake of brevity, I present here only two typical arguments concerning the category of relation to illustrate the types of difficulties that face the opposite position, represented by pseudo-Campsall in its most extreme form.

One type of argument is based on the separability of any two really distinct entities, at least by divine power. If, for example, the fatherhood of Socrates is distinct from both Socrates and his children, then it is possible for God to create this fatherhood in Socrates without Socrates begetting any children, and thus Socrates could be a father without having any children. Indeed, by the same token, God could create a man first, and then some others who would not be his children, nor would he be their son. However, if filiation (the relation of being somebody's son) is distinct from both father and son, God could create it in this man, and thus he would be a son. But he certainly would not be the son of anything but a man. However, all the men there are are younger than he, and thus the father would have to be younger than the son, which is a contradiction.[51]

Another type of objection concludes some physical absurdity. If any relation is really distinct from the things related, then so is the spatial relation of distance. If so, then any change of relative position by locomotion would entail the generation and corruption of an infinity of such relations in the things distant from one another on account of such a relation. Thus, whenever an ass would move over on earth, an infinity of such relations would be generated and corrupted in the heavenly bodies and their parts, for they would be related to the ass differently than they were before. But it seems physically absurd to claim that the movement of the ass could cause any change in the heavenly bodies.[52]

V. CONCLUSION: ONTOLOGICAL ALTERNATIVES VERSUS ALTERNATIVE SEMANTICS

Pseudo-Campsall was quite unmoved by these and similar arguments. Because he was explicitly committed to these distinct entities, he argued either that the alleged absurd conclusion does not follow from positing them, or that the conclusion is not absurd, or that the absurd conclusion follows only because of some contradictory assumption in the objection itself.[53]

However, whatever we should think of the merits and demerits of either Ockham's objections or pseudo-Campsall's replies, the interesting thing from our point of view is that Soto, for all his *via antiqua* semantics, is moved to reject the real distinction of relations and the remaining six categories on the basis of precisely the same type of arguments one can find in Ockham.[54] Indeed, if we look earlier, we can see that arguments of this type figured in the discussions of many authors before Ockham, especially concerning the hotly disputed issue of the real distinction of relations from their foundations.[55] What is more, we can safely assert that the uncompromisingly exuberant ontology of pseudo-Campsall was rather the exception than the rule even in pre-Ockhamist philosophy.[56] Thus, Ockham's ontological "reductions" were hardly as radical as he himself makes them appear by his contrast with the *moderni*. Nevertheless, Ockham is still an innovator, not with respect to *what* he achieves in his ontology but with respect to *how* he achieves it.

As we have seen, the driving force behind Ockham's ontological program is his new semantics. In fact, if Ockham's sole purpose had been to achieve a simplified ontology to avoid the sort of absurdities pseudo-Campsall was bound to handle, he could have done so simply by abandoning the critical assumption of the essentiality of abstract terms in all accidental categories, as many had done before him with respect to several categories, while leaving the main semantic framework intact. But Ockham had a much more ambitious project. He set out to simplify the conceptual edifice of all theoretical sciences by ridding them of what he perceived as unnecessary recent accretions that were unjustifiable both theoretically and on the grounds of "pure Aristotelian" principles.[57] It is only the requirements of this overall project that can explain why Ockham could not rest content with the ontological alternatives provided by the old semantic framework ranging from the extreme position of pseudo-Campsall to the much more parsimonious ontology of Soto and others. Therefore, despite whatever Ockham tells us about the ontological calamities allegedly inevitably incurred by the semantics of the "moderns," those calamities alone would not be sufficient to justify his abandonment of the old framework and the introduction of his alternative semantics.

NOTES

1 Substance and the nine categories of accidents: quantity, quality, relation, action, passion, time, place, position, and habit.

2 Obviously, this designation is quite tendentious in Ockham's usage: besides identifying his opponents as being relatively recent, and thus not carrying as much authority as well-established older authors, this enables him to pose as someone who only reclaims the genuine Aristotle from his more recent distorted interpretations.

3 The "most general genera" are the ten categories listed in n.1, which then are divided by specific differences into *their* species, which in turn are also divided by further differences into their species, of which they are the genera, but not the most general genera, for they are species of some higher genus. This process of subdivision continues until we reach "the most specific species," which cannot be divided further by any specific differences, for the individuals contained under them are essentially the same and are distinct from one another only by their individuating conditions. For example, descending the famous "tree of Porphyry" in the category of substance, we get the following series of divisions: A substance is either material or immaterial. A material substance is a body (and this is how we get the essential or quidditative definition of 'body,' constituted by its genus, 'substance,' and its specific difference, 'material'). A body is either living or nonliving. A living body is either sensitive or nonsensitive; nonsensitive living substances are plants, sensitive living substances are animals. An animal is either rational or irrational; irrational animals are brutes, rational animals are human beings. But human beings differ from one another only by nonessential differences such as gender, color, height, weight, virtues and vices, and so forth. Therefore, the species of humans is a most specific species, not divisible by any further essential differences. This is how we get the essential definition of 'man' ('*homo*,' of course, in the sense of 'human being,' not in the sense of 'human male') constituted by the genus 'animal' and the specific difference 'rational.'

4 To be sure, this sentence would be as strange in vernacular Latin as it is in English. However, we must not forget that in the technical Latin of Scholastic philosophy '*quando*' ('when') or its contrived abstract form '*quandoleitas*' or '*quandalitas*' ('when-ness') functioned precisely as our author describes it: as the most universal, essential predicate of all temporal determinations.

5 The "first movable" is the outermost sphere of the Aristotelian cosmos, the sphere of the fixed stars, the daily rotation of which was held to be the first movable cause (itself being moved by some immaterial, and hence locally immovable separate substance – for the Christian medievals, by some angel) and the first measure of every other motion of inferior things. According to our realist author, this motion causes in inferior things a "when-ness," a certain temporal determination that is a really inherent accident distinct from the substance as well as from the substance's other accidents.

6 Pseudo-Campsall 1982, 216–7 (§38.12). Unless otherwise indicated, translations are mine.

7 *SL* I.51. (Compare Loux 1974, 169.)

8 *SL* I.51. (Compare Loux 1974, 171.) Here Ockham explicitly claims this is the root of the errors of the moderns.

9 To be sure, this designation is both somewhat anachronistic and simplistic in this context. Nevertheless, it is not entirely unjustified and with proper reservations in mind can safely be applied to the set of semantic principles commonly endorsed by the majority of thinkers before Ockham and by those after Ockham who expressed their commitment to these or similar principles already in conscious opposition to Ockham's views or even later in opposition to the relevant views of the "nominalists" in general. In any case, I find this designation potentially less misleading than the term 'realist' (despite the fact that in late-medieval debates the opponents of the nominalists would often identify themselves as "realists"), which would inevitably suggest primarily some *ontological* difference in their treatment of universals. But the point here, as we shall see, is precisely that the difference between the treatment of the categories by the adherents of a *via antiqua* semantics and by Ockham is not primarily an ontological matter and not primarily a matter of how they treat universals. For a detailed historical discussion of the late-medieval contrast between *via antiqua* and *via moderna*, see Moore 1989.

10 That is, all or only some supposita are such, depending on whether the proposition is universal or particular. Also, we assume here that the proposition is interpreted as expressing some actual fact about the actually existing supposita of its subject, not as a definitive "eternal truth," in which case it may be true even if the supposita of its subject do not exist. According to the latter interpretation, such an affirmative proposition was analyzed by several authors in a number of different ways, either taking it to be equivalent to a hypothetical, or taking its subject to have natural supposition, or taking it to express some necessary possibility, or taking it to express a mere conceptual connection regardless of the existence of the supposita of its subject, and so forth. See Klima forthcoming b. See also n. 17.

11 *On Interpretation* 1.16^{a}3–8.

12 'Biltrix' is one of several standard examples of a meaningless utterance (along with 'bu,' 'ba,' 'buba,' etc.) one can find in medieval commentaries on Aristotle's passage and in the corresponding sections of medieval logical treatises.

13 Some authors also attributed supposition to terms outside the context of a proposition. Perhaps the most notable example is Peter of Spain's treatment of natural supposition. Peter of Spain 1972, 81 (tract. VI.4).

14 The Latin technical term for this function was '*supponere pro*,' which has often been transcribed in the secondary literature as 'to supposit for'

just to keep the medieval theory apart from the burgeoning contemporary theories of reference.

15 Or according to some realists, the universal nature immediately represented by the concept. (See n. 16.) But many authors were willing to call that nature an "objective" concept insofar as it was regarded as the direct, immediate object of the human mind considering the individualized natures of particulars in abstraction from their individuating conditions. See Suarez 1960, 360–1; Cajetan 1964, 67–71, 121–4. For a discussion of some complications involved especially in the case of Aquinas, see Klima 1993a, 25–59, and Klima 1993b, 489–504.

16 Or again, the universal nature of trees immediately represented by this concept. See, for example, Lambert of Auxerre 1971, 206–9; Burley 1955, 7. It should also be noted here that pseudo-Campsall reserves a different kind of supposition, "formal supposition," for reference to the nature immediately represented by the concept, to distinguish it from simple supposition, in which reference is made to the concept. In fact he attributes this formal supposition even to proper nouns. For example, in 'Socrates is numerically one, primarily and by himself,' the term 'Socrates' is taken to refer to Socrates' individual difference, his haecceity – Socraticity. Pseudo-Campsall 1982, 353 (§51.06).

17 Modifications in the referring function of terms caused by tense and modality were usually handled by medieval logicians in the theory of *ampliation*. For a detailed discussion and technical reconstruction, see Klima forthcoming b. Ockham's treatment was the exception, not the rule. See Priest and Read 1981; also *SL* I.72 ad 1.

18 Again, this proposition is being taken to express some actual fact about actually existing trees and not a definitive "eternal truth." See n. 10.

19 Most medieval "realist" authors would describe the ultimate significata of spoken terms as the *forms* signified by these terms. However, they would add the proviso that 'form' in logical contexts need not refer to something that is a form in the metaphysical sense, namely some determination of an act of real being. See Thomas Aquinas, *De potentia* 7.10, ad 8; Cajetan 1939, 18. In fact, Domingo Soto, a late-medieval "realist" who denies any ontological distinction between the ultimate significata and personal supposita of concrete common terms in the category of substance, would still draw the semantic distinction between their "formal" and "material" significata even though, according to him, ontologically these are one and the same thing. See Soto 1554, I.7, II.10, II.14. In any case, this is the reason I tried to provide an "ontologically neutral" formulation of the general semantic rule.

20 For more detailed discussion of this claim in connection with Aquinas, see Klima 1996.

21 For an explicit statement of this view, see Cajetan 1939, 16–17. For a detailed reconstruction, see Klima 1996.

22 De Rijk's "Introduction" to Abelard 1970, 37–8; Henry 1972, 55–6; Geach 1972.

23 Soto 1587, 28H (*In Isagogen*).

24 Ibid., 181B (*In Categorias* I.2).

25 Or, in the parlance of modern possible worlds semantics, this term refers nonrigidly to Socrates. For a more technical exposition of the connection between the modern notion of "rigid" reference and the medieval notion of essential predication, see Klima forthcoming a.

26 Compare n. 3. Pseudo-Campsall's work follows closely the structure of Ockham's *SL* in accordance with the author's intention to provide a thoroughgoing refutation of Ockham's doctrine.

27 See *SL* III-2.7.

28 *SL* I.41. See *Quodl.* V.22; *Expos. Praed.* 7.1.

29 *SL* I.41.

30 For the distinction between predication in a strict and in a broad sense, see ibid., I.31.

31 Pseudo-Campsall 1982, 217 (§38.13).

32 Although this is not precisely the characterization Ockham gives us, I believe this formulation covers his intention pretty well. In formal terms, this formulation says that the function that would assign the significata of an absolute term in a formal semantics would be a one-place function, whereas the one assigning the significata of a connotative term would be a many-place function. For technical details, see Klima 1993b and Klima 1991. For detailed analyses of Ockham's relevant texts, see Spade 1975 and 1990.

33 See, for example, Lambert of Auxerre 1971, 205–9; Burley 1955, 7; Soto 1554, I.7, II.10, II.14; pseudo-Campsall 1982, 101 (§9.4).

34 For a detailed explanation of this theory of abstraction in Aquinas in particular, see Klima 1996. It should be noted here that talking about "the nature of trees in general" need not commit anyone to the existence of an entity that is numerically one and distinct in real existence from individual trees and from their individual treenesses. In fact, such extreme realism concerning universals was regarded even by otherwise "realist" medievals as entirely absurd and as sufficiently refuted by Aristotle; thus, some even doubted whether Plato ever held the theory in this crude form. See Soto 1587, 30a (*In Isagogen* 1); Giles of Rome 1521, *In Sent.* I.9.ii.1, and Wyclif 1985, 61–9.

35 *SL* I.64. I am not dealing here with Ockham's earlier *fictum* theory. For that theory, see Adams 1987a, 71–109.

36 *SL* I.36, II.7.

37 Ibid., I.6. For the theological complications concerning 'man' and 'humanity' with respect to Christ, see ibid., I.7.

38 Ibid., I.6; *Quodl.* VI.25.

39 See n. 22.

40 *SL* II.2.

41 Aquinas, *In Sent.* III.5.3.3; *ST* I.13.12.

42 *Quodl.* V.22.

43 *SL* I.10. The translation is from Spade 1995.

44 *SL* I.10.

45 Ibid., Compare *SL* I.44 (137) (= Loux 1977, 145).

46 *SL* I.10.

47 Ibid., I.55; the translation is from Adams 1987a, 281. Compare *Quodl.* VII.2.

48 *SL* I.55. Quoted and translated by Adams 1987a, 281.

49 These considerations also quite clearly indicate the general reason this strategy cannot work for Ockham in the case of the other species of quality. The concepts of those qualities for Ockham simply admit of no such analysis. An analysis along these lines would probably have to involve explaining change in respect of these qualities in terms of the locomotion of the particles of a body, a theory dangerously close to Democritean atomism, which Ockham, following Aristotle, unequivocally rejects. For more discussion of this issue, see Adams 1987a, 283–5.

50 For Ockham's actual formulations of the principle and its applications, see ibid., Index of Subjects, s.v. "Razor, Ockham's."

51 *SL* I.50.

52 Ibid.

53 For his answers to the particular objections presented in the preceding, see pseudo-Campsall 1982, 280–7 (§§43.56–43.85). For detailed discussion of Ockham's arguments, see Adams 1987a, 169–285.

54 For Soto's consideration of the same arguments, see Soto 1587 (*In Categorias* 7.2).

55 For a comprehensive historical overview of the problem, see Henninger 1989.

56 For example, in view of Aristotle's discussion of motion in his *Physics*, it was typical to identify action and passion with the same motion. See, for example, Aquinas, *In Metaph.* I.9 §2313; *In Phys.* III.5. Here Aquinas argues that the categories are diversified in accordance with the diverse modes of predication, and thus it is not unacceptable to posit the same entity in diverse categories. On the other hand, concerning the nonrelational categories of quantity and quality (and concerning relations *secundum esse*), Aquinas clearly commits himself to the view that the abstract terms of these categories are essential predicates, species, and genera of the particulars of this genus in the same way pseudo-Campsall commits himself to the same view concerning all categories. See Aquinas, *De Ente et Essentia* 7.

57 See Moody 1935, especially 26–30.

7 Ockham's Philosophy of Nature

When Galileo Galilei succeeded in transforming physics into a quantitative, mathematical science, his effort was the culmination of a tradition that we can trace to the Greeks. At the same time, the success of Galileo's effort represents the end of the fundamentally qualitative approach to nature that is characteristic of Aristotelian natural philosophy.[1] Aristotle's philosophy of nature comprises all of the texts related to the study of nature, the metaphysical principles of nature, change and motion, earth, the heavens, his studies in biology, and the shorter treatises on the senses and perception, all culminating in his major work on the soul.

In the Middle Ages the interpretation of Aristotle's natural philosophy continued the classical tradition of interpretation in the context of Peripatetic, Neoplatonic, Stoic, Christian, Islamic, and other agendas.[2] Although there were scholars who contributed to the exact sciences,[3] in texts that fit in the tradition of medieval natural philosophy we find for the most part philosophical discussions of texts, typically of Peter Lombard's *Sentences*, Aristotle's *Physics*, and of other treatises by Aristotle as well as of the commentaries of Averroes. William of Ockham wrote two very long texts on natural philosophy, two shorter accounts, and numerous comments dealing with questions on natural philosophy in his massive *Commentary on the Sentences*. Yet, even when he shows himself to have some familiarity with a specific discipline (as in theories of vision), his use of it tends to be sketchy and highly selective. He says virtually nothing about astronomy, about the mathematical models of astronomy, or about their relation to the principles of Aristotelian physics. There is almost nothing in Ockham's texts about music and the mathematics of musical theory. Ockham does discuss topics in geometry, but here as elsewhere his focus is on ontological and logical issues, not on geometry as a discipline and certainly not on its application to the analysis of nature. In discussing Ockham's philosophy of nature, then, we focus on ontological and logical issues, and, above all, on his conception of nature.

As for Ockham's works, even some editors of the critical editions question the authenticity of his major treatises on natural philosophy, but no one doubts that the treatises are "Ockhamist" in character. The chief editor of the series and his colleagues at the Franciscan Institute in St. Bonaventure, New York, and Stephen Brown, the editor of several of Ockham's works, however, regard all these treatises as authentic.

This summary is in two parts. The first part focuses on Ockham's commentaries on Aristotle and on his relationship to Aristotle. The second part focuses on the principal subjects of physics: place, time, and motion.

I. OCKHAM AND ARISTOTLE

The *Expos. Phys.* contains Ockham's formal commentary on Aristotle's *Physics*. He wrote *Expos. Phys.* in 1322, two years before his departure for Avignon, but he broke off the commentary at the beginning of Book VIII. We do not know why he failed to complete it. This commentary and *Qq. Phys.*, written in the academic year 1323–4, are Ockham's most extensive and most important works on natural philosophy. We rely on *Expos. Phys.* and refer, where appropriate, to relevant texts from *Qq. Phys.*, the two shorter works in natural philosophy, *Phil. nat.* (1319?–24?), and *Brev. Phys.* (1322–23), Sent. (1317–21), *SL* (1322), and *Quodl.* (completed in 1327).

At the outset in *Expos. Phys.*, Ockham takes some pains to point out that his intention is merely to present Aristotle's meaning, not what he himself regards as true. Ockham regarded Aristotle with great respect. He clearly believed that Aristotle's texts, correctly interpreted, approximated the truth. Ockham had his own convictions, however, and thus he also believed either that his interpretation of Aristotle was correct or that Aristotle himself was in error on some point. The upshot is that we get Ockham's genuine view of what unaided reason would conclude however much he may have been willing to revise those conclusions in the light of Catholic orthodoxy.

We are barely a few lines into his major commentary on Aristotle's *Physics* before Ockham indicates his agenda: There are many confusions in the literature that arise because many people are insufficiently trained in logic. As Ockham saw it, these confusions could be avoided by consistently exercising a few simple precautions.[4]

To understand these precautions we must review briefly some of Ockham's principal doctrines in logic and how they were innovative and original.[5] Ockham's view that, typically, terms or words primarily signify things rather than concepts was not original, but his emphasis on the view that common terms signify individuals, not universal things, led to an original contribution in his theory of supposition. Because Ockham rejects any common reality existing in things, he rejects theories of simple supposition that hold a common reality as the significate of a common term. When a suppositing term stands for its significate (a thing), it has personal, not simple, supposition, according to Ockham, because the only true things are individual things. When a term has simple supposition, it stands for the concept, but the concept is typically not the significate of the term because a term that stands for its significate stands for true things, not for mental intentions.

In Ockham's account, then, individuals are the only significates; universals are concepts or words. Universal concepts or words can signify only individual things. A term that stands for a universal concept supposits nonsignificatively, and therefore it has *simple* supposition. When a term stands for individuals, it supposits significatively, and therefore it has *personal* supposition.

Ockham's move produces a reversal in supposition theory, and its cash value, so to speak, is the effect that reversal has on his interpretation of the categories. Substance terms and abstract quality terms are *absolute* terms that supposit significatively, and therefore there are real things these terms can refer to in personal supposition. Science in its most strict Aristotelian sense is of universals, and so science cannot be of things because there is no universal reality. Science is of concepts, then, but real science is a science in which the concepts stand for things, and rational science is a science in which the concepts stand for other concepts. Hence, natural philosophy is a real science, whereas logic is a rational science.

Concrete quality terms and terms in all of the other categories are *connotative* terms that supposit significatively for one thing primarily and another thing secondarily, and therefore there are real things these terms can refer to in personal supposition. Connotative terms do not signify things distinct from individual substances and inhering qualities. That is to say, the terms in all categories other than substance and quality signify something real but not a distinct thing existing subjectively in singular substances like individual inhering qualities. A relation such as 'similarity' signifies something real, namely that something (an essential characteristic, a property, a quality, or whatever) two things have that makes them similar, not similarity itself as an entity inhering subjectively in them. A term in the category of quantity signifies that something is quantified or numbered, not quantity itself as an entity inhering subjectively in the things quantified or numbered.

Ockham's doctrine of connotation has caused scholars many problems. Important differences in interpretation remain, but I focus on the consequences of his doctrine for natural philosophy and science. Every science is of concepts, not things. From Ockham's point of view most of the mistakes in philosophy and science have arisen from two fundamental errors: (1) the assumption that science is of things, which leads to fruitless searches for common realities and universal essences, and (2) the assumption that every term has some thing corresponding to it, which leads to the postulation of superfluous entities. As Ockham puts it, "This, however, is an abusive way of dealing with terms and leads people away from the truth."[6]

Connotative terms require descriptions that cannot be reduced to a single term, and so such concepts and words are often deceiving. Part of the difficulty with Ockham's doctrine is that he never found a general way of analyzing propositions that use connotative terms. What apparently defeated him was the use of such terms by philosophers in many different and even equivocal ways. It is impossible to produce an exhaustive general statement, and so Ockham accepted the unavoidable, though not without complaint. He would have preferred that abstract terms in categories other than substance and quality not be used at all. Ockham admits that he too must speak as others do, using their language and the very abstract terms he wants to avoid, but he insists that what *can* be avoided is positing totally distinct realities corresponding to them. The job of the philosopher, then, is to provide translations for terms that can be misleading. Many of Aristotle's expressions and examples should not be taken literally but figuratively. With such cautions repeated tirelessly, Ockham attempts to understand Aristotle's science, his use of concepts and terms, which is to say, his message about the physical world.[7]

In the Prologue to *Expos. Phys.*, Ockham makes other preliminary but fundamental points and distinctions to which he often refers the reader throughout the treatise. All speculative philosophy and theoretical science are composed of propositions. The propositions of natural philosophy and natural science are principally about sensible substances made up of matter and form. The propositions themselves are composed of terms or concepts that supposit for things, and in the case of natural science, the terms or concepts supposit for causes, principles, elements, and the like. Throughout, Ockham allows himself to be distracted by numerous issues that are central to his own agenda but peripheral to Aristotle's. Nevertheless, we may also observe that Ockham gets the principal point, for instance in *Expos. Phys.* I.1, that method in natural science begins with sense knowledge and confused generalizations that can lead to a clearer grasp of terms and their proper attributes. Still, Aristotle's central point tends to get bent to Ockham's own purpose.[8]

There are three principal subjects that will help clarify Ockham's natural philosophy and its relation to Aristotle's: hylomorphism and the divisibility of matter, Ockham's theory of connotation and its application to quantity and mathematics, and his views on causes and causal explanation.

1.1. Hylomorphism and the Divisibility of Matter

Aristotle adopted hylomorphism (the idea that things are compounded of matter and form) because his predecessors, in his view, maintained one-sided doctrines. They tended to reduce the principles of real physical things and of change either to matter (several pre-Socratics) or form (the Pythagoreans and Plato). In Aristotle's view, both principles are necessary to explain stability and change or motion.

The first principle is the idea of a substratum, some principle whereby the thing undergoing change has continuity with the new thing it becomes. Aristotle called this substratum "matter." The

matter of a thing is that in the thing that remains unchanged throughout all of its changes. Aristotle called that which changes the "form."
We can think of change, then, as involving a transformation whereby
one form replaces another form while the matter remains the same.
The matter is often compared with cookie dough and the form with
the molds that are used to shape the cookie dough. Such metaphors,
however, are misleading. There is an abstract character to Aristotle's
talk about principles that many later authors, including Ockham,
either could not grasp or did not accept.

Aristotle analyzed change and motion also in terms of the principles of the passive and the active. Matter is passive, that is, in potency to forms, whereas forms are in act. In Aristotle's discussions,
matter and passivity are principles of change and not really existing
things.

Medieval Aristotelianism adopted and utilized the theory of hylomorphism extensively. Ockham is no exception. Matter and form
are essential principles and causes. Ockham rejects the abstract character of the Aristotelian analysis, however, for Ockham considers
matter and form to be real, though not independent, constituents
of things. Matter cannot be pure potentiality, for it must serve as a
substratum of change. Matter is truly extended and therefore cannot
be numerically the same in distinct subjects and places.[9]

In Ockham's theory really existing physical things are composed
of matter and a hierarchy of substantial forms. Ockham inherited
the doctrine of a plurality of substantial forms from several authors.
Although the context is a discussion by Ockham on the plurality
of souls in human beings, critics of pluralism believed that Aristotle
had rejected that doctrine when he rejected atomism. Atoms are substances, and substances cannot be part of a larger substance. The
problem with atomism, as Aristotle saw it, is that the theory could
not account for the properties of substances and it could not define
the point at which a division produces a change in properties.

Medieval philosophers agreed with Aristotle on substances, but
some introduced changes in the theory that blunted his objections
to atomism. Even as Ockham retains hylomorphism and the reality
of qualities, he sees no difficulty with the idea that really distinct
parts can be added to or subtracted from a thing without affecting
the substantial unity of a thing and without affecting the essential
unity of an accidental form. In short, one finds in Ockham and other

medieval authors an Aristotelian theory about substantial and qualitative forms that is compatible in some respects with an atomistic
or corpuscular theory.

In Ockham's texts we find one interesting contribution to these
discussions. In his treatment of natural substances and elemental
substantial forms, and especially of the changes that such things undergo, Ockham reduces change to local motion of the parts. Even
where observable qualitative changes occur, such as in cases of rarefaction and condensation, Ockham reduces the explanation to a function of the local motions of the parts.[10] To us such a move suggests a
mechanistic explanation, the explanation of secondary qualities by
reduction to primary qualities and even to the motions of the parts
of a thing. Ockham himself, however, saw nothing more than an
economical and ontologically reductive version of the Aristotelian
account. Among late-medieval thinkers, only Nicholas of Autrecourt entertained an atomistic theory, and in his case our sources
are very deficient; nevertheless, the evidence shows that he relied
on Ockham's account of motion to support atomism.[11]

We may also point to some later discussions where authors thought
themselves to be applying an Ockhamist doctrine or appealing to
nominalism in support of a mechanistic analysis. The German ato-
mist Jungius referred to Democritus as an Ockhamist because the
principle of economy seemed to justify the elimination of superfluous qualities and forms from the account of the transmission of qualities. Jungius also saw no need to suppose the existence of *species in
medio*, a doctrine that Ockham had vigorously opposed. Digby and
Hobbes also appealed to nominalism and the principle of economy
in their defenses of atomism.[12] These references justify the assertion that later authors interpreted Ockham in ways compatible with
atomism, but it is misleading to attribute such views to Ockham
himself. How, then, can we characterize Ockham's role in these developments and still do justice to his intention?

Ockham's nominalism, his acceptance of the doctrine of a plurality of forms, his ontologically reductive analysis of transmission of
qualities, and his reductive account of rarefaction and condensation
were used by others to construct mechanistic accounts of qualitative
change. It bears repeating that Ockham, along with several other late-
medieval authors, vigorously defended the idea that some composite
things are composed of several really distinct things.

1.2. Connotative Concepts and the Interpretation of Quantity and Mathematics

Aristotle also analyzed qualities and qualitative characteristics in terms of matter and form. All physical things are made up of elements in various combinations. Aristotle accepted the view that there are four elements (earth, air, fire, and water) and that these elements are combinations of qualities (dry, cold, moist, and hot). Qualitative changes can be explained by the replacement of one quality by its opposite. When water (cold and moist) is changed to air or steam (moist and hot), the quality of cold is replaced by the quality of hot.

Aristotle also maintained that physically extended things are potentially divisible ad infinitum but are actually subject to a natural limit; that is, they cannot actually be divided beyond some point without destroying their substantial form.

Medieval Aristotelians explicitly raised several questions that Aristotle's principles suggested. For example, when water turns to steam, is there a point at which the water ceases and the steam begins? Does the cold lessen gradually and the hot replace it increasingly? If things cannot actually be divided ad infinitum, then is there not in fact some minimal extension that a particular substance has and beyond which its existence ceases or, at least, its qualitative characteristics change?

By raising such questions it seems that commentators put Aristotelian categories in the service of non-Aristotelian agendas. The questions challenged authors to be more precise and to devise more subtle logical distinctions. The discussions contributed to techniques of linguistic and logical analysis and to the use of mathematics to try to understand these subtleties with greater clarity, not to experimentation or more precise observation and measurement. Insofar as Ockham's views are relevant, they concern his contributions to linguistic, logical, and conceptual analysis. Ockham's views on quantity, mathematics, and connotation are the important considerations.

With respect to quantity and mathematics, we may briefly note that Ockham denied the existence of quantity as a thing distinguishable from a thing that is quantified. A quantity is not a real thing distinct from substance and quality. When a subject undergoes some real change – for example, if its length changes – then the change is real, and a proposition expressing that quantitative change expresses a real truth or a reality about the subject, but this does not require any *quantity* as an entity distinct from substances and qualities. Likewise, Ockham denied the existence of mathematical entities. He placed quantity terms and mathematical terms under connotative terms and concepts. We consider what motivated Ockham to adopt this approach to quantity and mathematics before describing the account itself.[13]

Modern science is inconceivable without mathematics. But what relation do mathematics and nature have in Aristotle's conception? As Aristotle maintains, mathematics abstracts from the things physics considers.[14] Ockham concludes, then, that mathematics and physics are distinct sciences because they consider diverse conclusions having diverse subjects or diverse predicates. Should they consider the same conclusion in such a way that the conclusion pertains essentially to both sciences, then it is possible that a part of physics may be subordinate to some part of mathematics, or the other way around. With respect to the middle sciences such as perspective, harmony, and astronomy, it was Ockham's view that they belong to physics more than they do to mathematics. Perspective and astronomy consider geometrical lines as physical, and they draw conclusions about attributes that are a part of natural philosophy. The sounds studied in harmony, however mathematical the relationships, are also physical. These sciences, then, are less abstract than the purely mathematical sciences. Ockham's reading here tends to support the standard Aristotelian view that mathematics is subordinate to natural philosophy.

On the other hand, in his theory of connotation, Ockham develops an interpretation of mathematical entities that subordinates ontological considerations to what we might call a more pragmatic conception of mathematics. It is a conception that makes mathematics into a language or into another tool of analysis. As such, mathematics can be used to clarify any subject matter. Ockham's interpretation seems to have influenced many authors of his time to use mathematics in sciences that do not involve measurement, where mathematics is a kind of theoretical formalism that enables us to resolve thorny questions about qualitative contraries, time, place, and the like.

Ockham rendered the connotative terms and concepts used in natural philosophy into "sets of explaining propositions." That is to say, such terms must always be thought of as shorthand for complex propositions that describe or summarize two or more facts and conditions or some relationship that the terms signify. In some instances Ockham denied altogether that the terms refer to anything existing.

For example, mathematical terms such as 'point,' 'line,' and 'surface' are fictive. The explaining propositions that render such terms are properly conditional, not assertoric in form. Euclid's fifth postulate provides a good example. It should be rendered thus: "If two parallel lines were extended to infinity, they would never intersect."[15] In Ockham's view, we need not assume the real existence of lines or suppose they can actually be extended to infinity. Mathematicians do not have to assume the real existence of lines to employ them usefully.

The view of mathematics as an inventory of objects was inflationary, according to Ockham. That Ockham's view was congenial to many authors follows from mathematical applications that were dictated by formal and not empirical considerations. Bradwardine's analysis that produced his famous law of motion, for example, proceeds from the mathematics of ratios, not from empirical considerations. If an analysis begins from some simplifying assumption, several results can be derived, whether empirically verified or not.

Although some fourteenth-century mathematicians were mathematical realists in fact (Bradwardine, for example), Ockham and others shifted attention away from mathematics as discussion about objects and entities to mathematics as a language and a formalism that can be interpreted in many ways and applied to all disciplines. Ockham refuted the Aristotelian prohibition against *metabasis*, the prohibition against using mathematics to represent other categories of being. If we think of mathematics primarily as a language and not as a category of being, then the prohibition loses its force.[16]

As an example of Ockham's criticism of the focus on ontological issues, we may consider an application of his refutation of Aristotle's prohibition against *metabasis*.

In the *Expositio* on *Physics* VII.4,[17] Ockham discusses at some length the question of whether motions of different kinds are comparable. The Aristotelian analysis recognizes obstacles or places a priori considerations in the way of comparison. Aristotle sees words being used equivocally. For example, when we say that a pencil and a musical note are sharp, we are obviously using the term 'sharp' differently. Aristotle regards circular and rectilinear as qualities whose properties or attributes cannot be compared. This follows from Aristotle's insistence that the two must have no specific difference from each other either in themselves or in that in which they are manifested. Ockham indicates in which respect such a comparison is invalid but then immediately objects that if you imagine someone walking in a circle, then that individual's motion in a circle is comparable to the motion of someone walking in a straight line, and hence that circular motion is comparable to rectilinear motion. In track events that require runners to sprint in curved lanes, the starting positions of the runners are staggered to ensure that all of the runners sprint exactly the same distance.

Ockham points out that a rope that is straight is not longer than the same rope when it is rolled up into a coil. In this sense, a circular line is longer, shorter, or equal to some straight line. Such examples lead Ockham to ask, What conditions must be satisfied for something to be comparable to another? Here is the point where Ockham directs his questioning of (attack on) the Aristotelian assumptions behind the analysis. If Aristotle insists that the movements and the tracks or trajectories in question are equivocal, then are we to add that the means of locomotion also establish specific differences in the motions themselves (e.g., walking with feet or flying with wings)? We may dismiss such distinctions and confine ourselves to the formation of the track and say that equal velocity means traversing the same distance in equal time; only the "sameness" must be specific in the case of the track and (consequently) in the case of the movement.

Ockham resolves such problems through an analysis of language. If abstract terms convey inherent entities, then such general terms are not comparable. But if abstract terms such as 'curved,' 'slow,' 'unequal,' 'swift,' and the like do not convey such things, then they are comparable because they do not convey specifically different things. In other words, if the unique, most specific definitions express the nominal definition, and if the nominal definition is predicated of both terms, then the terms are comparable.

Ockham goes on to interpret Aristotle as distinguishing between ontological claims and the use of nominal definitions, which do permit comparisons that would otherwise be ontologically incomparable. Ockham interprets Aristotle's text as a discussion about the use of terms and about genus and species, but in the end he rejects Aristotle's claim that the motion of a body on a curve cannot be compared with its motion on a straight line. For example, the sun moves more rapidly than a heavy or a light body because the sun covers a greater distance in a day than a heavy or light body does in any example known to us.

1.3. Causes and Causal Explanation

Material and formal causes are in their effects. Things composed of matter and form are said to have material and formal causes in the sense that the constituents of a thing partially explain what a thing is and why it acts in the way it does. The intellect does not stop asking questions about a thing until it has answers that provide all proximate and remote causes, and so the form and matter as explanatory can be viewed as causes. Whereas material and formal causes are in the effect, efficient causes are typically totally distinct from the effect. That without which something is not moved or changed is the efficient cause of why it is moved, and the same holds for rest. A final cause is that towards which a motion tends, or it is that for the sake of which a thing acts.

Efficient and material causes *can* be the same. When something acts on itself, for example, its efficient and material causes are identical. When a body moves itself downwards, when heated water cools itself, and when the will moves itself to love or hatred, in all of these cases the material and efficient causes are the same. Likewise, efficient, formal, and final causes can coincide, that is, belong to the same species, and formal and final causes can even be numerically identical.

Ockham's view on final cause is not a thoroughly orthodox Aristotelian one. He was uncomfortable with the doctrine for several reasons. To attribute ends to natural things struck Ockham as a metaphorical way of speaking that he believed Aristotle had adopted to refute atomism and like doctrines. Those doctrines produce accounts that explain actions as occurring by the necessity of matter, or accounts that rely on chance and luck as explanatory principles. In Ockham's hands, Aristotle's purposive language – that things act to an end intended by nature – is translated into the idea that where no impediment intervenes, some things become *as if* they acted for the sake of that end. In nature, 'end' refers to that which follows from an effect always or for the most part. For Ockham, then, the term 'final cause' requires numerous translations into statements about propensities, inclinations, and effects that occur frequently as long as nothing hinders the operation of an efficient cause.

Ockham's views on efficient cause require further comment. The real or true efficient causes of effects are the things that have the power or potency to produce the effects that we observe them to produce with regularity. It bears emphasis that Ockham does not identify efficient causes simply with necessary and sufficient conditions. The exclusive total sufficient cause of an effect is a thing that has the power to produce the effect sufficiently and without which such an effect cannot be produced. In other words, Ockham's view is very much in line with Aristotle's view, read parsimoniously, and not with a modern Humean analysis.

Indeed, Ockham's commitment to the principle of causality in general deserves some comment. His emphasis on the principle of economy explains his tolerance for incompleteness in explanation, especially with respect to the identification of causes. But he did not renounce completeness or explanation altogether as goals. Even with his willingness to abide incompleteness rather than tolerate bogus explanations, he was, for example, also willing to accept action at a distance for the sake of causal explanation.[18]

In conclusion to this first part of our analysis, we can see that Ockham transformed Aristotle's natural philosophy to a large extent into a logical analysis of Aristotle's assertions. The ultimately dialectical character of Aristotelian natural philosophy served to advance discussion within the Aristotelian tradition. Still, in the hands of all of his commentators, Aristotelian science remained intact.

In sum, Ockham was an Aristotelian, yet Aristotle's natural philosophy tends to get bent to Ockham's own purpose. We have provided three examples of how Ockham interpreted Aristotle, and we have hinted at the significance that Ockham's interpretation has for the eventual overthrow of Aristotelian science.

II. OCKHAM'S PHYSICS

In one text Ockham announced his intention to comment on all of natural philosophy (heavenly bodies, the elements, the rational animate soul, animals, and plants)[19]; in fact, he commented extensively on only the *Physics*. Ockham's four texts on physics suggest that he regarded physics as the most important of all of the topics treated in natural philosophy. The proper subject matters of physics are place, time, and motion. Here our order of exposition will be: (1) an initial and general discussion of motion and the infinite; (2) place and void; (3) time and eternity; and (4) continuity, infinity, and the physics of motion.

II.1. *Motion and the Infinite*[20]

Aristotle's definition of nature posits the notions of change and motion as essential parts of the definition.[21] Anyone ignorant of the causes of change and motion is ignorant of nature and of the nature of motion.

Motion, says Ockham, is not a really distinct thing, distinct from the body undergoing motion and from the successive places the body occupies. The change a body undergoes is not distinct from the body in the act of change. Such a change refers to the potential acquisition of a qualification or of a part the body now lacks or is in the process of acquiring. A sudden change refers to the acquisition of a form all at once. To refer to change and motion as distinct entities is to commit the mistake of taking a connotative term for an absolute term. 'Motion' is a connotative term, and the misuse of that term illustrates the dangers of using abstract terms as a kind of shorthand for more complex expressions and events.

Some commentators on Ockham have seen in his denial of the existence of motion a denial that motion itself can change, so that all motion has to be uniform and there can be no acceleration. But Ockham's point is different. He recognized that bodies undergo different kinds of motion and that each requires a description adequate to the kind of motion the body undergoes. Bodies that undergo a uniform acceleration, for example, do not require us to suppose that the motion exists independently of the body in motion and that the motion itself is increasing in a uniform way but merely that the body is moving with uniform acceleration.

On infinity, Ockham holds with Aristotle that we can talk of things as being infinite only in the potential sense. For example, a thing is potentially divisible to infinity. Where Ockham perhaps introduces a twist is in his explanation of the potentially infinite. If a continuous thing can be divided to infinity, then it must have an actually infinite number of parts; otherwise, we would be able to complete its division. Aristotle posits a potentially and not actually infinite number of parts, argues Ockham, not because an actually infinite number of parts are not present but because the parts are not, and cannot actually be, all separated. If they could actually be separated, then they would be finite, not infinite. To say that a thing is potentially infinitely divisible requires us to suppose that it has an actually infinite number of parts.

The relevance to natural science can be derived from the preceding examples. As Aristotle himself emphasized, spatial magnitudes, motion, and time are necessarily finite or infinite. Inasmuch as the science of nature is concerned with spatial magnitudes, motion, and time, it is concerned with the finite and infinite. Ockham tried to eliminate all of the ontological considerations and worries associated with these topics and replace them with talk about concepts. The clarification of concepts, in turn, would provide solutions to a wide array of pseudoproblems. Ockham's views on number and infinity represent one of several metalinguistic approaches to such problems. The approaches mark a shift in the interpretation and application of mathematics, and, as such, they are linked with later developments in acoustics, astronomy, and mechanics.[22]

II.2. Place and Void[23]

Although Aristotle never loses sight of the broader meanings of change and motion, the emphasis in the *Physics* from Book IV on tends to be on local motion, motion of a body from place to place. Ockham is led, then, to discuss the concepts following from locomotion or that are presuppositions of locomotion: place, time, continuity, and infinity.

In his discussion of place and void, Ockham takes up issues that had become central in the commentary tradition, and even though he adopts many of the standard views gives them his own emphasis. 'Place' is a relative and connotative concept. Place is not a real thing distinct from the containing body but is the limit of the body contiguous to the containing body. Ockham resolves many problems by interpreting the claims made according to the distinction between proper place and common place. Common place is in place and is immobile, but proper place is not strictly in place and is mobile. A whole river, for example, may be the common place of a boat, but the proper place of the boat is exactly that limit of the river that is contiguous to the boat, and because the water of the river moves past the boat, it follows that proper place is mobile. It was through that distinction that Ockham attempted to save assertions about a place not being in place and about a place that is mobile.

Aristotle's notion of natural place, that is, the place to which an element tends and in which it rests, caused commentators a great deal of trouble. Aristotle explains natural place as a function of, or relation between, the form of a thing and its final cause. Bodies in motion are striving, so to speak, to get to that place where they will naturally rest: the end of their motion. The implication is that natural place acts as a cause of motion. It follows as well that the direction of a motion is determined by a quality that a body has and that moves it to its natural place. A body that has the quality of heaviness tends downwards in an absolute sense towards the center of the universe, and it will continuously possess the tendency to move to the center until it reaches the center.

Ockham's interpretation of place has already made it clear that place is not a thing and hence cannot function as a cause of motion. This left Ockham with no choice but to reinterpret all of Aristotle's language here in metaphorical terms and to shift the emphasis in the causal explanation of the motions of elemental bodies from place to other characteristics: gravity and levity, the attraction and repulsion of the qualities of the elements, and the actions of the supracelestial heavens on inferior ones. It is tempting to say that Ockham shifts the emphasis to mechanical features, but the word 'mechanical' has connotations that are misleading and that Ockham did not intend. It is fair and accurate, however, to note that Ockham focuses his attention on efficient causes, on the qualitative characteristics of the elements, and on the motions generated by the circulating heavens. Ockham speaks of the attractive potency or power of a place as if place had such a power, but he quickly reinterprets this as meaning that bodies are naturally saved or preserved in certain places. In contexts where he speculates about other possible worlds, Ockham hypothesizes that if the heavens attracted the earth and even if the earth were not naturally in that place, we could still find a cause why the earth would rest there. Such texts confirm the non-Aristotelian arguments presented by Ockham in *Sent.* where he relativizes the notions of "up" and "down," "natural" and "violent." As Ockham saw it, the Aristotelian picture of the universe may be the empirically correct one, but it can claim no logical privilege over any other picture of the universe.

Aristotle had denied the existence of void because it could not serve as a cause of motion and hence as a principle of explanation. Ockham retains the idea that place provides a principle of explanation but not as a literal cause of motion. He is free, then, to examine the hypothesis of void from another perspective. The issue for Ockham is not whether void could be a cause of motion but whether void is compatible with motion. In other words, if there were a void, would a body be able to move through it?

Ockham's discussion was influenced by other commentators, but he makes an important contribution to our understanding of certain features of local motion. One of the issues that had troubled Aristotle is that if there were a void, then the limits of a motion would be together and either no time could elapse or the speed of a mobile would have no limit. Ockham rather imagines an empty space in which the limits are distinct and concludes that some time would elapse and that there would be a limit on the speed of a body through that space. The important issue here is that we need no longer suppose the existence of a medium offering physical resistance as a condition of motion. Imagining such a possibility requires a higher level of abstraction, and it permits Ockham to distinguish between the causes of local motion and the causes of greater or lesser speed.

II.3. Time and Eternity

'Time' is a connotative term. It follows that 'time' does not refer to a thing distinct from things that change and move. Because something changes or moves, the mind measures other changes or motions. Time is the number or measure of motion according to prior and posterior. Ockham acknowledged that the motions of the heavens are privileged by being the most rapid and most uniform motion numbered by the mind and are a standard by which other motions are measured. Yet other motions and perceptions can also serve as standards of motion. A blind person, after all, has a perception of time, and there are many daily and regular experiences that can function as measures of time. If we know that a horse can walk a given distance in half a day, then at the end of that distance we know that a half day has transpired. Workers know by their amount of work (piece work) what hour of the day it is. In sum, time in the strict sense is the most uniform, most regular, and swiftest motion of all. In a larger and more improper sense, time is any motion by means of which we measure other motions.

Every Scholastic had to come to grips with Aristotle's belief and reasons for believing in the eternity of the world. For Ockham the issues were not just related to theological orthodoxy but to the integrity of philosophy. He avoided the issue in *Expos. Phys.* by repeating his declaration about the commentary as an exposition of Aristotle's intention and not as an exposition of truth according to Catholic doctrine. What was Ockham's genuine view?

Ockham clearly used philosophy and philosophical discourse in theology, and he set restrictions on the application of theological conclusions to philosophical discourse and to the solution of problems in philosophy. In theology he accepted distinctions (e.g., the formal distinction in talk about the divine essence) that he clearly considered to be mistaken and inappropriate in philosophy. In the famous treatise on predestination, Ockham concluded that God knows future contingents, but we are unable to say *how* God knows them. As in other equally famous discussions where Ockham shows an ironic awareness of the possibility that well-educated Church officials may be in error about a doctrine that a little old lady holds correctly, the point is not that there are two truths but rather that there is a possibility of dissonance between what Church leaders teach and what the Church holds.[24]

In sum, Ockham's view on the proper discourse of philosophy preserves a healthy recognition of the limitations of human knowledge and relies on pragmatic principles derived from human success in negotiating our way around and through the world.[25] In concert with most medieval theologians, Ockham believed that philosophy can prepare us for theology, but he evidently parted company with most Scholastics on how far philosophy can lead us to theology. God's liberality, he believed, compensates for a great number of human mistakes, but the mistakes are an integral part of the human condition. We must not assume that we understand God's interventions infallibly, nor may we import the conclusions of dogmatic theology into philosophy without awareness of the mysteries and perplexities that remain. This is not a doctrine of double-truth nor a form of fideism but a theory that we can best characterize as a form of cognitive dissonance, according to which we may be in possession of the truth but be incapable of understanding it.

In brief, then, Ockham believed that only God is eternal, that the world had a beginning in time, and that in time the world will come to an end. The philosopher must confront the inconceivable. We cannot conceive of something that has no beginning, but we also cannot explain how something that exists could have come into existence from nothing. We must assume that something has existed from all eternity, either God or the world, but whichever we choose we cannot fully comprehend it. The consequence for natural philosophy is that as we examine features of time, change, and motion, the examination can lead us to the conclusion that something must exist eternally. It is not unreasonable for the philosopher to conclude that the world must exist eternally, but it follows that the conclusion could give way to another conclusion about something else that exists eternally and on which the world itself depends. But it is hardly a necessary conclusion and in either case leaves us to accept what our minds cannot fully grasp.

II.4. Continuity, Infinity, and the Physics of Motion

The Aristotelian analysis of change and motion follows from a clarification of the concepts that are prerequisites for all of our talk about change and motion. First, Aristotle discusses the species and properties of motion, then the continuity and divisibility of motion, and, finally, the perpetuity of motion.

Ockham argues that motion is not a thing distinct from the thing in motion. The question about the species and properties of motion is, then, a question about which categories can properly be said to undergo change or motion. There is no change or motion with respect to a *substance* because every change is from contrary to contrary, and a substance has no contrary. A thing in the category of substance is not acquired by a change or motion but only by substantial coming-to-be. Hence, generation and corruption are not changes or motions because they are sudden mutations. A *relation* does not itself undergo change. If a thing changes, then its relation to other things changes, but only because the thing itself changes. Hence, a relation is said to change only incidentally and not because relation itself is a thing that can change. *Action* and *reception* are also not subject to change or motion. Something that undergoes change or motion is either a subject of motion or the end of a motion. Action and reception are motions and, therefore, cannot be the subject of motion or the end of a motion. If they could be the subject or end of motion, then they could be at rest, which is a contradiction. Furthermore, if motion itself could change, this would imply that motion can be the end of a motion, which leads to an infinite regress.

Motion, then, is not itself a thing, and only five things are required for movement: a primary mover, a primary thing moved, time, a terminus from which (a beginning), and a terminus to which (an end).

Of the remaining categories, only *quantity*, *quality*, and *place* can be subjects of change or motion. Changes in quantity are called "increase" and "decrease." A change in quality is called "alteration." A change in place, strictly speaking, requires that a body of the same quantity move from one place to another. In a somewhat looser sense, Ockham regards increase and decrease that are due to rarefaction and condensation, respectively, as species of local motion.

Nature is a principle of motion in things that move themselves. Things that move themselves, or are moved by themselves, are understood to do so in two ways: largely and strictly. In the *large* sense, a thing that moves itself is anything that is not moved by an extrinsic mover, at least as a sufficient and precise cause of its motion. Hence, all simple bodies and all heavy and light bodies can move themselves and can be moved by themselves because the effective principle of motion is something existing subjectively in them. In the *strict* sense, a thing that moves itself refers to anything that has in itself the principle of motion and rest in such a way as to be able to stop its motion before the end of that motion. Taken in this sense, only animate bodies, not simple and elemental bodies, move themselves or are moved by themselves.

Ockham turns his attention to questions about the unity, continuity, and divisibility of motion. These are discussions that lay the groundwork for solving a number of traditional problems and paradoxes about change and motion. As we often find in Aristotle and in Ockham, they proceed by clarifying the concepts that are prerequisite to a meaningful discussion of the issues.

The continuous is said of things that are *contiguous*, that is, *successive* and *touching*, and *that constitute one thing*. Two things are said to be *touching* when there is nothing intermediate between the limits of the two things distinct in place. Lack of an intermediate, however, is not a sufficient condition for continuity. Someone playing a cithara, for example, may sound one note followed immediately by the octave, but this would not be a strictly continuous change in the sound. Succession refers to something that comes after another without anything of the same kind or genus in between. For example, two houses can be said to be in succession to one another if there is no house between them. This is true even if there is a great distance between them because we would refer to the second as the next house in succession. The *contiguous* refers to something that is *successive to something and touches it*. The contiguous, then, is a subdivision of the successive.

To summarize, two things are said to be continuous when they are contiguous and constitute one thing. For example, two bodies of water that constitute one body of water are said to be continuous. Continuous things touch, have nothing of the same kind in between, and constitute one thing. Continuity, then, is a subdivision of contiguity and a further subdivision of succession.

Something continuous cannot be composed of indivisibles because indivisible things cannot have limits that are touching; otherwise, they would be divisible. Much less can they be one. Continuous things are infinitely divisible. Continuity of time does not entail continuity of change or motion. Every magnitude, however, can be divided in principle, and thus if motion is a magnitude, then it cannot be composed of indivisibles and must be infinitely divisible. The distance through which a body moves is a magnitude. Because the distance is divisible, so is the motion over that distance.

Ockham follows Aristotle in refuting Zeno's paradoxes: the dichotomy, the Achilles, the flying arrow, and the stadium. The fundamental presuppositions in Zeno's paradoxes are that every body either always moves or is always at rest and that place, time, and motion are atomic, not continuous. The point of the paradoxes is to prove that motion or change is impossible. In refuting the paradoxes, Ockham and Aristotle argue that place, time, and motion are continuous, not atomic, and they argue for the reality of motion and change.

Note that while he is following Aristotle, Ockham places less emphasis on the distinction between act and potency, and although he agrees that terms such as 'more,' 'fewer,' 'equal,' and 'unequal' apply properly to finite quantities, Ockham also concedes that the whole of a continuum includes all of the parts in half of the continuum and more. In other words, Ockham thinks of the parts as actually existing but not separately from the whole, and he admits the notion of unequal infinite series.[26]

With the preceding clarifications and distinctions in place, Ockham turns to the analysis proper of local motion, asking whether there is an unmoved mover and whether motion and the unmoved mover are eternal and perpetual.

The Aristotelian analysis of motion explicates the causes, that is to say, the relation between what is moved and what moves or between mobiles and their movers. Aristotle maintained the principle that everything moved is moved by another, and he used the principle as a premise leading to the existence of a first unmoved mover. Aristotle evidently meant the principle in a highly abstract, metaphysical way, but even he applied the principle in a mechanical way to account for some forms of local motion. In the commentary tradition, one of the central questions involved the application of the principle to two cases – objects that move themselves and objects that are moved by other extrinsic things. Most discussions led to the application of the principle in an almost exclusively mechanical fashion.

Ockham followed some authors in the commentary tradition in distinguishing between objects moved by an intrinsic principle and those moved by an extrinsic principle. This distinction led almost unavoidably to a discussion of self-moved things, the natural motions of inanimate things, and violent motion. By the time Ockham began considering these issues, the notions had already been distinguished into distinct and separable principles. What in Aristotle had served as principles applying to absolutely distinct and simple motions were taken by several medieval authors as distinct and separable principles applying to actually complex motions. The natural motion of an inanimate elemental body, for instance, seems to be that of a body having the beginning of its motion, understood in a purely mechanical way, in the qualities of the element itself. Even though a projectile motion has the beginning of its motion in some extrinsic mover, its continued motion after it has left the mover is partly explained by the qualities of the elements of which the object is composed. Even some examples of qualitative alteration involve self-movement. Water can cool itself because it can be cooled by a part of water. In short, in natural motions and even in those parts of violent motions where natural principles continue to operate, a part can cause the motion of the whole.

Aristotle seemed to maintain, or so did many commentators understand him, that a mover must be and remain in contact with the mobile throughout its motion. In his comments on this principle, Ockham raises several objections that drive him to affirm the principle that motions are caused but to deny the requirement that the mover and the mobile must be in continuous contact. Accordingly, he denies that the continued motion of a projectile is due to the surrounding air or to the quality of impetus.[27]

In *Expos. Phys.*, Ockham would have completed his understanding of Aristotle's proof of the first unmoved mover, as the completed *Brev. Phys.* shows. Yet we must also suppose that he would have raised problems and objections that would have led readers to question fundamental principles and the conclusions drawn from them. From *Brev. Phys.*, we may venture the following conclusion: either motion is eternal or motion has a beginning. In either case there must be an extrinsic cause of motion. If eternal, then there must be a first unmoved mover; otherwise, there would be an infinite regress. Or if it has a beginning, then there must be a creator.[28]

For Ockham, 'nature' is a connotative term that refers, first, to all sensible substances, excluding artificial things, composed of matter and form and, secondarily, to some separate substances. Used in a wider sense, 'nature' refers to objects whose principle of motion is in themselves, whether the principle is understood actively or passively. Nature is a principle of motion and rest if the principle is in a thing in a primarily essential way or if it is an essential part of the mobile. With his view of divine creation, Ockham tends to interpret nature as a primarily passive principle of motion, for example, of heavenly motions, of elemental motion, and of generation and corruption. With respect to alterations in sensible qualities and some cases of qualitative increase and decrease, however, Ockham concludes that nature is an active principle of change. When vapor becomes light, it dissipates and heaviness returns. This happens because water is produced partly by the substantial form of water and partly by the qualities of water.[29]

However deviant he may appear, Ockham remained an Aristotelian or as Aristotelian as he could.[30] Ockham's principal contribution to Aristotelian philosophy was his effort to decode Aristotle's language and not reify concepts that were meant to be taken figuratively. There are individual things created by God that act for the most part in regular and predictable ways. When known by apprehending their terms or through repeated experience, statements about such things can be expressed in necessary and universal propositions, but the statements are not about natures considered absolutely but about that for which the terms stand, individual things created by God with the power to act for the most part in regular and predictable ways.

NOTES

1 McMullin 1965, 113–18.
2 Lang 1992; Bianchi and Randi 1990.
3 Lindberg 1992, xv–xvii, 1–4, 360–8.
4 *Expos. Phys.*, Prol.; *Brev. Phys.*, Prol. tract.
5 The next several paragraphs are heavily dependent on Brown 1981.
6 Brown 1981, 121; *SL* I.51 (171) (= Loux 1974, 171).
7 Brown 1981, 125–9.
8 *Expos. Phys.* I.1.2–5.
9 *Expos. Phys.* I.15.1–18.7; *Brev. Phys.* I.3; *Phil. nat.* I.1–15. See Adams 1987a, 633–69.
10 *Expos. Phys.* V.4.2; *Brev. Phys.* V.2; *Qq. Phys.* 92–7.
11 Dutton 1996; Adams 1987a, 644, 723.
12 Dijksterhuis 1961, 81, 432.
13 *Expos. Phys.* I.4.4–5; *Qq. Phys.* 58–65, 102–12. Compare Spade 1975, Adams 1985, Panaccio 1990, and Goddu 1993.
14 *Metaphysics* VI.1.1026^{a}6–15.
15 *Expos. Phys.* III.15.5; *Brev. Phys.* III.5.
16 *Expos. Phys.* II.3. Compare Livesey 1985, Murdoch 1981, and Goddu 1993.

17 From here to the end of this section, compare *Expos. Phys.* VII.5–6, *Brev. Phys.* VII.5.

18 *Expos. Phys.* II.4–13, VII.3.2–4; *Quodl.* I.1 (8); *Sent.* III.2; *Brev. Phys.* III; *Phil. nat.* II.6; *Qq. Phys.* 126–51. See Goddu 1984b.

19 *Phil. nat.*, praeam. (155); compare III.9.

20 With this section, see *Expos. Phys.* III; *Brev. Phys.* III; Murdoch 1981; Goddu 1993 and 1994.

21 *Physics* III.1.200^{b}12–13.

22 *Expos. Phys.* III; *Brev. Phys.* III; Murdoch 1981; Goddu 1993 and 1994.

23 With this section, see *Expos. Phys.* IV; *Qq. Phys.* 87–90; *Sent.* I.44; *Brev. Phys.* IV.1–4; *Phil. nat.* IV.17–18. Consult also Moody 1935.

24 *Expos. Phys.* IV.18–27; *Brev. Phys.* IV.5–7; *Sent.* III.1 ad 2; *OND* 120–3. Compare Miethke 1969, 295–7, 552–5, with McGrade 1974b, 48–67.

25 Kaufmann 1994, 229–38.

26 With the preceding paragraphs, see *Expos. Phys.* III.1–6, V.1–10.2, VI; *Brev. Phys.* III, V–VI; *Phil. nat.* III.1–30; *Qq. Phys.* 66–71.

27 *Expos. Phys.* VII.1–4; *Brev. Phys.* VII.1–4; *Sent.* III.2. See Goddu 1984a, 227–234; Boehner in Ockham 1990, xlviii.

28 *Brev. Phys.* VIII.1.

29 *Qq. Phys.* 123–5, 143.

30 Compare Adams 1987a, 741–98; Boehner in Ockham 1990, xlvi–xlviii; Boh 1966; Brown 1981; Corvino 1966; Goddu 1984a, 234–236; Wöhler 1994.

8   The Mechanisms of Cognition: Ockham on Mediating Species

After the death of Thomas Aquinas and well into the fourteenth century, medieval philosophers strenuously debated the nature of human cognition and the means by which it is achieved.[1] Ockham took a radical stand in that debate, rejecting the widely accepted view at the heart of Aquinas's account,[2] namely, that cognition is mediated by intelligible and sensible species.[3] (I will explain this technical use of 'species' in Section I.) In a variety of texts, Ockham went to great lengths to argue against not only what many scholars take to be Aquinas's own account but also a revised version of it adopted by Duns Scotus. Why did Ockham take such a stand? Why did he insist on rejecting species as a means of cognition, and what alternative theory did he adopt?

The full and complete answer to these questions would no doubt require a very lengthy book. I want to give only one part of the answer, focusing on Ockham's theory of the cognition of an individual extramental material object. Even so, for the sake of brevity, I will leave to one side an array of topics that are to some degree relevant. Thus, for example, I will leave largely unexamined Ockham's response to the optics of his time, which relied on species, and his reinterpretation of certain texts of Aristotle's, which seem to give species a prominent place. Instead I will focus just on Ockham's account of an ordinary and comparatively simple cognitive experience. I lift my eyes, look across the room, and see a coffee cup. What is it about me that explains my cognition of the cup for Ockham? And why does he feel impelled to reject Aquinas's view of the cognitive processes involved in perception of this sort?

To answer these questions, it is helpful to begin with a summary of Aquinas's account of perception. After that, I will say something about Ockham's understanding of the species account of cognition, which he inherited in a form that differs significantly from Aquinas's own account. In this context, the difference between Aquinas's account and the version of it that Ockham discusses is enlightening. With that background, I will turn to Ockham's theory itself.

One more preliminary point is worth making. Since in this chapter I want to concentrate just on the cognition we have when we look up and see a cup,[4] I will be dealing with what we would generally call a "perception" of the cup. Because there is considerable dispute about what exactly is required for perception, it will reduce confusion if I make clear at the outset how I am understanding perception in this chapter. I am not trying to give a full account of perception here or to adjudicate the disputes over perception but only to clarify the notion of perception I will be using. For purposes of this chapter, I will take perception in this way: To perceive an object such as a cup visually, at least three things are necessary. First, a person who visually perceives a cup needs to receive visually information about the cup; that is, she needs to be in epistemic contact with the cup through the medium of vision. Second, that visually gained information needs to be consciously available to her. And finally, by means of that visually gained information, she needs to recognize what she is seeing *as* a cup. (*Mutatis mutandis*, the same point holds for each of the other senses as well.)[5]

Perception as I am understanding it in this chapter, then, is incompatible with two widely discussed neurological conditions affecting perceptual ability in which a patient's sense organs are all functioning normally, namely, blindsight and visual agnosia. A blindsight patient claims, truthfully, to be unable to see. Yet if he is tested to see whether he can determine if a yardstick held up in front of him is horizontal or vertical, his responses are highly accurate. Such a patient has visual information about the yardstick and can use it, but that information is not consciously available to him, which is why he claims to be unable to see. Consequently, he does not count as perceiving the yardstick according to the view of perception adopted here. A patient with visual agnosia, by contrast, receives visual information and has that information available to consciousness, but, on the basis of the visually gained information alone, the patient cannot say what it is he sees. So, for example, if we hold a pen up before such a patient, the patient can describe the pen – black, long, thin, straight, and so on – but cannot say what the pen is. Forced to make a determination, he might well guess it is a ruler. Such a patient does not count as perceiving the pen either.[6] Perception, on the view of it I am adopting here, needs not only to be conscious but to contain a roughly correct categorization as well.[7]

I. AQUINAS'S ACCOUNT OF THE MECHANISMS OF PERCEPTION[8]

According to Aquinas, when a cup is presented to the sight of a cognitively normal person who perceives it, the first step in the process resulting in perception is that the sensible species of the cup are transmitted to some medium – for example, air – between the cup and the person, and the medium receives those species with spiritual reception (about which more will follow).

Sensible species are the accidental forms of the object perceived, and different sensible species are received by different sense organs. In the case of sight, the sensible species include the color and shape of a thing.[9] The sensible species for sight are thus sensibly receivable versions of those very forms, that very configuration, which, when imposed on the matter of what is being seen – the cup, for example – makes it brown and round, say, as distinct from red and square.

To say the sensible species are received in the medium with spiritual reception is to say that the forms are imposed on a medium such as air but in such a way that they do not make the air itself brown and round. The phrase 'spiritual reception' and the notion of imposing a form on air in any way are alien to us, but the phenomenon Aquinas was trying to capture is itself very familiar. Consider, for example, blueprints. In a blueprint of a library, the configuration of the library itself, that is, the very configuration that will be in the finished library, is captured on paper but in such a way that it does not make the paper itself into a library. Rather, the configuration is imposed on the paper in a different sort of way from the way it is imposed on the materials of the library. What Aquinas thinks of as transferring and preserving a configuration we tend to consider as a way of encoding information. Aquinas calls it "the spiritual reception of a form," or in the case of sensory cognition, "the spiritual reception of sensible species." For Aquinas, to say the sensible species of the cup is imposed on the air with spiritual reception is to say the configuration of the cup is preserved by some quality imposed on the air from the cup, but in such a way that the air does not itself take on the features of the cup.

After the medium has received the sensible species of the cup with spiritual reception, the medium in turn transmits those sensible species to the eye, which also receives them with spiritual reception. That is, the configuration of the cup that gives the cup the accidental features discernible by sight is received by the sense organ of sight, but in such a way that the sense organ does not itself take on the accidental features of the cup. The configuration of the cup is transferred to the eye, but in an "encoded" way.

One might suppose that at this stage the person whose eye is affected in this way sees the cup, but in fact we are still a long way from perception. That is because, on Aquinas's view, the sensible species is *not* what is cognized by the senses. It is only the means by which something is cognized. Aquinas does not have a notion that exactly mirrors our notion of consciousness, but certain things he says enable us to draw inferences regarding consciousness. To say the sensible species is not what is cognized is to say it isn't in any way the object of a sensory cognition of ours[10]; in that case, of course, it also isn't known consciously. A person who had sensible species and nothing more would, then, be like the blindsight patient. Visual information would have been received by him, but he wouldn't have conscious access to it.

The next step in the cognitive processing required for perception takes place in a cognitive power called "*phantasia*." On Aquinas's view, *phantasia* receives sensible species from the senses and turns them into phantasms, and all sensory cognition involves phantasms. Scholars of medieval philosophy disagree about *phantasia*, about what the medievals thought it was and what they supposed it contributed to cognitive processing. I have argued elsewhere that for Aquinas the contribution of *phantasia* is to render available to consciousness the information about the extramental material object that the senses have received.[11] At any rate, phantasms are responsible for the mental images one has in imagining as well as in all sensory cognition, and phantasms as mental images are certainly consciously accessible on Aquinas's view.

If this interpretation of the role of *phantasia* is correct, then a person who had sensible species and phantasms of a cognized cup, but nothing more, would be – in some but not all respects – like an agnosia patient agnosic for all sensory modalities.[12] That is because at this stage in the cognitive processing such a subject has consciously available only the accidents of the cup but not its quiddity; that is, nowhere in her cognitive structure does she have the concept *cup*. Consequently, the subject at this stage is conscious of the thing that is the cup and can see it in some sense of "see." She has visual information about the cup, and that information is conscious, but she doesn't not know what it is she sees. If we ask her if she sees a cup, she won't say "yes"; if we where the cup is, she will say she doesn't know, not because she can't locate the cup but because she doesn't know that what she can locate is a cup.

What is missing for the subject to recognize what she sees as a cup is provided by the intellect on Aquinas's account. The intellect abstracts a universal from the phantasm in *phantasia*. This universal is itself a form of the cup, but it is a "substantial" rather than an "accidental" form. Just as the senses receive the accidental forms of what is cognized, so the intellect gets the form that is the quiddity. Like the sensible species, this form, which is called "the intelligible species," is received in the intellect with spiritual reception. Again, like the sensible species, the intelligible species is *not* what is known but only the means by which an extramental thing is cognized.

One peculiarity of Aquinas's account of the abstraction of the intelligible species from the phantasm is important to notice here. The extramental material object acts as an efficient cause to impress a sensible species on the medium, which in turn acts with efficient causation on the subject's sense organ, which itself acts with efficient causation on *phantasia*. Up to this level of cognitive processing, the direction of causality runs from the object cognized to the cognizer. But at the level of the abstraction of intelligible species, the direction of causation reverses. *Phantasia* does not act with efficient causation on the intellect. Instead, the intellect, in abstracting the universal, acts with efficient causation on *phantasia*. If we ask what *makes* the intellect do this or what causes the intellect to abstract the universal, we are asking a misformulated question according to Aquinas. Nothing makes the intellect do so. This is part of what Aquinas means by speaking of the intellect as an agent intellect.[13] For Aquinas, the agent intellect is a top-down causer; that is, it initiates causal chains without itself being caused to do so by anything else.[14]

It is no doubt partly for this reason that Aquinas has no qualms about allowing the will to be determined (at least with final causality, if not with efficient causality) by the intellect. The intellect is not itself determined by anything outside the agent but is rather an initiator of a causal sequence. That is why Aquinas says, for example:

If the judgment of the cognitive [faculty] is not in a person's power but is determined extrinsically, then the appetite[15] will not be in his power either, and consequently neither will [his] motion or activity.[16]

Once the intellect has abstracted the intelligible species from the phantasm, it turns that species into what Aquinas calls a "concept" or an "intellected intention." I have argued elsewhere that on Aquinas's account a concept is to intellective cognitive processing what a phantasm is to sensory cognitive processing: it makes available to consciousness what was unavailable as a species.[17] A cognizer with the intelligible species *cup* but not the intellected intention would be like a visually agnosic person who has the concept *cup* but cannot gain conscious access to it in the visual modality. That is, such a person has the concept *cup* but cannot connect it to the thing visually sensed. What the intellect primarily provides for cognition, according to Aquinas, is thus the quiddity of the thing cognized – *cup* in the case of my example.

This part of Aquinas's account has occasioned consternation among some of his interpreters, as if Aquinas were supposing that human beings know directly only universals and have nothing but a ghostly, mediated, or indirect acquaintance with individual material objects, including, of course, other human beings. But this interpretation rests on a mistaken application of reductionist philosophical attitudes to Aquinas's thought.[18] Aquinas is an antireductionist. He does not think the intellect, strictly speaking, is any sort of cognizer. Cognizers are human beings, not components of human beings. And for Aquinas a human being can perceive a material object directly and immediately. Thus, for example, he says that

we say that corporeal creatures are seen *immediately* only when whatever in them can be conjoined to sight[19] is conjoined to it ... and so they are seen *immediately* when their similitude [or species] is conjoined to the intellect.[20]

In other words, Aquinas thinks that to cognize something immediately is compatible with the cognition's occurring by means of a whole series of processes,[21] as long as those processes and their parts are the means for cognizing the extramental object and are not themselves the objects cognized.[22] In the case of intellect, he thinks what the intellect first acquires in its cognitive processing is the universal. But he supposes that the intellect can connect the universal it acquires to the particular material object being cognized by relating that universal to the phantasm caused by the material object. In this way, the intellect cognizes individuals by working with *phantasia*. This claim is compatible, on Aquinas's view, with holding that a human being knows individuals directly and in themselves. Because Aquinas is not a reductionist, from the fact that one component of the cognitive apparatus grasps something indirectly, it does not follow that the cognizer perceives that thing only indirectly. That is why Aquinas says that

to cognize things by means of their similitudes [or species] existing in the cognizer is to cognize them in themselves or in their own natures.[23]

When the intellect has formed the intellected intention *cup* and has connected the universal *cup* with the phantasm caused by the cup, then, and only then, does the cognizer herself perceive the cup. That is, only at this stage in the cognitive processing does the cognizer have visual information about the cup, have that visual information consciously available, and have the recognition of the cup *as* a cup.

It would be a mistake to suppose the individual components of this process are, for Aquinas, psychologically separable or extended in time in a subjectively discernible way. Nothing in his account requires us to suppose anything but that the cognizer finds herself, all at once, perceiving this cup with its accidents. And it is certainly not part of his account that the components of this process are all discoverable by introspection. Aquinas clearly thinks some parts of our cognitive processing go on below or apart from consciousness. We can reason our way to the existence of sensible and intelligible species, but we cannot cognize them directly by introspection (or in any other direct way either). Thus, although he thinks the intellect can reflect on itself, it is not transparent; not all its acts are available for conscious, introspective inspection.

Once the cup is perceived, a variety of other cognitive acts can occur. The species of the cup can be stored in sensory or intellective memory, and the species stored in either memory can function just as the species did when it was first acquired in the cognitive structure. In this way, it is possible to remember the cup or to see it again in the mind's eye. Furthermore, the cognition of the cup is the cognition of a noncomplex; that is, in cognizing the cup the cognizer does not have to engage in compounding or dividing any other concepts or intellected intentions. Cognition of complexes, such as propositions, can occur once there is cognition of noncomplexes. But in what follows I will leave all other cognitive acts, except those involving remembering and imagining, to one side in the interests of concentrating on the noncomplex cognition involved in the perception of an extramental material object.

II. PROBLEMS WITH AQUINAS'S ACCOUNT OF PERCEPTION

Aquinas's account of the mechanisms of cognition is one kind falling under a genus of theories that I will call, collectively, "the species account of cognition." Many things about Aquinas's version of the species account, even just the fragment of it presented here, are perplexing. I want to call attention to only three, because it is easier to understand the shape Ockham's account of cognition takes if one is clear about these puzzling features of Aquinas's view.

To start with what is perhaps the most obvious puzzle, Aquinas's notion of the intellect (in one of its aspects) as active is hard to understand. The idea of a cognitive power that operates with top-down causation is of course perplexing all by itself. We expect, vaguely, that cognition – or at least the perception of material objects – occurs when a cognitive power receives impressions caused in it by something in the outside world. That is, we tend to have an untutored expectation that, at least for perception, our cognitive faculties are entirely passive in the sense that they just receive impressions from without; it is difficult to know what to make of an account of perception in which human cognitive powers are active.[24]

What is especially puzzling, however, and also worrisome, has to do with the reliability of perception if the intellect operates with top-down causation. On Aquinas's view, perception involves a cognitive power that acts on the incoming perceptual information with efficient causation rather than being acted on with efficient causation by causes that can be traced back to the object being perceived. Why should we think such an active cognitive power is reliable? That is, why should we suppose the concept that emerges from the intellect's active processing of the phantasms is a concept that matches the thing presented to the senses? And if we could find some way to support the claim that such a cognitive power is reliable, how would we explain its reliability? Not by its being in one state rather than another because it has been caused to be in that state by the material object being perceived. But by what then?

The second puzzle I want to call attention to here has to do with the intellect's abstracting the universal by acting on the phantasm. The senses receive only sensible species, and sensible species are only accidental forms of what is being perceived. Sensible species received by the eyes, for example, include color and shape; they do not include the substantial form of the thing presented to vision. The phantasm does not differ from the sensible species in this regard. How could it? The phantasm is derived from the sensible species. Since the sensible species do not include the substantial form of the thing being perceived, neither do the phantasms. Yet by acting on the phantasms, the intellect derives or acquires the substantial form. How is this possible? If the senses also apprehended the quiddity of things, that is, if the sensible species included the substantial form but it was just opaque in some way to the senses, then we could understand abstraction as a sort of whittling. The intellect would whittle down the sensible species, discarding the accidental forms and keeping the substantial form hidden within those accidental forms. But the senses receive only accidental forms, on Aquinas's view; they do not also receive the substantial forms.[25] So how does intellect acquire that form by processing the phantasms?

The third and most important puzzle, for my purposes here, arises in connection with Aquinas's account of stored species. What is it about perception that makes it different from imagining or remembering? According to Aquinas, when we perceive a cup, the forms of the cup are processed by our cognitive powers until intellect connects the universal *cup* to the phantasms of the accidental characteristics of the cup sensed, and at that point one perceives this cup. But the very same phantasms are stored in the memory and imagination. One can form a mental image of the cup by calling up the stored

phantasms and connecting them to intellect again, and one can remember the cup in the same way, by recalling the stored species from
memory.

Clearly, however, human beings in general (though, of course, not
always) recognize immediately the difference between perceiving
and remembering or imagining. No doubt we can tell some philosophical story in which it is difficult to distinguish perceiving from
remembering or imagining. And, of course, the theoretical difficulty
of telling the difference between perceiving and the imagining that
goes on in dreaming gives an impetus to skepticism. But these philosophical cases do not alter the fact that most human beings, virtually
all of the time, have a very powerful sense of the difference between
perceiving and imagining. A person who sees a cup, and then shuts
his eyes and forms an image, however vivid, of that same cup, will
not be in the least inclined to confuse the two experiences.

The difference has at least two elements to it. First, there is a difference in what we might call "the phenomenological feel" between the
experience of perceiving and the experience of remembering or imagining, so that we feel confident in our ability to tell the different experiences apart. And, second, generally, when we are perceiving, but
not when we are remembering or imagining, we are strongly inclined
to believe that the object of our cognitive act exists and is present
to us.[26] But how are these differences to be explained on Aquinas's
theory? In either case, we have the same set of phantasms, which
are stored in *phantasia* and acted upon by intellect. It is true that,
in the case of perceiving, those phantasms have come fresh from the
material object perceived, and in imagining and remembering they
have not. But the question does not have to do primarily with the
way perceiving *is* different from remembering and imagining; it has
to do rather with the way human perceivers are immediately attuned
to that difference. How could the species theory of cognition explain
the subjective discernibility of the difference between perceiving and
imagining or remembering?

I do not mean to suggest these three puzzles are all insuperable
difficulties for Aquinas's account. In fact, for the first two puzzles,
I think Aquinas does have something to say. As I have argued elsewhere,[27] on Aquinas's view, God's purpose in creating human cognitive faculties is to make human beings reliable cognizers. The reliability of the intellect and its ability to abstract a universal by acting

on phantasms are thus both explainable in the same way the computer's ability to generate the results of a mathematical computation is: it was designed to do that and to do it reliably. Not everyone will regard this as satisfactory, but it is at least *an* answer to the questions raised by the first two puzzles discussed in the preceding paragraphs.

For the third puzzle, I think Aquinas has no answer of any sort, and it is hard to see how he could provide one by using the species account.[28] The species account of human cognition is designed to explain the processes by which we come to cognize extramental reality. It is not designed to explain the differences among the ways we have access to the information gained by those processes. Something else besides the acquisition and storage of species is needed to distinguish our experience of perception from our experience of imagining or remembering.

III. OCKHAM'S VERSION OF THE SPECIES ACCOUNT

Ockham inherits a version of the species account of cognition that contains, in effect, a resolution of two of the puzzles raised by Aquinas's account. (In fact, it is possible that attempts by others after Aquinas to resolve these puzzles may be one part of the complicated explanation of why the species account takes the shape it does in Ockham's version of it.)[29]

To begin with the second puzzle regarding abstraction of the universal, Ockham assumes that on the species account the intellect can receive the universal from the phantasm because the universal is itself somehow included in the phantasm. Thus, for example, Ockham talks about the universal "existing in the phantasm"[30] or the phantasm representing the universal[31] on the species account.[32]

Furthermore, Ockham understands the species account as one in which the intelligible species is impressed on the intellect. For example, in one place he introduces the species account this way:

There is one view which supposes that one must suppose a species impressed on the intellect in order for the intellect to cognize intellectively.[33]

Elsewhere he describes the species account as holding that the intelligible species or the phantasm "determines" the intellect to cognize one thing or another.[34]

On this version of the species account, then, two of the puzzles I pointed out in the previous section are obviated. The puzzle about how the intellect can acquire the universal from the phantasm does not arise because the phantasm includes the universal. And the intellect does not act with efficient causation on the phantasms. Instead, the universal or intelligible species hidden in the phantasm is impressed on the intellect to cause an act of intellection. On this version of the species account, the intellect is not a top-down causer, and the direction of causation always goes one way, from the material object, through the senses and *phantasia*, to the intellect. In one place, Ockham asks what causes a particular act of intellect on the species account, and he canvasses what seem to him the possibilities:

I ask [regarding the intellect's cognition of a singular], "By what is it caused?" Either just by a phantasm, or by something in the sensitive part [of the soul], or by an intelligible species, or by an act of intellect which cognizes a universal.[35]

But, of course, Aquinas would think the proper answer to the question "What *causes* the intellect's cognition of a singular?" is just the intellect itself, not anything outside the intellect[36] or even any preceding act of intellect. Although the phantasm, the sensible species, the intelligible species, and the intellect's abstraction of the universal from the phantasm are all necessary for the intellect's cognition of a singular, none of these, taken singly or all together, is an efficient cause of the intellect's cognition of a material individual.

Although the species account Ockham considers lacks the first two puzzles arising in connection with Aquinas's account, it (or it together with certain views of Ockham's) raises serious problems in its own right.

To begin with, Ockham apparently thinks most intellective acts are conscious.[37] Acts of intellect we can think about are also in general acts of intellect known directly by the intellect.[38] Elsewhere he says, "every act of intellect is known evidently to [the intellect] itself."[39] Because he holds this view, he interprets the species account in such a way that every reception of species is a conscious cognitive act. So one argument he raises against the species account is just that introspection is against it:

No one sees a species intuitively, and therefore experience does not lead us to this [account of cognition].[40]

In the same spirit, he takes a sensible or intelligible species to be itself an object of cognition. It is, however, hard to make sense of the species account interpreted in this way. Ockham complains, for example, that on the species account the intellect first cognizes a universal and only afterwards cognizes a singular.[41] And it is clear that human perception does *not* work this way.

Moreover, on Ockham's version of the species account, a new and much more serious problem emerges as regards the reliability of our cognitive faculties. Because he supposes that the act of receiving a species is a conscious act and that the species is itself what is known in such an act, Ockham asks how we could ever know whether the species represents reality correctly. In fact, Ockham argues, we can know one thing is a good representation of another only if we can have independent access to the thing represented. We would not know if a statue of Hercules was a good likeness of Hercules unless we had knowledge of Hercules himself. But, he says,

according to those who posit species, a species is something antecedent to every act of intellectively cognizing an object,[42]

for there is no cognitive act without a species. Consequently, Ockham maintains, we cannot tell if a species is a good representation of the object being cognized. There is, therefore, no reason for supposing a species leads us to an accurate cognition of an extramental object.

Perhaps because he understands species in this way, Ockham seems not to recognize the notion of the spiritual reception of a form. Aquinas assumes that species are forms identical to the forms in the object being cognized but that these forms are received differently in the cognizer from the way they are received in the material object perceived. Ockham, on the other hand, wants to know whether species are the same in character as the forms in the object perceived.[43] On his view, the species account can give no satisfactory answer to this. If the species are the same in character, then receiving the forms that are the species will put real color or real sound into the soul; in virtue of receiving the sensible species *brown* from cognizing a brown cup, the soul will itself become brown. On the other hand, he thinks, if the species are different in character from the form in the object presented to the senses, then in virtue of cognizing the species the cognizer is not cognizing that object.[44]

These *are* worries for the species account in the version Ockham has inherited, but not for Aquinas's version. For Aquinas, these issues do not arise. He assumes the act of receiving a species is unconscious and that the species is not itself the object of cognition but only the means by which an extramental object is cognized. The fact that the species is received with spiritual reception means that it is the same in character as the form in the object perceived but that the soul is nonetheless not made brown, for example, by receiving such a form.

In these ways, the version of the species account Ockham discusses is different from and philosophically worse than Aquinas's account. Nonetheless, the two versions share one feature. For the version Ockham discusses as well as for Aquinas's, the third puzzle mentioned in the previous section remains. Neither version has the resources to explain our ability to discern readily the difference between perceiving and imagining or remembering.

IV. OCKHAM ON INTUITIVE
AND ABSTRACTIVE COGNITION

In the period after Aquinas, there is one notable innovation in discussions of human knowledge, namely the distinction between intuitive and abstractive cognition. The discovery or invention of this distinction is commonly attributed to Duns Scotus, though no doubt it can be found before him, and others have been proposed as the distinction's originator. Scotus's own theory of cognition is a combination of one version of the species account with the distinction between intuitive and abstractive cognition.[45] One way of understanding the addition of the distinction to the species account is to see the distinction as a remedy for the third puzzle of Aquinas's account, namely that regarding our ability to discern readily the differences between perceiving and imagining or remembering.[46] I am not here claiming that explicit reflection on this puzzle generated the distinction. I mean to suggest only that the inability of the species account to resolve this puzzle naturally led to some alternative approach to it in one context or another.[47] This way of thinking about the distinction between intuitive and abstractive cognition requires considerable explanation, but I think that explanation will come more easily in connection with an exposition of Ockham's own theory of human cognitive processes. Ockham rejects the species account entirely and substitutes a radically different theory, for which the difference between intuitive and abstractive cognition is foundational.

Ockham supposes that his own theory of cognition has the advantage over the species account of being simpler; one of his favorite arguments against the species account[48] is that we should not do with more entities what can be done with fewer.[49] It is in fact not at all clear, in the end, that Ockham's theory can do with fewer entities what could be done with more. As far as that goes, it is not clear that Ockham's theory really is simpler than the species account. I will return to these issues at the end of the chapter. For now, it is enough to say that Ockham's own account of cognition certainly *appears* simpler than the species account because it seems to posit nothing more in its account of human cognition than the thing cognized and the cognizer.

One advantage of this restraint as regards entities, in Ockham's view, is that we perceive material objects directly, something he supposes cannot be said on the species account. Thus he says,

I say that a thing itself is seen or apprehended immediately, without any intermediary between itself and the [cognitive] act.[50]

How, then, does Ockham himself explain cognition of an extra-mental material object? The heart of the answer has to do with intuitive and abstractive cognition, as he understands them.

For Ockham, when a material object is perceived, there is intuitive cognition of that object. Ockham thinks that for Scotus intuitive cognition is the sort of cognition one has of an object when that object is really present to the cognizer.[51] Although, as I will explain just below, Ockham explicitly repudiates this view of Scotus's, there is one sense in which he shares it. Thus, for example, he says, that

by nature, an intuitive cognition cannot be caused or sustained unless the object [of that cognition] exists.[52]

Elsewhere he gives a definition that is similar in spirit:

A simple cognition which is proper to a singular and first [in the order of generation] ... is an intuitive cognition.[53]

In another place, he says that,

intuitive knowledge is knowledge such that by virtue of it one can know whether a thing exists or not, in such a way that if the thing exists, the intellect immediately judges it to exist and evidently cognizes it to exist.[54]

Abstractive cognition is then defined as cognition that is not intuitive and abstracts from judgments of existence or nonexistence.[55]

The difference Aquinas could not explain satisfactorily, namely between perceiving and imagining or remembering, is in effect the difference between intuitive and abstractive cognition. The cognition one has of a cup when one remembers or imagines it can be caused and sustained when the cup no longer exists. Furthermore, the imagined or remembered cup is certainly not first in the order of generation of cognitive acts; some cup must be perceived before that cup can be seen in the mind's eye, and only a cup that has already been perceived can be remembered. Finally, neither remembering a cup nor imagining it is the sort of cognitive act by which one can know whether the cup exists. Therefore, imagining and remembering do not fit the descriptions of intuitive cognition in the passages quoted above. Perception, on the other hand, clearly does fit these descriptions and so counts as intuitive cognition.

In this way, the distinction between intuitive and abstractive cognition, whatever else it accomplishes, in effect fills in a serious gap in Aquinas's account. On this way of thinking about perception, perceiving an object carries with it a sense of the object as present, as imagining and remembering do not. And the fact that this occurs in perception but not in imagining and remembering also helps explain why we can readily discern the difference between these two sorts of experience.

Of course, if the sense of an object as present, which intuitive cognition includes, could also be had easily in imagining or remembering, that is, if one had a sense of an object as present when in fact it was not,[56] then the nature of intuitive cognition would not be enough to explain our ability to discern readily between perceiving and imagining or remembering. Clearly, then, if the distinction between intuitive and abstractive cognition is to play the role I am suggesting for it, intuitive cognition will have to be highly reliable. A person's having intuitive cognition of an object will have to be correlated very reliably with that object's being present to the cognizer. And, in fact, this is just the view Ockham takes. He says that

intuitive cognition cannot be naturally caused except when [its] object is present at a determinate distance.[57]

That is why, he goes on to say, Scotus's definition of intuitive cognition – "intuitive cognition is of a present and existing [thing] as it is present and existing" – makes sense as regards intuitive cognition when it is caused naturally. Elsewhere he says that

by nature, there cannot be intuitive knowledge without the existence of a thing which is truly the efficient cause of the intuitive knowledge.[58]

In this way, then, the distinction between intuitive and abstractive cognition in effect fills a gap left by the species account. It explains the readily apparent difference between perception and other sorts of cognition by associating perception with a special sort of cognition. It is true that the distinction between intuitive and abstractive cognition does not explain the *mechanisms* or *processes* that yield intuitive knowledge of material objects. But the proponents of the distinction seem to want to claim that for a certain sort of cognition, the kind had when we perceive some part of extramental material reality, there are *no* mechanisms or processes. There is just direct epistemic contact between the cognizer and the thing cognized. And that direct epistemic contact, which is not mediated by any process or mechanism, is what intuitive cognition is.

This fairly straightforward story is considerably complicated for Ockham, because he thinks God in his omnipotence could cause in a human being an intuitive cognition of a cup (for example) when there is no cup present to the cognizer. Insofar as the cognition of a cup is something really distinct from the cup, an omnipotent God could bring about the cognition without the cup. This complication subverts one useful advantage of the distinction between intuitive and abstractive cognition as I have been explaining it. One problem with the species account was that it could not explain our ability to discern immediately the difference between perceiving and remembering or imagining. If God can cause in us the state we are in when we are perceiving a cup, on an occasion in which we are not perceiving a cup and there is no cup present to us, then, apparently, we could take ourselves to be perceiving when in fact we are not.

Ockham's resolution of this problem is to concede the claim about the power of God but to deny the apparent implication of his concession. Although it is true, on his view, that God could give us intuitive cognition of a nonexistent thing, this intuitive cognition is such that it would cause in us the judgment that the object of the cognition did *not* exist. Consequently, it is not surprising that Ockham defines intuitive cognition differently from Scotus. For Ockham, intuitive cognition is that

by the mediation of which a thing is cognized to exist when it exists and not to exist when it does not exist.[59]

Or, as he puts it in another place,

by means of intuitive knowledge not only do I judge that a thing exists when it exists but also I judge that it does not exist when it does not exist; by means of abstractive cognition I judge in neither way.[60]

Two things are worth noticing about Ockham's position here.

In the first place, it is only by God's power that a human being could have intuitive cognition of something that does not exist. In one place, Ockham considers an objection against the possibility of the intuitive cognition of nonexistent things. If such intuitive cognition were possible, the objector says, God could bless the intellect by an intuitive cognition of deity, even on the supposition that God did not exist. The objection is not prepossessing, but Ockham's answer is interesting. "That God does not exist and yet that there is intuitive cognition of God is a contradiction," he says, "and so it's no wonder that absurdity results [from such a supposition]."[61] Why is there a contradiction here, in Ockham's view? If we can have intuitive cognition of nonexistents, why could we not have intuitive cognition of God if God were nonexistent? The answer is that nothing other than God can produce in human beings intuitive cognition of nonexistents; therefore, there is a contradiction in supposing simultaneously that we have intuitive cognition of any nonexistent thing whatsoever and that God does not exist. That is also why Ockham says, somewhat earlier in the same text, that although it is not absurd to suppose we can have intuitive cognition of nonexistent things, "this cannot happen naturally."[62]

The second thing worth seeing about Ockham's position is that when there is a judgment based on intuitive cognition, that judgment is not only reliable but in fact invariably right. An intuitive cognition need not be followed by any judgment at all,[63] and God can substitute a false judgment produced by God in place of the judgment that would have been caused by an intuitive cognition.[64] Nonetheless, when an intuitive cognition, whether of something existent or of something nonexistent, is naturally followed by a judgment, that judgment is always right.

Ockham makes this point clear in various places. For example, he says:

This suffices for intuitive knowledge, that, considered in itself, [the intuitive knowledge] is sufficient to produce a right judgment concerning the existence or nonexistence of a thing.[65]

But the most telling passage comes in a response to an objection from Chatton. Chatton claims that according to Ockham,

God could not cause in us an act of cognizing by means of which something which is absent would appear to us to be present.[66]

According to Chatton, Ockham is stuck with this view – which Chatton thinks is absurd since it appears to limit God's power – because of Ockham's view of the nature of intuitive cognition. If a person had an intuitive cognition of a nonexistent or absent thing, then on Ockham's view of intuitive cognition, Chatton thinks, the judgment that intuitive cognition gave rise to would be the judgment that that thing did not exist or was not present. On the other hand, abstractive cognition for Ockham is not the kind of cognition that gives rise to judgments about existence or nonexistence. So either way, on Ockham's view – according to Chatton – even God in his omnipotence could not cause an intuitive cognition of a nonexistent thing that in turn caused a false judgment that that thing existed.

If Ockham in fact thought it was possible for there to be an intuitive cognition that gave rise to a false judgment, then his response to Chatton would be obvious and straightforward. He would simply need to explain that Chatton had misunderstood his position: for him, as for Chatton, God could cause an intuitive cognition that leads to a false judgment.

But that is not the answer Ockham gives. Instead he grants Chatton's claim, namely, that on Ockham's view even God cannot cause an intuitive cognition that gives rise to a false judgment. His response to Chatton's objection consists in trying to blunt the impact of this concession. There is no limitation on God's power on his own view, Ockham says, because he holds that God can cause a false belief directly in us, although this will not be a case in which the judgment is formed in virtue of an intuitive cognition.[67]

Since Ockham does not deny the view Chatton attributes to him, that even God cannot cause in us an intuitive cognition that leads to a false judgment, and since for Ockham God can do anything that does not involve a contradiction, it is clear that Ockham thinks an intuitive cognition cannot lead to a false judgment.[68] Aquinas needs to explain the reliability of the intellect with theological considerations, as I explained in Section II. For Ockham the reliability of the cognitive powers responsible for intuitive cognition is built into those powers themselves; it is not possible for them to produce false judgments.

In fact, Ockham is so determined not to allow the possibility that an intuitive cognition could lead to a false judgment that he goes so far as to allow that qualities impressed on the eye are among the things that can be seen.[69]

Consider afterimages of the sun, for example. In this case, one apparently still sees the sun after turning away from it, and one is led to believe that one is seeing an afterimage. If the afterimage were nothing at all, just an optical illusion, then we would have an intuitive cognition of a nonexistent (namely, the afterimage) that led to a mistaken judgment (mistaken because afterimages are nonexistent): *An afterimage exists*, or *There is an afterimage*. In the case of afterimages, it looks as if Ockham is stuck with holding that one has an intuitive cognition of a nonexistent and that this intuitive cognition of a nonexistent yields a false judgment.

Ockham handles this difficult case by the simple expedient of denying that such an afterimage is a nonexistent. Consequently, intuitive cognition of it is an intuitive cognition of something that is really existent. After one has turned away from the sun, he says, there remains a real quality that is impressed on the eye, and *this quality* is itself what is seen.[70] The intuitive cognition is thus of something that exists, namely an afterimage that is a quality in the eye, and it leads naturally to the *true* judgment that that afterimage exists. That

is why Ockham begins this discussion of optical illusions by saying
that

by nature, an intuitive cognition can be neither caused nor sustained when
[its] object does not exist.[71]

For Ockham, therefore, an intuitive cognition is a cognition in
virtue of which the cognizer knows what is here and now present
to him, if the cognition in question is natural; if it is a cognition of
nonexistents that is produced by God, then it is also a cognition by
which the cognizer knows that what God is presenting to his senses
is *not* here and now present to him. So although an intuitive cognition need not lead to a judgment, when it does do so, the judgment it
leads to is a correct judgment regarding what is present or absent to
the cognizer. On Ockham's view, then, built into the soul is an infallibly correct detector of the presentness of things.[72] God can keep
it from operating, and God can substitute a false judgment for any
true judgment it might have produced, but even God cannot cause
it to give false results. Intuitive cognition is such that we just know
when what appears before us is really present and when it is not. Perception thus includes a sense of the object perceived as present that
imagination and memory of that object lack. Ockham's distinction
between intuitive and abstractive cognition thus accounts for a feature of human cognition that cannot be handled by any version of the
species account, namely the subjective difference between perceiving, on the one hand, and remembering or imagining, on the other.

V. PERCEPTION WITHOUT SPECIES:
OCKHAM'S ACCOUNT

With this background, we can turn to Ockham's account of the perception of an extramental material object. When a person sees a cup
and recognizes it for what it is, what is happening in his cognitive
apparatus? How does the cognition take place, on Ockham's view?

The first thing that happens is that the cup acts on the senses
with efficient causation to produce an intuitive cognition of the cup
in the senses.[73] Next, the intuitive cognition in the senses causes
an intuitive cognition in the intellect.[74] The sensory intuitive cognition and the intellective intuitive cognition are of the very same

thing, namely that individual thing that has operated on the senses with efficient causation.[75]

Unlike Aquinas, then, Ockham does not think what the intellect acquires first or primarily is a universal. When a person sees a cup, there is first sensory intuitive cognition of this cup, caused by the cup itself, and then – caused by that sensory intuitive cognition – intellective intuitive cognition of the very same cup. Thus, Ockham says

that very same singular which is sensed first by the sense is itself, under the same description, intellectively cognized first with intuitive cognition by the intellect.[76]

If a judgment is formed at all in virtue of intuitive cognition, then intuitive sensory and intuitive intellective cognition together naturally result in a true judgment about the existence or nonexistence of what has been intuitively cognized. This judgment is not itself an intuitive cognition, although it is formed in virtue of intuitive cognition. Thus, for example, Ockham says that

When I apprehend some extremes [that is, noncomplexes] perfectly with intuitive cognition, then immediately I can form a complex that these extremes are united (or not united), and I can assent [to it] (or dissent [from it]). For example, if I see with intuitive cognition a body and whiteness, immediately [my] intellect can form this complex: 'There is a body,' 'There is a white thing,' or 'A body is white.' And once these complexes have been formed, the intellect immediately assents, and [it does] this in virtue of the intuitive cognition which it has concerning the extremes .... One should nonetheless know that although the intellect can form a complex from these intuitively cognized non-complexes in the way just explained, while the intuitive cognition of these non-complexes both in the sense and in the intellect remains, nonetheless neither the formation of the complex nor the act of assenting to the complex is an intuitive cognition, because either of these cognitions is a complex cognition, and intuitive cognition is a non-complex cognition.[77]

Furthermore, the intellect's apprehension of a universal is not an intuitive cognition either but rather an abstractive cognition that occurs after the intuitive cognition on which it relies.[78] Thus, for example, in one place, in discussing the senses of abstractive cognition, Ockham gives as one sense of the phrase just the cognition of universals:

And in this [sense] abstractive cognition is nothing other than the cognition of a universal abstractable from many things.[79]

Finally, we might wonder how Ockham handles that capacity of our cognitive apparatus that seems to need the species account, namely, memory. For Ockham, what accounts for our ability to recall something of which we have had intuitive cognition when the intuitive cognition is past and the thing cognized is absent is not, as Aquinas supposed, a stored species. Rather, it is simply a habit. Once something has been cognized intuitively by the intellect, there is left in the intellect an inclination to the same sort of act. By this means, Ockham thinks, we can adequately account for the phenomena others try to explain with species.[80] He says that

everything which can be saved by a species can be saved by a habit. Therefore, a habit is required, and a species is superfluous.[81]

He takes this line not only for remembering but also for imagining. According to him,

what is left [in the imagination by a previous act of intuitive cognition] has more the character of something inclining to and partially eliciting an act of imagining than the character of something terminating [that act of imagining as its object].[82]

And just a little later in the same text Ockham describes this feature of the imagination this way:

This has more the character of a habit which inclines [to an act] than the character of an image which represents [an object previously cognized].[83]

In this way, then, Ockham thinks he has an account of human cognition that can do what the species account can do and more, without admitting any more entities than the object cognized and the cognizer.

VI. REFLECTION ON OCKHAM'S ACCOUNT

There are details and nuances in even just this part of Ockham's account that I am leaving to one side, including his distinction between perfect and imperfect intuitive cognition, his view of the role of *phantasia*,[84] and the way God's general influence is a concurrent cause in any act of cognition. I have given enough of his account, however, to bring out certain features of it I think are noteworthy.

First, it is clear that, for one reason or another, Ockham is working with a version of the species account significantly different from Aquinas's.[85] On the version Ockham rejects, the intellect is largely passive, the universal is hidden in the phantasm and impressed on the intellect, and the object of cognition is a representation of reality rather than an extramental object. This version of the species account lacks two of the three puzzling claims I called attention to in connection with Aquinas's account, namely that the intellect is a top-down causer and that it acquires a universal, the quiddity of the object cognized, by processing the solely accidental forms in the phantasms. But it does so at the cost of leaving the cognizer epistemically disconnected from the world, cognizing representations only. Furthermore, though it leaves in place the puzzle Aquinas's account seems unable to address, namely the cognizer's recognition of perception as different from remembering or imagining, it takes away the activeness of the intellect on which Aquinas insisted. Ockham is right to reject this version of the species account. Aquinas would have rejected it too.

Secondly, there is an interesting split between Ockham and Aquinas on the question whether all perceiving is perceiving *as*. For Aquinas, the answer is "yes." Because the first object of the intellect is the universal, and because the intellect works together with the senses to cognize a material object, when a person sees a cup, in the normal course of things she sees it *as* a cup because the intellect's grasp of the universal *cup* is part of her perception of *this*. But on Ockham's view, it is the very opposite. No perception is perception *as*. In the first place, the senses and the intellect intuitively cognize the thing that is a cup, and only afterward, in an act of abstractive cognition, does the intellect grasp the universal *cup*. Therefore, in the act of perception itself, a person sees the cup but does not see it *as* a cup because grasp of the universal *cup* is subsequent to the intuitive cognition of the cup itself. Ockham therefore would not accept the description of perception I gave at the outset of this chapter. On his view, it will be enough for perception if a person has perceptual information of an extramental material object and that information is consciously available to her; she need not also know *what* it is that she sees. For Ockham, a patient with visual agnosia still counts as visually perceiving a cup.

Additional support for this interpretation of Ockham's account comes from a question in which Ockham considers the objection that cognition of a singular is impossible without cognition of what that singular is. Responding to the objector's claim that a thing cannot be distinctly cognized unless the intellect also grasps the universal that is the substantial form of that thing, he says that

the distinct knowledge of a singular does not necessarily require distinct knowledge of any universal.[86]

And he ends this question by saying that

a thing can be distinctly cognized without [the cognition of] its defining characteristic.[87]

Thirdly, at least in its foundational acts of intuitive cognition, the intellect is largely passive or externally determined on Ockham's account.[88] An extramental material object acts causally on the senses. The resultant sensory cognition then causes an act of intuitive intellective cognition; if an abstractive judgment is formed at all, the first one formed is caused in its turn by the intuitive cognition. In this way, the states of the intellect are determined, ultimately, by something outside the cognizer, either by some object that acts on the senses or by God himself, who acts directly on the cognizer to produce some state of sense or intellect.

This feature of Ockham's account obviates some puzzles raised by Aquinas's. For Ockham, intellect does not operate with top-down causation, at least in its first and fundamental acts. Furthermore, on Ockham's account there is no longer the puzzling question how intellect extracts a universal from incoming sensory information that concerns only individual accidents. For Ockham, the intellect does not actively extract anything in perception. Rather, in perceiving, the intellect is acted upon, and its acts are caused to be what they are by the way reality is because some real extramental object or quality causes it to be in a certain state. It is true that God can act directly on the intellect. But in the intellect's foundational epistemic contact with reality, in intellective intuitive cognition of individual things, even God in his omnipotence cannot cause an intuitive cognition that leads to a false judgment. God can cause the false judgment directly, but the reality-tracking intuitive cognition of the intellect cannot itself deceive. The reliability of human cognitive functioning is thus a feature of the nature of the human cognitive apparatus itself for Ockham; it isn't grounded in theological considerations, as I suggested Aquinas's account is.

Ockham adopts a theory of free will very different from Aquinas's, and it is not hard to see why, given his account of the way cognition works. For Ockham, in order for a will to be free, not only does it have to be uncaused by anything outside the agent but it also cannot be determined in any way by the intellect.[89] For Aquinas, it is not possible for the intellect to form a judgment that what is good (in some sense of 'good,' in these circumstances, at this time, under this description) is A, and for the will to form a volition for not-A.[90] But for Ockham, unless the will is able to will either A or not-A regardless of the determinations of the intellect, the will is not free; to be free, the will has to be independent of the intellect as well as of causal influence on the will from outside the willer.

Whatever other motivations there might have been for Ockham to adopt such a theory of the will, his account of cognition will also have pushed him in this direction. Because for Ockham the intellect itself is largely determined by something outside the agent, if he thought the will were also determined by the intellect, as Aquinas does, it is hard to see in what way the will would be free. Not only would it not be clear that the willer was able to will otherwise, it would not be clear that the agent was ultimately responsible, in any meaningful sense, for what he chose to do.[91]

Finally, what can be said about Ockham's repeated claim that his theory of cognition is to be preferred over the species account on the grounds that it can do with fewer elements what the species account does with more? Is it true that Ockham's account of cognition is a simpler theory than the species account? For three reasons, the answer is not a resounding affirmative.

First, it is true that Ockham eliminates species from his theory. But it is not immediately apparent that he ends up with fewer entities than the species account does.[92] In order to deal with the way qualities imposed on sense organs by material objects strengthen or weaken the relevant faculty of perception, Ockham has to postulate a novel kind of quality, different from any standard qualities of the sort found in the Aristotelian categories Aquinas would also have recognized. Thus, Ockham says about these qualities that

in sight a certain quality is impressed which strengthens or weakens the organ of sight ... but this is a kind of quality which is not in any species of quality enumerated by Aristotle.[93]

Second, even if we did not suppose that the postulation of this odd sort of quality left his theory on a par with the species account as regards the number of entities, it is still an open question whether his theory is the simpler. A theory can be simple in the number of entities it postulates but complicated in the relationships and processes it assigns to these entities. On Ockham's account, there is an odd doubling of cognition. Like the senses, the intellect apprehends a singular directly; in this act of apprehension, the intellect doesn't apprehend something the senses did not apprehend or fail to apprehend something the senses did apprehend. That is why Ockham thinks both the senses and the intellect cognize the same thing under the same description. On Aquinas's account, it is clear why we need both the senses and the intellect for the perception of a material individual, because each cognitive faculty contributes a different part of the cognition. Intellect delivers the quiddity; the senses provide the accidents and also anchor the quiddity to *this thing sensed*. But in Ockham's account, the operations of the two cognitive faculties seem completely redundant.[94] If Ockham's theory fails to have superfluous entities, it seems to substitute superfluous processes.

Third, a simpler theory is to be preferred to a more complicated one only if the simpler theory can explain as well what the more complicated theory can explain. But it is not clear that Ockham's theory can explain all the species account can explain or even that it is meant to do so. The species account tries to give some explanation of the way human beings achieve cognition. But Ockham's theory, however much it remedies defects in the species account, does not give any answer to the puzzle the species account was intended to address. On Ockham's account, our cognitive faculties are a black box.[95] He gives a taxonomy of cognitive acts ordered in their causal relations to one another. But in the case of intuitive cognition, which is the way human beings make their first and fundamental epistemic contact with the material world around them, Ockham gives no explanation at all how that epistemic contact is achieved. It is as if in response to the question, "How do we cognize a material object?," which the species account answered in terms of the processing of species, Ockham's reply is that we just do. It is not clear, therefore, that his theory, even if it were simpler, can do what the species account does, however incompletely or inadequately.[96]

NOTES

1 For helpful discussions not only of this debate but also of Ockham's theory of cognition and the large literature that has grown up around it, see Pasnau 1997, Spruit 1994, Tachau 1988, and Adams 1987a.

2 I do not mean to suggest that Ockham knew Aquinas's views directly. Some scholars suppose that, although Aquinas was one of Ockham's main targets, Ockham knew Aquinas's account only indirectly through the work of one of Aquinas's disciples. See Spruit 1994, 293 n. 175.

3 For an excellent introduction to Ockham, see Adams 1987a. For a helpful discussion of Ockham's theory of the means of cognition as it relates to his philosophy of language, see Panaccio 1992.

4 Or reach out and touch a cup. The particular sensory modality is irrelevant to the discussion.

5 I am, of course, also assuming other things in this account of perception, such as that there is an objective reality to be perceived and that perception is a reliable cognitive faculty that puts us in epistemic contact with that objective reality. Notice, too, that what is at issue here is just perception of some thing – what the medievals called a noncomplex cognition – and not beliefs about that thing arising from such a perception. Thus, for example, perception of a cup (even perception of a cup *as a cup*) is not the same as the belief *that thing is a cup*, *I see a cup*, or *I am being appeared to cuply*, and it is possible to perceive a cup without having any such belief. A person who drives to work listening to the morning news on the radio sees the other cars on the road and sees them as cars but is not forming beliefs about what he sees because he is driving "on automatic pilot" while his mind is occupied with the news.

6 For a good discussion of these neurological conditions, their relations to consciousness, and what they teach us about the nature of perception, see Weiskrantz 1997.

7 It is not easy to explain with any precision what kind of ability to categorize an agnosic patient has lost. The agnosic patient in my example could no doubt categorize the pen accurately as an inanimate object. It is more nearly what medievals would have called "the lowest species"

that an agnosic is at a loss to recognize. But it would not be quite right to describe a visual agnosic as someone unable to categorize objects into their lowest species by using the visual sense. Any normal human being who was presented with a novel and, to him, mysterious object might also be unable to categorize it into its lowest species, but such a person would not count as agnosic. Perhaps this is more nearly correct as a description of an agnosic: a visual agnosic is someone who has a concept of the quiddity of objects of a certain type but who cannot apply that concept to objects of that type when they are presented to his visual sense organs, although those sense organs are functioning normally; the same holds, mutatis mutandis, for agnosias connected with the other sense organs. For a helpful discussion of visual agnosia, see Farah 1990.

8 I have presented and argued for a detailed account of Aquinas's theory of the mechanisms of cognition in Stump 1998 and forthcoming. Because this is an essay on Ockham, not Aquinas, I will simply summarize here the conclusions of those papers.

9 I am abbreviating a complicated story with this claim. For Aquinas, each sense has both proper and common sensibles. For sight, color is a proper sensible; shape is a common sensible. Common sensibles are those features of an object that can be apprehended by more than one sense. The common sensibles for sight include movement, rest, number, shape, and size.

10 Insofar as we can theorize about species, they are, of course, something we can cognize in some way. What is at issue here is whether sensible species are the sort of thing that can be apprehended directly by the senses.

11 See Stump forthcoming.

12 I say "some but not all respects" because the agnosia patient presumably would have the concept *cup* somewhere in her cognitive structure. Nonetheless, the concept would be disassociated from sensory cognition; like the person with sensory cognition but no intellective cognition, she wouldn't be able to perceive anything *as* a cup.

13 Agent intellect is just one aspect of intellect for Aquinas; there is also the aspect of intellect that receives and stores the forms agent intellect abstracts.

14 Aquinas does think an intellective state or act is sometimes caused by something other than the intellect. For example, Satan can introduce a thought into the intellect. The will also can act on the intellect with efficient causation. These concessions, however, do not do much to undermine Aquinas's view of the intellect as engaged in top-down causation. Any thought introduced into the intellect is subject to review by the intellect as a whole, and thus whether that thought is accepted or rejected

depends only on the intellect itself. As for the effects of will on intellect, any act of will has to be preceded by an act of intellect. Therefore, when the will acts causally on the intellect, it does so in virtue of some determination on the part of the intellect that the will's doing so is a good thing at that time, in those circumstances, under some description.

15 That is, the rational appetite or will.

16 Aquinas, *De veritate* 24.2. Although Aquinas was wrong in supposing that for human beings in this life intellect requires no material organ, he has been amply vindicated in his view that the intellect actively processes information from the senses and is not just determined by it. In fact, it turns out that even for sensory cognition considerable active processing is required. See, for example, Zeki 1993.

17 See Stump 1998.

18 See Kretzmann 1991.

19 Namely, the forms that are the sensible species.

20 Aquinas, *In Sent.* IV.49.2.1 ad 16. My emphasis. (I am indebted to Robert Pasnau for this reference.) For the sake of clarity, and because in Aquinas's view a species is a kind of similitude, I have added 'species' in brackets in the appropriate place in this and the next quotation. Notice that for Aquinas, although sight begins with the sensory faculty of sight, it is not completed until intelligible species are processed in the intellect and intellective cognition occurs as well.

21 The question arises whether a cognitive process that proceeds by means – media, in effect – counts as cognizing something immediately. The answer depends not only on our reading of Aquinas but also on what we mean by 'direct' and 'unmediated'. If by 'direct cognition' we mean that the cognizer apprehends the object of cognition in one indivisible act of cognition, without anything that counts as a means of cognition or a mechanism causing cognition, then, on contemporary neurobiological accounts of the way human beings perceive things, no human being knows any extramental object with direct and unmediated cognition. This is a fairly stringent notion of direct and unmediated cognition! We might also consider a more plausible notion. On this less stringent account, by "direct" cognition we mean just that the cognizer does not know the object of cognition solely in virtue of having something else as the primary object of cognition – as the television viewer at home is aware of what is happening in the football game solely in virtue of cognizing the images on the television screen. There is a correspondingly more moderate interpretation of 'unmediated cognition' too. In this sense, a cognition is unmediated if there is no mechanism external to the cognizer that significantly filters the cognition; on this interpretation, what is seen through an electron microscope is mediated cognition, but what

is seen unaided is unmediated cognition even after all the brain's processing of incoming visual data. On this more moderate interpretation, Aquinas's account of cognition does ascribe direct and unmediated cognition to human beings.

22 There is a small complication I am leaving to one side here. Because the intellect is reflexive, it can know its own acts as well as extramental objects. So when the intellect introspects, certain parts of the intellective process can become the direct objects of cognitive apprehension.

23 *ST* I.12.9.

24 I say "vague" and "untutored" because contemporary neurobiology tends to take the brain as active, too. See n. 16.

25 Each perceptual faculty has both proper and common sensibles; these are what that perceptual faculty apprehends. In the case of sight, the proper sensible is color, and the common sensibles include such things as motion and shape. In none of these is the quiddity of the thing being sensed included, nor is the quiddity readily deduced from the accidental features of the thing captured in the common sensibles. Something that is black, narrow, and long in shape and at rest might be any number of things.

26 I am grateful to Paul Vincent Spade for helping me find this formulation of the third puzzle.

27 See Stump 1991.

28 He could, of course, hold that God just hardwires us to be able to tell the difference, though this seems more like a restatement of our ability than like an explanation of it. I owe this point to Norman Kretzmann.

29 See Spruit's account of the history of the controversy over species. Spruit 1994, 175–256.

30 *Sent.* I.3.6 (484, 492).

31 *Sent.* II.13 (301).

32 There are many other things about the species account Ockham disagrees with besides those explicitly discussed in this chapter, including, for example, the nature of a universal.

33 *Sent.* II.13 (253–4).

34 *Sent.* I.3.6 (493).

35 Ibid. (490).

36 Of course, without the singular, the sensible species and phantasm of that singular, the medium that transmits the singular, and no doubt other things as well, there would be no intellective cognition either; these things constrain without causing the intellect's act of cognition.

37 To say there is no unconscious intellective state is not to say a person is always attending to all her conscious states. As is clear from the example in n. 5, a person can be conscious of a great deal without explicitly attending to it or having it in the forefront of her mind.

38 *Quodl.* I.14.

39 *Sent.* I.Prol.7 (191). Although in this quotation Ockham appears to commit himself to the view that all intellective acts are available for conscious introspection, Elizabeth Karger has persuaded me that there are exceptions to this claim for Ockham, and for that reason I have ascribed to him only the weaker claim that most intellective acts are conscious.

40 *Sent.* II.13 (268).

41 *Sent.* I.3.6 (490, 491).

42 *Sent.* II.13 (274).

43 Ockham's argument here seems uncharacteristically lacking in insight. It is as if he were to ask whether the written word 'dog' were the same in its character or definition as the spoken word 'dog.' If it is, the analogous argument would go, then we should be able to hear the written word just as we do the spoken word, and we should be able to see the spoken word just as we do the written word. On the other hand, if the written and spoken words are different in definition, then they cannot be the same word. The problem with this argument, as with Ockham's argument about species here, is that it fails to take into consideration the possibility that information can be faithfully preserved but in an encoded form. I owe this way of explaining the issue to Norman Kretzmann.

44 *Sent.* III.3 (115–16). See the related issue having to do with species in the medium, *Sent.* III.2 (47–8). In both passages, Ockham also raises an argument to this effect: If the species were different in character from the material object whose species they are, we would expect the cognizer's cognitive power to discern this difference. But we discover no such cognitive experience in ourselves. This is an odd argument for him to give, since in his presentation of the example of the statue of Hercules, he supposes that on the species account there is no way to discern the difference between a species and the object it is the species of, in virtue of the fact that on the species account as Ockham understands it there is no epistemic access to objects except through species.

45 That Scotus can combine the distinction between intuitive cognition and abstractive cognition with the species account shows that at least for Scotus the distinction can be taken as supplementing a deficiency in the species account rather than serving as a substitute for the account as a whole.

46 Here and in the rest of this chapter, for the sake of simplicity, I discuss intuitive and abstractive cognition in the context of the perception of extramental material objects. But it is clear that for the medievals something very like perception operates to cognize extramental immaterial

objects and also the immaterial objects of introspection. These cases are slightly complicated, since in them we have something like perception but without the operation of the senses. I will leave such cases to one side in what follows.

47 For a helpful discussion of Scotus's view of the distinction between intuitive and abstractive cognition and the context in which that distinction is used, see Dumont 1989. Dumont is particularly concerned to show the connection of the distinction to certain theological debates such as whether theology is a science. In these debates, epistemological issues make a significant difference to theological doctrine.

48 Ockham argues against the species account in many places. In addition to those already cited, see *Sent.* II.13 (294–310), III.3.

49 See, for example, *Sent.* II.13 (268), III.2 (59).

50 *Sent.* I.27.3 (241). See also *Sent.* III.3 (121).

51 See, for example, †*Sent.* I. Prol.1 (33).

52 *Quodl.* VI.6.

53 *Quodl.* I.13 (73).

54 *Sent.* I.Prol.1 (31) (= Boehner 1990, 23).

55 In Chapter 9, Elizabeth Karger discusses abstractive cognition in some detail. On her view, for Ockham abstractive cognition can be restricted simply to acts of apprehension that are not intuitive, or it can range so widely as to cover all acts of cognition that are not intuitive. She says there is "a wide sense [of 'abstractive cognition'] in which all acts of cognition that are not intuitive are abstractive, including acts of apprehension of a mental sentence and even acts of judgment." (Chap. 9, Sec. I.1.) My primary focus in this chapter is intuitive cognition; I will leave abstractive cognition largely unexplored.

56 There would, of course, also be a problem if we failed to have a sense of an object as present when it was; we might then suppose that we were not perceiving when we were.

57 *Sent.* II.13 (259).

58 †*Sent.* I.Prol.1 (38).

59 *Sent.* II.13 (256). It may be helpful to ward off a possible misunderstanding of the phrase 'by the mediation of which' in this claim and analogous phrases in similar claims. However exactly we are to understand that phrase, it is clear from everything else Ockham has to say about intuitive cognition that intuitive cognition does not function as evidence for a judgment. In the same way, my belief *That's a cup* is based on my perception of the cup, but the perception is not evidence I consult in trying to determine whether to assent to the proposition 'That's a cup'. I am grateful to John Boler for calling to my attention the need to ward off such a misconception.

60 *Quodl.* V.5.

61 †*Sent.* I.Prol.1 (71).

62 †Ibid. (70).

63 †Ibid. As this claim makes clear, Ockham does not suppose all cognitions are judgments, and on this score he is clearly right. I can perceive an object without going on to form perceptual beliefs about it. See also n. 5.

64 See, for example, †*Sent.* I. Prol. 1 (71).

65 †Ibid.

66 *Quodl.* V.5.

67 Ibid.

68 Here I am agreeing with most recent interpreters of Ockham and disagreeing with Karger's views in Chap. 9. As far as I can see, Karger and I do not disagree on the nature of Ockham's central claim but only on what is entailed by it. She says (Chap. 9, Sec. II.1,) that Ockham "is implicitly denying the possibility Chatton had asserted, namely, that God cause in us a[n] [intuitive] cognition of a nonexistent thing which would, in turn, [in itself] cause us to judge erroneously the thing to exist." (It is clear in Karger's chapter as well as in the primary sources that intuitive cognition is what is at issue here; consequently, for the sake of clarity, I inserted the bracketed 'intuitive' in the quotation. In correspondence, Karger has told me that the bracketed 'in itself' also needs to be added for her claim to be interpreted correctly.) I am inclined to think that if the claim in the quotation represents Ockham accurately, then contemporary scholars are right to suppose that for Ockham intuitive cognition infallibly leads to right judgment if it leads to judgment at all. It is compatible with this view ascribed to Ockham that if God were to prevent an intuitive cognition from having its natural effect, God could substitute a false judgment in place of the correct one the intuitive cognition would have given rise to.

69 As is clear in what follows, I am not persuaded by the analysis of Ockham's view of optical illusions Karger gives in her chapter.

70 *Quodl.* VI.6.

71 Ibid.

72 It need not also be an infallibly correct detector of the absence of things. Apart from the special case in which a person has an intuitive cognition, caused by God, of a nonexistent thing, there is no reason for supposing Ockham thought human beings have a highly reliable ability to detect the absence of things. My having a naturally caused intuitive cognition of a cup occurs only when there is a cup present. But my having no intuitive cognition of a cup is not a reliable indicator that no cup is present, since I might simply not be aware of the cup in my presence; it

might be hidden under a pile of papers or otherwise not available to my sight.

73 *Sent.* II.13 (276).

74 *Sent.* III.2 (65).

75 Ockham's theory that there are these two different intuitive cognitions of the same thing is based on his view that a human being has a sensory soul as well as an intellective soul, but this by itself does not make clear why intuitive cognition in both souls is necessary for the cognition of a single material object. For some very helpful discussion of this issue, see Adams 1987a, 507–9. It seems to me the closest Ockham comes to a plausible explanation of why we need to posit such overlap is that in very young children we get sensory intuitive cognition but not intellective intuitive cognition, and in the separated soul, after death, there is intellective intuitive cognition but not sensory intuitive cognition. (*Quodl.* I.15 [84–6].) I say this explanation has some plausibility, but I do not think it makes Ockham's case, since it seems to me more reasonable to suppose there is some intellective intuitive cognition (however rudimentary) even in infants, who would not be able to make any sense of their world if they got no quiddities at all of what they were sensing, and there are alternative ways of explaining the cognition of separated souls, as Aquinas's account of such cognition makes clear.

76 *Sent.* I.3.6 (494). Of course, the same singular can also be the object of abstractive cognition, as when one forms a thought about that singular when the singular is no longer present.

77 *Sent.* II.13 (256–7).

78 *Sent.* III.2 (65).

79 *Sent.* I.Prol.1 (30) (= Boehner 1990, 22).

80 *Sent.* II.13 (271–2).

81 Ibid.

82 *Sent.* III.3 (116).

83 Ibid. (117).

84 For some helpful remarks on *phantasia*, see, for example, *Sent.* II.13 (302–3).

85 For a good tracing of the complicated history by which Aquinas's account becomes transmuted into the account Ockham rejects, see Spruit 1994, 175–256. In his discussion of Ockham's rejection of the species account, Spruit himself is clear that the account Ockham is rejecting differs in important ways from the one Aquinas defends; see ibid., 291–8.

86 *Sent.* I.3.6 (521).

87 Ibid. (523).

88 This is a point Adams 1987a, 500, also remarks on in another context.

89 For a good and helpful discussion of Ockham's theory of free will, see Adams 1987a, 1115–37. For a good statement of Ockham's view of free will, see †*Sent.* I.38 (580).

90 I have presented Aquinas's theory of the will and argued for it as a species of libertarianism in various publications, including Stump 1993, 1996a, 1996b, 1997.

91 For this way of thinking about free will in terms of alternative possibilities and ultimate responsibility, see Kane 1996.

92 Pasnau 1997, 190–2, also argues for this claim, though in a different way.

93 *Sent.* III.3 (117). I am grateful to Elizabeth Karger for help in sorting out Ockham's position here.

94 For some discussion of this point, see n. 75.

95 I take this way of putting the point from Spruit 1994, 298, who calls attention to this feature of Ockham's account in a different context.

96 I am indebted to John Boler, Norman Kretzmann, and Paul Vincent Spade for helpful comments on an earlier draft of this essay.

9 Ockham's Misunderstood Theory of Intuitive and Abstractive Cognition

In 1943, Philotheus Boehner, the distinguished Ockham scholar, published an article entitled "The Notitia Intuitiva of Non-existents according to William Ockham,"[1] an article that has been extremely influential ever since.

This date can be regarded as a turning point in the history of the misunderstanding, in whole or in part, of Ockham's theory of intuitive and abstractive cognition in this century. Before that date, eminent scholars[2] had ascribed to Ockham the very doctrine of intuitive cognition of nonexistents he had rejected.[3] In his article, Boehner proceeded to denounce their mistake.[4] Ironically, however, in the very same article, he introduced a new mistake, now bearing on the whole of the theory. Unaware that he had misread a certain text, he ascribed to Ockham a theory of intuitive and abstractive cognition that neither he, nor anyone else as far as I know, ever subscribed to. Though this mistake was introduced in the literature more than fifty years ago, not only has it gone undetected, it has been repeated by most subsequent scholars who have written on the subject, all of whom have studied Boehner's article. As a result, the mistake has become completely entrenched, and many scholarly discussions on Ockham's epistemology have been based on the assumption that Ockham held a certain doctrine which, in fact, he never subscribed to, nor even conceived of.

It is high time that this mistake be denounced, which is what I propose to do here, by first providing a succinct account of the theory of intuitive and abstractive cognition to which Ockham did in fact subscribe (Section I). I will then explain how the misunderstanding of what he says in a certain quodlibetal text led scholars to ascribe to Ockham a different theory (Section II). I will finally show that this other theory, which is not contained in the quodlibetal text at all, is, moreover, incompatible with some of Ockham's explicit statements (Section III).[5]

Ockham's theory of intuitive and abstractive cognition is a theory of special kinds of cognitive acts. Before we look at his theory of those special cognitive acts, we need to know something of the more general theory.

I.I. Intellective Acts of Cognition

Acts in general are always ascribed to a subject, as, for example, the act of walking to a human being or to an animal. All cognitive acts are ascribed to a soul. There are, however, according to Ockham, two kinds of souls capable of cognition: sensitive souls and rational souls.[6] Whereas animals have only a sensitive soul and angels only a rational soul, humans have both a sensitive and a rational soul. Sensitive souls exist only as extended in a body, whereas rational souls can exist separately from any body and, when they do exist in a body, as the rational souls of humans do in this life, they are not extended in it.[7] In this section, I will consider only the cognitive acts a rational soul is capable of; a brief account of the cognitive acts a sensitive soul is capable of is included in Section III.

A rational soul is not capable only of acts of cognition; it is also capable of acts of willing. A rational soul considered as capable of acts of willing is called a will; considered as capable of acts of cognition it is called an intellect.[8] From the ontological point of view, all acts of the soul, of the rational soul in particular, are identified with individual concrete entities inhering in the soul called "qualities."[9] They are entities of relatively short duration because acts in general, acts of willing and acts of cognition in particular, are typically of relatively short duration.

Besides the qualities that are acts, there are in a rational soul other qualities, according to Ockham. They are of much longer duration than acts, and the soul is never aware of them, whereas it can, by introspection, become aware of some of its acts. These relatively permanent qualities are dispositions, called "habits," caused by an act, which stay in the mind, awaiting as it were the opportunity to cause an act similar to the first. Because it has such dispositions, a soul can rehearse thoughts it has previously had.[10]

Intellective acts of cognition are of two very different kinds. Some are acts of apprehension of an object, which may be an individual thing, or a general concept, or a certain complex object formed (we shall see how) of individuals, concepts, or both, and that is a mental sentence. Others are acts by which the intellect not only apprehends a mental sentence but assents to it. Acts of the first kind are called acts of apprehension; acts of the second kind are acts of assent or of judgment.[11]

Elementary mental sentences, which are of the subject–predicate form, have as their subject and predicate, called their "terms," either a general concept, used to refer to the things it applies to, or an individual thing, used to refer to itself.[12] Such a sentence is formed when the intellect apprehends together chosen individuals, general concepts, or both, in conjunction with one or several syncategorematics that do the job of linking those entities with one another in a statement-forming way (the copula) and of making the sentence affirmative or negative, universal or particular (if is not a singular sentence) as well as present, past, or future tensed, and so on, as the intellect intends. The act of apprehending a mental sentence is the act of apprehending its components together so as to form the sentence.[13]

Acts of apprehension are not all acts of cognition of the same kind. Acts of apprehension that have objects of different types are of different kinds. An act of apprehension of an individual thing is thus not of the same kind as an act of apprehension of a general concept and neither is of the same kind as an act of apprehension of a mental sentence. Acts of intuitive and acts of abstractive cognition are acts of apprehension of objects of the same type, for they are all acts of apprehension of an individual. They are *not*, however, acts of the same kind.[14]

A parenthetical remark should be inserted here: I have just now been using the term "abstractive cognition" in one of its senses, the sense in which it applies to apprehensions of individuals. But there is another sense of the term in which an act of apprehension of a general concept is an act of abstractive cognition and a wide sense in which all acts of cognition that are not intuitive are abstractive, including acts of apprehension of a mental sentence and even acts of judgment.[15] We shall see later the importance of keeping these other senses in mind, in particular the wide sense, but for now I continue to use 'abstractive cognition' in its first sense, the sense in which acts of intuitive and acts of abstractive cognition, though different in kind, are acts of apprehension of individuals.

By calling upon our everyday experience, the difference between these acts of apprehension of individuals can be made a familiar one. An act by which we apprehend a material object via one or several of our five senses is an act of intuitive cognition, whereas an act by which we think of the same material thing when it is no longer present is an act of abstractive cognition. For example, during the walk I took yesterday, when my attention was arrested by a majestic oak tree, I was apprehending the tree intuitively via my sense of sight. When, later, back in my study, I started thinking of that tree, recalling how majestic it looked, I was apprehending it abstractively. It cannot be too strongly stressed that, according to Ockham, the very same thing – that tree – has been apprehended by my intellect on both occasions.

These apprehensions surely have different causes. My intuitive apprehension of the oak tree was caused by the tree itself acting on my sense of sight and thereby on my intellect, according to Ockham.[16] The abstractive act of cognition I later had of the same tree cannot have had the tree itself as a cause; for the tree was no longer present and could not, therefore, have been acting either on my senses or on my intellect. According to Ockham, the abstractive cognition was caused instead by a disposition to think of that tree, a disposition or "habit" that was itself caused when I first apprehended the tree intuitively via my sense of sight.[17]

That these two acts of cognition are not caused in the same way is not regarded by Ockham as the reason they are not of the same kind. For, according to him, they *could* have been caused in the same way (we shall see later how).[18] Rather these acts of cognition are not of the same kind, he believes, because they are not capable of causing the same effects. As he sets out to explain, acts of intuitive cognition are, by nature, capable of causing certain cognitive acts that acts of abstractive cognition are not capable of causing.

The cognitive acts that only acts of intuitive cognition are capable of causing are, Ockham tells us, very special acts of evident assent.

We shall not understand what these acts are, however, unless we know something of Ockham's theory of evident assent.

1.2. Evident Assent

Recall that an act of assent is always to a mental sentence. For an act of assent to be evident, three conditions are required:

- The mental sentence assented to must be true.[19]
- Given the cognitive acts it is having (acts of apprehension and, possibly, acts of evident assent to other mental sentences), the intellect must have no choice but to assent to the sentence.[20]
- Any other intellect, if it were having equivalent cognitive acts, would also have no choice but to assent.[21]

The three requirements are probably not independent because the first is probably fulfilled if the other two are. The second requirement is not fulfilled if the intellect assents because it has the will to do so. Such is the case, for example, when a believer assents to an article of faith.[22] The third requirement is not fulfilled if, for example, the intellect is so impressed by an argument that it has no choice but to assent to what the argument purports to establish, whereas other intellects with more logical expertise are not so impressed and either dissent or remain in doubt.[23]

Acts of evident assent fall into two main categories: (1) those made to the conclusion of an evidently valid inference and caused by acts of evident assent to its premises, and (2) those that are not so caused and are, instead, caused by the apprehension of the terms of the very sentence assented to.[24] Acts of evident assent of the second category could be called acts of "immediately evident" assent.

Acts of immediately evident assent subdivide. Some are acts of assent to a mental sentence, all the terms of which are general concepts; others are acts of assent to a mental sentence, one of the terms of which is an individual, or both of the terms of which are individuals.

Acts of immediately evident assent to a mental sentence of the second sort again subdivide. In some cases the sentence assented to is necessarily true; in others it is of the present tense and contingently true. There are other cases, which, in this succinct account of

Ockham's doctrine, we may disregard.[25] Let us see examples of each of the two main cases.

Suppose I form a mental sentence with the oak tree I admired yesterday and am thinking of today as a self-referring subject term and with the concept "plant" as predicate term, a sentence saying of the tree that it can be a plant. That sentence, equivalent in import to a sentence saying of the tree that, if it exists, it is a plant, is necessarily true. According to Ockham, this is a mental sentence to which, as soon as I have formed it, I am caused to assent by the mere act of apprehending its terms, which are the tree and the concept "plant," no other mental act being required to bring about that effect. Moreover, I am caused to assent to the sentence whether I am now standing once again in front of that tree, looking at it, or whether I am thinking of it in my study, that is, whether my apprehension of the tree is intuitive or abstractive.[26] And the same would hold of any intellect.

Suppose now that I form a mental sentence again with that oak tree as self-referring subject term but with the complex concept (formed in much the same way as a mental sentence is) of having golden-colored leaves as its predicate, a sentence saying of the tree that it has golden-colored leaves. Suppose that the sentence is true at present, it being the right season for leaves to be golden. If I am now looking at the tree, apprehending it intuitively, then again I shall be caused to assent to the sentence, as soon as I have formed it, by the mere act of apprehending its terms, in particular that of apprehending the tree intuitively, no further mental act being required. And the same would hold of any intellect. Not so, however, if I am thinking of the tree in my study and apprehending it abstractively. In that case, the act of apprehending the terms of the sentence, in particular that of apprehending the tree abstractively, is insufficient to cause me to assent and, in the absence of any other considerations, I will be left in doubt as to whether the sentence is now true or not.[27]

1.3. Intuitive and Abstractive Cognition Defined

Here we have, at last, the type of cognitive acts that intuitive acts of cognition are, by nature, capable of causing and that abstractive acts are not. They are acts of immediately evident assent to a present-tensed, contingently true mental sentence, one of the terms of which is a self-referring individual or both of the terms of which are. This suggests defining intuitive and abstractive cognition as follows:

(D1) Acts of intuitive and of abstractive cognition are acts of apprehension of an individual. But acts of intuitive cognition are by nature capable of causing acts of evident assent to present-tensed contingent truths about the individual apprehended, whereas acts of abstractive cognition by nature lack that capacity.[28]

If D1 is adequate, the capacity it assigns to acts of intuitive cognition must belong to all possible instances of such. We have, however, considered only acts of intuitive cognition familiar to us in experience, which are all naturally caused acts, caused by the very thing apprehended. Yet, there is a theological principle Ockham never loses sight of, a principle according to which, though nothing ever causes any effect without God's cooperation, God, on the other hand, can act alone to cause any of the effects any given thing is capable of causing.[29] When one applies this principle to acts of cognition (which, it will be recalled, are qualities inhering in an intellect), it will have to be recognized that acts of intuitive cognition can exist which, if they had been naturally caused, would have been caused by the things that are their objects, but that are caused instead by God acting alone to produce them in an intellect. But, for any act of intuitive cognition, if it is caused by God alone, the thing that is the object of the act is taking no part in causing the act. That thing need not, then, be present or even exist for the act to exist. It follows that acts of intuitive cognition can exist *the objects of which are nonexistent things.* Any such act, however, would have to be caused supernaturally by God acting alone to produce it in an intellect.[30]

Now the question is, Would an act of intuitive cognition of a nonexistent thing be capable of causing an act of evident assent to a present-tensed contingent mental sentence containing the apprehended object as a self-referring term and, if so, what could the sentence be? Ockham answers that it would and that the sentence assented to would be one saying that the object does not exist.[31]

If such an extraordinary instance of an act of intuitive cognition has the capacity that D1 ascribes to cognitive acts of that kind, surely all possible acts of that kind have that capacity. If so, D1 effectively distinguishes acts of intuitive cognition in all their possible instances from acts of abstractive cognition. Thus, D1 is an adequate definition of intuitive and abstractive cognition.

Given what we have just seen, and excepting one single case,[32] the following alternative definition of intuitive and abstractive cognition is also adequate:

(D2) Acts of intuitive and of abstractive cognition are acts of apprehension of an individual. But, where the individual is a contingently existing thing, an act of intuitive cognition is by nature capable of causing the intellect to judge evidently that the thing exists if it does or that it does not exist if it does not, whereas an act of abstractive cognition by nature lacks that capacity.[33]

On Ockham's doctrine, acts of intuitive cognition differ from acts of abstractive cognition in the way indicated by D1 or by D2 in all their possible instances. If instances of acts of each kind are naturally caused, they differ additionally by the way they are caused, as we saw earlier. But if instances of acts of each kind are supernaturally caused, they do not differ by the way they are caused since they are caused in exactly the same way, namely by God acting alone to produce them. If they are of the same object, they differ only in the way indicated by D1 or by D2.

II. THE MISUNDERSTANDING OF A QUODLIBETAL TEXT

Since Boehner wrote his influential 1943 article, scholars have regarded the definitions of intuitive and abstractive cognition provided by Ockham, to which D1 and D2 correspond, as failing to mention other, no less important features characteristic, on his full doctrine, of each kind of cognitive act.

Evidence for this view was thought to be found in a quodlibetal text. The text consists of Ockham's responses to two objections leveled against his doctrine of intuitive cognition, one by his confrere Walter Chatton, the other by an unidentified opponent. These responses are largely variants of one another.[34] It is, however, in his response to Chatton's objection that the point thought by Boehner to be of such momentous consequence is explicitly made. Accordingly, we need consider only Chatton's objection and Ockham's response to it.[35]

II.I. *Chatton's Objection and Ockham's Response*

Chatton's objection is directed against Ockham's doctrine that an intuitive cognition[36] of a nonexistent object, a cognition supernaturally caused by God, would cause the intellect that has it to judge correctly that the thing does not exist.

If this were so, Chatton argues, it would follow that God could not cause in us a cognition by which we would judge[37] a nonexistent thing to exist,[38] though this is something he can do since the idea involves no contradiction. For the cognition would have to be either intuitive or abstractive. If it were intuitive, it would, on Ockham's doctrine, cause the intellect to judge the thing not to exist and would not, therefore, cause it to judge the thing to exist. If it were abstractive, then again it would not cause the intellect to judge the thing to exist, as everyone would acknowledge, Ockham included, who had said of abstractive cognitions of individuals that they abstract from the existence and nonexistence of their objects.[39]

Chatton himself believed God can cause us to have the false belief in question by causing in us an intuitive cognition of the nonexistent object. For, on his doctrine, that cognition would naturally cause the intellect to judge the thing to exist, such being the effect of every intuitive cognition, *whether its object exists or not*.[40] He takes, of course, the preceding argument as showing that his doctrine, not Ockham's, is the correct one.

In his response,[41] Ockham acknowledges that God can cause in us a cognition by which we judge a nonexistent thing to exist while denying that this is a possibility his doctrine would rule out. For, on his doctrine, God could achieve that effect by causing directly in us the very act of judgment itself, which is itself correctly described as the cognitive act by which we judge the nonexistent thing to exist. God would have to be acting alone to bring about that cognitive act, but that is something he can do. For, as we have seen, an act of judgment is, on Ockham's doctrine, a quality in the intellect and, just as God can act alone to produce any given thing, quality, or substance, so he can act alone to produce that quality in the intellect. Being an act of judgment, that cognition is not of course an intuitive cognition. It is, however, in the wide sense of the term, the sense in which every cognition that is not intuitive is abstractive, an abstractive cognition.[42] On this basis, Ockham can respond briefly to Chatton by pointing out that, on his doctrine, God can indeed cause in us a cognition by which we judge (or believe) a nonexistent thing to exist, a cognition that is however abstractive, not intuitive, as it might have been if Chatton's doctrine had been the correct one.

Ockham only seems to be answering Chatton on his own terms, however. For he is implicitly denying the possibility Chatton had asserted, that God cause in us a cognition of a nonexistent thing that would, in turn, cause us to judge erroneously the thing to exist. The possibility Ockham is asserting instead is that God cause in us directly the very act by which we judge the nonexistent thing to exist, an act that is not a cause of the judgment but the judgment itself.

It is important to realize that, when God is deceiving us in that way, causing us to judge a nonexistent thing to exist by causing in us the very act of judgment itself, the cognition we are having of the thing plays no part at all in causing the judgment, the sole cause of which is God himself. It follows that the cognition the intellect is having of the thing may well be intuitive (though it need not be). For, on Ockham's doctrine, God can prevent any given thing from exercising its natural causal powers by simply not cooperating with it. It is, then, possible that God should first cause in us an intuitive cognition of a nonexistent thing, that he should next prevent that cognition from exercising its natural capacity of causing us to judge the thing not to exist, and that he should finally cause in us instead an erroneous act of judgment by which we judge the thing to exist. In such a case God would have miraculously intervened three times by causing the intuitive cognition, by preventing it from causing its natural effect, and by causing the act of erroneously judging the thing to exist. Though extraordinary, such a conjunction of miracles is possible.

A simpler case, simpler in that it involves only two miracles, not three, is envisaged by Ockham in *Sent.*[43] There he acknowledges that God can first prevent a given naturally caused intuitive cognition from exercising its natural capacity of causing the intellect to judge the thing to exist and then act alone to cause instead in the intellect the false belief that the thing does not exist.

Such is Ockham's doctrine of the possibility that God cause the intellect to judge a nonexistent thing to exist or an existent thing not to exist, a doctrine he subscribes to in *Sent.* and in *Quodl.*[44]

II.2. Boehner's Misunderstanding of Ockham's Response to Chatton

The quodlibetal text has, however, been misunderstood first by Boehner in his 1943 article[45] and later by subsequent scholars, all of whom knew Boehner's article, failed to detect the mistake he had committed, and then repeated that mistake in their own writings.[46]

Boehner took Ockham to have not only apparently but effectively answered Chatton on his own terms, believing Ockham to have conceded Chatton's premise that it is possible for God to cause us to judge a nonexistent thing to exist by causing in us a cognition *of that thing* which, in turn, would cause the false judgment. Having assumed that much, he thought that Ockham's response to Chatton consisted in denying that that cognition would be intuitive and in asserting instead that it would be abstractive, a possibility Chatton would have been wrong to rule out.[47]

On the basis of this misunderstanding of Ockham's reply to Chatton, Boehner and subsequent scholars inferred that, on Ockham's doctrine, intuitive cognitions are *infallible* and abstractive cognitions *deceptive*. Intuitive cognitions are infallible, they reasoned, since it follows from this quodlibetal text that even God, for whom nothing is impossible save what involves a contradiction, cannot, by producing in an intellect an intuitive cognition of a thing, cause a false judgment about the thing – in particular a judgment ascribing to the thing a present contingent property it does not have (including existence if the thing does not exist); he must resort instead to an abstractive cognition. The reason must be, it was thought, that it would involve a contradiction that an intuitive cognition cause a false judgment, whereas no contradiction is involved by an abstractive cognition having that effect. Indeed, since God can rely on an abstractive cognition to cause the intellect to judge the apprehended thing to have a present contingent property it does not have (including existence when the thing does not exist), it must even be assumed that abstractive cognitions have, by nature, the capacity of causing such erroneous judgments. If so, they can be called deceptive.

Scholars were thus led to believe that, on Ockham's "full account," [48] the following definition of intuitive and abstractive cognition should be added to D1 and D2:

(D3) Acts of intuitive and of abstractive cognition are acts of apprehension of an individual. But it is impossible, on pain of contradiction, that an act of intuitive cognition cause a false judgment, in particular a judgment ascribing to the apprehended thing a present contingent property it does not have, whereas an abstractive cognition is by nature capable of causing just that effect.

The quodlibetal text by which this alleged "full account" of intuitive and abstractive cognition was thought to be implied, implies, however, no such doctrine. Correctly understood, the text implies that the definition of intuitive cognition by D2, and not the one given by Chatton, is valid, and it makes no reference at all to abstractive cognitions of individuals. It implies neither the thesis that abstractive cognitions are deceptive cognitions nor the thesis that intuitive cognitions are infallible cognitions.

As we will now see, both theses are, moreover, incompatible with some of Ockham's explicit statements.

III. TWO THESES OCKHAM WOULD HAVE REJECTED

Consider first the thesis ascribing a deceptive nature to abstractive cognitions.

III.1. *The Nondeceptive Nature of Cognitions*

If the thesis that abstractive cognitions are, by nature, capable of causing the intellect to ascribe to the apprehended thing a present contingent property it does not have had been submitted to Ockham, he would surely have rejected it. For he characterizes abstractive cognitions of individuals by saying they "abstract" from the existence and nonexistence of the apprehended thing and from all other present contingent properties it may have.[49] But it would be paradoxical, to say the least, that a cognition that excludes from consideration a certain range of properties should cause the intellect to ascribe to its object – truly or falsely – a property chosen in that very range.

Ockham further admitted the general principle that "nothing which leads the intellect into error should be posited in the intellect."[50] In other words, no cognition should be admitted that would have a deceptive nature – a cognition that would, by its very nature, cause the intellect to make false judgments. Ockham applies this principle to intuitive cognitions, using it to rule out that an intuitive cognition of a thing should, by nature, cause the intellect to judge the thing to exist, whether it does or not, since that would necessarily lead to a false judgment whenever the thing does not exist.[51] But he could have applied this principle to abstractive cognitions as well, using it to rule out that abstractive cognitions should be capable by nature of causing the intellect to make false judgments.

Finally, it follows from Ockham's theory of evidence that abstractive cognitions, no less than intuitive ones, are, by nature, capable of causing evident judgments. What sets them apart from intuitive cognitions is that they can cause evident assents to necessary truths about the apprehended object, not to present-tensed contingent truths about it, whereas intuitive cognitions can cause both.[52] Nevertheless, both kinds of cognitive acts share the property that they are, by nature, capable of causing true judgments, not false ones.

That a cognition is not, by its very nature, capable of causing a false judgment does not entail that it is absolutely impossible that it should do so. For, on a particular occasion, the circumstances might be such as to determine a cognition to cause a false judgment in a given intellect, which it would not have caused had no such circumstances been present. It is, I believe, in this light that Ockham's doctrine of sensory illusions can be understood – a doctrine that entails, as we shall see, that intuitive cognitions, far from being infallible, can and sometimes do cause false judgments. Before we look at Ockham's discussion of sensory illusions, we need to have some knowledge of his doctrine of sensory cognition that it presupposes – a doctrine that was, moreover, also presupposed by some aspects of the theory of intellective cognitions sketched in Section I.

III.2. Ockham's Theory of Sensory Cognition

Recall that, according to Ockham, humans have, in this life, two souls, a rational and a sensitive soul. Both souls are in a body, but the sensitive soul is extended in it, part of the soul being in part of the body, another part in another, whereas the rational soul is in the body without being extended in it.

The body is endowed with sensory organs, which are of two sorts. Some are external,[53] located on the surface of the body, and one is internal,[54] located within the body. The sensitive soul, insofar as part of it is extended in a given sense organ is called a "sense." Thus, insofar as part of the sensitive soul is extended in each of the external sensory organs, it divides into the five external senses.[55] Insofar as the sensitive soul is extended in the internal sense organ, it is the so-called internal sense or the imagination. All acts of cognition or apprehension by the senses, external or internal, are thus acts of apprehension by one part or the other of the sensitive soul.

Acts of apprehension, by the external senses and by the internal sense, are acts by which a material thing is apprehended. Acts of the external senses are acts by which the thing is perceived (i.e., seen, heard, felt, smelled or tasted), whereas acts of the internal sense are acts by which the thing is imagined. An act of the first kind, if it is naturally caused, must be caused by the thing apprehended acting on the sensitive soul by acting on an external sense.[56] An act of the second kind is not caused by the object apprehended since an object can be, and generally is, imagined in its absence. According to Ockham, if the act is naturally caused, it is caused by a disposition or "habit" that was itself caused in the sensitive soul when its object was first apprehended by an external sense.[57]

The sensitive soul is not, according to Ockham, capable of any other acts of cognition than acts of apprehension of individual things. It is, therefore, not capable of acts of judgment. Only the intellect can judge. It follows that no sensory act of apprehension of a thing can cause an act of judgment about that thing in the sensitive soul. Provided the sensitive soul is that of a human, and thus conjoined with a rational soul, a sensory act of apprehension of a thing can, however, cause an act of judgment about that thing in the rational soul of the human. But a sensory act of apprehension can do so only indirectly. For the judgment will have to be an act of assent to a mental sentence containing the thing as a term. Consequently, before judging, the rational soul will first have to form that sentence, which is something it can do only if it apprehends its terms. It follows that the sensory act of apprehension will cause an act of judgment about its object in the rational soul or intellect only if the apprehension first causes in the rational soul an intellective apprehension of the same object. But once the intellective act of apprehension is present in the intellect, *it* will cause the act of judgment, not the sensory one. The situation will, then, be the following: the sensory apprehension causes in the intellect an intellective apprehension of the same object, and that intellective apprehension causes an act of judgment about that object. A sensory act of apprehension can, therefore, cause an act of judgment about its object, but always as an indirect cause, one step removed from its effect, not as a direct or proximate cause.[58]

On that basis, it is possible to extend the definitions of intellective acts of intuitive and abstractive cognition so as to make them apply to sensory acts of intuitive and abstractive cognition. We could say that a sensory act of cognition of a thing, had by a human, is intuitive if it is by nature capable of being the indirect cause of an act of evident assent to a present-tensed contingent mental sentence about the thing and that it is abstractive if it by nature lacks that capacity.

On that definition, all acts of the external senses are intuitive,[59] whereas acts of the internal sense are acts of the imagination and, as such, typically abstractive. Ockham considers, however, the possibility that acts of the internal sense should include some acts of intuitive cognition as well. But he rejects that possibility. There is, he argues, no reason to posit any other sensory acts of intuitive cognition than those of the external senses. All acts of the internal sense must, therefore, be abstractive.[60]

Ockham acknowledges that, in this life, our intellect can apprehend a material thing intuitively only via the external senses.[61] Given the doctrine that humans have two souls, that can happen only if we are having two intuitive apprehensions of the same thing, one by the sensitive soul, caused by the material thing, the other by the rational soul, caused both by the material thing and by the sensory apprehension of it.[62] There is, however, no introspective difference between the two cognitions because we are not even aware of apprehending the same thing twice over.

We can now examine Ockham's discussion of sensory illusions.

III.3. Ockham's Doctrine of Sensory Illusions

Ockham discusses sensory illusions in *Sent.*[63] In the text in which that discussion is included, his main purpose is to refute a certain theory of objects of thought defended by his French confrere, Peter Auriol. He rejects Auriol's claim that sensory illusions are apprehensions by the external senses of objects having mere intentional being that are apprehended as actually present real things. He insists that a sensory illusion, when it is had by a human, is, instead, an erroneous judgment ascribing to a real thing some present contingent property it does not have, a judgment caused (indirectly, of course) in the intellect by a sensory apprehension of that thing.[64]

For example, the visual illusion we sometimes have that a straight stick, half immerged in water, is bent, is not, as Auriol believes, an apprehension of a purely intentional bend in the stick taken to be really present in it; rather it is the erroneous judgment that the stick is bent caused by the visual apprehension of the stick.[65]

Some scholars amongst those who had ascribed to Ockham the doctrine that abstractive cognitions, not intuitive ones, are capable of causing false judgments, inferred that the sensory apprehensions that in sensory illusions cause erroneous judgments had to be abstractive.[66] But this is incompatible with Ockham's theory of sensory apprehension, as they failed to realize. For the sensory apprehensions in question are acknowledged by both Auriol and Ockham as being apprehensions by an external sense.[67] But, as we have just seen, all apprehensions by an external sense are, on Ockham's doctrine, intuitive apprehensions.[68]

The fact staring us in the eye is that, contrary to current scholarly consensus, Ockham admitted there to be cases where an intuitive cognition causes a false judgment.

No intuitive cognition, however, has that effect except owing to special circumstances in which it is had. For example, because the stick is seen partly through one medium, partly through another, the visual apprehension of it causes the intellect to judge the stick to be bent. One could say that, on Ockham's doctrine, the causing of an erroneous judgment by an intuitive cognition is always itself causally dependent on there being special circumstances in which the cognition is had.

An intuitive cognition that, owing to the special circumstances in which it is had, causes in an intellect an erroneous judgment about the apprehended object, is nevertheless by its very nature capable of causing some true and evident judgments about the same object. It follows that in some cases an intuitive cognition will cause both some true and evident judgments and some false ones. Ockham provides an example of this possibility. It is that of an object seen in a mirror.[69] By virtue of that act of vision, which is an act of intuitive cognition, some present contingent properties of the object can be evidently known, such as the fact that it exists or that it is red (if such is its color). But other properties cannot be known by virtue of that act of vision, such as the location of the object. Why not? Because in this case, Ockham explains, the object is not seen as it normally is, by a direct line of vision, but by a reflected one.[70] As a result, the object, appearing to be at a place where it is not, behind the mirror,[71] is judged to be where it is not.[72] Thus, the special circumstance in which the act of vision is had, namely the circumstance that the object is seen not by a direct line of vision but by a reflected one, prevents that act from causing a judgment ascribing to the object the location it has.[73] The circumstance has that effect, however, because it determines the act of vision to cause instead a judgment ascribing to the object a location it does not have.

Not all intellects, however, by seeing an object in a mirror, are caused to judge the object to be behind the mirror. An intellect that understands mirrors and the way things are seen in them will not do so. For it would instead invoke compelling reasons to judge the thing to be in front of the mirror, not behind it.[74] But that is just as it should be: only an evident judgment, caused in a given intellect by certain cognitions, would be caused in any intellect having equivalent cognitions.[75]

Ockham's discussion of sensory illusions shows that, on his doctrine, it is by no means impossible that an intuitive cognition cause a false judgment, though it is always because of special circumstances in which the intuitive cognition is had that it does so.

IV. CONCLUSION

The doctrine of intuitive and abstractive cognition that, by their misreading of a certain quodlibetal text, scholars have been led to ascribe to Ockham never was a doctrine of his. In particular, he did not regard abstractive cognitions as capable by nature of causing false judgments, nor did he consider it absolutely impossible, on pain of contradiction, that an intuitive cognition cause a false judgment.

Convinced that he did hold these views, scholars speculated that the purpose of his doctrine of abstractive and intuitive cognition must have been, while allowing for error, to provide a basis on which to ground absolutely certain knowledge "safe from any intrusion of natural or supernatural scepticism," as Boehner wrote.[76]

The doctrine thus ascribed to Ockham was, however, a lame one. Some scholars recognized the fact and raised the question whether Ockham had effectively achieved by it the purpose they thought must have been his, namely that of defeating skepticism.[77] Others defended the doctrine by arguing its extreme sophistication.[78] Others still, aware of Ockham's indifference to skeptical arguments, abandoned the idea that the purpose of the doctrine was that of defeating skepticism, some suggesting a rather obscure alternative purpose[79] and others suggesting that its purpose was to defeat not Academic skepticism but some more mundane form of skepticism without explaining why such a heavy machinery might be required to that purpose.[80] The underlying belief that this really was Ockham's doctrine was never called into question, however.

Once it is realized that this belief was, in fact, mistaken, the speculations based on it can be dismissed as groundless, and features of Ockham's genuine doctrine can be recognized instead. One such feature is that there *is no privileged connection between intuition and evidence*. On Ockham's genuine doctrine, both intuitive and abstractive cognitions have, as we saw, the capacity of causing immediately evident judgments. The difference is one of greater power on the part of intuitive cognitions, for they can cause evident judgments that abstractive cognitions cannot; they cannot, however, cause more evident ones.

Suppose God were to provide intellect A with abstractive cognitions of just the three individuals a, b, and c while preventing it from having any intuitive cognitions at all. Suppose further that he were to provide intellect B with intuitive cognitions of just the same three individuals while preventing it from having any abstractive cognitions of individuals at all. Because neither act implies contradiction, God can bring about both states of affairs. On Ockham's doctrine, intellect A would know some necessary truths about a, b, and c, but it would know no contingent truths about any of those individuals. Intellect B, however, would know both some necessary truths about those individuals and some present-tensed contingent truths about them. The knowledge of truths about a, b, and c that intellect A has is thus more limited than the knowledge intellect B has; it is not, however, less evident nor less certain. Only a third intellect that, let us suppose, has been provided by God with both intuitive and abstractive cognitions of just the three individuals a, b, and c would know some of the truths known by the other two intellects more evidently than they do. For it would know the same necessary truths about *a*, *b*, and *c* as they do but by means of two specifically different cognitions of those individuals, one intuitive and the other abstractive; but Ockham has granted that "a truth is known more evidently when it is known by several means than when it is known just by one."[81]

NOTES

1 Boehner 1943.

2 In particular Konstanty Michalski, Erich Hochstetter, Étienne Gilson, and Anton Pegis, but *not* Paul Vignaux.

3 A doctrine Ockham rejected when he encountered it in writings by his French confrere, Peter Auriol. On this doctrine, as defended against Ockham by another confrere, Walter Chatton, see Sec. II.1.

4 A task he continued, responding to Anton Pegis in Boehner 1945.

5 In support of the views I ascribe to Ockham, I will rarely quote him directly but will refer instead in a footnote to the relevant text. The works by Ockham I will be referring to all belong to his theological works because it is in the context of theology that the doctrine of intuitive and abstractive cognition was developed by him.

6 *Quodl.* II.10.

7 Ibid.

8 *Sent.* II.20 (435).

9 *Quodl.* I.18.

10 *Sent.* IV.14 (297).

11 *Sent.* I. Prol.1 (16) (= Boehner 1990, 18).

12 This theory of mental sentences is the theory Ockham first subscribed to, which he abandoned later in favor of a theory identifying the terms of mental sentences not with objects of thought but with acts by which objects are apprehended. This early theory is, however, the one that is basic to his first and main account of intuitive and abstractive cognition (an account contained in his *Sent.* I. Prol.1), and he never produced a complete revision of that account that would bring it into harmony with his later theory of mental sentences. Because of this, the only theory of mental sentences I will take into account here is Ockham's early theory. It is remarkable that, on this theory, mental language is a "Lagadonian" language since it includes things used as names of themselves. See Lewis 1986, 145–6.

13 This account of how mental sentences are formed is contained in †*Sent.* II.12–13 (279–81) except that no mention is made there of any other syncategorematic than the copula.

14 *Sent.* I.Prol.1 (15) (= Boehner 1990, 18), †(62– 3).

15 *Sent.* II.12–13 (257) (= Hyman and Walsh 1983, 671).

16 The process involved will be explained in Section III.2.

17 †*Sent.* I. Prol.1 (61).

18 In Sec. I.3.

19 †*Sent.* I. Prol.1 (5).

20 *Sent.* I. Prol.7 (192).

21 *Sent.* I. Prol.1 (6).

22 *De intellectu agente* (187–8).

23 *Quodl.* IV.6.

24 *De intellectu agente* (188).

25 The case I will disregard is that of immediately evident assent to sentences in the past tense that are contingently true, a case acknowledged by Ockham in †*Sent.* II.12–13 (261–3).

26 †*Sent.* I. Prol.1 (6).

27 †Ibid.

28 Ibid., (31–2): "And generally every incomplex cognition of a term or of terms ... by virtue of which some contingent truth can be known, especially one of the present tense, is intuitive ... [whereas] by an abstractive cognition no contingent truth, especially of the present tense, can be evidently known." (= Boehner 1990, 23–4.)

29 †*Sent.* I. Prol.1 (35): "Whatever God can bring about by a mediate efficient cause, He can bring about directly by Himself."

30 †Ibid.

31 The reason Ockham has for giving this answer can obviously be only an a priori one, for neither he nor anyone else has had any experience of the underlying acts. It is beyond the scope of this introductory exposition to explain what this reason may have been.

32 The case to except is the one where the individual apprehended is the only necessary existent there is, namely God.

33 *Sent.* I. Prol.1 (31–2): "An intuitive cognition of a thing is a cognition such that, by virtue of it, it can be known whether the thing exists or not, so that, if the thing exists, the intellect ... evidently knows that it exists ... and ... if the cognition were by God's power preserved in existence [by continued causation] though the thing does not exist, by virtue of that incomplex cognition the thing would be evidently known not to exist ... Whereas an abstractive cognition of a contingent thing is one by virtue of which it is not possible to know evidently whether the thing exists or not." (= Boehner 1990, 23.)

34 *Quodl.* V.5.

35 Chatton's objection is ibid. (496) and Ockham's response ibid. (498).

36 Following Ockham, who often uses the term '*cognitio*' in that sense, I will often be using 'cognition' for 'act of cognition.'

37 Chatton does not talk of a cognition by which we would *judge* the thing
    to exist but of a cognition by which it would *appear* to us that it does.
    Ockham would, however, consider the difference to be merely verbal,
    and Chatton would either agree or consider the difference to be irrele-
    vant to the point he is making.

38 Chatton talks here of presence and of absence rather than of existence
    and of nonexistence. But presence entails, of course, existence and nonex-
    istence entails absence, and it makes no difference to his argument or to
    Ockham's response to it if one substitutes one set of notions for the other.

39 *Sent.* I. Prol.1 (31) (= Boehner 1990, 22).

40 See Walter Chatton 1989, 102.120–121 (in his *Sent.* I. Prol.2.3).

41 Ockham's response is a two-pronged one. One part of it, however, is not
    relevant to Chatton's objection at all, for Chatton had not claimed for
    God the capacity of causing a cognition by which we would *evidently*
    judge a nonexistent thing to exist and did not, therefore, need to be told
    that this is something impossible, given that evidence entails truth. The
    part of Ockham's response that effectively addresses Chatton's objection
    takes up but a few lines, namely *Quod.* V.5 (498.72–75).

42 See Sec. I.1.

43 †*Sent.* I. Prol.1 (70).

44 Because she failed to notice the text from *Sent.* just referred to, Anneliese
    Maier mistakenly believed that Ockham had acknowledged that God
    can cause directly in us a false judgment of existence about a thing in-
    tuitively apprehended in *Quodl.* only, not in his earlier work. See Maier
    1963, 373–76.

45 Boehner may have taken his cue from Paul Vignaux who, in a masterly
    encyclopedia article on medieval nominalism published in 1931, known
    to Boehner, briefly suggested such a misreading of that text. See Paul
    Vignaux 1930–50, especially the section "La vérité de la connaissance"
    (cols. 768–9).

46 The list of those scholars who followed Boehner in his misreading of
    this quodlibetal text would be very long indeed. In fact, the only scholar
    I know who read the text correctly is Maier 1953, 375–6. She did not,
    however, denounce Boehner's misreading of it. Of the very many scholars
    who misread the text as Boehner had, I shall mention here only those who
    were most intent in following through the epistemological consequences
    of the doctrine they ascribed to Ockham on that basis. They are, listed in
    chronological order of their relevant writings: Baudry 1958, entry "noti-
    tia," 177; Scott 1969, 45; Adams 1970, 394; Boler 1973, 103; Streveler
    1975, 228; Adams 1987a, 590. I know of only one scholar who, writing
    on the subject after Boehner, disregarded the quodlibetal text: Day 1947.

47 Boehner 1943, 281–2, 285–6.

48 The expression is that of Marilyn McCord Adams, who writes (Adams 1970, 391 n. 8): "On Ockham's full account, intuitive cognitions differ from abstractive cognitions precisely in the fact that they cannot be the cause of any false judgments, while abstractive cognitions can."

49 *Sent.* I. Prol.1 (31) (= Boehner 1990, 22).

50 †*Sent.* II.12–13 (281).

51 †Ibid. (286–7).

52 See Sec. I.2.

53 *Sent.* III.3 (105).

54 Ibid. (114).

55 †*Sent.* III.4 (136–7).

56 *Sent.* III.3 (111).

57 Ibid. (115, 117).

58 *Sent.* I. Prol.1 (22) (= Boehner 1990, 19–20).

59 In *Sent.* III.3 (110) it is claimed that "the sense of sight has no other cognition than intuitive." Though the claim is made by an opponent, the subsequent discussion shows that Ockham agrees. The same claim could be made of the other external senses.

60 *Sent.* III.3 (124–5).

61 †*Sent.* II.12–13 (285).

62 *Sent.* III.2 (64–5), together with *Quodl.* I.15.

63 *Sent.* I.27.3 (238–51).

64 Ockham also attempts to characterize a sensory illusion when it is had, not by a human, but by an animal, in which case it cannot be identified with a false judgment, for animals are incapable of judging. I will disregard these attempts and consider here only sensory illusions as they are had by humans.

65 *Sent.* I.27.3 (247).

66 Scott 1969, 45 n. 65, takes the idea for granted.

67 *Sent.* I.27.3 (230) for Auriol, quoted by Ockham; ibid. (243) for Ockham.

68 One author, having repeated Boehner's misreading of the quodlibetal text, was so convinced that sensory apprehensions that cause false judgments must be abstractive that he invented an obscure theory of "abstractive sensations," as he calls them, supposed to be of the external senses, which he presents as if he had read it in Ockham. This exercise in deception (or is it shoddy thinking?) is owed to Michon 1994, 89–90 and 103–4. Michon would have been correct had he pointed out that, if Ockham had held the doctrine of intuitive and abstractive cognition ascribed to him nowadays by common consensus, he would have developed a theory of abstractive sensations of the external senses. But he did not do so, nor did he hold the doctrine of intuitive and abstractive cognition commonly ascribed to him.

69 *Sent.* III.2 (97), where Ockham answers an objection made earlier (78).

70 Ibid. (95).

71 Ibid. (78).

72 To say that something appears to be the case is, Ockham believes, just another way of saying that it is judged to be the case. See n. 37.

73 As Ockham acknowledges in *Sent.* I. Prol.1 (33), an act of intuitive cognition can be prevented from exercising the capacity, which it has by nature, of causing the intellect to assent evidently to some contingent truths about the object "because of its imperfection (because it is quite imperfect and obscure), or because of some impediments on the part of the object or because of other impediments." (= Boehner 1990, 24–5.)

74 *Sent.* I.27.3 (246), where the example is not that of misjudging a thing seen in a mirror as being behind the mirror but of misjudging trees seen from a moving boat as being in motion.

75 See Sec. I.2.

76 Boehner 1943, 285.

77 The question was first raised by Baudry 1958, 177, later by Scott 1969, and in the most searching manner, by Adams 1970.

78 Streveler 1975.

79 Boler 1973.

80 Adams 1987a, 594–601.

81 *Quodl.* V.4.

10 Ockham's Ethical Theory

William of Ockham presents his ethical theory not systematically but in remarks and discussions scattered throughout his writings, a fact that has obscured the structure of his views. He worked within a tradition of moral philosophy that took the basic normative principles to be given in the Bible and the conceptual tools of moral theory to be given by Aristotle; with these materials he put forward an original, powerful, and subtle theory. Ockham holds the rightness or wrongness of an act to depend not on any feature or characteristic of the act itself or its consequences but on the agent's intentions and character (elaborated in Ockham's theory of the will and of the virtues respectively). The goodness or badness of the agent's will, in turn, depends on its conformity to the dictates of right reason in the first stage and to God's will in the final stage.

I. THE NATURE OF MORALITY

Morality deals with human acts that are in our control – more exactly, with acts that are subject to the power of the will according to the natural dictate of reason and other circumstances.[1] The requirement that morality be a matter of reason and will rules out brute animals as moral agents[2] while allowing angels and humans to qualify. But before one attempts to spell out the respective contributions of reason and will to moral action, a fundamental question needs to be addressed, Is morality a rational enterprise in the first place? Are there moral truths, and if so, can we know them?

In *Quodl.* II.14 Ockham asks whether there can be demonstrative knowledge with respect to morality. He distinguishes two parts of ethical theory[3]: (1) positive moral knowledge, which "contains

227

human and divine laws that obligate one to pursue or to avoid things that are good or evil only because they are prohibited or commanded by a superior whose role it is to establish the laws," namely a superior such as a legislator or God; (2) nonpositive moral knowledge, which "directs human actions without any precept from a superior, as principles that are either known per se or by experience direct them." The former is like the knowledge jurists have with regard to human laws; it is regulated by logic and reason but is based on positive laws or commands that need not be evidently known. The latter, however, is a matter of principles that are evidently known and the conclusions that can be drawn from them and so can be formulated in demonstrative form. Hence, ethical theory is not only a matter of nonpositive morality (principles) but may take into account positive morality (authoritative commands) as well.

Positive morality, consisting of divine commands, can clearly provide substantive moral content to human action. Its knowability is a matter of God's informing us of his commands, which poses no theoretical problems. However, why following such commands should be a matter of morality is a question that needs to be addressed. We will take up Ockham's discussion of divine commands in Section VI.

Nonpositive morality consists of ethical principles that are either known per se or derived from experience. Now there seem to be two kinds of ethical principles knowable per se. On the one hand, some principles connect fundamental ethical notions at a high level of abstraction: everything right should be pursued and everything wrong should be avoided[4]; the will should conform itself to right reason[5]; anything dictated by right reason should be done.[6] These ethical principles connect the virtues by regulating permissible behavior.[7] On the other hand, some principles classify kinds of wrongful acts. In *Sent.* II.15 Ockham tells us that theft, adultery, murder, and the like are by definition not to be done: the very names do not pick out acts absolutely but connote that "the one performing such acts is obligated by divine precept to do the opposite."[8] Murder, for instance, is wrongful killing. Hence, principles such as "Murder is wrong" or "Theft is wrong" are knowable per se. Nonpositive morality, then, includes principles that are analytically true: one should do the right and avoid the wrong, not commit murder, and the like. But these principles, though discoverable by reason, do not tell us what the right is, or whether a given instance of killing is murder, and so do not provide us with any substantive moral content.

Nonpositive morality also includes ethical principles derived from experience – that is, particular propositions regarding what is to be done, which an agent devises on the basis of his particular experiences. These propositions may then be generalized into universal propositions; Ockham gives as a standard example: "An angry person should be calmed down with soothing words."[9] This is commonly called "prudence," although it is really nothing more than an application of reason to the situations in which the agent finds himself. Ockham holds that prudence is necessary for moral action,[10] although in itself it does not necessitate it; one can have prudence but not act morally.[11] In part this is a corollary of Ockham's claim that the will is naturally free and hence can diverge from the dictates of the intellect. But there is a deeper question here. What does human reason have to work on when it tries to cope with particular situations? For example, is there some objective rightness or wrongness that human reason can come to know in acts or types of acts?

II. THE MORAL NEUTRALITY OF ACTS

Ockham holds that all acts are morally neutral, neither good nor bad in themselves – except for the act of loving God above all else for his own sake (considered in Section III). He argues for this claim in *Quodl.* I.20 in two basic ways. First, one and the same act is good when combined with one intention and evil when combined with another. His typical example is of a person who sets off to church intending to praise and honor God but at some point continues his journey out of vainglory.[12] So too for the case of someone who hurls himself from a cliff intending to commit suicide but sincerely repents halfway down.[13] In each case the act – walking to church, falling to one's death – remains the same in respect of multiple acts of the will,[14] although it changes its moral quality: from good to evil in the former case, conversely in the latter case. Hence, "the act is neither morally good nor evil but neutral and indifferent"[15] and only called good or evil in virtue of the agent's intentions. Strictly speaking, only the agent's intentions are good or evil, although the acts corresponding to them may be extrinsically denominated as such. He summarizes the neutrality thesis sharply:

If you were to ask what the goodness or evilness of the act adds beyond the substance of the act that is called "good" or "evil" only by a certain extrinsic denomination, such as an act of the sensitive part and likewise an act of the will, I say that it adds nothing positive that is distinct from the act, whether absolute or relative, which has being in the act through any cause. Instead, the goodness is only a name or a connotative concept, principally signifying the act itself as neutral and connoting an act of the will that is perfectly virtuous and the right reason it is elicited in conformity with. Hence such an act is called "virtuous" by an extrinsic denomination.[16]

Therefore, acts have no intrinsic moral qualities at all.

Second, Ockham argues that the performance or nonperformance of the act does not affect moral evaluation – this is, in effect, an argument against moral luck. If each of two people wants to perform a virtuous deed and attempts to do so, and one succeeds while the other fails through no fault of his own, we still hold that they have equal moral goodness. To hold otherwise would be to allow luck to play a role in moral evaluation. Likewise, a person who would commit adultery given the opportunity is no less guilty than the one caught in the act.[17] Ockham's intuition here is that act-centered morality loses any counterfactual purchase on what might have been the case and so cannot separate moral from nonmoral factors. To allow for the possible and the might-have-been, something other than the actual deed has to enter into the determination of moral worth. Intentions need not be discharged for the agent to be praised or blamed, and hence they are able to provide a counterfactual foothold for moral assessment.

Ockham draws a further conclusion from his arguments, namely that there is no identifiable feature or set of features common to acts that correspond to good intentions or to bad intentions. That is, there is no type–type correspondence between acts and morally good or morally bad intentions. Consequently, there is no way to pick out morally permissible or impermissible acts as such without reference to the agent's intentions. This conclusion clashes with the contemporary consensus of Ockham's day on normative principles taken from the Bible, traditionally understood to be absolute prohibitions regarding the performance or nonperformance of specific acts: we are enjoined not to kill, not to bear false witness, and so on. (Some forbidden acts are arguably acts of the will, e.g., those involving covetousness, but as such they do not pose a problem for Ockham's view.) Ockham offers two replies to this line of criticism. On the one hand, the performance of the act may lead to further sinfulness by intensifying the (evil) intention, either in its own right or through enjoyment of the pleasure the performance of the act generates; on the other hand, acts and intentions are prohibited together in the Decalogue so that ordinary people do not mistakenly think that only the performance of the act is morally reprehensible.[18] The Biblical prohibitions are absolute, but they apply to intentions and not to acts.

Ockham's thesis that exterior acts are morally indifferent has other equally counterintuitive consequences, as he himself was aware. For example, it seems to countenance the literal truth of the claim that God wills evil: God wills us to give alms to the poor, an act that Jones performs out of vanity (say); Jones's act is evil, and so God wills something that is an evil – hence God wills evil.[19] After pointing out that one cannot conclude God is evil because he wills evil in this literal sense, Ockham is careful to say he has only been considering this view as one that might be held, whereas he himself rejects this manner of speech even if it is literally true.[20] What matters, Ockham tells us, is not that one performs just acts but that one does so justly.[21]

III. THE WILL

To the negative thesis that exterior acts are morally indifferent Ockham counterposes the positive thesis that acts of will are the bearers of moral worth. More exactly, he argues first that there must be some (interior) act "necessarily and intrinsically virtuous." His reasoning is as follows[22]: Take any interior act that is granted to be virtuous; it is either intrinsically virtuous or not. If it is, the conclusion is established. If it is not, then it is at best only contingently virtuous, that is, virtuous through its conformity with some other act. Consider the second act; is it intrinsically virtuous or not? If it is, the conclusion is established; if it is not, it must be contingently virtuous in virtue of its conformity to some third act, and so on to infinity. But there can not be an infinite regress here. Hence, at some point there must be an act virtuous in itself rather than by its contingent relation to another act. Therefore, some interior act is intrinsically virtuous.

Second, the interior act in question must be an act of the will[23]: only an agent's intentions are primarily praiseworthy or blameworthy, for these alone are clearly and immediately in the power of the will – and "it is a necessary condition for the goodness of an act that it be in the power of the will of the agent who has the act."[24] Other interior acts, such as passions or acts of the intellect, are produced by faculties only indirectly controlled by the will, whereas acts of will are directly in our control.

Third, the act of the will that is intrinsically virtuous is an act of loving God:

> I state that the act that is necessarily virtuous in the way described above is an act of the will, because the act in which God is loved above all else and for his own sake is an act of this kind; for this act is virtuous in such a way that it cannot be vicious, and this act cannot be caused by a created will without being virtuous – because on the one hand everyone, no matter where or when, is obligated to love God above all else, and consequently this act cannot be vicious; and, on the other hand, because this act is the first of all good acts.[25]

The act of loving God above all else for his own sake is good in itself and generates or tends to generate a virtuous habit in the agent's will (properly identified as the virtue). This act is good whenever it is elicited, and it is the intrinsic good on which the goodness of other acts depends, including the goodness of other acts of will. The proviso "whenever it is elicited" is meant to sidestep a logical puzzle, namely whether the act of loving God above all else for his own sake is virtuous in the circumstances where God commands that he not be loved. Ockham's response is to hold that in such circumstances the agent cannot in fact elicit the act of loving God above all else for his own sake, for to love God means to do as God commands, and hence not to love God, which is contradictory. Hence, the love of God above all else for his own sake cannot be elicited in this singular set of circumstances, although even here the agent can love God "with a simple and natural affection though not above all else."[26] The logical puzzle, in other words, has to do with the conditions of eliciting the act and not with the content of the act itself, which is not affected by its circumstances.

IV. THE STAGES OF MORAL ACTION

In *Connex.*, Ockham describes what he calls "five stages" for each moral virtue. His presentation is misleading on two counts. First, although the first four stages are sequential, the fifth is not clearly like the others. Second, the stages are as much about moral motivation and the agent's intentions as they are about the virtues and thereby address a wider variety of concerns than merely the theory of character (though they do that as well). The five stages – or at least the first four – explicate the nature of moral action.

The first stage, on which the next three are grounded, is described in detail as follows:

The first stage is when someone wills to perform just works in conformity with right reason, which dictates that such works ought to be done, in the appropriate circumstances, looking precisely to the work itself for the sake of the rightness of the work insofar as it is an end. For example, the intellect dictates that such a work should be done at such a place and at such a time, for the sake of the rightness of the work, or for the sake of peace or something of the sort, and the will elicits an act of willing such works in conformity with the dictate of the intellect.[27]

There is nothing peculiar to the virtues here; Ockham's mention of "just" works at the beginning is inessential – he could as easily have said "when someone wills to perform works in conformity," and so forth. What is most striking about the first stage is that it seems to characterize an agent who is doing what he can to act morally. Right reason dictates that a given work should be done; the circumstances are apt; the agent does the work because it is right (while remaining morally neutral in itself). Yet although it seems the very picture of Aristotelian morality, Ockham finds it incomplete.

The second stage adds one of the missing elements: it is the same as the first stage "along with the intention of not putting such things aside at all for anything that is against right reason; not even for death, if right reason were to dictate that such a work not be put aside for death."[28] The missing element is that morality should be an overriding concern of the agent – or at least a concern to the extent prescribed by right reason, itself a moral arbiter. The agent should not put aside moral reasons for immoral ones; one who does is not taking morality seriously. The very seriousness of morality is one of the key features that sets it apart from other legitimate but nonultimate concerns an agent may have in his life.

The third stage builds on the second stage, adding to it that the agent "wills to do such a work in the aforementioned circumstances precisely and solely because it has been so dictated by right reason."[29] That is, the agent should act from a purely moral motive. It is not enough merely to do the right thing, or even to hold to doing it in the face of other temptations. The right thing should be done for moral reasons – or, in Ockham's terminology, it should be done precisely because right reason dictates it should be done, no more and no less. Even if the agent has other motives for action, they should not be what move him to do what should be done. More exactly, it is better for an agent to be motivated only by a concern for acting rightly than for any other reason. Such an agent, it seems, acts from a purely moral motive.

When we come to the fourth stage, it is not clear whether any moral feature is added to the preceding three:

The fourth stage is when the agent wills to do such a work in line with all the aforementioned conditions and circumstances, and beyond this precisely for the love of God, e.g., because the intellect so dictates that such works should be done precisely for the love of God. And this stage alone is the true and perfect moral virtue of which the Saints speak.[30]

The intention to act out of the love of God does not move us out of the realm of moral virtue, not even to the theological virtues; Ockham allows that justice, for instance, may exist in a fourth-stage form that is recognizably higher and still a matter of morality rather than theology. Ockham offers three arguments to prove that fourth-stage action is properly moral[31]: (1) it is generated by and in turn is directive of moral actions; (2) the mere variation in the agent's end does not alter the action in question from moral to nonmoral; (3) the vice opposite to this virtue is moral vice strictly speaking, and so the action must be morally virtuous. Yet these essentially technical arguments let the larger question go begging, What moral features are missing from third-stage action that are provided in fourth-stage action?

No clue is forthcoming from the fifth and final stage. Whereas the first through fourth stages are hierarchically ordered, Ockham is explicit that the fifth stage can build on either the third or the fourth stage of action[32]: if one puts aside the end of the action, "which can come about indifferently for the sake of God, or rightness, or peace, or something of the sort," what is distinctive about fifth-stage action is that the agent acts in a way that far transcends the ordinary human condition, either by supererogation or heroic perseverance. The person who deliberately commits himself to the flames rather than perform an immoral act has done something the ordinary person probably could not nerve himself to do and deserves our respect and praise accordingly. But this will not help in understanding how fourth-stage action is a moral improvement over the third stage. To put the problem sharply, What moral feature does the love of God add to acting from purely moral motives?

V. GOD AND RIGHT REASON

Ockham returns to a slightly simplified version of his distinction among moral stages in *Dial*. I.vi.77,[33] where he contrasts only three possibilities: an action may be done for the sake of God, or because it is dictated by right reason, or for the sake of some useful or pleasurable good to be pursued. He raises the last possibility only to dismiss it as not a kind of moral motivation at all. Hence, we are left with the contrast between third-stage and fourth-stage action. Here Ockham tells us that actions performed for the sake of God are instances of perfect virtue, whereas actions performed because they are dictated by right reason are instances of true virtue, though imperfect with respect to actions performed for the sake of God. His example, framed in terms of the context in which he is discussing the veracity of witnesses, suggests an interpretation of the difference:

Wanting to tell the truth for the sake of God is much more perfect an action than wanting to tell the truth only because right reason dictates the truth should be told, even as God is more perfect than right reason, and so this truth is more imperfect than the other ... There were such moral virtues, some people think, in many pagans. For many of them tried to live and did live according to right reason.[34]

Ockham argues that even as God is more perfect than right reason, so too the truth told is more perfect from one of the devout than from an upright pagan. Now he cannot mean that the devout truthteller is more veracious than the pagan truthteller. Both, he admits, are telling truths; they are each virtuous. (It might be that the devout are less likely to lie, owing to their fear of divine retribution, than pagans are, but that is a different matter altogether.) Nor is there a difference in the result: God and right reason each prescribe telling the truth. Instead, the difference lies in where one puts one's trust for a source of truth – God or reason.

Reason is, first and foremost, an individual cognitive capacity, as sight is an individual perceptual capacity; when Ockham and others speak of "right" reason they mean an intellectual capacity that is not disordered. One of the signs that reason is functioning properly is its ability to recognize evident truths, including those discussed in Section II (e.g., "Murder is wrong"). Now it is by no means wrong to trust right reason. Yet our finite and limited cognitive capacities can take us only so far. Human reason does not tend to converge on nonevident truths (witness long-standing philosophical disagreements). Fortunately we are not limited to cognitive capacities; in good Franciscan fashion, Ockham holds that the will can reach beyond the intellect and even help to guide it. In more traditional terminology, faith can extend the grasp of reason.

Ockham holds it cannot be proved by natural reason that we require any "supernatural habit" (such as faith or charity) for our ultimate end; faith is not enjoined by reason,[35] though it may complement and extend it. Recall from Ockham's definition of the fourth stage of moral action that it builds on the third stage: the agent performs an action precisely because it is dictated by right reason and precisely for the love of God. That is, one expresses the love of God by acting in accordance with the dictates of right reason. The feature added in the fourth stage is to see moral action itself as expressing one's love of God. This deepens the ordinary notion of the moral but does not alter or replace it. Hence Ockham can maintain some pagan thinkers led lives of perfect moral rectitude and were deserving of final reward: "It is not impossible that God ordain that one who lives according to the right dictate of reason, in such a way that he believes only what he concludes through natural reason he ought to believe, be worthy of eternal life."[36] This is true even though there is an important sense in which the moral virtues of the pagan philosophers are systematically different from the moral virtues of Ockham and his contemporaries, the latter inspired as they are by faith.[37]

VI. SUBORDINATION OF THE WILL

The highest stage of moral behavior, then, is to act out of the love of God above all else for his own sake. What does this formula entail? How is moral action structured by this end? Ockham has already suggested the answer in the discussion of the logical puzzle presented at the end of Section III – "to love God above all else is this: to love whatever God wants to be loved."[38] Again, "anyone who rightly loves God loves all that God wants to be loved."[39] In short, the will binds itself to God by subordination. We love God above all else by wanting what God wants precisely for the reason that God wants it. For Ockham, then, the core of ethics is the love of God (the intrinsically good act), and the love of God is a matter of conforming one's own will to God's will.

In *Sent.* I.48, Ockham asks whether every created will is bound to conform itself to God's will. In the course of his answer he draws a series of distinctions to make precise the sense in which we subordinate our wills to God's will. The first and most important distinction is that one will can conform itself to another in three ways[40]: (1) to will what has been willed by another will; (2) to will what another will wills it to will; (3) to will something in a way similar to that in which another will wills it. Ockham puts the last of these aside and concentrates on the first two. The natural way of interpreting the phrase "loving what God wants to be loved" is in line with (1), where the agent adopts the will of another. Brown wants to make Smith happy; Jones, who wants to conform his will to Brown's, adopts the desire to make Smith happy. However, Ockham holds (2) to be the better interpretation, where the agent takes his will to be directed by the will of another and not merely to adopt whatever desires the other has.[41] Thus, the appropriate desires on the part of those conforming their will may differ systematically from one another, and any or all desires may differ from the will of the one to whom they conform their wills. For example, Brown may want to make Smith happy but wants Jones to do something that would make Smith sad (perhaps so that Smith can thereafter be made happy by contrast); Jones, in conforming his will to Brown's, should thereby want to make Smith sad rather than happy. Ockham elsewhere offers a pair of examples where (1) and (2) come apart[42]: God from eternity willed the death of Christ and yet wanted the Jews not to want Christ's death in the way they brought death upon him; God wills my father to die and yet wants me not to want my father's death. To love God above all else, then, involves willing what God wants one to will.

More precisely, Ockham argues in *Sent.* I.48 that any given created will is bound to will habitually and mediately what God wills it to will precisely because God wills it, thereby manifesting the love of God above all else for his own sake. Ockham unpacks this claim as follows:

And if the question were raised what the habit is that inclines one to will everything willed by God, it should be said that it is some such habit by which one's will is pleased by everything that pleases the divine will, and this should always exist in everyone having the use of reason after he achieves (or can achieve) a cognition of God. Yet this habit doesn't incline one immediately to everything willed by God. For it has to presuppose a cognition in which it is known that this is willed by God, and it inclines one to act through the mediation of this cognition.[43]

The will is not a blind faculty; it operates through the mediation of right reason, though it need not follow its dictates; the will is free. To act properly, therefore, an agent must try to be the sort of person who wills what God wants him to will precisely because he knows God wills him to will it.

This is, roughly, a general condition on rational action: to be habitually disposed to carry out God's will. When it comes to the actual cognition of God's will, Ockham points out that we are not bound to know everything willed by God, for this is simply impossible for our finite capacities. However, if we do know something is willed by God, then we are bound to conform our will to it; such is the case for particular precepts as well as general moral rules.[44] Ockham says the expected things about our epistemic responsibilities: the will can elicit a right act even with an error in the intellect, provided the error could not be overcome and the agent is in no way culpable,[45] for "a created will following reason that is erroneous through an invincible error is right."[46] If God wants us to act in a certain way, then he can make his will known to us, and we are bound to carry out his will, as described earlier in this section.

VII. DIVINE COMMANDS

God can issue commands that differ systematically from one agent to another,[47] but he cannot give anyone contradictory commands, nor can he will a contradiction.[48] Because the very notions of theft, murder, adultery, and the like involve the notion of someone performing an action who is under the obligation by divine command to the opposite, it follows that God cannot make such actions the objects of his commands, that is, God cannot make murder or theft right; he can, however, enjoin the acts commonly described by these names, for the acts in themselves are morally neutral.[49] Ockham offers a lively illustration: when God commanded the sons of Israel to despoil the Egyptians, this, it turns out, was not a case of theft at all; "it was a good thing rather than an evil."[50]

Given the moral neutrality of acts, it seems as though God could command any given act or type of act to be obligatory or prohibited, and indeed that his command would be constitutive of the rightness or wrongness of these acts. Yet the matter is not quite so straightforward. In *Sent.* I.46.1,[51] Ockham discusses the case in which Abraham is told he must sacrifice his son Isaac. He is reluctant simply to assert God's freedom to command anything; he recognizes God granted Abraham the power to sacrifice Isaac and gave him the command to do so but maintains God did not want to be a coparticipant in the sacrifice.[52] But why not? It would no more have been murder than despoiling the Egyptians was theft. Ockham even hints that the reason God did not permit the sacrifice to occur was that "God neither commands nor counsels sin."[53]

Now God devised humans in such a way that clear cases of murder, theft, and the like would appear to be such. (There may be difficult borderline cases.) Were God to command that some class of acts is obligatory or forbidden that appears to our faculties to be otherwise, then we should have been designed otherwise. This is, of course, compatible with God's informing us of special cases that might appear to be theft (despoiling the Egyptians) or murder (sacrificing Isaac) but in fact are not such. However, the tension between God's freedom to command and the apparently wrongful acts that are commanded is one of the most controverted points in scholarship on Ockham's ethics, and there is no consensus about his response to the difficulty or even whether he recognized a difficulty at all.

No matter how this issue is resolved, it is clear that Ockham's ethics ultimately rests on at least the possibility of different divine commands to different agents. Yet there is something that underlies all of their actions, namely their virtue.

VIII. THE VIRTUES

In *Sent.* III.11, Ockham asks where the virtues are located in human psychology: the intellect? the will? the passions? He offers a complex and subtle argument that advances the following theses[54]: First, we should postulate a habit in the sensitive appetite that inclines one to act – roughly, that we have or can develop patterns of emotional responses. Second, this habit is not, strictly speaking, a virtue, although it is often loosely called one. Third, for every such habit postulated in the sensitive appetite a corresponding habit should be postulated in the will. Fourth, this habit in the will is properly the virtue.

The will is a free potency and so of its nature is no more inclined to one alternative than to another in a choice situation. Yet after eliciting several acts of the same sort there does seem to be an effect on the will such that it is inclined (but not determined) to act in that way, or at least to act more easily in that way than in other ways. In fact, we experience this effect in ourselves. We can call it a "habit" and recognize it in other faculties as well; habits are a fundamental part of Ockham's philosophy of mind. Our ability to train our responses, emotional and otherwise, is also a phenomenon of habit.

Ockham's argument for the crucial fourth thesis presented earlier is short and to the point. The only thing that can properly be called a virtue is that whose act is strictly virtuous; but only the act of the will is virtuous; hence, virtue must be a habit of the will.[55] Now traditionally the virtues were taken to be patterns of emotional and motivational responses to situations. Those that were stable and abiding could be identified as character traits. Ockham rejects this traditional account and replaces it with the idea of an inclination to choose in certain ways. On his account, the virtues are much more closely linked with the will.

Ockham recognizes two kinds of virtues: theological and moral. The theological virtues are those of faith, hope, and charity; the moral virtues include justice, temperance, and fortitude. (Ockham does not treat prudence as a virtue.) He occasionally refers to other virtuous conditions, such as chastity and virginity, abstinence, and the like, but for the most part his discussion is only concerned with the specific virtues listed have. As noted in Section IV, each of the moral virtues may occur in various stages.

Ockham has an extensive discussion of the nature of the virtues and their interrelations in *Connex.*; most of the following discussion will be indebted to his analysis there. But before turning to it, we can summarize its main results by looking at Ockham's more compact discussion in *Sent.* III.12.[56] His conclusion can be summed up in a slogan: the moral virtues are connected dispositively but not formally. That is, no given moral virtue of its nature involves any other moral virtue; they are formally independent. They are of course each compatible with one another. Yet in addition to their formal independence and their actual compatibility, there is an important fact about the moral virtues: the possession of one may dispose their bearer to the possession of another (or all the others). They are connected "dispositively."

In *Connex.* Ockham again inquires into the connection of the virtues but this time in the context of the stages outlined in Section IV and adds a treatment of the theological virtues. His analysis defies summary. However, a statement of some of the main points can provide a feeling for the subtleties and nuance of which Ockham was capable.

Start with the moral virtues. Ockham holds that third-or fourth-stage moral virtues are such as to incline their possessor to engage in acts generative of other virtues. For instance, someone with third-stage justice would be so unwilling to perpetrate injustice or to see it done that he would at least begin to resist, even in the face of danger – which is to say, he would thereby make a start on the virtue of fortitude as well. An agent who merely had a second-stage moral virtue might or might not be so inclined; it would depend on the virtue and on the case. But first-stage moral virtue does not so incline its possessor for the agent would presumably be willing to abandon the moral pursuit for another concern (because the distinction between first- and second-stage moral virtue amounts to this).

Matters become more complex when we take the vices contrary to these moral virtues into account. Any given first- or second-stage moral virtue may coexist in an agent with the vice contrary to some other moral virtue. But this is not the case for third- and fourth-stage moral virtue, which, as just noted, tend to reinforce other moral virtues and thereby drive out the corresponding contrary vices. The only exceptions for the latter are instances of nonculpable ignorance; an agent may have fourth-stage justice, for example, and as the result of unavoidable ignorance commit an intemperate act.

The theological virtues do not admit of stages; they all express the agent's love of God by their very nature. They are formally independent of one another; as Ockham remarks in *Sent.* IV, God can make charity without faith or hope, at least by his absolute power.[57] Because the theological virtues usually occur together, though, it is clear they are mutually compatible.

Returning to the discussion in *Connex.*, Ockham notes that the theological virtues can be possessed without all the moral virtues, although they are directly incompatible with the moral vices. Clearly fourth-stage moral virtues require the theological virtues. But none of the preceding stages of moral virtue requires the theological virtues, and the first two stages of moral virtue are also compatible with the theological vices (contrary to the theological virtues). The third stage of moral virtue, however, is only compatible with a theological vice through some form of reasoning error.

IX. CONCLUSION

Ockham's scattered and fragmentary presentation of his ethical views belies the systematic rigor and unity they possess. His insistence on the moral centrality of the agent as well as the moral centrality of God gives shape to his distinctive and original claims regarding actions, the will, divine commands, and the virtues. Ockham's ethical theory, centered on the subordination of the human will, serves as a marked contrast to our modern insistence on the autonomy of the will as a fundamental ethical principle. It is a testament to Ockham's philosophical creativity that he could devise such a powerful and original theory – not to mention having done so within the traditional constraints of Biblical and Aristotelian morality. Ockham's theory deserves more attention than it has received.[58]

NOTES

1 *Quodl.* II.14.
2 *Sent.* III.11 (359–60).
3 *Quodl.* II.14.
4 Ibid.; *Connex.* 3.143.
5 *Quodl.* II.14.
6 *Sent.* III.12 (425); *Connex.* 3.144–5.
7 Ibid., 3.142–143.
8 *Sent.* II.15 (352).
9 *Connex.* 2.14–26.
10 Ibid., 3. 493–4.
11 Ibid., 3.521–2.
12 *Sent.* III.11 (360).
13 *Quodl.* I.20 (103).
14 *Sent.* III.11 (383).
15 Ibid. (384).
16 Ibid. (388–9).
17 *Quodl.* I.20 (103–4), following Augustine.
18 *Sent.* III.11 (375–6). See also *Quodl.* I.20 (104–5).
19 *Sent.* I.47 (681).
20 Ibid. (684).
21 Ibid. (683).
22 *Connex.* 1.99–130; *Quodl.* III.14.
23 *Connex.* 1.132–44; *Quodl.* III.14.
24 *Sent.* III.11 (389).
25 *Quodl.* III.14.
26 Ibid.
27 *Connex.* 2.116–23.
28 Ibid., 2.125–8.
29 Ibid., 2.132–6.
30 Ibid., 2.137–42.
31 Ibid., 2.143–51.
32 Ibid., 2.152–80.
33 *Dial.* I.vi.77 (Goldast 1614, 590).
34 Ibid.
35 *Sent.* III.9 (279).
36 Ibid. (280). See also *Sent.* I.17.1 (452–3).
37 *Sent.* IV.3–5 (58).
38 *Quodl.* III.14.
39 *Connex.* 3.416–7.
40 *Sent.* I.48 (687).
41 Ibid. (689–90).

42 *Act. virt.* (434.575–435.580).
43 *Sent.* I.48 (688).
44 Ibid. (689).
45 *Act. virt.* (423).
46 Ibid. (436).
47 *Sent.* I.47 (683).
48 *Sent.* II.15 (353).
49 Ibid. (352).
50 *Sent.* I.47 (685).
51 *Sent.* I.46.1.
52 Ibid.
53 Ibid.
54 *Sent.* III.11 (358). See also *Quodl.* II.16.
55 *Sent.* III.11 (366).
56 *Sent.* III.12 (424–5).
57 *Sent.* IV.3–5 (48). See also *Quodl.* III.9.
58 Recommended reading with this chapter: Adams 1986; Freppert 1988; Suk 1950; Urban 1973; Wood 1997.

11 Ockham on Will, Nature, and Morality

Among other things, Ockham is notorious for his doctrine of the liberty of indifference[1]: the notion that created willpower is power to will, to nill,[2] or to do nothing with respect to any object.[3] By contrast with his great medieval predecessors, many estimate, Ockham has staked out a position fraught with disadvantages. First, it cuts will off from nature. The liberty of indifference turns created wills into *neutral* potencies unshaped by natural inclinations.[4] Second, it "frees" will from reason's rule: no matter what reason dictates, created willpower can disobey.[5]

To some, such consequences have seemed momentous for ethics because they are inconsistent with a kind of naturalism. For example, Maurer writes that

the scholastics prior to Ockham looked upon goodness as a property of being. Saint Thomas, for example, speaks of goodness as the perfection of being that renders it desirable. Because God is all-perfect and supremely desirable, he is supremely good. A creature is good to the extent that it achieves the perfection demanded by its nature. Moral goodness consists in man's acting in accordance with his nature, with a view to attaining his final end (happiness), which is identical with the perfection of his being. For Saint Thomas, therefore, morality has a metaphysical foundation, and it links man with God, giving him a share in the divine goodness and perfection.

Ockham, on the other hand, severs the bond between metaphysics and ethics and bases morality not upon the perfection of human nature (whose reality he denies), nor upon the teleological relation between man and God, but upon man's obligation to follow the laws freely laid down for him by God.[6]

Likewise, Bourke sees Ockham as challenging the teleology of human nature – as rejecting eudaemonism (the notion that humans are

naturally ordered to the pursuit of personal well-being or happiness),
as well as denying that philosophy can prove "the finality" of human
nature (in particular, that God is its ultimate end).[7] Bourke infers
that Ockham cannot regard either the properties of moral goodness
or badness or moral laws as a function of natural human proprieties[8]
and concludes with Maurer that Ockham must embrace an authoritarian, divine-command theory of ethics. Because, for Ockham, the
divine will is unencumbered by obligations and free to will anything
that does not involve a contradiction, moral demands will be arbitrary and contingent, even changeable![9]

Nevertheless, caution is in order. However distinctive, Ockham's
theories of will and morality are developed within the broad outlines
of an Aristotelian theory of rational self-government, according to
which it belongs to the intellect to deliberate and legislate, whereas
implementation pertains to the will. Not only does Ockham subscribe to the truism that agents cannot will what they do not think
of,[10] he also upholds the Aristotelian doctrine that an agent's own
practical dictates are morally *normative* for willing,[11] that not only
right reason but erring conscience binds.[12] Likewise, Ockham retains
the distinction between nonpositive morality or ethics – which is
based on principles known per se or through experience quite apart
from the commands of any authority – and positive morality – which
pertains to human or divine laws having to do with matters that are
neither good nor bad except insofar as they are commanded or prohibited by the authority.[13]

In fact, more detailed examination of Ockham's writings shows
how he weaves a complex tapestry of continuity and innovation. Although his critics rightly suspect Ockham of significant departures
regarding relations between will and nature, they drastically overes-
timate the consequences for ethics.

I. NATURAL EXCELLENCE VERSUS
NATURAL TELEOLOGY?

I.I. Mapping the Issues

Where nature and goodness are concerned, Ockham is supposed to
have rejected a variety of theses his eminent predecessors held:

(T1) Good/'good' and being/'being' convert.

(T2) Natures form an excellence hierarchy descending under a maximum value.

(T3) Natures constitute norms for individuals of their kind.

(T4) Natures other than the divine have a teleological structure: (a) they aim at God as ultimate and external end and (b) at their own perfection as proximate and internal end.

These claims fit together easily in the thought of Anselm, who holds that to be is either to *be* Supreme Goodness or a way of striving towards it (hence [T1]). Supreme Goodness is the paradigm, created natures constituted as ways of imperfectly imitating it.[14] The Supreme Nature (= Supreme Goodness = Supreme Being = God) and created natures form a hierarchy of natural excellence, and each of the created natures is ranked lower or higher according to its degree of God-likeness (thus [T2]). Created natures have a double teleological structure. Most fundamentally, nature-constituting powers collectively aim at Supreme Goodness (their "ultimate" and "ecstatic" end); their unsuccessful effort to reach it attains a characteristic "proximate" or "internal" end, the *that-for-which-they-came-to-be* of that nature (that is, [T4]).[15] Thus, Beulah the cow's nature-constituting powers aim at being Supreme Goodness, but the most they can produce is the bovine imitation she is. Anselm takes a further step, reasoning that, because *each* nature-constituting power must be *telos*-promoting insofar as each contributes to the definition of the nature's internal end, each – taken singly – can aim only at some good. Because all creatures owe their being to the Supreme Nature (insofar as the Supreme Nature causes them to exist), all "owe" their being to the Supreme Nature (that is, they owe it to the Supreme Nature to be and to do that-for-which-they-came-to-be (and so [T3]). Thus, fire owes it to the Supreme Nature to heat nearby combustibles, earth to seek the center, and so on. Barring obstructions, nonrational natures fulfill such obligations by natural necessity. By contrast, rational creatures (angels and humans) should do so freely.

If Aquinas and Henry of Ghent share Anselm's notion that created natures are constituted by imitability relations, Duns Scotus rejects it. Scotus argues that relata are metaphysically and epistemologically prior to their relations. If creatable natures owe any being (real or intelligible) they have to God, their "contents" (nonrelational formal constitutive principles, e.g., rationality and animality in the case of human nature) and their possibility pertain to them of themselves.[16] Thus, for Scotus, the active and passive efficient causal tendencies constituting creatable natures do not, of themselves, have an ecstatic focus on God. Instead, they converge on because they define the "internal" end of the nature, which is the completion or perfection of the being they constitute.[17] Following Aristotle, Scotus conceives of natural powers and inclinations as deterministic in the sense that (a) given appropriate, obstacle-free circumstances, they necessarily act to their limit, and (b) given "Aristotelian optimism," obstacles are rare.

1.2. Embracing Natural Excellence

Contrary to his recent reputation, Ockham appropriates much of Scotus's metaphysical picture. In *Sent.* and *SL*, Ockham employs the notion of transcendental goodness (and thus endorses [T1])[18] and embraces the category of natural (as distinct from moral) goodness.[19] Further, Ockham takes hierarchies of natural excellence for granted: angels are better than humans, humans than donkeys[20]; the human intellectual is superior to the human sensory soul[21]; substances are more excellent than inherent accidents[22]; and within the same species, qualities of greater are better than those of lesser intensity.[23] In *Quodl.* I.1, he mounts an argument from a hierarchy of natural perfection or excellence to establish the existence but not (*pace* Scotus) the unity of God, where 'God' is understood to mean that than which nothing is better or more perfect.[24] That God alone is the highest good[25] and most worthy of honor[26] is given by faith. Moreover, Ockham assumes that the natural perfection of the divine essence as well as that of created substance and accident natures is prior in the order of explanation to, and furnishes reasons for, divine or created choice.[27] (Accordingly, Ockham's acceptance of [T2] is unproblematic.)

Like Scotus, Ockham denies that creatable natures are constituted by imitability relations. Although none could have any *being* apart from God, their constitutive contents are defined independently of God's essence as much as the divine will.[28] In his *Physics* commentaries, Ockham views "Aristotelian" natures as reified complex active and passive efficient causal powers, the coordinated operation of which converges on forms or functional states that constitute the substantial or accidental perfection of things of that kind. Because obstructions are rare, natural powers act deterministically, by natural necessity, to produce such agent perfection always or for the most part.[29] Such forms or functional states constitute norms relative to which particulars may be judged to be perfect or imperfect specimens (hence, [T3]). Likewise, although the unaided active powers of created rational agency are unable to reach it, the nature-constituting powers still make it the case that beatific vision and enjoyment of God would satisfy in the weak sense of putting the rational creature beyond any need or pain. Thus, Ockham's endorsement of (T1)–(T3) is unhesitating. It is with the meaning and truth of (T4) that he has difficulties.

1.3. Teleological Troubles

For Anselm, Goodness explains being. The Supreme Nature is too good not to be real.[30] Goodness explains creatable natures, too, insofar as they are metaphysically defined as ways of imitating it[31] and insofar as Goodness is the transcendent object of their constitutive powers. Likewise, especially in *Physics* II, Aristotle assigns a nature's proximate and internal end (the perfection-constituting forms or functional states) explanatory value, and numbers final along with material, formal, and efficient causes. Ockham finds such claims problematic.[32]

Once again, Ockham does not deny that efficient, causal nature-constituting powers act always or for the most part to produce forms or functional states that complete or perfect the being of things of that kind (compare [T3]).[33] Sometimes, Ockham is willing to speak of such states as the "end" the nature "intends" or "for the sake of which" it acts[34]; in *Quodl.* IV.1, he dismisses such talk as a category mistake.[35] Because he regards efficient causality as fundamental, Ockham can think of only one way for ends to have explanatory value – by helping to account for the motion of the efficient cause.[36] According to him, intelligent voluntary agency is the one clear case where this happens: when cognition and love of, or desire for, an end give the agent a *reason* and likewise function as *efficient partial causes* of the agent's efficaciously willing something else.[37] Here the explanatory link is forged by the intelligent voluntary agent's actually intending the end and efficaciously willing something for its sake. In *Expos. Phys.*[38] and *Phil. nat.*,[39] Ockham interprets Aristotle as beginning with paradigm-purposive agency (intelligent voluntary agency) and mounting an argument from analogy for teleology in nature. Ockham worries that this inference is undermined by a double disanalogy: that nature lacks cognition and so cannot act for a reason and that, although thought and love of an end "trigger" the efficacious willing of something else in voluntary agents, there is no comparable way for the not-yet-extant perfecting end products to "trigger" natural agents; moreover – because natural agents act always or for the most part by natural necessity – such triggers are superfluous.[40] Thus, in *Expos. Phys.*, Ockham concedes as "true but not evident"[41] what in *Quodl.* IV.1 he denies: that ends in nature add anything to the explanation over and above what efficient causal powers provide.

Such scruples explain why Ockham defines transcendental goodness not as "being considered as proper object of appetite" but as "being considered as willable[42] or lovable[43] or lovable according to right reason."[44] At best, Ockham treats natural teleology as a second-class citizen and 'appetite' as an analogical term. What remains uncontroversial is that natural goodness provides genuine (if often defeasible) *reason* for intelligent voluntary agents to love it and so is that upon which right reason bases its practical calculations.

Likewise, Ockham gives up the idea that goodness, by virtue of its very normative force, explains being. For what makes ends causally salient is their *actually* being so loved or desired that the efficient cause produces something for their sake. Because of the liberty of indifference, however, goodness is incidental to an object's filling that explanatory role. True, natural goodness supplies the agent with a *reason* to will it. But if the intelligent voluntary agent freely does not will in accordance with right reason or even wills against it, what *ought* to be the end may not be.[45] Nor does Ockham accept Anselm's notion that goodness explains being by virtue of being the object of nature-constituting powers. For Ockham, efficient causal powers are fundamental. Their being what they are comes first; their mutual coordination determines what completes or perfects things of their kind.

II. WILL AND NATURE

Ockham's vacillations about natural teleology prove his recent critics' hunch about another point: he does not begin with a generalized account of natural agency and subsume intelligent voluntary agency as a special case, nor does he treat will simply as a species of natural power driven by natural inclinations.

II.1. Anselm's Account – Beginning With Nature

By contrast, Anselm understands rational natures (angelic and human) within his comprehensive theory of natural goodness, teleology, and obligation. Reason is given for discerning relative goodness,[46] and will for loving in accord with correct excellence estimates – in particular for upholding justice for its own sake[47] and for loving God above all and for God's own sake and Elsewhere he says rational creatures were created for happy eternal intimacy with God,[48] an ecstatic goal for which we must strive with all our power but which we cannot reach without divine aid. As essential, the will and its freedom must be *telos*-promoting powers. Anselm concludes that freedom of the will cannot consist in a power for opposites – to sin or not to sin – because the former aims away from the agent's proximate and remote ends.[49] Rather it is the power to uphold justice for its own sake.[50]

Because rational creatures (angelic and human) are the crown of creation, Anselm's God wants them to be as God-like as possible: in particular, to imitate him in being just somehow of themselves. Divine self-determination requires no power for opposites in God because Anselm's God is and does whatever God is and does through Himself. God *is* Justice Itself, through Godself.[51] By contrast, Anselm reasons, because creatures get their natures from God, they are not self-determining with respect to whatever they do by natural necessity. To get spontaneity into rational creatures, Anselm concludes, God must build into them a power for opposites after all by endowing created wills with the affection for justice and the affection for advantage, which metaphysically define them as a power to aim at the Good in two ways: by willing the apparent maximum of the agent's advantage, or by willing the agent's advantage only to the extent that justice allows. For Anselm, no unmotivated willing is possible: agents can will less than their apparent maximum advantage only if considerations of justice appear to tell against it; conversely, they can will less-than-maximal justice only if considerations of advantage seem to oppose it.[52] These twin affections will not suffice to put Anselmian

created rational agents in a position to be self-determining with respect to preserving justice for its own sake, if they have full relevant
information. For if they know God will punish sin, they recognize
they have nothing to gain by willing more advantage than justice
permits, and so they will only what justice permits by natural necessity. Further, such knowledge would make it impossible for them
to will justice *precisely* for its own sake or to choose it in preference
to their own apparent advantage.[53] Anselm concludes that God will
have to withhold full knowledge, if he is to give rational creatures
the opportunity to transcend concern for their own advantage, to be
just *somehow of themselves*.

Notice, although Anselmian agents can will things only under the
aspect of good, their spontaneity is not restricted to choice of means
or proximate ends. Rather Anselm's God has the project of giving rational creatures the opportunity to be self-determining with respect
to willing their ultimate end. That is, they are able to choose whether
to preserve the orientation to justice with which they were created or
to desert justice in favor of greater apparent advantage. Notice, too,
how Anselm's understanding of the relation between reason and will
in rational creatures makes it impossible for fully informed agents
to have the relevant power for opposites apart from some measure of
ignorance.

II.2. Duns Scotus's Dichotomizing – Natural Versus Voluntary Agency

Although willpower is essential to, and so constitutive of, intelligent or rational agency (divine, angelic, human), Scotus contends,
it is contrary both to experience and to the systematic demands of
ethics and religion to style willpower as such a deterministic *natural*
power. For voluntary action (inaction) is supposed to be *imputable* to
the agent for praise or blame, reward or punishment, which would be
inappropriate unless it were within the agent's power to act or not.
Moreover, morality and virtue require that an agent reach beyond its
own (individual or species) perfection, to love goods for their own
intrinsic worth quite apart from whether they are (really or apparently) good for the agent or its kind. Likewise, merit involves the
agent in loving God above all and for God's own sake.[54]

Thus, Scotus understands willpower, first of all, to be a self-determining power for opposites (both of contradiction and contrariety).[55] As such it possesses a "superabundant sufficiency" insofar as it is not exhaustively constituted by any tendency or tendencies toward object(s); rather over and above the latter, there is power to act or not with respect to its object(s) and to act in contrary ways.[56] Scotus concludes that because will alone possesses "superabundant sufficiency," it is the only rational power (in Aristotle's *Metaphysics* IX sense).[57]

Reworking Anselm's doctrine of the dual affections, Scotus sees the affection for advantage as analogous to the natural inclinations of nonrational natures because it tends towards objects insofar as they contribute to the agent's own (individual or species) completion or perfection.[58] If willpower were constituted by the affection for advantage alone, it would lack the ecstatic reach required for moral virtue or merit, which Scotus takes to be the glory of created rational agency.[59] Concluding that capacity for such must be essential, Scotus declares the affection for justice as well as the affection for advantage to be native and inalienable.[60] Although conceptually distinct and logically independent, the "superabundant sufficiency" and the affection for justice go together when considered teleologically. If imputability is in service of morals and merit, then a self-determining power for opposites would be otiose without the affection for justice that makes self-transcendent aim possible.[61] Conversely, as Anselm argued, if the point of an affection for justice is to enable the agent, not simply to act justly, but to *be* just, to have justice *imputed* to it, then it would be incongruous to have the affection for justice without the "superabundant sufficiency" as well.[62] Thus, when in different passages Scotus identifies the will's freedom with one apart from mentioning the other, this is against the background understanding that each brings the other in its wake.

Interestingly, although for Scotus willpower is not exhausted by object tendencies (insofar as it includes "superabundant sufficiency") and its object tendencies transgress the aim of "Aristotelian" natural powers at the agent's own (individual or species) perfection, the Subtle Doctor retains the notion that at the most generic level the proper object of willing is good and that of nilling evil or bad. Thus, humans can will or not will but cannot nill happiness, can nill or not nill but cannot will misery.[63]

II.3. *Ockham's Irony – Beginning with Morals*

Methodologically, Ockham takes his cue from Scotus, insisting that the philosophical portrait of willpower must reflect our experience of self-determination and be drawn from moral and religious requirements for imputability. Ockham's doctrine of self-determining liberty of indifference is part of his answer to these empirical and systematic demands. Thus, from Ockham's point of view, his recent critics have it backwards. They think his rejection of natural teleology and refusal to cast will as a natural power jeopardize ethics. But he reasons that morals force us with Scotus to see voluntary and natural as fundamentally disjoint types of agency – so much so, Ockham thinks, as to place natural teleology in doubt[64]!

Moral evaluation targets intelligent voluntary agency. Ockham declares that no act can be morally virtuous unless it is done with knowledge and freedom.[65]

II.3.1. REASON'S ROLE True to his Aristotelian inspiration, Ockham consistently presents will as rational appetite in multiple equivocal senses. First, and most obviously, no one can will or nill what he or she never actually thinks of.[66] Second, the agent's own intellectual noncomplex and complex cognitions normally are efficient partial causes of the will's acts[67]; and were God to suspend that causal connection, the resultant action or inaction would not qualify as morally appraisable.[68] Third, the agent's own practical reason enjoys a *normative* function as rightful regulator of the agent's will. Agents are bound to make their own practical calculations (neither mindless nor slavish actions are candidates for virtue) and to do so correctly insofar as they are able.[69] If incorrigible ignorance excuses, conquerable ignorance places the agent in a double-bind: to conform is wrong because the dictated course is contrary to right reason, to disobey wrong because it shows contempt for conscience[70] inasmuch as the agent does not actually know it to be erroneous.[71]

Nevertheless, Ockham denies that any deliverance of reason *determines* the will's action (inaction), for the principal systematic reason that then the will's action (inaction) would not be within the agent's power and so would not be imputable.[72] Scotus had already challenged Giles of Rome and Godfrey of Fontaines precisely on this ground – the determination of the will by the intellect would turn the former into a passive rather than an active power; for Scotus, no matter what reason dictates, the will retains power to act or not. This is not enough control for Ockham, who insists that *experience* shows that "no matter how much reason dictates something, the will still has power to will or not to will or to nill it."[73] Moreover, systematic considerations require it: the power of inaction contrary to reason opens the possibility of sins of omission, but created will power must extend further to sins of commission![74] In the same vein, Ockham finds it counterintuitive to explain sins of incontinence and malice in terms of ignorance; rather they are instances of action against full knowledge.[75]

II.3.2. FREEDOM AMIDST INCLINATIONS As to freedom, Ockham focuses on what Scotus calls "superabundant sufficiency," remodeling Scotus's characterization of the self-determining power for opposites into his own doctrine of the liberty of indifference. Given the required cognition of the object and divine will to concur with the will in its action or inaction, "the will can by its liberty – apart from any other determination by act or habit – elicit or not elicit that act or its opposite."[76] That is, it can will it or not, and it can nill it or not. Nevertheless, Ockham does not use this definition to empty willpower of any and all object tendencies. Contrary to what recent critics suggest, Ockham recognizes that many inclinations pertain to the human will in and of itself – for example, the Anselmian inclinations for advantage and for justice and against disadvantage and injustice[77]; inclinations to will (nill) things that produce sensory pleasure (harm, sorrow, anger, fear, etc.), which function as efficient partial causes to make certain acts difficult or easy,[78] not to mention acquired habits that may function as efficient partial causes to make certain actions barely resistible.[79] But he denies that any inclination is *natural*, either in the sense of defining the will's scope or in the sense of causally determining its actions. Where others (including Anselm, Aquinas, and even Scotus) allow the will's object tendencies to define the proper object of willing as good and of nilling as bad or evil, Ockham lets the will's self-determining power plus the agent's intellectual capacities define the will's scope. For the nondefectible power of an omnipotent and omniscient God, the non-complex object of willing is being-in-general, and the complex object is whatever does not involve a contradiction.[80] For created wills, the scope of each willing and nilling is delineated by what the agent's intellect can conceive of. Moreover, no matter how strong (Ockham admits the inclination to accommodate the senses is very powerful), none causally determines the will's choice.[81] In these twin senses, willpower is a *neutral* potency.[82]

II.3.3. CAUSALLY DETERMINED WILLING AND NILLING? Ockham reasons that, because the will's inclinations are not natural in the strict sense of Aristotle's *Physics*, motion contrary to them does not count as "violent,"[83] nor can the will be coerced in the strict sense of being forced to act contrary to its natural inclinations.[84] Nevertheless, in sponsoring the liberty of indifference, Ockham does not mean to imply that willpower is not the kind of thing whose acts can be causally determined. If voluntary and natural are fundamentally different forms of agency, the More than Subtle Doctor finds counterexamples to Scotus's claim that it is impossible for the *same* power to produce some effects by natural necessity and others by free choice.[85] The divine will necessarily wills the procession of the Holy Spirit and freely and contingently wills to produce creatures.[86] Moreover, if neither the intellectual apprehensions, the will's inclinations or habits, nor their combination can determine the will, the will's own acts in the form of efficacious generic volitions can combine with beliefs and virtuous habits, or the native inclination, to will objects whose sensory apprehension is pleasure-producing to determine its later acts.[87] For example, the efficacious generic volition to do whatever right reason dictates, or to eat all available sweets, combines with the belief that right reason dictates this, or that this food is sweet, to determine a volition to do this act commanded by right reason, or a volition to consume this particular sweet. Moreover, created acts of will can be necessitated or prevented because divine omnipotence can act alone to produce any created act, and God can obstruct any created act by withdrawing divine concurrence.[88] Ockham suggests that God used the latter tack to keep the Blessed Virgin Mary from sins of commission,[89] whereas God suspends the efficient causal agency of the created will in the blessed and acts as the total efficient cause of their acts of beatific love and enjoyment.[90] No necessitated acts of will are within the created agent's power; thus, none is imputable, virtuous or vicious, worthy of merit or demerit. But acts of will necessitated by the agent's own generic volitions are *indirectly* within the agent's power insofar as the agent can revoke or sustain the generic volition.

II.3.4. STARTLING SCOPE Ockham's recent critics begin with the view that human nature has a natural inclination towards happiness, indeed towards God as its ultimate end, and that the will as a nature-constituting power aims at goodness as its proper object. Because such inclinations define human nature and willpower, respectively, these critics conclude it would be impossible for the will to nill the good-in-general, the agent's own happiness, or God. As we have seen, Ockham believes ethics requires us to reject these critics' premises, to deny the created will any *natural* inclinations, and to match the will's to the intellect's scope. He contends further that a consideration of Aristotelian rational self-government forces us to contradict their conclusion, to affirm that *humans can nill so-called "ultimate" goods.*

On the Aristotelian model, rational agency includes cognitive power to calculate what ought to be done and willpower to implement it. Where nonpositive morality is concerned, the agent's own right reason is the primary norm. But suitably informed right reason will derive divine commands as a secondary norm via the argument "God is the highest good; the highest good ought to be loved above all and for its own sake; therefore, God ought to be loved above all and for God's own sake; therefore one ought to will whatever God wills one to will and nill whatever God wills one to nill."[91] Thus, the proper function of rational agency requires the following:

(T5) Will *can* conform to its norms – can will (nill) whatever (a) right reason[92] or (b) God dictates to be willed (nilled), respectively.[93]

Rational agency deliberates by weighing up goods and evils and their consequences.[94] Ockham concludes the relevance of such deliberative function presupposes the following:

(T6) Will can will (nill) the consequences of what it wills (nills).[95]

All agree that the point of moral science generally and prudence specifically is to put the agent in a position to refuse what is disadvantageous or unjust, to pursue what contributes to justice or the perfection of the agent's own nature. Surely, then, in well-made rational agency, the following obtains:

(T7) Will can nill what reason judges cannot satisfy.[96]

On the other hand, Ockham maintains, *experience* shows created rational agency to be "defectible" or "divertible." Everyone admits our cognitive powers are fallible in such a way that the following can be asserted:

(T8) Created reason can make false judgments about what is good, bad or evil and to what degree.

And Ockham believes experience shows what systematic considerations demand[97]:

(T9) Will can fail to conform to its norms.[98]

According to Ockham, (T7)–(T8) by themselves show "ultimate" goods can be nilled, and (T7) shows the possibility of nilling the good-in-general because the good-in-general would not satisfy – only particular goods would.[99] Likewise, he claims, we can nill each particular good (perhaps because by [T8] we could believe of each that it would not satisfy); by universal generalization, he infers, we could nill the good-in-general. In addition, (T7)–(T8) combine with the obvious possibility that one could believe happiness impossible (say, if one rejected post mortem survival and found ante mortem existence unsatisfying) to entail the possibility of nilling happiness.[100] Likewise, Ockham points out, (T7)[101] combines with the belief that God does (will eternally to) punish the agent, to yield the conclusion that *God can be nilled under the aspect of disadvantage, even by someone who has a clear vision of the divine essence!*[102]

A further argument that we can nill happiness is supplied by (T6). For experience shows that believers as well as unbelievers in post mortem existence commit suicide, or voluntarily expose themselves to death, or both. But if we can nill existence, it follows by (T6) that we can nill happiness, which logically and metaphysically presupposes existence.[103]

For good measure, Ockham expands his premise set to include (what we may style) "the Indifference Principle":

(T10) Whatever the will can will for (a) one time,[104] (b) one individual of a given species,[105] or (c) in relation to one practical dictate,[106] it can will for or in relation to any and all other(s).

Ockham expresses his understanding of the omnipotent scope of divine will as follows:

(T11) God can will whatever does not involve a contradiction.

Moreover, Ockham advances further, perhaps more controversial arguments for his scope claims. Thus, Ockham's disputed belief that each particular good can be nilled – whether supported via experience, by (T7) and instances of (T8) (for each particular good, the belief that it is unsatisfying), and alternatively by (T9) – yields, by universal generalization, the conclusion that we can nill the whole category of good-in-general.[107] Likewise, (T5) combines with the fact that both right reason and God can will that a person forever lack happiness (an instantiation of [T11]), to yield the conclusion that he or she can nill it.[108] Again, using his controversial tenet that people commit mortal sin with eyes fully open as to its consequences, Ockham infers by (T6) that we can nill both happiness in general and happiness in particular.[109] Similarly, experience shows that we can will unhappiness for others; by (T10), it follows that we can nill it for ourselves as well.[110] Again, Ockham reasons, it follows from (T5b) and a distinctive instance of (T11) – that God can command us to hate God[111] or forbid us to love God[112] – that we can nill God. Of course, (T9) interpreted via (T10) suffices by itself to yield the scope claims. Note that, except for arguments involving (T9) and (T10c), Ockham's claims here about what can be nilled do not essentially depend upon disputing conventional action-theory wisdom that something can be nilled only under a bad or evil aspect.

Everyone agrees that evils are often willed because they appear somehow good. Those who make good the proper object of willing maintain this is the only possible way of willing evils. In Ockham's estimation, this action-theory "axiom" undermines ethics and religion because imputability presupposes our ability to will evil under the aspect of evil. Arguing this time from the category of merit,

Ockham declares that "according to commonly ordained divine laws, the will of a person in this life cannot earn merit in connection with anything unless it can earn demerit with respect to the same thing."[113] But if the will could not wittingly will what right reason dictates to be evil – for example, the worship of false gods – it could not sin by a sin of commission. Consequently, it could not earn merit by refusing, for example, to worship false gods or willing to worship the true one.[114] Moreover, all such options must be *witting*. To get full credit (blame) for an action, it is not enough (*pace* Scotus) to have the option of witting action versus witting inaction; one must be able wittingly to perform the opposite action as well!

To the statement in *Ethics* III[115] that "Every evil [person] is ignorant," Ockham replies that this is not because it is metaphysically impossible to act contrary to the judgment of reason but because the wicked miss out on the practical wisdom they would acquire by acting well.[116] Indeed, he declares, on one and the same occasion, the will can act in accord with some dictates of right reason while wittingly acting contrary to others.[117] Appropriately enough, Ockham affirms that such action contrary to the dictates of right reason would be *irrational*: Anselm's "affection for advantage" and "affection for justice" define the scope, not of what is willable or nillable, but what can be elicited *according* to *the dictates of reason*.[118] Likewise, Ockham numbers 'Whatever is honorable ought to be done/made/produced,' 'Whatever is just ought to be done,' 'Whatever is good ought to be loved,' 'Whatever is dictated by right reason ought to be done,' 'Whatever is pleasing to God ought to be done,' 'No one ought to be led to do something contrary to the precepts of his or her God,' among self-evident truths.[119] Ignorance of them could never explain or excuse anyone's action contrary to norms. Thus, Ockham uses words that startle his opponents – that we can will evil under the aspect of evil – to express a ready consequence of liberty of indifference: that we can will evil wittingly!

Liberty of indifference reaches further, however, to imply not only that we can will evil under the aspect of evil but that we can will things *for evil's sake*! Ockham repeatedly explains that for agent *a* to make *E* an end, properly speaking, is for *a* to will or nill *E* and because of that love or hatred for *E* efficaciously to will or nill something else. For *E* to be one's end is for love or hatred of *E* to be both one's reason and also an efficient partial cause of one's efficaciously

willing something else.[120] Liberty of indifference implies we could
have such love for evil-in-general, or such hatred for goodness-in-
general, right reason, or God, as to adopt these as our reason and have
them as efficient partial causes of our efficaciously willing something
else.

Although Ockham himself does not spell out the derivations, such
claims follow from some of his action-theory assumptions. Thus, he
could with equal ease or difficulty infer our ability to will evil-in-
general from our capacity to will each particular evil just as he can
conclude our ability to nill good-in-general from our power to nill
each particular good. The same style of argument could (via [T10c])
be deployed to prove our ability to hate right reason. We have already noted Ockham's claim in Sent. IV.16 that we can hate God
because (T5b) the will can conform itself to divine commands, and
God can command it.[121] In Quodl. III.14, Ockham observes that if
God were to command us not to love him, we would not be able to
love God above all and for God's own sake. For the latter involves
a generalized commitment to obey all God's commands,[122] and in
this case one of these commands forbids love of him.[123] Presumably, he would have by the same token to acknowledge that divine
commands to hate God in this generalized way (hatred of God that
involves commitment to disobey all relevant divine commands) are
self-referential in such a way as to make generalized hatred of God
impossible. For if we disobeyed all God's commands, we would obey
that command; and if we obeyed it, we would disobey it. Yet, if such
reflections make divine commands to hate God counterexamples to
(T5b) and so undermine Ockham's argument that we can hate God,
they do not show that generalized hatred of God is impossible for us
but only that "generalized hatred of God when generalized hatred of
God is commanded" is. For proof that generalized hatred of God is
possible for us, Ockham might fall back on his argument that God
can appear under the aspect of disadvantage or on (T9), his doctrine
of the liberty of indifference.

In Connex., Ockham takes some of these results for granted. If
loving God above all and for God's own sake is intrinsically virtuous,
Ockham claims it is intrinsically vicious to will to pray for the sake
of vainglory and because it is contrary to God's precept and contrary
to right reason.[124] Later, he assesses the compatibility with acquired
habitual virtue of acts of willing to do unjust works because they

are dishonorable and contrary to right reason.[125] Still further on, he makes it criterial for mortal sin that the agent do something that God does not will (refrains from doing what God does will) *because* God prohibits (commands) it.[126] Once again, Ockham does not count such willings and nillings as *violent* motion because he denies the will any *natural* inclination to act for the sake of the good, of right reason, or for God's sake!

III. DIVINE LIBERTY OF INDIFFERENCE

Ockham's recent critics charge that his doubts about natural teleology deprive morals of their metaphysical foundation and thereby abolish the category of nonpositive morality, leaving only an authoritarian base. They also fear that his portrait of willpower as neutral potency so cuts off will from nature, from natural inclinations to goodness and perfection, as to make it arbitrary in a pejorative sense. The consequences are unsalutary enough when focused on the human will alone. Applying Ockham's doctrine of liberty of indifference to the divine will conjures for them the specter of the reckless divine commander who might enjoin anything at all! Once again, these impressions must be sorted into insights and confusions.

III.1. *Divine Will and Nature*

Ockham affirms that God is a being who acts by intellect and will. Because the divine intellect is omniscient and infallible, the scope of divine will cannot be restricted by lack of conceptual imagination. Because the divine will is of all wills the most excellent, nothing essential to willpower itself would keep any being from falling within its scope. Ockham concludes that the scope of nondefectible divine willpower is equivalent to omnipotence itself: being, or whatever does not involve a contradiction![127]

Ockham is on conventional ground in maintaining that, because of divine simplicity, the act that constitutes divine willing or nilling as well as divine understanding is identical with the divine essence and so exists by natural necessity and eternally. Thus, in God's case there is no question of anything's being an *efficient* cause of (the thing that is) a divine act of willing or nilling or understanding, and so on. What requires explanation is the intentionality of that act.

Just as in the case of creatures, one and the same act can be an act of willing one object and nilling another, willing one for its own sake and willing another only for the sake of something else, so also, and all the more so, with the divine will.

Recent critics are simply wrong to say that Ockham cuts off the divine will from nature. In agreement with many, but contrary to Scotus, Ockham maintains the divine will acts in relation to some objects by natural necessity (in particular, God loves Godself, the Father begets the Son, and the Holy Spirit proceeds from the Father and the Son by natural necessity) but with respect to others (the actual existence and disposition of creatures) freely and contingently.[128] For God as for creatures, natural excellence furnishes reasons for loving. Ockham merely joins theological consensus in asserting that only infinite divine goodness constitutes a *decisive* reason to love it; the finite natural goodness of creatable natures is too slight by itself to constitute a nondefeasible reason for God to create or benefit them.

Nevertheless, many of Ockham's predecessors thought God's love of infinite divine natural goodness and truth to himself could combine with considerations of what is suitable for created natures individually or collectively to generate decisive reasons for God to treat such creatures one way rather than another. For example, Anselm analyzes divine policies towards creation in terms of the integration of justice and mercy.[129] Aquinas sees divine goodness as guaranteeing God will order whatever creatures he makes into the best collective God-likeness they can show,[130] one in which a variety if not all degrees of being will be represented[131] but in which the good of particulars may be sacrificed to the good of the whole.[132] Conceiving of God as the most well organized of lovers, by nature consistent of purpose, Scotus infers that divine election of the soul of Christ (an incomplete substance) requires the follow-through intention to create the rest of the hylomorphic composite along with a material world to sustain it. Such ideas are in the background when Albert the Great contrasts absolute divine power (divine power considered in abstraction from other divine attributes) with God's ordered power, the scope of which is constricted by his goodness.[133] By contrast, Ockham envisions no such scope-contraction and reduces the distinction between God's absolute and ordered power to a contrast between what he could do and what he actually does.[134]

Thus, relatively speaking, Ockham does loosen the grip of creatable natural excellence on the divine will when he denies such considerations of natural suitability as decisive for divine policy. If the finite goodness of a created nature does not constitute a *decisive* reason for God to love it enough to create it, the fact that certain conditions are required for its finite flourishing does not combine with divine self-love to generate an overriding reason to situate the nature in advantageous circumstances either. The same goes for creatures collectively. For because an actual infinity of simultaneously existing real things is metaphysically impossible,[135] any collection of creatures would still have only finite goodness and be capable of at most finite excellence. Thus, if nature does not so much oblige as necessitate divine self-love, the ontological "size-gap" between God and created natures is so great that nature cannot oblige God to love or benefit created natures individually or collectively.

If divine natural excellence and created natural proprieties are not enough to obligate God to creatures, can God bind himself to creatures by the laws he establishes? Objectors in *Sent.* IV.3–5 suggest he does: "God is a debtor Who owes rewards for merits"[136] and likewise punishment for guilt.[137] The wording of Ockham's replies suggests that after all he agrees: "God is a debtor to none *unless He so ordained it*,"[138] and "punishment is owed because God has ordained it."[139] In fact, however, the immediate context of both passages explains away this obligation language as follows: because the laws God freely and contingently lays down governing salvation simply express his *actual* policies, he will reward and punish the acts and conditions that thereby qualify. But God had no obligation to adopt those or any policies.

Ockham troubles himself to spell out the ways in which nature does not constrain God to will good in relation to creatures. Once again, God cannot will badly or maliciously because willing badly or maliciously is a matter of willing contrary to one's own obligations, whereas God is a debtor to no one and so has no obligations.[140] Nevertheless, Ockham declares several times, both in earlier and later works, that literally, so far as logic is concerned, 'God wills bad or evil' should turn out true because 'bad' or 'evil' is a connotative term signifying things that are contrary to someone's obligations, and God is an efficient partial cause of any absolute things signified by those terms. Because saints and authorities conflate 'God wills badly or maliciously' with 'God wills bad or evil,' the latter has come to *sound* bad. Consequently, Ockham agrees to the more explicit formulation 'God wills what is in fact bad or evil.'[141]

Further, although he does not put it this way, Ockham allows that God can will what is *bad* for creatures. Like everyone else, Ockham agrees that created rational powers exercised under optimal conditions will not suffice with general concurrence alone to bring the rational creature to beatific vision and enjoyment. These require a further assertion of divine willpower, which, Ockham claims, is free to frustrate rational creatures' pursuit of their ends, whether of happiness or uprightness. God could accomplish the former by inverse matching of eternal rewards and punishment with virtuous and vicious ante mortem careers. Even if such a divine policy, misery for the good and happiness for the wicked, were revealed, there would still be room for heroic human dignity that pursues loyalty to right reason, God, or both, at the expense of their own advantage. But as we have seen, Ockham's God could also thwart such attempted sacrificial loyalty to himself by commanding rational creatures not to love[142] or commanding them to hate Him.[143] This external circumstance would put rational creatures in the bind of not being able to conform to their norms (contrary to [T5b]).

III.2. *The Wreckage of Morality?*

Ockham's recent critics are mistaken to suppose that liberty of indifference simply collapses nonpositive into positive morality. On the contrary, Ockham accepts an Aristotelian model of rational self-government in which considerations of natural excellence undergird right reasons that are normative for action. Thus, for Ockham, ethics is not authoritarian the way the category of merit is. If no creature is intrinsically worthy of being loved by God enough to be created, a fortiori, nothing a rational creature could do or be would make it intrinsically worthy of eternal beatific intimacy and enjoyment of God. It is entirely a matter of free and contingent divine volition whether or not there are any regulations according to which a creature qualifies, and of what sort.

Nevertheless, Ockham's moral theory does inherit difficulties kindred to those confronting authoritarian divine command theories. For right reason infers from divine natural excellence that God ought to be loved above all and for God's own sake; suitably informed right reason, that divine commands are a secondary ethical norm. But according to Ockham, divine liberty of indifference means God could forbid us to love or even command us to hate him.[144] Likewise, God could command the opposite of what right reason dictates, whether in general or in particular. Given such divine precepts, right reason would enjoin contradictory dictates. And this would mean the breakdown of Ockham's ideal of the moral life as one in which at the highest degrees of virtue agents freely commit themselves to do whatever right reason dictates for right reason's sake or whatever God commands for God's sake, or both, and do so to a heroic degree at the cost of advantage or life. Ockham's doctrine of divine liberty of indifference makes such a breakdown logically possible.

In accepting this logical possibility, Ockham insists on the controversial assumption that it is enough for the coherence of moral theory if the two criteria for morally virtuous action, right reason and divine precepts, *in fact* yield extensionally equivalent results. God actually commands rational creatures to follow the dictates of right reason and in fact rewards adherence to right reason and sacramental participation with eternal life. The two norms could break apart but they do not and will not!

III.3. *Self-Transcendent Aseity*

Persistent is the worry that liberty of indifference is power to act outside the bounds of reason. Why does Ockham want to allow that reasons underdetermine divine action in creation, that creatures can act contrary to the dictates of right reason, indeed even make rebellion against reason's norms their aim? How can the capacity for arbitrary and perverse action be an excellence in the best of agents? The heart of Ockham's answer, I believe, is that the liberty of indifference is a necessary condition of self-transcendent aseity.

Willing without a reason or contrary to reason when good and sufficient reasons are available is often subject to moral censure. But where creatures are concerned, Ockham's God is never in this position. Nor is to will or nill without decisive reasons the same as to act for no reasons at all. If chocolate and raspberry are equally delicious, or I like them equally well, or both, my choice of chocolate when chocolate and raspberry are available has my love of chocolate as its reason just as opting for raspberry would have love of raspberry as its reason. Thus, Ockham maintains, divine creation and government must choose among nondecisive reasons because it is metaphysically impossible for created nature to constitute any other kind. At the same time, God's choice among nondecisive reasons to will something besides his own infinite goodness, to create and to benefit something else, is an act of divine self-transcendence, a manifestation of divine "liberality," "sheer grace."[145]

Similarly, as Anselm and Scotus insist, the dignity of rational creatures, the crown of moral life, lies in their capacity for self-determined commitment to something else – to right reason, or to God loved above all and for his own sake, or to both, even to a heroic degree at the cost of life and happiness.[146] Following Aristotle, like Aquinas, but contrary to Anselm, Ockham believes "ignorance diminishes the voluntary" so significantly that God could not create the opportunity for such self-determination by withholding relevant information. Ockham seizes the alternative action-theory option, rejected by Anselm, of assigning will the power to act wittingly contrary to the dictates of reason, to do so not only in selecting means but more importantly in pledging allegiance to an end.

Like Anselm, Ockham sees the capacity for self-determination as opening the way for greater God-likeness, but his emphasis is different. Ockham's God and rational creatures both choose whether to act for the reasons available to them: the divine will for nondecisive reasons and rational creatures for decisive reasons to commit themselves to right reason, or to infinite goodness, or both – to will whatever right reason dictates, or whatever God commands, or both. Thus, for Ockham, the liberty of indifference allows God and rational creatures to be assimilated in performing mirroring acts of self-transcendent love.

NOTES

1 *Sent.* I.1.6 (501–2).
2 To nill that *p* is to will that not-*p*.
3 *Sent.* IV.16 (359); *Expos. Phys.* II.8.1 (319–20).
4 *Sent.* III.6 (174–6); *Quodl.* IV.1 (300).
5 *Quodl.* I.16.
6 Maurer 1962, 285–6.

7 Bourke 1968, 104–5, 122.

8 Ibid., 104, 123.

9 Maurer 1962, 286–7; Bourke 1968, 106–7.

10 *Sent.* III.11 (364); *Act. virt.* (425); *Quodl.* III.20.

11 *Act. virt.* (409, 411).

12 Ibid. (429–30, 411).

13 *Quodl.* II.14.

14 *Monologion* 4 (Sch., I.16–8), 31 (Sch., I.47, 49).

15 Ibid., 68–9 (Sch., I.78–79); *De veritate* 3 (Sch., I.180–2).

16 Scotus, *Ordinatio* I.35.5, §§30–2 (Scotus 1950-, VI.258–9), I.43.7, §§14–8 (Scotus 1950-, VI.358–61). See Adams 1987a, 1075–6; Adams 1989.

17 Scotus, *Ordinatio* IV.suppl. 49.9–10 (Scotus 1986, 184–6), III.17 (Scotus 1986, 180).

18 *Sent.* I.Prol.2 (114–5), III.7 (215–6); *SL* I.11.

19 Ibid., III-3.6 (610).

20 *Quodl.* II.13 (168).

21 *Sent.* II.20 (442).

22 *Sent.* I.17.1 (450–1).

23 *Quodl.* II.13 (168).

24 *Quodl.* I.1 (1–3).

25 Ibid. (3); *Quodl.* VII.15 (761).

26 *Sent.* I.Prol.12 (365).

27 See *Sent.* I.10.2 (341), where the natural perfection of the divine essence explains God's willing Godself necessarily. Also ibid., I.44 – "Could God make a *better* world than this world?" – where an excellence hierarchy among creatable substance and accident natures is presupposed for divine choice to create.

28 This is documented in detail in Adams 1989.

29 *Expos. Phys.* II.12.4–6.

30 This is the point of his so-called "ontological" arguments in *Proslogion* 2–3 (Sch., I.101–3).

31 *Monologion* 4 (Sch., I.16–18), 31 (Sch., I.47, 49).

32 For a more detailed discussion of this issue, see Adams 1998.

33 *Expos. Phys.* II.12.11–12, 13.1 (395); *Quodl.* IV.2 (302, 307).

34 *De fine* (99–100, 103–4, 106); *Expos. Phys.* II.12.11–12, 16; *Quodl.* II.2.

35 *Quodl.* IV.1 (297, 299–300).

36 *Sent.* I.Prol.11 (305).

37 *De fine* (107–9, 113–4, 120–4, 143–54); *Sent.* I.Prol.11 (306); *Phil. nat.* II.4, 6.

38 *Expos. Phys.* II.12.6, 18. See *Brev. Phys.* II.6.

39 *Phil. nat.* II.6.

40 *Expos. Phys.* II.12.6, 11–12; ibid., 13.1.

41 Ibid., II.12.11–12, II.13.7.

42 *Sent.* I.Prol.2 (114–15).

43 *Sent.* III.7 (215–16).

44 *SL* I.11 (38).

45 *Sent.* I.Prol.11 (305–6, 308); *Phil. nat.* II.4, 6; *Expos. Phys.* II.12.18; *Quodl.* IV.1 (298).

46 *Monologion* 68 (Sch. I.78–9); *De veritate* 3 (Sch. I.180); *Cur deus homo* II.1 (Sch. II.97).

47 *Monologion* 68 (Sch. I.78–9); *De veritate* 4 (Sch. I.181).

48 *Monologion* 74 (Sch. I.83); *Proslogion* 1 (Sch. I.98, 100); *Cur deus homo* II.1 (Sch. II.97–8).

49 *De libertate arbitrii* 1 (Sch. I.207–8).

50 Ibid., 1 (Sch. I.211), 3 (Sch. I.212); *De concordia* I.6 (Sch. II.257).

51 *Monologion* 1 (Sch. I.15), 3 (Sch. I.16), 6 (Sch. I.20), 16 (Sch. I.30).

52 *De casu diaboli* 12–14 (Sch. I.254–9).

53 Ibid., 21–4 (Sch. I.268–72).

54 Wolter 1972 and 1990a; Scotus 1986, 3–29 (abbreviated in Wolter 1990b, 181–206); Boler 1990 and 1993; Adams 1995a.

55 The will is "lord of its act" (Scotus, *Ordinatio* III.17 [Scotus 1986, 182], compare IV.29 [Scotus 1986, 176]). See also Scotus 1975, 390 (§17.8), 406–7 (§§18.24–25).

56 Scotus, *Quaestiones in Metaphysicam* IX.15 (Scotus 1986, 152, 194).

57 Ibid., (Scotus 1986, 157); Scotus, *Ordinatio* III.suppl. 3; (Scotus 1986, 331, 333).

58 Ibid., suppl. 26 (Scotus 1986, 178), III.17 (Scotus 1986, 180).

59 Ibid., suppl. 26 (Scotus 1986, 178).

60 Ibid., III.17 (Scotus 1986, 180, 182).

61 I owe this point to Jeffrey Hause, who offered the teleological angle in discussions of my spring 1996 seminar on John Duns Scotus at Yale University.

62 Adams 1995a.

63 Scotus, *Ordinatio* IV. suppl. 49 (Scotus 1986, 193). Compare Scotus 1975, 374–5 (§§16.19–20).

64 See Sec. I.3

65 *Connex.* 3.499–501.

66 *Sent.* III.11 (364); *Act. virt.* (425); *Quodl.* III.20.

67 *Sent.* IV.3–4 (50); *Expos. Phys.* II.5.7; *Connex.* 3.510–18; *Act. virt.* (447).

68 *Act. virt.* (416, 418).

69 Ibid. (409, 411).

70 Ibid. (429 – 30).

71 Ibid. (411).

72 *Connex.* 3.521–48.

73 *Quodl.* I.16.
74 *Act. virt.* (443).
75 *Connex.* 3.597–612.
76 *Sent.* IV.16 (359). See *Expos. Phys.* II.8.1 (319–20).
77 *Sent.* I.1.6 (502).
78 *Act. virt.* (446–7).
79 *Sent.* III.7 (209–10).
80 *Quodl.* II.9 (154–5).
81 *Sent.* I.1.2 (399).
82 *Sent.* III.6 (174–6). Compare *Quodl.* IV.1 (300).
83 *Sent.* I.1.3 (410), II.15 (351), IV.16 (353).
84 *Sent.* II.15 (351, 355). Compare Aquinas, *ST* I.82.1 resp., who defines "coercion" the same way.
85 *Sent.* I.1.6 (490–1). See *Sent.* I.10.10 (333–5, 340–1); *Qq. Phys.* 127.
86 *Sent.* I.1.6 (490).
87 *Sent.* III.7 (210–11). See *De fine* (126, 133, 134–5).
88 *Sent.* III.7 (205–6).
89 *Sent.* III.5 (153).
90 *Sent.* II.15 (355–6).
91 Adams 1986.
92 *Sent.* I.1.6 (503), IV.16 (350).
93 *Sent.* I.1.4 (443). See *Sent.* I.48 (686–90).
94 Ockham discusses deliberation at length in *De fine* (143–51).
95 *Sent.* I.1.6 (504). See *Sent.* IV.16 (350).
96 *Sent.* I.1.6 (503).
97 See Sec. II.3.1.
98 *Sent.* I.1.6 (350–1)
99 *Sent.* IV.16 (351).
100 *Sent.* I.1.6 (503).
101 Perhaps better, (T7)–(T8) because the agent's belief about God's punishing policies may or may not be true.
102 *Sent.* I.1.6 (505–6).
103 Ibid. (504). Abbreviated in *Sent.* IV.16 (350).
104 *Sent.* I.1.6 (505).
105 *Sent.* IV.16 (351).
106 Ibid. (350–1).
107 Ibid. (351).
108 *Sent.* I.1.6 (504–5).
109 Ibid. (504).
110 *Sent.* IV.16 (351).
111 Ibid. (352).

112 See *Quodl.* III.14, where Ockham has an objector raise this possibility as a counterexample to Ockham's claim that the act of loving God above all and for God's own sake is necessarily virtuous. Despite waffling with 'if' and 'it seems,' Ockham on balance allows the possibility of such a command.

113 *Act. virt.* (443).

114 Ibid. (442–3).

115 Aristotle, *Nicomachean Ethics* III.1.1110^{b}28.

116 *Sent.* IV.16 (354, 357–8).

117 *Circa virtutes et vitia* (285).

118 *Sent.* I.1.6 (502).

119 *Connex.* 3.143–5, 562–3, 583–4.

120 *Sent.* I.1.1 (375). See *Sent.* I.Prol.11 (306); *De fine* (103–7, 120–43); *Phil. nat.* II.4, 6; *Quodl.* IV.1 (293).

121 *Sent.* IV.16 (352). See n. 111.

122 See *Connex.* 3.416–7.

123 *Quodl.* III.14.

124 *Connex.* 2.204–5.

125 Ibid., 3.250–2.

126 Ibid., 4.336–9.

127 For Ockham's understanding of omnipotence, see Adams 1987a, 1151–231.

128 *Sent.* I.1.6 (490).

129 *Proslogion* 9–11 (Sch., I.106–10); *Cur deus homo*, passim (Sch. II.37–133).

130 *ST* I.25.5 resp., I.25.6 ad 3.

131 *ST* I.23.5 ad 3, I.22.4 resp.

132 *ST* I.22.2 ad 2.

133 For an extensive discussion of medieval ways of distinguishing absolute from ordered divine power, see Desharnais 1966. See also Adams 1987a, 1186–207.

134 Roughly speaking. See Adams 1987a, 1186–207.

135 *Quodl.* III.1 (204). Compare ibid. (201); *Qq. Phys.* 136.

136 *Sent.* IV.3–5 (45).

137 Ibid. (53).

138 Ibid. (45).

139 Ibid. (55).

140 In *Sent.* II.15 (342), Ockham remarks, "everything that does not include a contradiction or an evil of guilt can be done by God alone," but quickly goes on to rule out the latter disjunct: "Now God is not bound or obligated to anyone like a debtor, and therefore he cannot do what he ought

not to do, or not do what he ought to do" (ibid., (343)), and so is not strictly speaking morally good or evil (bad) because "moral goodness or badness connotes that the agent is obliged to that act or its opposite" (ibid., (353)). Likewise in *Sent.* II.3–4 (59). Compare *Sent.* IV.3–4 (55); *Connex.* 4.320–5; *Quodl.* III.4.

141 See *Sent.* I.47 (682–5), where Ockham explains the view that 'God wills evil' is true literally as what "some" would say and only *"recitative,"* and at the end locates the grounds for his hesitation to endorse the view in what the saints say. See *SL* III-4.6 (773–4); *Quodl.* III.2.

142 *Quodl.* III.14.

143 *Sent.* II.15 (348, 352–3).

144 See Secs. II.3.4 and III.1.

145 *Sent.* IV.3–5 (55). See *Sent.* I.17.1 (455, 463–4), I.17.2 (470).

146 This is explicit in the way Ockham distinguishes the highest degrees (third, fourth, some versions of fifth) of virtue from others in terms of a generalized commitment to a transcendent end – right reason, God, or both. See *Connex.* 2.111–67.

12 Natural Law and Moral Omnipotence

What follows is as much reconstruction provoked by Ockham as a study of Ockham. My main aim is to provide a framework to accommodate various things Ockham said but did not put together as neatly as we might wish.[1]

What provokes this project is the apparent tension between obedience to divine will, which figures so prominently in Ockham's academic writings, and the nonsacral reasonableness so prominent in his political works. Granted, both divine command ethics and a demonstrative science of morals are found in the academic writings, and extensive references to God's will as well as astute Aristotelian political analysis are found in the political works. Ockham did not abandon God's will in favor of philosophical reason when he abandoned John XXII for the protection of Ludwig of Bavaria. Yet there is, I believe, something to the impression that Ockham, especially the earlier Ockham, held God's will to be a uniquely supreme, comprehensive, unrestricted moral principle, and also something to the impression that the later, political Ockham was distinctive in arguing for a secular political order operating according to a rationally ascertainable natural law but lacking any inherent religious orientation. At any rate, such impressions set the problem I want to grapple with in this chapter.[2]

The problem is to understand how something like the following propositions go together (grounds for ascribing them to Ockham will emerge as we proceed):

P1 Correct ethical and social norms can often be determined by purely rational means, without reference to God's will.

P2 All and only valid norms are divine commands. (Obedience to God is in some way a comprehensive or uniquely basic practical principle.)

P3 God can command virtually anything.

The difficulty P2 poses for P1 concerns the rationality of ethics or natural law. It is sometimes held that for Ockham natural law is simply a product of divine will, that our actions are morally neutral apart from God's command.[3] The difficulty P3 poses for P1 concerns the stability of natural law. If God can command anything, what is divinely commanded on Thursday may be divinely forbidden on Saturday. A natural law based on divine commands emanating from "Ockham's God" would thus seem to be less stable than one grounded in the enduring natures of things or in the nature or character of the divine in other theologies. If P2 makes morality authoritarian, P3 threatens to make it capriciously authoritarian.

I. NATURAL LAW AS TACIT DIVINE COMMAND

My reconstructive strategy for putting P1 and P2 together begins by distinguishing two possible moral frameworks, which I call "Moral Naturalism" and "Natural Law." Moral Naturalism is the framework of someone who

MN1 appreciates the intrinsic value of such things as justice, gratitude, marital fidelity, science, and pleasure but

MN2 has no beliefs about God.

That Ockham accepted the intrinsic value of pleasure and of moral and intellectual virtues is evident from his approval of Aristotle's claim that we would choose honor, pleasure, understanding, and the virtues for their own sake, even if nothing further came of them.[4] That Ockham would call Moral Naturalism a *moral* framework, despite the moral naturalist's ignorance of God, is suggested by his contention that it is not necessarily morally bad to act for the sake of goods less than the highest possible good. An act is inordinate, however, when something that should not be loved as supremely good *is* loved as supremely good.[5] For Ockham, Moral Naturalism would have been the position of pagan philosophers. In contrast with some earlier Christian thinkers, Ockham believed the philosophers could attain genuine moral virtue, including rejection of idolatry and respect for the inherent value of rationality, although not any certain positive knowledge of God.[6] They would be aware of some intrinsic goods or reasons for action, and they would have everything needed for an objective ethic, a science of morals.

Natural Law I construe as a specifically religious moral framework of a peculiar kind. It is the moral framework of someone who

NL1 appreciates the same intrinsic values as the moral naturalist, but

NL2 recognizes an additional intrinsic value: loving God above all and for God's own sake – *praeter omnia* and *propter se* (call this the value of godliness) – but beyond this believes about God only that

NL3 God's free action is a causally necessary condition for anything that exists other than God.

What is peculiar about this conception of natural law is that it both brings God into the moral picture and yet stipulates an artificially limited set of beliefs about God. Historically, those who hold there is such a value as loving God *praeter omnia* and *propter se* and who believe God's free causality is required for everything else in the universe typically believe a good many other things about God, including things about God's will for human beings. It might be better to say natural law in the present sense *would be* the moral framework of someone for whom NL1–3 obtained, if such a person existed. My aim in putting other beliefs about God to one side is to show as clearly as possible the congruence in content of a large area of secular and religious morality in an Ockhamist perspective while preserving as sharply as possible their difference of essential form.

I suppose agents operating in these two frameworks would perform the same actions, materially speaking (or, in Ockham's terms, as to anything "absolute" in their actions). Even their reasons for action would coincide, as far as the moral naturalist's reasons went. The difference is that moral naturalists, having no beliefs about God, do not regard their moral principles as having to do with God, and hence they cannot regard them as principles of natural law in my sense of the term.

How do NL2 and NL3 affect actions performed on the basis of NL1? I want to argue that operating by natural law in my sense involves regarding God as the decisive determiner of all one's reasons for action. The problem is to understand how God determines reasons for action in such a way that we maintain a general coincidence in content between natural law and moral naturalism and also preserve whatever is authentic in religion's claim to represent a unique and supreme moral value. This is a problem of maintaining the distinctness of godliness from other goods, and even the supremacy of godliness in comparison with the other goods, while finding a systematic connection between them. If this is to be done under Ockham's aegis, it seems natural law must be interpreted as a kind of divine command but one whose content necessarily corresponds to the dictates of rational morality, even though, as a command, it is determined solely by God.

Here is another statement of the problem, in Ockham's own terms. In *Connex.*, Ockham distinguishes degrees or grades of moral virtue. One grade (the third among five Ockham recognizes) is found when someone wills to do something that accords with right reason and, besides this, "wills the performance of such a work ... precisely and solely because it is dictated by right reason." The next highest grade (fourth among Ockham's five) is when someone "wills ... according to all the conditions and circumstances discussed above [in preceding grades] and beyond this wills that work precisely on account of love of God – because, for example, the intellect has dictated that such works should be performed precisely for the sake of love of God."[7] The question is whether the transition from Grade 3 to Grade 4 moral virtue is in some sense natural. For Ockham, does the understanding *always* tell us that something dictated by right reason should *also* be done for the love of God? Can the dictates of right reason or natural law reasonably be regarded as divine commands?

Partly on the basis of a text I will cite,[8] but mainly as a friendly supplement to what Ockham says, I suggest natural law can indeed be understood as divine command, but as *tacit* divine command. The form or structure as well as the basic motive of a Natural Law moral framework thus understood is properly religious, the basic principle being godliness. But its content needs to be derived by purely natural or rational means. For this suggestion to work, we need a plausible concept of tacit command. If we can understand what is involved in one person's tacitly commanding another to do something, we may be able to understand rational morality as in some cases a response to God's will.

With a bow to a Gricean account of speech acts,[9] I propose the following rough analysis.[10] *A* tacitly commands *B* to do *X* (in preference to *Y*) if and only if

TC1 *A* brings it about that there is reason for *B* to do *X* rather than *Y*.

TC2 *A* also brings it about that *B* is in a position to see there is reason for her to do *X* rather than *Y*.

TC3 *A* could have brought it about that TC1–2 did not obtain.

TC4 *B* is aware that TC1–3 do obtain.

TC5 *A* does not *directly* (or conventionally) command *B* to do *X*.

TC6 *A* does not *directly* command *B* to do *Y*.

The idea is to treat our having reason to do one thing rather than another as the token of a speech act, if it is plausible to regard that fact as produced by the intentional action of a "speaker." At one point in his political writings, Ockham gives two arguments for extending the concept of divine law to cover all natural law. One is that God is the creator or author of nature.[11] I offer the concept of tacit command as a way of spelling out how God writes to us in nature.

The point of conditions TC1–6 will become clear as we see how they are met when *A* is God and *B* is someone who accepts the premises of my Natural Law framework – someone who believes in God's goodness and power but has no further morally relevant religious knowledge or beliefs. According to NL3, God's action is causally necessary for anything that exists other than God. If this is true, TC1–3 are satisfied whenever *B* can see there is reason for her to do something. That is, if there is reason for *B* to do *X*, then it is true that God brings it about that there is reason for *B* to do *X*, and if *B* can see there is reason for her to do *X*, then it is true that God brings it about that she can see there is reason for her to do *X*. Condition TC3 stipulates that *A* must have been able to bring it about that TC1–2 did not obtain. (A speech act or its vehicle or token must normally be in the speaker's power to produce or not produce at will.) This condition is met by the assumption in NL3 that God is a freely acting cause. Now for a command to be effectively given, the intended recipient must *recognize* the command. There must be uptake. This is the point of TC4. Condition TC4 will be met if *B*, instead of being a moral naturalist, accepts the basic framework of NL1–3. Or at least TC4 can readily be satisfied if *B* herself places the reasons she has for doing *X* and her awareness of those reasons among the facts ascribed to God's causality in NL3. Finally, in order that a command be merely tacit, what it prescribes must not be directly or conventionally commanded (TC5), and for it to be in force it must not be *cancelled* by a contrary order (TC6). Conditions TC5–6 are satisfied by the stipulation that *B* has no beliefs about God beyond NL2–3. She has no relevant direct divine commands or prohibitions to consider.

Because the value of acting to conform with another person's will can be realized whenever that will is known, it follows on the preceding analysis that acting rationally will be a way of achieving the supreme value of godliness for anyone operating in the framework NL1–3. A connection is established between God's will and the norms of moral naturalism via the causal relation traditionally held to obtain between God and the world. There is no need to define specifically religious values in terms of an external, nonreligious conception of holiness, as Kant tried to do, but neither is there need to regard other values as inapprehensible apart from religion, the position frequently but falsely ascribed to Ockham. Insofar as the connection between religion and morality suggested here is in Ockham's spirit, we may conclude that, contrary to objections sometimes raised against it, Ockham's emphasis on obedience to God as a basic practical principle allows due weight to the essential rationality of natural law. The detailed theory of rationality need not be religious, but its practice, in this framework, is a sacred activity.

If P1–2 are thus consistent with one another and an Ockhamist conception of natural law can claim to be fully rational, what about the relation of P1 to P3, the nub of the charge that Ockham deprives natural law of stability by allowing that God can command virtually anything? On the preceding analysis God could indeed change our obligations under natural law but only by creating a world with different laws of nature in the physicist's or biologist's sense. The virtue of temperance, for example, would have no place in a world where rational creatures had no physical desires or in one where our appetites were wholly unaffected by habituation. But there is no loss of *moral* stability in such scenarios. Similarly, improved knowledge of the world God actually has made, including improved knowledge of our own nature, could change our conception of what is dictated by natural law, and hence by God. But in this situation, instability, if we call it that, would be a virtue – moral enlightenment or, in religious terms, clearer discernment of God's will.

Like Augustine, Aquinas, and all other pre-Enlightenment Christian theologians, however, Ockham held that God could change our reasons for action in another way – not by changing the laws of nature or our knowledge of the natural world but by directly ordering us to do things we would otherwise have no reason to do. In my terminology, God could issue *direct* commands – which brings us to Section II.

II. DIRECT DIVINE COMMANDS: GOD'S MORAL OMNIPOTENCE

The most straightforward examples Ockham cites of direct divine commands are land grants recorded in Scripture. Ockham holds that no divine grants of particular territories to particular individuals or groups are presently in force, but in his political writings he repeatedly refers to such grants in the Old Testament precisely to highlight his contention that there is nothing like them in the New Testament or any later revelation.[12] Other examples Ockham considers of direct divine commands will be discussed in this section.

What is the scope of such direct divine commands? As is well known, Ockham's position concerning limits on God's *power* is that the only limit is the law of noncontradiction. God can do anything it does not involve a contradiction for God to do.[13] For Ockham are there any further limits to what God can *will* or *command*? I argue that in substance there are not. God can command virtually anything.[14]

If God cannot do anything it would be contradictory for God to do, does it follow that God cannot command someone else to do something involving a contradiction? Ockham's discussions of the possibility of a divine command to hate God suggest that God could issue a command it would be impossible to obey. Ockham holds at one point that God could command someone to hate him and that the individual could *conform* to the command,[15] but elsewhere he asserts that love and hatred of God are incompatible.[16] So, as he concludes in still another passage, although it seems God can without contradiction command someone to hate him, such a command could not be *obeyed*. "For ... by the very fact that it elicited such an act it [the will] would love God above all things and, as a result, would fulfill the divine precept ... and by the very fact that it loved in this way it would fail to fulfill the divine precept in this particular case. As a result, by loving in this way [the will] would both love and not love God."[17] God presumably cannot wish for the impossible (as we ourselves do so often). This would imply that God cannot will the *fulfillment* of an impossible command,[18] but as far as Ockham's general principle is concerned, God could wish us to *attempt* the impossible and hence order us to do so. According to Saint Paul,[19] God keeps faith and does not permit us to be tested beyond our powers, but for Ockham this seems to be a matter of divine choice, not a limitation on divine moral power.

Does God's *goodness* limit the things God can command? Ockham holds that God is "supremely good" and "a cause of every good." "Properly speaking, God does not *have* justice. Properly speaking, the highest nature *is* justice." "From the fact that God does something it is done justly." "God cannot will evil." Even the act of hating God, if it is caused in a creature solely by God, "will always be for a good end."[20] Such statements provide backing for Ockham's assertions that it seems "self-evident" that one should never act against God's command and that "from the very fact that the divine will wills something right reason dictates that it should be willed."[21] None of this entails, however, that there are any physically or psychologically performable acts God cannot command. God's goodness does entail that God cannot will badly (*male*). In this sense God cannot will evil (*malum*),[22] but Ockham is clear in holding that the same act may be evil when caused by a created will but good when willed by God. In discussing sin, for example, he argues that

if we speak of a sin of commission, ... the efficient cause of that act is not solely the created will, but God himself, who is as much the immediate cause of every act as any second cause. ...Someone might say that then God would sin by causing such a deformed act, just as a created will sins by causing such an act. My reply is that God is a debtor to no one, and therefore he is not obligated to cause either that act or the opposite act; nor is he obligated not to cause that act. Therefore, however much he might cause that act, God does not sin. But the created will is obligated by divine precept not to cause that act, and consequently it sins by causing that act because it does what it ought not to do. Hence, if the created will were not obligated not to cause that act or its opposite, however much it caused that act, it would not sin, just as God does not sin.[23]

But if right reason dictates that we should will what God wills us to will, and if God's lack of indebtedness is transferable by divine command, then God's goodness does not seem to foreclose the possibility of God's commanding any conceivable action.[24]

Is God's lack of indebtedness transferable by divine command, or does the *rationality of natural law* place limits on what God can command or the actions we might be obliged to perform in obedience to God? Ockham's distinction between the third and fourth grades of moral virtue may suggest that the independent rationality of an action is a precondition for its being motivated by love of God, for virtuous action for God's sake presupposes that the conditions for virtuous action at the level of rationality for its own sake have been met. As stated earlier, there is Grade 3 moral virtue when someone wills to do something that accords with right reason and, besides this, wills to do it "precisely because it is dictated by right reason." There is Grade 4 virtue when someone "wills ... *according to all the conditions and circumstances discussed above* [in preceding grades] and beyond this wills that work precisely on account of love of God."[25] Is Ockham saying an act must independently accord with right reason before it can be done from love of God? This would mean that all religious morality is the morality of natural law in the sense discussed in Section I, or at least that religious obligations cannot legitimately conflict with natural law. One could still imagine God's issuing commands contrary to reason, but, as with hating God, such commands would be impossible to obey.

Ockham's treatment of theft, adultery, and fornication indicates this would be a misreading. He cites Aristotle and the saints to the effect that such actions are inherently bad[26] but argues that their badness depends on our being obligated not to perform them. Anything "absolute" in such an action could be done well, not badly, in response to a divine command, in which case the action would not count as theft or adultery.[27] I take Ockham to mean here that the same physical acts that would count as theft or adultery in the absence of a divine command to perform them would not count as theft or adultery when performed in obedience to divine command. The moral seems to be not that God can command the irrational but rather that what would *otherwise* be irrational or wrong would not be irrational or wrong if done in obedience to divine command.[28] There is a sense, then, in which God cannot command anyone to commit adultery – because, if God commanded a person to have intercourse with someone else's spouse, it would not *be* adulterous.[29]

In terms of Ockham's grades of moral virtue, then, the presence or absence of divine commands is something for an agent to consider at Grade 3. It is always rational to obey a divine command, Ockham holds. Thus, an agent who both does what right reason dictates, simply and precisely because right reason dictates it, and recognizes a divine command will obey the divine command on the ground that it is rational to do so, even if recognition of the command depends on faith or revelation. Ockham discusses something like this solution in the *OND*, when he argues it is a matter of "natural equity" for Christians to support preachers of the gospel, given that what they preach is true, beneficial, and necessary, even though the value of their preaching cannot be proved by pure natural reason.[30] He makes what looks like the same point in terms of right reason when discussing Eleazar's refusal to eat pork in violation of divine law.[31] What happens, then, when we move to Grade 4 moral virtue? Here love of God above all and for God's own sake is a new and transforming *motive* for acting as one is rationally bound to act anyway. Instead of respect for a rational principle, love of a person moves us. Or perhaps 'instead of' is the wrong term. For Ockham holds it is rational not only to obey God but to love God, for God is supremely lovable.

Is the independently ascertainable rationality of some actions of no consequence, then? There are, as I understand it, some things God cannot bring about in the moral sphere. God cannot bring it about that, in the *absence* of direct divine command to the contrary, it is right to commit adultery, or wrong, other things being equal, to benefit benefactors, at least in a world like ours, or that it is wrong to love God *praeter omnia* and *propter se* in any world whatever. If it really is self-evident that adultery is wrong or that benefactors are to be benefited, God cannot bring it about that these things are not self-evident.[32] The conditional character of these norms – that their validity depends on no contrary direct command being in force –

does not affect their validity *on that condition*. For example, a direct divine command to kill an innocent child (such as the command to Abraham to sacrifice Isaac) would not make it false that in the absence of such a command such an action is horribly wrong. To suppose, as Ockham does, that a direct divine command to kill an innocent child would make the action right does not at all imply that, absent such a command, the action is morally neutral, that we have no reason to reject it.[33]

One could go a step further to suggest that the rationality or irrationality of an action apart from direct divine command properly affects one's interpretation of what one might take to be a direct divine command. Perhaps a very strong impulse to have an affair with someone else's spouse is less likely to be a prompting of the Holy Spirit than is a weaker impulse to help a friend (or an enemy) in need. More broadly, perhaps an interpretation of a sacred text that makes the divine will fly in the face of all that otherwise seems reasonable is, other things being equal, less acceptable than a reading in which the independently rational and the revealed are in accord.

The hermeneutical principle of employing reason in the interpretation of revelation finds support in Ockham's interpretation of revelation itself. I mentioned earlier that Ockham had two arguments in favor of extending the concept of divine law to cover all natural law. The first was that God is the creator or author of nature. Section I of this chapter was a way of spelling out that argument. Ockham's second argument was that the principles of natural law are to be found in Scripture:

Every law that is contained explicitly or implicitly in the divine Scriptures can be called a divine law ... but every natural law is contained explicitly or implicitly in the divine Scriptures, because in the divine Scriptures there are certain general propositions from which, either alone or with other [premises], can be inferred every natural law ... though it may not be found in them explicitly.[34]

Thus, what I construed earlier in an artificially restricted Natural Law moral framework as tacit divine commands are confirmed as direct divine commands for those who accept the Bible as revealing God's will. Ockham presumably has the Decalogue's prohibitions of adultery and bearing false witness in mind when he offers "Do not commit adultery" and "Do not lie" as examples of a kind of natural law or natural reason that "in no case fails."[35]

Given his earlier treatment of theft and adultery, however, we must understand Ockham as allowing *apparent* failures of such natural law precepts in the face of what I have called cancellation of one divine command by another. Whether or not he should have done so, Ockham would not have agreed with Kant that the command to sacrifice Isaac could not have come from God simply because deliberately taking innocent human life "flatly contradicts morality."[36] It seems, then, that for Ockham the irrationality of an action apart from direct divine command is a good but not always a conclusive reason for rejecting what appeared to be a direct divine command to the contrary. The inclusion of the principles of natural law in Scripture gives these principles the status of direct divine commands, but this does not rule out the possibility of more specific or later contrary commands.

The thought that God might on occasion command actions that look very much like adultery may not strike terror in a twentieth-century heart; hope might be a more common reaction. There are cases that may be more difficult to imagine, however – cases even more difficult in some ways than that of Abraham and Isaac. The last thesis of *Centil.*, a work formerly attributed to Ockham, implies that the damned ought to will their own damnation, for "they are equally bound to love God for damning them as the blessed are bound to love God for beatifying them."[37] Ockham does not consider quite this situation, but he comes close. For he holds that in obedience to divine command a person might will not to have the beatific vision.[38] The difficulty in trying to obey a divine command to hate God would not be involved here, for not having the beatific vision does not imply one hates God. For the same reason, willing not to have the beatific vision is not the same as willing one's own damnation. For the damned do hate God.

If Ockham does not envision the possibility of God's ordering us to will our own damnation, he does consider it possible that God assign eternal punishment to those who love him and eternal blessedness to those who hate him – or at least that God might have done so.[39] God is debtor to no one and hence is not required in the nature of the case to reward any creaturely act, including the act of loving God *praeter omnia* and *propter se*, an act intrinsically virtuous of its own nature.[40] For Ockham, the category of merit – eternal reward and punishment – is an entirely gratuitous one, as Adams has rightly emphasized.[41]

Ockham believes God has arranged the conditions for salvation and damnation in a way that has traditionally struck Christians as more than reasonable. Those who accept Christ and do all that is in them to love God above all else will be saved. That is God's offer. But this raises an obvious question. Is God obligated to keep his word? Does the thesis that God is not a debtor to anyone apply even after God has announced the terms of salvation? Granted no one else can obligate God, can God obligate himself?

Common sense, the Bible,[42] and, for philosophers not reliant on either, Searle's derivation of 'ought' from 'is' (arguing from the fact of a promise to an obligation to fulfill it)[43] support an affirmative answer. By promise or covenant, it seems, God can obligate himself, and because nothing other than God could prevent God from keeping his promises, they seem to provide complete assurance that what was promised will occur.

Ockham sometimes seems to speak as if this is his view. Can God *not* grant eternal life to someone in whose soul the supernaturally created form of charity is present? Absolutely speaking (*de potentia absoluta*) yes, but in accordance with the order of things God has established (*de potentia ordinata*) no. "God will give [eternal life] freely and purely from his own grace to whomever he will give it, although *de potentia ordinata* he cannot do otherwise [than bestow it on those in charity] because of laws voluntarily and contingently ordained by God."[44] In parallel contexts Ockham claims, similarly, that "according to the laws now ordained by God, no human being will ever be saved or be able to be saved without created grace" and that "if one is speaking about conditional necessity, then God of necessity accepts an act elicited out of charity."[45]

Ockham's treatment of theft and adultery suggests, however, either that God cannot make a binding promise or – what amounts to the same thing – that any eventuality could count as God's keeping his promises. For a promise is fulfilled, arguably, when the promiser provides something better than what was promised. Now Christians ask God to fulfill their desires and petitions as may be best for them, but much of Ockham's discussion of these issues suggests that what is best for all of us is whatever God wants for us. It is important to recall here that the love of God Ockham commends as the noblest act of the created will is love of God above all and for God's own sake. It is the noblest example of love of a friend for whose sake one acts (*amor amicitiae*), not desire for a result (*amor concupiscentiae*), even for the result of having the beatific vision.[46] If what is best for us is what best serves what we best love, then what is best for us is what God wills for us.[47]

Christians may find it blasphemous to suppose God's promises will not, or might not, be kept, and it is natural to expect that promises be kept in a manner consonant with one's understanding of them (whatever the basis for that understanding).[48] The question is whether confidence in God's promises should rest on the idea that such promises limit God's power, that we should think of God as *bound* to keep those promises.

III. OCKHAM'S GOD AND MORALITY

As I have construed his position, Ockham's affirmation of God's will as the uniquely supreme principle of right and wrong is perfectly consistent with his espousal of an ethic of right reason and natural law not dependent on reference to a superior's will. On one hand, it is self-evidently reasonable to obey divine commands, for God is the highest good, and whatever God commands is by that fact just. On the other hand, there are also self-evident normative principles and intrinsic goods apprehensible even by a natural reason that knows little or nothing of God. Philosophers and saints share many values. The difference is that for achieving even these shared values the saint has a motive not necessarily operative for the philosopher: love of God. Love of God above all else and for God's own sake, the one human act that cannot possibly be vicious (or irrational), supports the pursuit of philosophically intelligible human goods both directly and indirectly: directly in scriptural endorsements of the principles of natural law and indirectly through reflection on God's authorship of nature and the consequent reasonableness of interpreting our natural grounds for action as divine precepts. To love God perfectly involves acting as God wishes us to act, and both directly and indirectly God orders us to act reasonably.

The apparent tension between P1–2 discussed at the beginning of this chapter has thus been resolved. Correct ethical and social norms can often be determined purely rationally, without reference to God's will (P1), while all and only valid norms are divine commands (P2). But the question remains whether P3 can be satisfactorily accommodated. If I am right in taking Ockham to hold that God can command virtually anything (P3), will not the consistency of rational and divine-command moralities summarized in the last paragraph turn to chaos? To put it otherwise, is it reasonable to love and obey a God understood in Ockham's terms?

In Ockham the impulse to theodicy is severely tested. The problem is not with justifying what God actually does or commands. Ockham is in as good a position here as any medieval theologian. The fearful difficulty is with Ockham's emphasis on the contingent character of God's actions, especially with what appears to be the morally contingent character of the future in God's hands. In Ockham's terms, it is fair to ask whether God, who can still command or will or justly do anything, is indeed the highest possible good. Is God the best of all possible gods? It is under this description, in effect, that Ockham presents God as the due and proper ultimate object of creaturely love, the only being capable of "quieting" or satisfying a reasonable will.[49]

The divine authorship of creation gives us continuing reason to believe God wishes us to do what creation (including our own creation) gives us reason to do. This includes using reason to aid in interpreting scriptural revelation, though not as a warrant for rewriting it. The idea that "Ockham's God" is hostile to human reason is unfounded, as is the implication that for Ockham our actions are morally neutral in the absence of direct communications of the divine will.

Furthermore, if God makes promises – if God "swears by himself," for example[50] – that does provide reason to believe that what was promised will occur. There could be no better reason.

Should we ask for more? Granted, if I read Ockham correctly, then no matter what occurs, one is never in a position to blame God for nonperformance or unsatisfactory performance of a contractual obligation. But the ultimate poverty of our legal position in relation to God is perhaps the right and therefore rationally more satisfying position to take. To look for more may amount to converting God from a trustworthy person into a moral machine.[51] Ockham holds that God is supremely lovable (*diligendus*, to be delighted in or cherished), but this is because God is God, the highest good, not because of past or prospective benefits granted to us or others. (This is not to say that gratitude, hope, fear, and longing to live in God's presence are out of place in an Ockhamist relationship with God, but their proper placement depends on loving God for God's sake.) To love God *praeter omnia* and *propter se* is the supreme and supremely reasonable act of the human spirit, a necessary condition for complete satisfaction of the human will. That is the point of *Sent.* I.1, at the beginning of Ockham's major theological work.[52] The rest of his theology unfolds from this beginning. That he renounces all claims to power over the beloved in so thoroughly Franciscan a manner is not an inconsequent result.

IV. MORAL THEOLOGY AND SECULAR POLITICS

What are the consequences of this position for politics, which is the question that provoked this chapter?[53] Theocracy, personally or biblically based, is one possible consequence of taking seriously the assertion of God's moral omnipotence that I attribute to Ockham. According to the position I have presented, anyone who knows God's will is bound to attempt to put it into effect, no matter what circumstances obtain. An individual possessing such knowledge from personal revelation seems entitled to dictate to everyone accordingly. Theological experts qualified to elicit God's will from a sacred text seem entitled to dictate to all who accepted the text as sacred. Institutions claiming scriptural support for their authority seem entitled to obedience from those who accepted the texts or interpretations being alleged. Why did Ockham's political thought not follow this path?

The first thing to say is that it did. The second is that in following the path of theologically motivated political reflection, Ockham, consistent with his initial principles, arrived at a relatively liberal conception of religious authority and a distinctly secular conception of politics.

Ockham never claimed personal revelation,[54] but he considered himself obligated, as a theologian, to make God's will as revealed in Scripture clear to his fellow Christians.[55] Indeed, his political writings so abound in references to the Bible and its interpreters that the editor of one of these works questioned whether Ockham was a political thinker at all. "He was above all a theologian, and nothing can lead to greater errors than considering his political views apart from his theological starting point."[56]

The most obvious theological starting point for Ockham's political views was his commitment to a particular Franciscan understanding of the life and teachings of Jesus Christ. As God and human being, Christ had "demonstrated" that God most wants us to live as much as possible without private property or political entanglements. Convinced as Ockham was that the way of life exemplified and taught as most perfect by Christ and the apostles called for complete absence of property, he became equally convinced that John XXII had fallen into heresy in denying even the moral possibility of such poverty. So persuaded, Ockham wrote the final treatise in the poverty controversy, *OND*, and the most systematic medieval treatise on heresy, Part I of *Dial.*, which is concerned especially with papal heresy (a possibility recognized but not thoroughly explored by other theologians and canon lawyers of the day).

Two other biblical starting points for Ockham's political views must be mentioned, one positive and one negative. The positive starting point, easily overlooked by those shocked or dazzled by his life of radical opposition to John XXII and his successors, is Ockham's acceptance of the traditional basis for papal authority, the interpretation of certain passages in the gospels as showing that Christ had conferred power over the other apostles on Saint Peter.[57]

The most important biblical starting point for understanding Ockham's conception of politics as secular is negative, the *absence* in Scripture of specific directions for the general organization of political and economic life. On Ockham's reading of the Gospels, the most perfect way of life for a Christian is one without property or humanly established legal rights. He acknowledged that such a life is not possible for everyone, not even for every Christian. Positive law, government, and property are necessary for most of us. But Ockham does not find in Scripture specific instructions for arranging such matters. We are left to our own devices, although not our own uninhibited desires.

Given the view of God's moral omnipotence I have attributed to Ockham, he would allow that all three of these biblical starting points could have been different. God in Christ could have set forth a life of philosophy, crime, or industrious capitalism as most perfectly meritorious. He could have conferred supreme ecclesiastical authority on anyone or ones other than Peter, or on no one. He could have prescribed divine right of kings, the U. S. constitution, or the syndicalist state as an obligatory basis for all political arrangements.

With respect to his actual biblical starting points, however, Ockham's understanding of what God has or has not commanded fits his own conception of what is reasonable apart from divine command. (Disagreement with Ockham's interpretation of the biblical passages might accordingly be a result or a cause of disagreement with his conception of what is reasonable.)

Startling as Saint Francis's dedication to poverty was to his contemporaries and is to many others who go beyond the more anodyne popular images of him, love of "Lady Poverty" jibes well with the emphasis in Ockham's academic theology on loving God for God's own goodness and denying all limits to God's will. A leitmotif in the writings of Ockham's group of friars in their attacks on John XXII is Peter's statement to Jesus (on behalf of all the apostles), "Behold, we have forsaken all and followed you."[58] Ockham's concentration on God's goodness is not a denial that other things are good, but it involves a sometimes startling (yet for Ockham perfectly reasonable) displacement of other values from any possible competing position.

Ockham found Christ's decision to set up a monarchical government for the church perfectly reasonable. The greater part of a book of *Dial.* is devoted to showing, largely from Aristotle's *Politics*, that it is beneficial for the whole congregation of believers to be under one faithful head, leader, and prelate subordinated to Christ. For Ockham, however, the reasonableness of papal monarchy depends on conditions not respected in absolutist theories of authors like Giles of Rome, James of Viterbo, and Augustinus de Ancona. First is respect for the freedom of the pope's subjects in religious matters not requiring authoritative regulation. Of comparable importance is respect for the normal autonomy of secular political processes. Ockham found what he took to be ample support in Scripture and many of its interpreters for a pastorally mild, normally apolitical ideal of papal government. He went beyond the Western tradition of his time in arguing that drastic failure of the pope or his subjects to rule and be ruled according to this ideal justified temporary recourse to other forms of administration. He thus interpreted the gospel texts supporting papal primacy as allowing the community of believers power to change this form of Church government temporarily as circumstances might require.[59] Acute disillusionment with his papal and papalist contemporaries, realistic but not deeply pessimistic longer-term philosophical considerations, and a desire to discern Christ's will as revealed in Scripture are tensely balanced at this point in Ockham's thought, but balanced they are.

Finally, for Ockham, politics' secular character depends on an absence of direct divine commands establishing political institutions on specifically religious foundations. It would, however, be a great error to conclude from this that for Ockham God has left the political arena vacant for amoral combat (or compact) among blind human wills. As we ought to expect from the commitment to right reason in Ockham's academic works, Ockhamist secular politics is to operate within a framework of rationally construed natural law and natural rights.[60] Within that framework, granted, there is room for reasonable choice among a variety of governmental and economic arrangements, depending on historical circumstances, including what people are willing to agree to at particular times and places.[61] Nevertheless, nothing could be more opposed to Ockham's spirit than a politics of absolute sovereignty or blind decision. The medieval models for modern theories like this are rather to be found in the curialism Ockham so strongly opposed.

The apparent shift of emphasis from divine command to natural law between Ockham's academic and political writings is thus not so much a volte-face on his part as a reversal of figure and ground in the eye of the beholder. What stands out about Ockham in the context of Scholastic academic theology is the extent to which he holds the revealed, believed truth of faith apart from the conclusions of natural reason. He holds that theology is not strictly a science or wisdom, that God's uniqueness and infinite power cannot be philosophically demonstrated, that God's will is not constrained by a metaphysic of perfection. Struck by these aspects of his thought, we are apt to ignore his constant affirmation of natural human powers. His epistemology is not skeptical. It allows the existence of sciences in the strict sense, in some of which he had a contributing interest. His refined analysis of moral conduct centers on commitment to the dictates of right reason, including the dictate to act from love of God, but he by no means takes that dictate as warrant for ignoring the fruits of purely philosophical and scientific reflection on ourselves and our circumstances.

What stands out about Ockham in the context of late-medieval political controversy is the extent to which he holds what we can recognize as politics apart from religious control. Spiritual and secular institutions are normally to operate independently. The pope's fullness of power does not include power to command just anything consistent with divine or natural law. He must especially respect rights of secular rulers, his approval is not required to make civil government legitimate, and even within his own sphere he must not govern harshly. Struck by these aspects, we may glide over the dense apparatus of biblical, patristic, and earlier medieval theological citations Ockham uses to make room for a reasonable secular politics (as readers of Locke are apt to glide over the biblical references in his works). It may not occur to us to imagine that the ultimate raison d'être of politics might be (in Ockham as in Locke) to provide a framework where individuals are safe to seek God.[62]

The different saliences in our perceptions of Ockham at different stages of his career are natural enough in view of his circumstances and our own. Thus, there is indeed something to the diverse impressions of the More Than Subtle Doctor with which we began. But an image in depth must show the same mind at work consistently throughout. Ockham does not produce a finished system at any stage, let alone a formula for deducing his politics from his academic theology or vice versa. I have not meant to neaten him up in a way that suggests such constructions. Ockham's synthesizing of reason and revelation, of human autonomy and love of God, of P1, P2, and P3, is more in the nature of a strenuous ongoing project. The disquieting personal demands of the project in the last twenty years of Ockham's life give energetic point to his early contention that the enjoyment of God "on the road" in this life and in the homeland of the blessed, different as they are in other respects, have an identical focus, an ultimate if unsystematic unifier. In an Ockhamist framework it is in all circumstances fitting and by nature pleasant to rejoice and delight in God.[63]

NOTES

1 Section I is based on a paper I gave on "tacit divine command" in Ockham at the American Philosophical Association Eastern Division meetings (abstract McGrade 1974a). Section II considers the scope of "direct" divine commands in an Ockhamist framework. I then consider the two

sorts of dictates together. I am indebted to discussions of Ockham's ethics that have appeared since 1974, especially Adams 1986 and 1987b, Holopainen 1991, Kilcullen 1993, Wood 1994, and Kaye 1997.

2 Compare Cross 1997 (review of McGrade and Kilcullen 1995): "The editors' introduction leaves at least one question unanswered. In the texts printed, Ockham consistently defends natural law: whereas in his earlier, non-political discussions he rejects such a theory in favour of a divine-command meta-ethic. The volte face seems to me worthy of comment."

3 Oakley 1961. Compare Knowles 1962, 324, "Acts are not good or bad of themselves, but solely because they are commanded or prohibited by God." (As quoted, along with similar judgments, by Adams 1986, 2.) Recently Mann 1991, 257, has argued that, "Because God's will determines what counts as created goodness and because God's perfect goodness places no constraints on what he could have willed for creatures, Ockham's position assigns God's perfect goodness to a kind of explanatory limbo."

4 *Nicomachean Ethics* I.5.1097^{b}3–5; *Sent.* I.1.1 (378). Ockham argues that "in moral philosophy there are many principles that are known per se" on which a demonstrative science can be based which "directs human acts apart from any precept of a superior." (*Quodl.* II.14. Translations from *Quodl.* in this essay are from Freddoso and Kelly 1991.) This is in contrast to a "positive" moral science containing "human and divine laws that obligate one to pursue or to avoid what is neither good nor evil except because it is commanded or prohibited by a superior whose role it is to establish laws." (Ibid.) See also *Connex.* 2.1–74. The demonstrative moral science of Ockham's academic writings is linked to the natural law of his political works by the fact that, for Ockham, natural law is not a matter of instinct but of evident rationality. See *Dial.* III-2.i.15 and III-2.iii.6 (= McGrade and Kilcullen 1995, 273–4, 285–93). See also Kilcullen 1993.

5 *Sent.* I.1.1 (374–5, 376–9), 1.4 (431). In arguing that there can be a demonstrative science of morals, Ockham defines 'moral' broadly, as referring to "human acts subject to the will – without further qualification," and more strictly, as referring to "habits or acts that are subject to the power of the will insofar as they are measured by the natural dictate of reason and by the other circumstances." (*Quodl.* II.14.) I take it "the other circumstances" include the facts of a situation. These might include a command from a human or divine superior, which would bring positive moral science into the situation. But Ockham argues here that positive moral science is not always a demonstrative science, "even though it is regulated by a demonstrative science in many ways." On the grades of moral virtue recognized by Ockham, some of which involve no reference to God, see later in this section.

6 See McGrade 1974b, 101–2, 134, 201.

7 *Connex.* 2.132–41. Translations from *Connex.* in this essay are taken from Wood 1997.

8 See n. 11.

9 Grice 1990. Compare Strawson 1991. I am grateful to Ruth Millikan for these references.

10 I follow current custom in discussing the theological dimensions of Ockham's ethics in terms of divine *commands*. His own term '*prae-ceptum*' is sometimes better translated 'precept.' If we bear in mind Ockham's view that the proper religious motive in life is eagerness, born of love, to be in accord with the mind and gracious will of a loving God, it seems clear that 'command' will often set the wrong tone. Other divine speech acts deserve thinking about. The analysis I propose doubtless also needs refining on other grounds.

11 "Every law that is from God, who is the creator ['*conditor,*' also translatable as "author"] of nature, can be called a divine law; but every natural law is from God who is the creator of nature; therefore etc." (*Dial.* III-2.iii.6 [= McGrade and Kilcullen 1995, 290].) The idea of the natural order as a book written by God is traditional, but it is typically used to argue that creation tells us something about God's nature or that God's authority over creation serves as a model for authority in human affairs. Neither of these uses is involved here.

12 *Brev.* III.10; *OND* 88 (657–8; McGrade and Kilcullen 1995, 64).

13 There is room to question whether this should be called a limit. See Ockham's discussion of whether it more primarily pertains to God to be unable to do the impossible or to the impossible to be unable to be done by God. Ockham concludes it is a draw. *Sent.* I.43.2 (648–50) (= Bosley and Tweedale 1997, 88–9; Wippel and Wolter 1969, 452–3).

14 I agree with Adams 1987b, 241, that for Ockham, "[t]he scope of God's options matches the range of His omnipotent power (whose boundaries are defined only by the principle of noncontradiction."

15 *Sent.* IV.16 (352).

16 *Connex.* 4.349–52.

17 *Quodl.* III.14.

18 Perhaps this is what Ockham has in mind when he says "opposites cannot fall under a divine command at the same time." (*Sent.* II.15 [352].) In any case, this passage is earlier than *Quodl.* III.14, where Ockham recognizes the possibility of a divine command impossible of fulfillment. According to the *Rule of St. Benedict* 68 (Benedict 1982, 70), the proper response to a monastic superior's command to do the impossible is first to point out the difficulty but then, if the superior persists, to attempt to comply.

19 I Cor. 10:13.

20 *Sent.* I.1.5 (464), I.47 (683); *SL* I.7; *Sent.* IV.3–5 (55), I.47 (680), II.15 (353).

21 *Sent.* I.41 (610). Compare *Connex.* 3.580–9.

22 *Sent.* I.47 (684–5).

23 *Connex.* 4.310–30.

24 Ockham's assertion that "from the very fact that God does something it is done justly" is not based on an obligation on God's part to do anything positive that is owing to anyone, but just the reverse: "God is debtor to no one, but whatever he does to us, he does purely from grace. And *hence* from the very fact that God does something, it is done justly." (*Sent.* IV.3–4 [55], my emphasis.) Again, Ockham's claim that hatred of God, if caused in a creature solely by God, "will always be for a good end" does not depend on supposing that God will always have a *further* good in mind as a reason for causing what is ordinarily the worst of all possible acts when caused by the creature itself. The argument is rather that God suffers no harm from such hatred. (*Sent.* II.15 [353–4].) (To be sure, God is not harmed when a creature hates him of its own volition, but as some manuscripts make explicit here, in "the worst hatred" of God the intention would be that God not exist.)

25 *Connex.* 2.135–141. Emphasis added.

26 Theft and adultery in Aristotle, *Nicomachean Ethics* II.6.1107^{a}8–12; theft and fornication in Ockham, *Connex.* 2.216–26.

27 *Sent.* II.15 (347, 352–3); *Connex.* 4.353–66.

28 "If God had not given them [the children of Israel] the land of the Chanaanites through a particular revelation they would not have had the power to appropriate that land rather than another." *Brev.* III.10.

29 Ockham's position here seems substantially identical with Aquinas's (*ST* IaIIae.94.5 ad 2). Aquinas considers three divine commands apparently contrary to natural law: to Abraham to sacrifice his innocent son Isaac, to the Israelites to plunder the Egyptians at the Exodus, and to Hosea to marry a prostitute. In each case he holds that God's position vis-à-vis human beings exempts the action from being a violation of the natural precept. He notes that death was introduced into the world as a consequence of sin, but he does not say God must have had some rationally intelligible further end in view to justify these apparently contrarational commands.

30 *OND* 65 (OPol II.574–5) (= McGrade and Kilcullen 1995, 51).

31 *Circa virtutes et vitia* (280).

32 The situation with principles and conclusions of demonstrative moral science is analogous to that with demonstrative natural science. As Leppin argues, Ockham consistently maintains both the utter contingency of creatures with regard to their existence and the possibility

of necessary truths regarding their natures and natural operations. (Leppin 1995, 51–8, with references to the secondary literature). Compare Adams 1987a, 784–98; Adams 1987b, 227–8. My contention has been that Ockhamist nonpositive moral science and natural law are similarly grounded in objective assessments of how it is reasonable for creatures like us to act in our world. In both the physical and moral cases, however, God can nullify the natural effects of creatures. In the physical world nullification is by miracle. Can pigs fly? No, and necessarily no. But God can carry a pig through the air with an indetectable hand (in which case the pig is being flown, not flying) or instantaneously metamorphose it into an avian look-alike equipped with scientifically intelligible means of flight. We can think of direct divine commands as capable of effecting similar nullification in the moral order. That it is in principle impossible for us to understand miracles may suggest that it is in principle impossible for us to understand how God could rightly do or command some of the things Christians and others have traditionally supposed him to have done or commanded.

33 Ockham offers killing an innocent person as an example of something obviously wrong on even the briefest consideration. (*Dial.* III-2.i.15 [= McGrade and Kilcullen 1995, 273].) There is no doubt that for Ockham the clearest example of an intrinsically virtuous act is the act of loving God *praeter omnia* and *propter se*. But besides holding that some acts are good in their general character he is prepared to call an act intrinsically virtuous without reference to God if a person wills to perform it because it is dictated by right reason. "An act can be called virtuous, either intrinsically or extrinsically.... Here is an example: In abstraction from any [particular] circumstance someone wills [to] study. That act [*A*] is generically good. Subsequently the intellect dictates that that act of will should be continued according to all requisite circumstances, and the will wills to continue the first act according to the dictate of right reason. That second act [the act of willing to continue *A* in accordance with reason] is perfectly virtuous, since it conforms to a complete dictate of right reason, and it is intrinsically virtuous. The first act [*A*] is virtuous only by extrinsic denomination – namely, because it conforms to the second act." (*Connex.* 4.184–98.) This is consistent with his occasional qualifications of judgments about virtue as valid "as long as the [relevant] divine precept remains in force" (*Quodl.* III.14), if we understand him to be presupposing God can cancel or override any obligation we might otherwise have. There is one odd passage where Ockham appears to say that "loving God is the sole virtuous act" (*Quodl.* III.14). Two early manuscripts used in the critical edition of *Quodl.* observe that this seems nonsensical, perhaps because what the argument logically requires here is a different

proposition, that "loving God is solely an act of will" (a difference of one word in Latin, 'voluntatis' for 'virtuosus'). In any case, a claim that loving God is the only virtuous act would go counter to the passage cited earlier in this note and to the whole conception of Grade 3 moral virtue.

34 *Dial.* III-2.iii.6 (= McGrade and Kilcullen 1995, 290).

35 Ibid. (= McGrade and Kilcullen 1995, 285). I understand in this light the biblical command to love God. Ockham's recognition that there can be a difference between a "natural" and a meritorious love of God (the latter an effect of the infused virtue of charity) might seem to suggest that the dictate to love God holds only in the context of revelation and grace. Ockham's point is rather the reverse. His contention in this passage is that natural and meritorious acts of loving God *are* of the same species when they have the same object. They are specifically different acts when they have different objects. The example Ockham gives to illustrate difference of objects does not mention grace or divine command: "As if someone loved God above all [but] not according to any required circumstance, and the same individual later loved God above all according to all [required?] circumstances, say according to right reason, because he is the ultimate end, and so about the other [circumstances?]." (*Dubitationes addititiae* [292–3]).

36 Kant 1960, 81–2 (II, General Observation). Compare ibid., 175 (IV.4).

37 *Centil.* §100.

38 *Sent.* I.1.4 (443).

39 *Sent.* I.17.1 (454–6), IV.3–5 (55); *De necessitate caritatis* (17–9).

40 Ockham distinguishes two ways something could be called intrinsically good: from its own nature, or because some extrinsic cause accepts it as such. Acts of understanding could be intrinsically good in the second way (as some acts of will now are) if God accepted them, but nothing can be intrinsically good from its own nature except an act of will. (*Connex.* 4.144–54.)

41 Adams 1987b, 243–7; Adams 1986, 18–37. The thesis that God is free to reward or punish whomever he pleases on whatever basis he pleases obviously *can* be used as a basis for conjuring up scenarios even more terrifying than *sinners* in the hands of an angry God, but the initiative here lies with the conjurer. Adams suggests a more plausible motive for Ockham's emphasis on God's freedom in setting up the conditions for salvation as he has. "When Ockham draws out the implications of how He didn't *have* to do it, he is not trying to scare people, but trying to offer a measure of His generosity." (Adams 1987b, 246.) Rega Wood rightly points out that in Ockham's view God is merciful, not cruel, more prone to forgive and to reward than to punish. His mercy ordains that no good act will go unrewarded, and even unjustified sinners sometimes

escape punishment. Wood 1994, 44, citing *Sent.* IV.10–11 (237); *Praedest.* 4; *Sent.* I.1 (603–4, 606), IV.3–5 (61).

42 Heb. 6:13–8.

43 Searle 1969, 175–98.

44 *Sent.* I.17.1 (455).

45 *Quodl.* VI.1–2.

46 *Sent.* I.1.4 (441, 444).

47 In *Quodl.* VI.1, Ockham compares God's absolute and ordained power with the pope's power in a way that suggests God is not bound to observe the order he has established. "There are many things God is able to do that he does not will to do.... And these things God is said to be able to do by his absolute power. In the same way there are some things that the pope is unable to do in accordance with the laws established by him, and yet he is able to do those things absolutely." It is not self-evident that legislators are bound to act in accordance with the laws they have established, although it seems reasonable to require justification for their not doing so if we are speaking of human legislators. This is Ockham's position with regard to promises by a secular ruler. "*Student* Say, therefore, whether ... just as it is not permissible for [the emperor] to assert something false or to promise deceitfully or fraudulently anything he does not intend to perform, so it would not be permissible for him to revoke in any way something promised, or not fulfill it, or postpone it. *Master* Some think [that], although the emperor should not fulfill things promised badly or things he promised licitly and afterwards considers are beginning to be harmful but should rescind them ... yet he should not in any way revoke other promises or postpone them without manifest necessity." *Dial.* III-2.i.17 (= McGrade and Kilcullen 1995, 279).

48 One could perhaps argue that a divine promise is a basis for claims against God, even insistent claims. (Some Christians, relying on Paul's assertion that God wills all human beings to be saved [1 Tim 2:3], may find it reasonable to hope and pray urgently that *that* should occur.) But who would be the appropriate judge? Ockham's papalist contemporary Augustinus de Ancona rejected the possibility of the pope's appointing a third party to judge an appeal against his own sentence by arguing that the pope would then be denying he was pope, head of the whole Church, just as God would be denying he was God if he permitted anything to be exempt from his jurisdiction in the natural order (Augustinus de Ancona 1584, VI.7).

Could one *know* that divine promise will be kept? Ockham begins *Sent.* I. Prol. by arguing it is consistent with the conditions of human understanding in this life for God to cause someone to have "evident" (objectively certain) knowledge of at least some truths of theology, but he expressly excludes here both contingent truths ('God is incarnate,'

'There will be a resurrection of the dead,' 'A blessed soul will be blessed in perpetuity') and necessary truths involving reference to contingent truths not evidently knowable in this life ('God is capable of incarnation'). (*Sent.* I. Prol.1.5 [49–51].) In a later work he holds that God can cause in a human being an evident awareness of future contingents. (For God himself has such an awareness. Hence it can exist; hence it can be caused and revealed by God to someone else.) But since the foretold event will occur contingently, it is possible that it not occur. In that case the proposition about the future that God had caused would turn out not to have been a revelation (since revelation implies that what has been revealed is true). (*Quodl.* IV.4.) For an acute and approving presentation of this position as amounting to the thesis that God can lie (a formulation not in Ockham), see Kaye 1997, chap. 2.

49 *Sent.* I.1.4 (429–47).

50 Heb. 6:13, referring to Gen. 22:16–17.

51 Thomas 1990 distinguishes trust from reliance insofar as trust assumes a possibility of nonfulfillment, whereas reliance sometimes does not, as when we rely on the laws of physics or when a creature's metaphysical constitution is such that it necessarily chooses to do what is moral. "Trust is anchored in the belief that a person will choose *not* to perform the action that he has been trusted not to perform, rather in the belief that he *cannot* perform it. Trust is unnecessary if the person is incapable of performing the action (or if it is highly improbable that he could perform it)." (Ibid., 245.) "I maintain that wholly rational moral selves are metaphysically constituted so that they necessarily choose to do what is moral." (Ibid., 246.) Thomas concludes, "It has been brought to my attention . . . that a most untoward consequence of the conception of trust that I offer is that it is not possible to trust God. Surprisingly, perhaps, I accept this, if it were possible to know how God should behave and what God would deem right. But clearly, whatever relationship there might be between God and human beings, it is surely one of radical uncertainty, owing, presumably, to the inability of human beings both to fathom God's will and to determine whether they measure up to it." (Ibid. 257, n. 14.) I am grateful to Jessica Prata-Miller for bringing this article to my attention.

Following Ockham, we can, I think, rely on God not to do anything *wrong.* If there is a Platonic Good beyond God or some feature of divine nature that restricts what God can rightly will, Ockham's contention that God *is* justice would seem to entail that God would not do anything contrary to such a Good or to such a normatively limiting natural feature. Therefore, insofar as trusting human beings involves the possibility of their doing wrong, the situation is different with respect to God.

Ockham's apparent conviction that nothing logically possible is morally foreclosed from being actually willed by God emphasizes, however, that, in Thomas's words, we do not "know how God should behave." To this extent, trust in God is possible and (on the basis of Ockham's reading of God's actions in creation and history) appropriate.

52 For fuller discussion of some of the issues Ockham considers in *Sent.* I.1, see McGrade 1981. I have discussed later treatments of the subject in McGrade 1987.

53 I more fully present the view of Ockham's political thought sketched here in McGrade 1974b, the introductions to McGrade and Kilcullen 1992 and 1995, and McGrade 1994–97.

54 Leppin 1995, 127–35 suggests that Ockham's account of Saint Paul's rapture (2 Cor. 12:1–4) as a beatific vision of the divine essence (*Quodl.* VI.1) may have been one stimulus for a sermon by John XXII inveighing against this interpretation. The issues are connected with the pope's deep disquiet about the teaching of Joachim of Fiore and Peter John Olivi. See Lambert 1977, 182–206, and Tierney 1988. In *Dial.* I.ii.5, 27, Ockham presents the possibility of postbiblical revelation as a source of Catholic truths, belief in which would be required for salvation, but he avers (if, as I suppose, the opinion recited in chap. 27 is his) that the Church has never based itself on such revelation in condemning heresy.

55 See especially *Epist.; Dial.* I.i and I.vii.48; *Brev.* I.

56 Scholz 1944, 1. I have discussed the theological interpretation of Ockham's political works in McGrade 1974b, 34–7, 210–1. Leppin 1995, 325, is primarily concerned with Ockham's academic writings, but in a chapter on the postacademic works he concludes it is the question of theology, the search for believed truth, that binds the parts of Ockham's life together. "His life was in certain respects lived theology" (ibid., 331). The conclusion of Kaye 1997 is that in some ways Ockham's entire twofold career can be understood as a defense of the belief that we are free to love God.

57 See especially *Dial.* III-1.iv.8–11 and III-1.iv.22 for Ockham's rejection of Marsilius of Padua's conciliarism and his affirmation of Peter's superior authority.

58 Matt. 19:27, Mark 10:28, Luke 18:28.

59 Ockham's defense of monarchy as regularly the best form of Church government and his arguments for the possibility of temporary shifts to other regimes are in *Dial.* III-1.ii. For Ockham's criticism of curialism, see *Brev.*

60 In Ockham's usage '*ius naturale*' is sometimes best translated "natural law," sometimes "natural right" in the sense of "a" right. On Ockham's considerable contributions to the idea of natural rights (rationally conceived), see Tierney 1997, Brett 1997, McGrade 1980 and 1996.

61 Ockham holds that monarchy is normally the best form of government in secular affairs for the world as a whole, but even if such a government has been legitimately established, its claims should not be pressed in all circumstances. (*Dial.* III-2.i.6–10.)

62 The comparison of Ockham with Locke is suggested by Gewirth 1951, 258. On religious motives in Locke's political thought, see Dunne 1969 and 1979, 36–40.

63 *Sent.* I.1.3, 4 (414–22, 443). On love of God as a source of pleasure, see McGrade 1981.

13   The Political Writings

In the year 1328 Ockham and certain leading members of the Franciscan order became convinced that the pope of the day, Pope John XXII, was a heretic and therefore no pope. From then until his death in 1347 Ockham wrote nothing more (or almost nothing) on logic, natural philosophy, or speculative philosophy but produced a large body of books and pamphlets, commonly called his "political" writings, advocating the deposition of John XXII and his successors, Benedict XII and Clement VI.[1] The quarrel with these popes began when John XXII issued several documents attacking doctrines and practices of the Franciscan order on the subject of poverty, doctrines the Franciscans believed to be based on the Bible and the accepted teaching of the Church. To understand Ockham's political writings, therefore, we must first consider Franciscan ideas about poverty.

I. FRANCISCAN POVERTY

Most people today, including most Christians, see nothing ideal in poverty. God provides for us partly by giving us the intelligence to provide for the future, for example by gathering a moderate amount of money and property, without which it may be more difficult to advance worthwhile purposes in future. In the New Testament, however, many passages seem to idealize poverty and improvidence. Jesus himself was poor: "Foxes have holes, and birds of the air have nests; but the Son of Man [i.e., Jesus] has nowhere to lay his head."[2] "If you would be perfect, go, sell what you possess and give to the poor, and you will have treasure in heaven; and come, follow me."[3] And

No one can serve two masters. ... You cannot serve God and Mammon. Look at the birds of the air; they neither sow nor reap nor gather into barns, and yet your heavenly Father feeds them. Are you not of more value than they? Therefore I tell you, do not be anxious about your life, what you shall eat or what you shall drink, nor about your body, what you shall put on ... your heavenly Father knows that you need [these things]. But seek first his kingdom and his righteousness, and all these things shall be yours as well. Therefore, do not be anxious about tomorrow.[4]

By voluntary poverty medieval Christians hoped to humble themselves and do penance for sin, to acknowledge the superiority of spiritual over worldly values, to be set free from worldly cares to serve God, and to express faith in God's providence; for the Franciscans poverty was also a way of identifying with the poor to whom they preached the gospel.

Saint Francis of Assisi, the founder of the Franciscans,[5] was the son of a rich merchant who renounced his inheritance to follow Christ. At Mass one day he was struck by the words of the Gospel in which Jesus addresses the disciples he is sending out to preach: "Take no gold, nor silver, nor copper in your belts, no bag for your journey, nor two tunics, nor sandals, nor a staff; for the laborer deserves his food."[6] Francis took this text as the charter of the Order of Lesser Brothers; they were to be itinerant preachers without money or possessions, depending for the necessities of life on gifts made by the people they preached to. Looking back at the end of his life, Francis wrote in his "Testament": "Those who embraced this life gave everything they had to the poor. They were satisfied with one habit [i.e. tunic] which was patched inside and outside, and a cord, and trousers. We refused to have anything more."[7] But even before Francis died, controversies had begun, both within the Order and between the Franciscans and others, about the theory and practice of poverty.

In matters of poverty, Francis was an extremist. He did make prudent provision for the needs of sick Brothers and for possession of basic clothing, but these were about all the concessions he made. Theologians at the time drew a distinction between duties incumbent on all and "counsels of perfection" not binding on all: "*If* you would be perfect, go, sell what you possess and give to the poor" – but we are allowed to choose not to aspire to this degree of perfection. Francis seemed to want his Brothers to bind themselves by vow to observe the counsels of perfection. In particular, he wanted his order to exemplify the highest poverty. "The friars should be delighted to follow the lowliness and poverty of our Lord Jesus Christ, remembering that of the whole world we must own nothing; 'but having food and sufficient clothing, with these let us be content,'[8] as Saint Paul says. They should be glad to live among social outcasts, among the poor and helpless, the sick and the lepers, and those who beg by the wayside."[9] "The friars are to appropriate nothing for themselves, neither a house, nor a place, nor anything else. As 'strangers and pilgrims'[10] in this world, who serve God in poverty and humility, they should beg alms trustingly."[11] Once when he and his companions were living in an old shed, a peasant who wanted to claim the shed but expected to be repulsed sent his ass into it; Francis and his companions simply moved out of the shed and left it to him.[12] "No matter where they are, in hermitages or elsewhere, the friars must be careful not to claim the ownership of any place, or try to hold it against someone else."[13] "They should give to every man who asks, and if a man takes what is theirs, they should not ask him to restore it."[14] Francis was especially opposed to the use of money. "All the friars, no matter where they are or where they go, are forbidden to take or accept money in any way or under any form, or have it accepted for them, for clothing or books, or as wages, or in any other necessity, except to provide for the urgent needs of those who are ill."[15] When they went begging, it was for food and things they needed, not for money to buy them.

Francis and his first companions had been laymen. Soon, however, priests joined the Order, and before long most of its members were priests. The approach to preaching and priestly ministry became more professional. Brothers became students, eventually there were Franciscan schools of theology in the universities, there were Franciscan convents, churches and other buildings. Attitudes began to change. It seemed to some in the Order that more thought needed to be taken for tomorrow, that a somewhat more assured access to material means might be required, that it might be useful to gain and exercise some legal rights (at least indirectly, through agents). Changing attitudes led to conflict among the Franciscans between those who modeled themselves most closely on Francis (notably those who had been his closest companions at the end of his life, when he was no longer the head of the Order) and those who made plans for the morrow. The zealots told stories about Francis illustrating the authentic Franciscan attitudes: "He ordered the friar who did the cooking for the brothers, when he wanted to give them vegetables to eat, not to put them in hot water in the evening ready for the following day, as is usually done, so that they might obey that saying of the holy Gospel, 'Take no thought for the morrow.'"[16] When the citizens of Assisi (with an eye to the tourist dollar already?) built a house for the brothers coming to a general chapter of the order, Francis started to tear it down: "He got up on the roof and with strong hands tore off the slates and tiles. He also commanded the brothers to come up and to tear down this monstrous thing contrary to poverty.... He therefore would have destroyed the house to its very foundations, except that a knight who was standing by cooled the ardor of his spirit when he said that the house belonged to the commune and not to the brothers."[17]

This last story implies the compromise that the majority of the Order (the "conventual" party) adopted: the Franciscans themselves owned nothing (they had no *dominium*, i.e. "lordship," or *proprietas*), but they had the use (*usus*) of things that always remained the property of the donors. The zealots (or "spirituals") seem to have accepted this theory but emphasized that Franciscans should practice "poor use," that is not use an abundance of good things made available by donors but be content with poor houses, simple food, and short and patched habits. The "minister general" who did much to stabilize the order, Bonaventure, defined the evangelical (i.e., "gospel") poverty practiced in the order as follows: "Since there are two things to be considered with regard to the possession of temporal goods, *dominium* and *usus*, and *usus* is necessarily annexed to the present life; it is the nature of evangelical poverty to renounce earthly possessions in respect of *dominium* and *proprietas*, and, not to reject *usus* utterly, but to restrain it."[18] The members of every religious order took a vow of poverty. What distinguished the poverty of the Franciscans was, they claimed, that not only individual members of the Order, *but also the Order itself as a body*, had no lordship over any thing – no property either individually or in common. Everything the brothers used belonged to someone else, either the original donors or the pope. According to the Franciscans, Jesus and the Apostles had also been poor in this sense: that is, they owned nothing, either individually or as a group, but made use of things that others made available to them. The theory of poverty elaborated by Bonaventure was endorsed in the constitution *Exiit qui seminat* issued by Pope Nicholas III in 1279.[19]

II. JOHN XXII'S ATTACK ON FRANCISCAN POVERTY

In the years 1322 and 1323, after much intervening controversy,[20] Pope John XXII acted to repudiate the Franciscan theory. In his constitution *Ad conditorem* (December 1332; second version January 1323)[21] he decreed that in future (with the exception of church buildings, vestments, and other things used in divine worship) the papacy would not accept ownership of things given to the Franciscans; the Franciscan Order would be the owners themselves. This destroyed in practice their claim that as a body they held no property. He also rejected their theory. The idea that the papacy can own something of which the Franciscans permanently have the use is incompatible with the Roman law principle that ownership and usufruct cannot be separated permanently. Ownership permanently separated from use would be "simple" or "bare" and useless, and the Franciscans' lack of it would not constitute poverty. In respect of things consumed by use (such as food), there can be no separation, even temporary, between ownership and use: In the technical sense the word had in the Roman law, "use" is a right to use something without destroying its substance, but the use of things consumed by use destroys their substance; to give the use of a consumable thing is therefore to give ownership. Simple use of fact without any right to use would be unjust because just use of a thing requires a right to use it. In the everyday "factual" sense of 'use,' it is impossible for an owner to grant use to another person, for the act of using is already necessarily the act of the person using; the owner merely gives the other a right to perform that person's own act (e.g., riding) upon the owner's thing (e.g., the horse). In another constitution, *Cum inter nonnullos* (November 1323), John rejected the doctrine that Jesus and the Apostles had nothing either individually or as a group. In a third constitution, *Quia quorundam* (November 1324), he defended *Ad conditorem* and *Cum inter* against critics who alleged it was beyond his power to contradict the teachings of Nicholas III in the decretal *Exiit*. On the topic of property, he once again argued that no one can justly use things without some right of use.

In 1328 Ockham studied these three at documents "at the command of a superior," perhaps the head of the Order, Michael of Cesena. Ockham found in them "a great many things that were heretical, erroneous, silly, ridiculous, fantastic, insane and defamatory, contrary ... to orthodox faith, good morals, natural reason, certain experience, and fraternal charity."[22] After they broke with the pope and left Avignon, Michael published an *Appeal* (in a long version and a short version), to which William of Ockham was a signatory, subjecting John's constitutions to close criticism.[23] In another constitution, *Quia vir reprobus* (1329), John replied to these criticisms, quoting them extensively. (What modern church or political leader would give a critic so much publicity, or undertake to answer in detail?) In three months early in 1332 Ockham wrote *OND* to answer John's answer to Michael's criticisms.[24]

The *OND* is a "recitative" work; others include *Dial.* and *OQ*. In *OND* Ockham reports ("recites") the arguments of "the attackers" without any assertion by Ockham himself on the matters in dispute. Ockham was one of the dissident group, so presumably his own opinions are included; but because "the attackers" disagreed among themselves on some points,[25] there is a problem about ascribing the arguments in *OND* to Ockham. However, believing that Christians have a duty to speak out plainly in defense of the truth,[26] he also wrote "assertive" works, including *Brev.*, *IPP*, and *CB*. These can guide our interpretation of the recitative works. Thus, the restatement in *Brev.* of the main elements of the theory of property in *OND* justifies ascribing it to Ockham (though not as original to him). Even within the recitative works themselves there are clues to the author's opinions, such as repetition, especial subtlety of thought, or some emphasis in presentation – for example, in *Dial.* the Student sometimes expresses surprise or disbelief and asks for a thorough explanation.[27] The recitative works are in a sense academic, offering an objective treatment of the issues and leaving readers to decide on the weight of evidence. Books written in that way would be more likely to circulate and be read, and no doubt Ockham was sure what he regarded as the truth would prevail in argument. He wanted readers to forget personalities and focus on the arguments. It seems reasonable, however, to attribute to Ockham himself opinions found in the recitative works, especially when there are clues such as those mentioned earlier in this paragraph, if they are not refuted elsewhere, if they are consistent with opinions expressed in assertive writings, and if they support purposes pursued in those works.

III. PROPERTY IN THE WORK OF NINETY DAYS

Pope John had made two main points: (1) No one can justly use a thing without having some right in it, at least a right of using, and (2) no one can justly "use" a thing consumed by use (i.e., consume it) without having a particular right in it, namely property. According to John, property existed as soon as human beings began to consume; Adam, even before Eve was created, had property in the Garden of Eden, granted to him by God. Property is essential to human existence, and it exists by positive divine law.

The answer given by "the attackers" to John's first point[28] is based on a distinction between *iura fori* and *iura poli*, respectively rights under human law and rights under natural or moral law.[29] To use things justly a legal right under human law is not required; a moral right is enough. There were no property rights in the Garden of Eden; originally everyone had a natural right to use anything at all. After Adam's sin the human race (not only Adam, but human beings collectively) acquired, by God's grant, the power to establish the institution of property in view of its likely benefits in the new situation of human sinfulness. Once property was actually established by human custom or agreement ("human law"), the original natural right to use any thing at all was tied, restricted, or impeded, because there is a moral duty to respect the legal rights of others. However, in situations of necessity the original moral right revives and overrides the owner's legal right to exclude use by others. The moral right can also be untied by the owner's permission. Permission sometimes confers a legal right, but not always; it may be what the civil law calls a *precarium*, and this is the kind of permission the Franciscans have. They do not claim or exercise any legal rights, either individually or as an order. They have a moral right to use things because the owners give them precarious permission, but if permission is withdrawn (for any reason, or none), the Franciscans have no right they can enforce in court. This is "simple use of fact." In this context the phrase does not mean the act of using, it means a right; but it is a moral right, not a legal right. Simple use of fact is "a licit power of using ... to which there is not necessarily" – in the Franciscans' case, not actually – "annexed any right by which one might claim use in court."[30]

The answer to the second point – that permission to "use" a thing consumed by use (i.e., to consume it) transfers ownership – is made chiefly by examples. According to civil law a slave cannot acquire ownership, yet a master can permit or direct a slave to use consumables. Ownership implies a right to give or sell, but if a host invites guests to eat and drink, they do not thereby acquire a right to take away any of the food and give or sell it to anyone else. In other religious orders individuals must eat food the order owns, yet the individual monk has renounced property.[31]

Ockham's thesis that property did not exist in the Garden of Eden and is an institution of human law was the standard view of theologians before John XXII (Aquinas included), and later theologians judged that in *OND* Ockham had got the better of the dispute with the pope.[32] However, it must be said that the Michaelist theory of apostolic poverty was a little odd. On their account the poverty of the Franciscans, like the poverty of the Apostles, consisted in the fact that property in the things they used was not vested in them individually or as a body but in the larger body of which their body was a part, namely the Church. A business school could just as well claim to be in absolute poverty because all its splendid facilities belong to the university. Poverty should have something to do with "poor use," about which the Michaelists had little to say.

IV. HERESY AND HERETICS

In the last two chapters of *OND*, Ockham explains why "the attackers" say John XXII is a heretic. John's predecessors had defined doctrines on the poverty of Christ and the Apostles, matters within the scope of "faith and morals," and because their teachings had been accepted by the Universal Church they must be Catholic truth. Because John's teachings were inconsistent with this Catholic truth, they were heresies, and his attempt to define his teachings and impose them on all Catholics showed that he was pertinacious in his heresies and therefore a heretic.

Part I of the *Dialogue Between Master and Student Concerning Matters Disputed Among Christians* (= *Dial.*) was a thorough discussion of questions about heresy and heretics. Dial. is a "recitative" work, but to summarize boldly, Ockham seems to be intending to suggest the following. A heresy is a doctrine inconsistent with Catholic truth.[33] Catholic truth includes anything taught in the Bible, anything at any time accepted as Catholic truth by all Catholics without dissent, and any new revelation attested by miracle.[34] A heretic is not merely someone who believes a heresy but someone who holds a heretical belief *pertinaciously*. There are various indicators of pertinacity: for example, a person who tries to impose a heresy on others by threats is pertinacious. On the other hand, not to lay heretical opinion aside at the mere behest of a prelate is not proof of pertinacity; anyone, including a lay person, is entitled to defend a heretical belief a thousand times, even in the court of the pope, until that person is *shown* that the belief is a heresy. Being shown that one's belief is heretical is what Ockham calls "legitimate correction"; someone who holds a heresy but is open to "legitimate correction" is not a heretic, but someone who believes a heresy and refuses to listen to attempts to show that it is a heresy is pertinacious and a heretic.[35] Anyone can become a heretic – the pope and the cardinals, all the clergy, a general council, and so on of every part of the Church; no part of the Church is infallible. Christ's promise, "I will be with you all days, until the end of the age,"[36] guarantees it will never happen that all Catholics become heretics at the same time, but any Catholic may become a heretic at any time.[37] If it is claimed that a man generally accepted as pope is in fact a heretic, many people will not know whether the claim is correct or not, and nonculpable ignorance will excuse them if they reject the claim when it is correct; but they are obliged to protect the accusers against coercion until it has become clear to them that the accusation is unjustified – no one can be nonculpably ignorant of the fact that the accusers, if they are indeed right, are obliged to campaign in defense of the Catholic faith and ought to get a hearing.[38]

The practical outcome is that a pope who (like John) tries to impose a heresy on others by threats is a heretic, even if he claims to be ready to be corrected; and on the other hand those who (like the dissident Franciscans) merely argue in public without trying to coerce others are not heretics, even if their beliefs are in fact heresies, as long as they have not been "legitimately corrected," that is, as long as no one has answered their arguments and shown to them that their position is heretical. Meanwhile they should not be coerced, and faithful Catholics, even if they do not know whether their accusations against the pope are right, should protect them against coercion.

Ockham's argument amounts to a defense of a limited right of freedom of thought and discussion.[39] The limitation is that Ockham is defending the rights of true Catholics; he is not advocating freedom of speech for atheists, heretics, Jews, or Muslims. His argument is that Catholics should not punish, silence, or coerce people who merely argue for a certain interpretation of the Catholic faith, even if their beliefs are in fact heresies, unless they persist after that fact has been shown to them.

V. THE PAPACY

In the first stage of Ockham's campaign against John XXII his general line of argument was that because John is a heretic he is not pope and should be removed from office; the main premise is that a pope who becomes a heretic automatically ceases to be pope. In later writings Ockham began to use a second main line of argument: because John is a tyrant who threatens the rights of others, including emperors, kings and other lay persons, he is therefore a grave sinner and should be removed from the papacy; the main premise is that grave sin justifies deposition of a pope even if he has not automatically ceased to be pope by becoming a heretic.[40] The two lines of argument were brought together by the concept of "fullness of power." Ockham presents John and his successor Benedict XII as claiming full power to define and redefine the Catholic faith and to grant or cancel rights of all sorts. Strong doctrines of papal power were in the air. Without knowing Plato's *Republic*, theologians were moving toward a doctrine that made the pope a kind of "theologian king," a superexpert on the matters most important to human existence, not normally occupied with the details of secular government but able to intervene at any time by superior right untrammeled by man-made laws.[41] In opposition to this development and in defense of the older medieval idea that the world is ruled by *two* powers,[42] Ockham labored to define and limit the power of the pope.[43]

Ockham does not deny that the pope has "fullness of power" in some sense of the term. The conception he attacks is that the pope has such fullness of power that he can do anything not contrary to natural law or divine positive law. The main argument for attributing such "fullness of power" to the pope was formulated by Pope Innocent III: "The Lord said to Peter, and in Peter to his successors,

'Whatever you bind on earth will be bound also in heaven,'[44] truly making no exceptions – '*whatever* you bind.'"[45] Ockham answers that even if Christ mentioned no exceptions, there must be exceptions. General statements are not always to be taken generally. This is true even of statements found in the Bible: Paul says, "Children, obey your parents in all things," "Slaves, obey your lords in the flesh in all things," "As the Church is subject to Christ, so also are women to men in all things" – yet "in many things children are not bound to obey their parents, since they are not slaves but free, or wives their husbands, since they are not maidservants but are judged to be entitled to equality in many things ..., and slaves are not bound to obey their masters in all things without any exception."[46] The main exception to papal power that Ockham wants to assert is that popes must respect *liberties* as well as rights, including those that exist under *human law* (which included the "law of nations" and the civil law, that is, laws or customs made or observed by a particular people) and other rights and liberties acquired by agreement – provided, of course, they are consistent with natural and divine positive law.

Ockham does not seem to have believed there would be any philosophical objection to the combination of supreme religious and secular authority in one person.[47] The objection is theological. It is clear from the Bible and the writings of the Fathers of the Church that the clergy should avoid entangling themselves in secular affairs so that they can devote themselves to religious activities. For this reason the two powers must be separate. His main argument against papal "fullness of power" in the sense he rejects is that if Christ had given so much power to the pope, Christians would be the pope's slaves. It is clear from the Bible that Christ did not intend this and that he recognized rights existing under human law, including rights of unbelievers. It is also clear from the Bible and the Fathers that (though as God he could have done so) Christ did not in fact abolish or abridge the rights and liberties rulers and others legitimately had before the time of Christ. These rights included the right of an independent people to establish rulers for themselves and the already-established rights of the Roman Empire, which Christ himself recognized as legitimate.

So from the power of the pope "there must be excepted the legitimate rights of emperors, kings and the rest, believers or nonbelievers, which do not conflict with good morals, God's honor and the observance of the gospel law." This is not a blanket endorsement of existing rights: the pope must respect the "legitimate rights ... which *do not conflict with good morals*," and so forth. This might seem to open a wide door to papal intervention. But the passage continues, "according as ... Christ, the evangelists, and the apostles have more fully taught and more clearly explained" somewhere in the Bible: that is, those who wish to argue that the pope may interfere because the rights in question are not legitimate must prove they are not legitimate from the Bible.[48] There are other limits. The pope must respect not only the rights but also "the liberties granted to mortals by God and nature," and "in the things he can do by right ... the Roman pontiff should not exceed due measure" – that is, he must not impose unnecessary burdens. It is clear from the Bible that Christ meant the gospel law to be a "law of liberty," less burdensome than the Old Law had been.[49]

Such are the limitations on the pope's power. What power does he actually have, then? Ockham distinguishes between power the pope has from Christ and other powers that he may have by human law (for example, his powers as temporal ruler of certain regions of Italy). As for the power he has from Christ, Ockham distinguishes between the pope's "regular" power and the powers he may have "on occasion."[50] In *spiritual* matters (i.e., matters relating to eternal salvation and peculiar to the Christian religion) that are *of necessity* (as distinct from those that are supererogatory or merely useful), the pope *regularly* has over Christian believers (not over unbelievers) full authority on earth. In temporal matters he regularly has no authority at all (though he is entitled by divine law to a reasonable supply of temporal goods, not necessarily in the form of property,[51] for his sustenance and for carrying out his duties). *On occasion*, however, "in a situation of necessity, or of utility tantamount to necessity," both in temporal matters and in spiritual matters that are not normally necessary for salvation, the pope may do whatever is necessary (for example, to ward off some imminent danger to the Christian community or to the faith) if it is not being done by whoever is normally responsible (and, in the case of temporal matters, if the laity will not do it). The legitimate conception of "fullness of power" is that the pope can do all of the above, either "regularly" or "on occasion." Ockham never settled on a neat formula summing up the exceptional powers of the pope. "It is not easy to give a particular description of all the cases in which he can do these things, or some of them. And perhaps no universal doctrine can be given about them by which it may be known with certainty and without error, especially by the simple, when the pope can do such things and when he cannot."[52]

It should be noted that Ockham is not an opponent of the papacy as such, only of certain pseudopopes and of a certain conception of papal power. Besides opposing the extreme doctrine of fullness of power, Ockham also opposed a doctrine that attributed to the pope very little power indeed, that of Marsilius of Padua. According to Marsilius, Christ did not make Peter head over the other apostles and gave him no more power than he gave the others; the papacy is a purely human creation.[53] It seems clear that Ockham's main purpose in *Dial.* III-1 is to refute Marsilius.[54] After a discussion in Book One of various opinions about papal power, including that of Marsilius, Book Two discusses whether it is more beneficial for the Church to be ruled by one or by many. Most of the commonplace arguments for rule by one[55] are in fact arguments for unified government, whether by one person or by a committee. The main advantages specific to monarchy are that it is easier for subjects to get access to one person than to many, a single bad ruler is more easily removed, the ruler need not wait for colleagues to concur before taking action, the ruler can manage the process of deliberation more flexibly, and there is less likely to be conflict within the rulership.[56] The main objections come from three points made by Aristotle: (1) Monarchy is unjust unless the monarch is clearly superior in virtue and wisdom; (2) decisions made by many consulting together are wiser than decisions made by one person; and (3) a community should be able to adapt its form of government to circumstances.[57] The answer to the first is that rule by one ruler who is good and wise enough but not outstanding is just if his equals and betters consent, as they should do if monarchy is otherwise best for the community.[58] The answer to the second is that provided the ruler is willing to take wise advice, it is better to have one sufficiently good and wise ruler than many good and wise rulers obliged to act together.[59] The difficulty with the third point is that, if the papal monarchy was established by Christ, the Christian community cannot go against his command. The answer is that Christ can be assumed to intend (except when he explicitly says otherwise) that exceptions can be made to his commands when necessity or great utility requires.[60] If Christ did establish a monarchy in the Church, it will nevertheless be possible, when necessity demands, to have several popes jointly in office at the same time, or to have no pope but independent patriarchs ruling separately in different parts of the world; but a single pope must be elected as soon as circumstances permit.[61]

Whether monarchy is more advantageous or not, the question remains, Did Christ in fact establish monarchy in the Church? Book Three discusses the preliminary question, What counts as evidence of Christ's intentions? Marsilius held that no Christian is obliged to believe anything except the Bible and General Councils of the Church.[62] The Master presents arguments against the infallibility of General Councils and also arguments to show that the testimony of even fallible writers on factual matters within their knowledge must be presumed to be true unless there is some specific reason for disbelief.[63] In Book Four we reach the main question. The Master presents Marsilius's arguments against belief in Peter's headship and the traditional arguments in favor. Because (as the argument of Book Three implies) we must accept the testimony of early Christian writers as to the meaning of Christ's words, the traditional belief that Christ meant Peter to be head of the Church is vindicated.[64] The papacy exists not by the choice of Christians, still less by the choice of the secular ruler, but by divine institution.

VI. THE EMPIRE

When Michael of Cesena and his companions fled from Avignon, they went for protection to the court of the "Roman Emperor," Ludwig of Bavaria.[65] Ludwig had been excommunicated by John XXII for exercising imperial rights without first obtaining the pope's approval of his election. According to advocates of papal supremacy in temporal matters, the emperor-elect needed papal approval because the Empire was subject to the Church, as had been demonstrated by its transfer from the Greeks to Charlemagne by Pope Leo III. The Michaelists, on the other hand, alleged that John's interference with the government of the Empire was an injustice and that such injustices flowed from principles threatening not only the rights of the Empire (about which many people outside Germany would not have cared) but also the rights of all secular rulers and indeed of all mortals. Hence the second of the two lines of argument mentioned at the beginning of Section V above, that even if he were not a heretic, John should be deposed for serious and incorrigible sins of injustice.

In *Dial.*, the Master recites the arguments for the opinion that the world should be ruled by one secular ruler, "not inappropriately called emperor." Mostly they are arguments for world government of some sort – perhaps no more than a United Nations and a World Court – that would keep the peace and restrain the wicked.[66] The best arguments specifically for a world monarchy (or at least for a strong Secretary General) are again in terms of the importance of flexibility in consultation and action. The answer to the argument that committee government is best because many are less likely to err than one, is that although advice is needed, it is useful for one person to control the process of deliberation.[67] Monarchy is therefore regularly the best regime for the world, but under some circumstances – for example, if there are powerful groups who will not submit – the best regime should be suspended, perhaps for an extended period,[68] though it could not be abolished or impaired permanently.[69] The Empire need not be a unitary state. The emperor can establish parts of the Empire as independent kingdoms or dukedoms or grant exemptions to individuals or groups,[70] and such a grant gives the recipient a right the emperor cannot revoke unless there is some fault on that person's part or some good reason in terms of the common good.[71] No sovereignty is absolute; the emperor must be able on occasion to correct governments or individuals who are normally independent and conversely, on occasion others may need to correct or depose a bad emperor – one of the advantages of monarchy is that one ruler is easier to remove if he rules badly. The ruler should therefore not have so much control that he can evade correction. It is unnecessary, indeed dangerous, for everyone in the state to be subject regularly and in every case to the supreme ruler.[72] Thus Ockham rejects the view of Marsilius[73] (and Hobbes, and many others) that government power must be absolutely unified.

On Ockham's view world government has existed since ancient times in the form of the Roman Empire. All peoples not already subject to a superior have a natural right to make laws for themselves and to establish a government for themselves.[74] This is true also of unbelievers.[75] Like other peoples, the pagan Romans established their own government, and in course of time it obtained power over other peoples. It may be that their rule over others was first established by unjust force,[76] but by Christ's time it had become legitimate, as the New Testament proves.[77] How it became legitimate Ockham does not know, but perhaps it was by the consent of their subjects, in view of the usefulness to the world of Roman rule.[78] The world Empire belongs fundamentally to the peoples of the world, but by consenting to Roman rule they have entrusted it to the Romans, who therefore have a right to it that they cannot lose without some fault or for some other good reason, and there is no reason to think that they have ever lost it.[79] The Romans, in turn, entrusted their government to one person, namely the first emperor, Augustus, with the right to provide for succession. As befits the highest level of government, succession is determined by the best method, namely, election – that is, deliberate choice, either by the emperor or by an electoral college. The Empire has never been hereditary, though there have been times when the emperor chose his eldest son as his successor. In more recent times the successor has been elected by an electoral college, existing by the emperor's choice, consisting of certain German princes.[80] Their election is enough to give the elect full right to administer the Empire without waiting for papal confirmation or coronation. When a people establish a government, they can impose whatever conditions they think appropriate, and they could provide that a successor should not take office until he has been approved by the pope or crowned, but if the people impose no such condition the monarch can determine the conditions under which his successor will assume administration of the government. Immediate power upon election has many advantages for the common good and is the practice established for the Roman Empire by the emperors.[81]

Ockham's account of the Empire is developed mainly in opposition to the opinion that the emperor derives his power from the pope.[82] According to Ockham, the power of the emperor comes from God, not through the pope but through the people. The Empire was established by the Roman people, and through any "transfer" it remained the same Empire: later emperors therefore succeeded in the same right as the first emperors,[83] that is, as empowered by the Roman people. The pope does not have any regular power over the Empire, but on occasion popes may have intervened legitimately in the affairs of the Empire, either with the consent of the Romans, or to remedy the Romans' negligence or incapacity in situations of urgent necessity when the laity would not or could not act.[84] Conversely, after the emperors became Christians, there have been cases when the emperor (not as emperor but as a leading Roman Christian) has legitimately intervened in Church affairs, either with the consent of the Catholic Romans, who by divine law have the right to choose the pope, or with the consent of some person or persons to whom the Romans have entrusted some right in Church affairs.[85]

Ockham's account of the power of the emperor parallels his account of the power of the pope. Both are limited by the rights of free subjects and by the requirement that whatever is imposed be for the common good. In *Dial.* III there is a discussion of whether the emperor has "fullness of power."[86] One opinion is that in temporal affairs the emperor can command anything not contrary to divine or natural law; this corresponds to the doctrine of papal "fullness of power" to which Ockham was so much opposed. Another opinion is that "his power is limited, so that, with respect to his free subjects and their property, he can do only the things that are useful to the common benefit." If he had more power than that, his subjects would be slaves, which would be incompatible with the character of the Empire as the best form of government.[87] The emperor has his power from the people, and the people never had power to impose on anyone anything that is not necessary without that person's consent; the emperor's power has the same limit. According to this second opinion, the emperor is bound not only by natural and divine law but by the law of nations. On behalf of those who hold the second opinion the Master answers the famous "absolutist" texts of Roman law: That the emperor is "released from the laws" is not true, because he is bound not only by natural and divine law but also by the law of nations (a branch of human positive law), according to which at least some are free and not slaves. "What pleases the prince has the force of law," but only when it is something reasonable and just for the sake of the common good and when this is manifestly expressed.

VII. WOMEN

Ockham does not say much about women. What he says is consistent with the views of Aristotle and Augustine, according to whom

women are naturally subordinate to men. But there are some qualifications. Like Aristotle, Ockham acknowledges that there are exceptions to the natural superiority of men over women.[88] Even when the
natural superiority does obtain, a husband does not have "fullness
of power" over his wife "because she is not a maidservant, and in
many things is judged to be entitled to equality."[89] In the Garden
of Eden God granted lordship not only to Adam, but to "Adam and
his wife for themselves and all their posterity"[90]; if (as John XXII
claimed) Adam had lordship before Eve was made, he had no power
to withhold it from Eve, and no act on Adam's part (for example, no
grant) was necessary for Eve to acquire it.[91] Matters of faith concern
women as well as men, for "in the new man there is neither male
nor female."[92] Women should (when necessary) take part in general
councils of the Church: "Where the wisdom, goodness or power of
a woman is necessary to the discussion of the faith ... the woman
should not be excluded from the general council."[93]

VIII. CONCLUSION

Ockham did not write "political" writings as a contribution to political philosophy; he wrote as a theologian engaged in a campaign
to remove a pseudopope from office. His premises were drawn from
traditional sources in theology, philosophy, and law; many of his conclusions were also traditional, but some were new justifications for
a radical activity, the attempt to depose a pope. Even this activity
had conservative aims: to preserve the Franciscan way of life, to re-
instate the practices that had been observed in the Church before the
late-medieval inflation of papal claims, to defend the ancient rights
of the Roman Empire, and above all to preserve the Church from
heresy.

However, there is a political philosophy in his "political writings," and in some ways it resembles nineteenth-century liberalism.
Ockham's Utilitarian theory of property, his defense of civil and
(within limits) religious liberty, and his emphasis on the inevitability
of exceptions to rules and the need to adapt institutions to changing
circumstances anticipate John Stuart Mill. The connecting link is
Aristotle: there is an analogy between Aristotle's criterion, the common good, and the Utilitarian criterion, the general happiness. That
government is for the sake of the common good is the leading idea of

Ockham's political philosophy. In combination with his belief that human affairs are unpredictable, it leads to his characteristic formulation of Aristotle's idea of "equity," namely the contrast between what is "regularly" right and what is right "occasionally." Rules are needed, but because no humanly made rules can guarantee the common good in all the multifarious cases that will arise, individuals must be prepared on occasion to act without the rules or against the rules – a line of thought Mill would have endorsed. Such comparisons with other writers may help place Ockham's political thought into a larger historical context, but the real interest is in the details, in the thoroughness and subtlety with which he applied his leading ideas to the complexities of his own world. His theological arguments may have little appeal to non-Christians (though they may find them interesting historically), but any reasonably persistent reader will come to respect the intelligence, seriousness, courage, and moderation with which Ockham wrote about some of the major issues of his time.

NOTES

1 For the Latin text of Ockham's "political writings," see Ockham 1956–97. An edition of *Dial.* with Latin text and English translation in parallel columns is in progress at http:// britac3.britac.ac.uk/ockdial.html. *Translations*: McGrade and Kilcullen, 1992 and 1995; Kilcullen and Scott 1998; Lewis 1954; Miethke 1992 and 1995; Santidrian 1992. *Studies*: Baudry 1950; Miethke, 1969; McGrade 1974b; Knysh 1996. See also the reading suggestions in McGrade and Kilcullen 1992 and 1995.
2 Matt. 8:20. (All quotations from the Bible are taken from the Revised Standard Version.)
3 Matt. 19:21.
4 Matt. 6:24–34.
5 He did not call his fellowship after himself, of course. The official name was "The Order of Friars Minor," that is, "of lesser brothers."
6 Matt. 10:9. See Habig 1983, 646.
7 Habig 1983, 68.
8 1 Tim. 6:8.
9 Habig 1983, 39.
10 1 Pet. 2:11.
11 Habig 1983, 61.
12 Ibid., 265.

13 Ibid., 38.

14 Ibid., 42.

15 Ibid., 38.

16 Brooke 1970, 95.

17 Habig 1983, 412.

18 Lambert 1961, 127, quoting Bonaventure, *Apologia pauperum*. For the complete work see Bonaventure 1966.

19 A rough translation of *Exiit* is available at http://www.mq.edu.au/~ockham/wexiit.html.

20 See Douie 1932; Lambert 1961; Leff 1967; Tierney 1988. For Aquinas's part in the controversy between seculars and mendicants (the "mendicants" included the Franciscans and Dominicans), see Weisheipl 1974, 80–92, 263–72, 383–4.

21 For rough translations of some of John's constitutions see http://www.mq.edu.au/~ockham/opgeock.html.

22 *Epist.* (6) (= McGrade and Kilcullen 1995, 3–4). He goes on to list the errors and heresies.

23 For a list of Michael's writings, see Dolcini 1977, 11–12.

24 For dates of Ockham's political works, see Offler's introductions in OPol.

25 See *OND* 124.462–6. For expression of differences, see *OND* 94.327–32, 103.85–98, 106.66–114, 124. 96. Sometimes it sounds as if the attackers are a collective author with Ockham merely holding the pen; see *OND* 105.19–21.

26 *Dial.* III-1.iv.22 (= McGrade and Kilcullen 1995, 229). This duty seems to be an implication of Ockham's interpretation of Christ's promise to be with the Church all days; see *Dial.* III-1.ii.30 (= McGrade and Kilcullen 1995, 206) and *Tractatus contra Ioannem* 14 (67.22–34). However, it is "not necessary on every occasion to confess with one's mouth the truth, even if it is catholic, since it falls under an affirmative precept, which always obliges but not for always" (*Dial.* III-1.Prol.); hence, the legitimacy of recitative works.

27 See, for example, *Dial.* III-2.iii.6 (= McGrade and Kilcullen 1995, 288); *Dial.* III-1.iii.4, III-2.ii.8. However, some of the theories we might expect Ockham to favor are not asserted elsewhere; it seems likely that some of the discussion is simply exploratory. (Notice the warnings at the beginning of *Dial.* I.v.34.) On the interpretation of *Dial.*, see Knysh 1996, 237–64. On the interpretation of *OQ* see Offler's introduction, OPol I.13; he suggests that in *OQ* IV and VIII Ockham's opinion is the one ascribed to the German princes.

28 *OND* 28, 65. See also *Brev.* III.7–10.

29 Natural law and natural rights figure prominently in Ockham's political thought. See *Dial.* III-2.iii.6.

30 *OND* 6.260–71.

31 *OND* 4.255–86, 6.231–56.

32 Kilcullen 1995, §§2–3. De Soto says John XXII had acted illegitimately out of hatred of Ockham; Molina says John was only "disputing and arguing" and not intending to define anything.

33 *Dial.* I.ii.6.

34 *Dial.* I.ii.2–5. This has been called Ockham's "three source" theory, but behind these the one source is God.

35 On legitimate correction, see McGrade 1974b, 53 ff. On the indicators of pertinacity, see *Dial.* I.iv.

36 Matt. 28:20.

37 On the fallibility of every part of the Church, see *Dial.* I.v.

38 *Dial.* I.vii.37, 40, 45, 47.

39 The medieval practice of disputation (within which Ockham's recitative works fall) already allowed a measure of free thought and free speech, and Ockham's inquiry into papal power, though he felt a need to justify it, would probably have been recognized as legitimate by other theologians; see *Brev.*, especially I.2; McGrade and Kilcullen 1992, 5–6, nn. 4, 10.

40 See Tierney 1955, 57–67. For statements of these premises, see *CB* VII.1, 13.

41 For example, according to Aquinas 1949, 62, "Those to whom pertains the care of intermediate ends [i.e., kings] should be subject to him [i.e., the Roman Pontiff] to whom pertains the care of the ultimate end." For telling criticism, see John of Paris 1971, 184–6. For other arguments for papal supremacy (in some sense) over secular government, see Giles of Rome 1986; James of Viterbo 1995; Tierney 1980, 123–4, 131–8, 143–4, 147–9, 153–7.

42 See Pope Gelasius, *Duo sunt*, translated in Tierney 1980, 13.

43 Ockham's first references to "fullness of power" are in *CB* IV.12, VI.2. It is discussed also in *Brev.* II, *OQ* I, *Dial.* III–1.i, *AP* 1–6, and *IPP*. See extracts in Lewis 1954, 606–15. Marsilius of Padua had also seen the doctrine of "fullness of power" as the main source of the revolutionary encroachments of the papacy on secular government. Marsilius of Padua 1980, 313–64.

44 Matt. 16:19.

45 *Brev.* II.2.

46 *Brev.* II.14. For discussion whether and when it is permitted to make exceptions where the words of the Bible do not mention any exception, see *Dial.* III-1.ii.23–4.

47 See the arguments reported in *OQ* V.5.

48 Or, presumably, from one of the other "sources" of Catholic truth.

49 For the quotations in this paragraph, see *Brev.* II.16, 17, 18.

50 For this distinction, see *Brev.* IV.4. See Bayley 1949; Bayley relates it
   to the traditional concepts of equity (in the Aristotelian sense – setting
   aside the letter of the law for the sake of its purpose), the common good,
   and necessity ("What is not licit by the law, necessity makes licit").

51 *Brev.* I.7. See also McGrade and Kilcullen 1992, 12 n. 30, and *OND*
   88.201–4 (= McGrade and Kilcullen 1995, 66).

52 *Dial.* III-1.i.16; see also i.17. For other passages in which Ockham tries
   to sum up, see *Brev.* II.20; McGrade and Kilcullen 1992, 62–3 nn. 95, 96;
   and OQ I.7.30–87.

53 Marsilius of Padua 1980, 233 ff. (II.xv, xvi).

54 Ockham seems to have written *Dial.* III-1 partly because he had obtained
   a copy of Marsilius's book, to which he had not previously had access
   (*Dial.* III-1.iii.1).

55 *Dial.* III-1.ii.1, 9–10.

56 Ibid., ii.18. The discussion is not about a monarch succeeding by inheritance (which Ockham regarded as an inferior mode of succession), but
   about a monarch elected for life.

57 Although Book Two contains an exposition of Aristotle's political
   thought (*Dial.* III-1.ii.3–8), one of its chief purposes is to counter Aristotle's practical opposition to monarchy. Aristotle echoes Plato's preference for monarchy but with a qualification that makes the preference
   merely academic, namely, that the monarch must be clearly superior to
   all his subjects.

58 Ibid., ii.17.

59 Ibid., ii.19, III-2.i.13, 15. The ruler will need to be wise enough to know
   when he needs advice and where to get it – and good enough to take it.

60 *Dial.* III-1.ii.20–4. A command by Christ is an item of divine positive law.
   No exception can be made to *natural* law except when God explicitly
   commands it (ibid., ii.20). That God can command exceptions to natural
   laws does not imply that they hold (when they do hold) by virtue of
   a divine command or that the exceptions could become the rule. For
   discussion of these issues see Chap. 12.

61 *Dial.* III-1.ii.26–8, III-2.i.8 (the election of a pope "could licitly be deferred
   for a hundred years, or two hundred, or more"); *Dial.* III-1.iv.24. In the
   seventeenth century some Anglicans argued that, although episcopacy
   was of divine right, by reason of necessity a church might live for a time
   without bishops. See Sykes 1956, 69 ff.

62 Marsilius 1980, 274ff. (II.xix).

63 For Ockham's opinion, see *Dial.* III-1.iii.4–7, 22–6, and iv.13, 14, 22.

64 *Dial.* III-1.iv.13–7, 22.

65 What Ockham called the "Roman Empire" was later called "The Holy
   Roman Empire of the German People"; it lasted until Napoleon.

Constantine transferred the capital of the Roman Empire to Constantinople, and Pope Leo III transferred the Empire from the Greeks to the Franks; it was then transferred to the Germans. The kingdoms of Spain, France, and England did not recognize its authority; the spokesmen for the Empire claimed that the independence of their kingdoms was de facto, not de iure. Like the pope, the Emperor was an elective monarch for life; the cardinals elected the pope, the German Princes Electors elected the Emperor.

66 *Dial.* III-2.i.1.

67 Ibid., i.13.

68 Ibid., i.5–10.

69 Ibid., i.8; *OQ* III.11, VIII.4.210–7; *Dial.* III-2.i.31.

70 *OQ* III.9.1–12.93 (= McGrade and Kilcullen 1995, 320–6); *OQ* VIII.4.237–44.

71 *OQ* IV.4.115–23, VIII.4.276–84.

72 *OQ* III.3.34–9 (= McGrade and Kilcullen 1995, 310, last paragraph).

73 Marsilius of Padua 1980, 80 ff. (II.xvii).

74 *Brev.* IV.10; *Dial.* III-1.ii.28.

75 *Brev.* III.

76 Ibid., IV.9.

77 Ibid., III.3, 10.

78 Ibid. The consent of a majority would have been sufficient: *Dial.* III-2.i.27, Master's third speech. In *Brev.*, Ockham mentions just war as a way of legitimating empire, but see *OQ* IV.4.63–95.

79 *Brev.* IV.13; *Dial.* III-2.i.29 (Master's last speech), ii.5.

80 *OQ* IV.6.161–95, IV.7.8–17, IV.9.50–66, VIII.4.218–36. The Electors represent the Romans: *Brev.* VI.2.

81 *Dial.* III-2.ii.29; *OQ* IV.10, V.6; *CB* VI.6 (283.35–284.5).

82 See *CB* VI.2, 5; *OQ* II; *Brev.* IV, V; *Dial.* III-2.i.18–25, 28. Ockham also criticizes the views of Lupold of Bebenburg, who tried to reconcile the papal view with the view of the German princes. According to Lupold, election makes the elect "King of the Romans" as successor to Charlemagne with immediate administrative power in the lands that belonged to Charlemagne before Pope Leo crowned him Emperor, but he needs to be crowned by the pope before he has power in other lands. For Ockham's criticisms see *OQ* IV, VIII, especially VIII.4.

83 *OQ* IV.2.29–40; *Brev.* IV.1, 9.

84 *OQ* II.10.14–33, IV.6.72–97, VIII.6.21–32, 6.48–62. See similar remarks about the transfer of the kingdom of the Franks, *Brev.* VI.2; *OQ* IV.3.132–50. See also *Dial.* III-2.ii.13–19 on supplying the deficiencies of secular judges.

85 *Dial.* III-2.iii.3–7. Also ibid., iii.11–4.

86 *Dial.* III-2.ii.26–8.
87 *OQ* III.6, 7.
88 *Dial.* III-1.ii.3.
89 *Brev.* II.6; see II.14. See also *Dial.* III–1.ii.4.
90 *Brev.* III.7.
91 *OND* 27.71–84 (= McGrade and Kilcullen 1995, 40).
92 Gal. 3:28.
93 *Dial.* I.vi.85.

14   Ockham on Faith and Reason

Analytic philosophers specializing in medieval philosophy have tended to focus on those aspects of Catholic medieval thought that seem relevant to research programs already firmly established within the mainstream of contemporary academic philosophy. In this way they have tried to convince other philosophers that the Catholic medieval thinkers, despite their theological presuppositions, have something useful to contribute to current discussions.[1] The tendency in question has been especially pronounced in the case of William of Ockham because he is at his best when doing ontology and philosophical semantics, two areas that have figured prominently in recent analytic philosophy and that seem safely removed from distinctively Catholic beliefs.

Undeniably, much valuable reflection on Catholic medieval thought has been generated by this desire to show how certain parts of the works of Ockham and the others might bear on contemporary problematics or even inspire us to reconfigure those problematics; indeed, many academic philosophers who would not otherwise have noticed the medievals have thereby been led to treat them as full-fledged interlocutors. Still, to limit ourselves to this fragmentary approach prevents us from understanding these thinkers as they understood themselves and renders us vulnerable to the abiding temptation to refashion their work so as to make it suit our own cultural and philosophical biases.

But how can we hope to understand the intellectual projects of the Catholic medieval thinkers as they themselves understood them? A first step in the right direction is to ask how they perceived their own relationship to the classical non-Christian philosophical traditions they had inherited. The Middle Ages were, of course, marked by spirited and sometimes bitter debates about how, or even whether, a given one or another of those traditions might contribute to the systematic articulation of the Catholic faith. But the question I mean to raise here is a more basic one, Did the Catholic medieval thinkers see themselves in any philosophically interesting sense as the successors of classical philosophical inquirers such as Socrates, Plato, Aristotle, and the Stoics?

Here I will explore answers to this question gleaned from Ockham on the one hand and from his predecessors, especially Thomas Aquinas and John Duns Scotus, on the other. In so doing I will touch upon the most important general issues that have come to be lumped together under the rubric "Faith and Reason" in studies of Catholic medieval thought.

I. CATHOLIC TRADITION ON THE FRAILTY OF NATURAL REASON

If the term 'successor' is taken in a suitably broad sense, then the answer to our question is unequivocally affirmative, once we grant three important assumptions that were shared by all the thinkers to be discussed here. The first is the Socratic conviction that the aim of an intellectually and morally integrated philosophical life is the attainment of wisdom – that is, the attainment of a comprehensive and systematic elaboration of the first principles of being that provides definitive answers to ultimate questions about the origins, nature, and destiny of the universe and about the good for human beings and the ways to attain it. In Aquinas's more precise formula, unqualified wisdom, which enables its possessor to "order things rightly and govern them well," consists in (1) knowledge of God as he is in himself, (2) knowledge of creatures insofar as they proceed from God as their origin, and (3) knowledge of creatures insofar as they are ordered to God as their end.[2] The second assumption is that in the pursuit of wisdom, so conceived, philosophers should draw upon all the cognitive resources available to them. The third and final assumption is that one indispensable cognitive resource is the Catholic faith itself.

Given these assumptions, the Catholic medieval thinkers found it easy to identify Christian wisdom, personified in the incarnate Son of God and articulated systematically by Christian theology, as the real (albeit hidden) object of the quest for wisdom that the classical philosophical inquirers had initiated but had been incapable of bringing to fulfillment in the absence of Christian revelation. Indeed, this commonly shared perception of themselves as the intellectual heirs of the classical philosophers helps explain the naturalness with which the Catholic medievals carried out their interestingly diverse attempts to assimilate, or at least make use of, a wide variety of non-Christian philosophical traditions.

As we will see in Section II, agreement on this general point did not preclude an animated dispute over the precise sense in which Christian theology can claim to be the successor of classical philosophical inquiry. However, I want to pause for a moment to consider an important implication of what has been said thus far, namely the (perhaps surprising) extent to which the Catholic faith itself deflates the pretensions of natural reason unaided by divine revelation. For it is a central Catholic doctrine that our natural cognitive powers, both theoretical and practical, are severely limited to begin with and, to make matters worse, have been gravely wounded by sin, with the result that they cannot lead us to genuine wisdom unless they are healed and elevated by the supernatural virtue of faith graciously bestowed upon us by God.[3]

To be sure, the Catholic tradition has time and again repudiated what it considers to be insufficiently circumspect condemnations of the influence of non-Christian philosophical traditions within Christian thought. I have in mind the sort of radical intellectual separatism championed in different historical contexts by the likes of Tertullian, Eusebius of Caesarea, Martin Luther, and Karl Barth.[4] Yet it is important to see that this combative intellectual separatism, with its animus against pagan and secular philosophy and its characteristic call for a "return to Scripture," has its origins in a central Christian teaching, namely that as long as human reason is cut off from the illumination made available through the salvific action of Jesus Christ, it cannot perceive fully or definitively the metaphysical and moral truths that constitute the object of the classical search for philosophical wisdom. Thus, although while the Catholic tradition has always viewed radical intellectual separatism as a misguided exaggeration, it has nonetheless seen such separatism as the excess of a genuine virtue, to wit, an intellectual modesty that might lead even the greatest of pagan and secular philosophers to acknowledge that, as Aquinas puts it, "in divine matters natural reason is greatly deficient,"[5] and to remain open, at least in principle, to the possibility of divine revelation.

All this is necessary by way of a preface to Ockham on faith and reason. Ockham is not a radical intellectual separatist, but he is in fact less hopeful than Aquinas or even Scotus in his assessment of just how much philosophical truth natural reason is capable of acquiring without the aid of divine revelation; nor, in what follows, will I underplay the resulting differences or suggest that they are not significant. Still, I want to emphasize from the beginning that the differences, great as they might be, are no more impressive than the similarities.

The reason this point is not commonly emphasized is that Scotus and especially Aquinas have often been cast as veritable rationalists in order to contrast their views on faith and reason with Ockham's alleged "fideism." To some extent this is to be expected, for historians of philosophy who follow the chronological progression from Aquinas and Scotus to Ockham have naturally tended to underscore what is distinctive to Ockham. But more recent cultural and historical factors have also engendered exaggerated estimates of the degree of confidence that Aquinas and Scotus repose in natural reason. For instance, at various times since the seventeenth century the Catholic intellectual tradition, including the Church as an institution, has deemed it necessary to defend the basic integrity of natural reason against those forms of skepticism regarding philosophical wisdom that Chesterton aptly grouped under the title "The Suicide of Thought" in his early-twentieth-century apologetic work *Orthodoxy*.[6] Then too, given the increasingly pluralistic character of Western liberal democracies, Catholic thinkers have felt an added pressure to find common ground with nonbelievers on important metaphysical and moral issues, and this has helped generate, to put it bluntly, unconscionably optimistic assessments of the power of natural reason to fashion a lingua franca that is wholly independent of specifically Christian revelation. Yet if the resulting picture is taken myopically to imply that natural reason can provide a wide range of substantive and easily discernible points of agreement between believers and nonbelievers regardless of other historical, cultural, and moral differences in their respective epistemic situations, then it is contrary to the positions of Aquinas and Scotus no less than to that of Ockham. In short, a good dose of wariness about the capacity of natural reason, as situated in concrete historical and cultural settings, to discern with clarity even relatively fundamental metaphysical and moral truths is and must be endemic to any authentically Catholic philosophy.

An analogy might be useful here. Radical and universal Christian pacifism is often portrayed within mainline Catholic circles as a (perhaps dangerous) aberration in order to contrast it with what are taken to be the more reasonable requirements of classical just war theory. Yet although not entirely misleading, such a portrayal conceals the extent to which just war theory, if applied rigorously to concrete historical situations, is itself a modified pacifism that attempts to respond faithfully to the very same gospel imperatives that inspire universal pacifism. In the same way, Ockham's emphasis on the limitations of unaided human reason is often portrayed within mainline Catholic circles as a (perhaps dangerous) aberration in order to contrast it with the less gloomy assessment of natural reason associated with thinkers such as Anselm, Aquinas, Scotus, and Suarez, who constructed elaborate natural theologies and were convinced that the Catholic faith could in principle be shown to satisfy any plausible standards of rationality. Although not entirely misleading, such a portrayal obscures the firmness with which *all* the important Catholic medieval thinkers held to the conviction that divine revelation is absolutely necessary for us to flourish as human beings and that, as far as ultimate metaphysical and moral questions are concerned, we remain in an utterly perilous state of ignorance without it.

By way of corroboration one need only cite *SCG* I.4, where Aquinas argues in great detail that even though God's existence and many of the divine attributes can in principle be discovered by natural reason, hardly anyone, even the most astute philosophers, would have a sufficiently accurate and secure cognition of God were it not for divine revelation – and this just a few chapters before Aquinas lays out his most sophisticated rendering of the proof for an unmoved mover.[7] Likewise, in *ST* IaIIae.94.4 and 6, he claims that, although we have a sort of "connatural" cognition of the moral law, even fundamental moral precepts such as the prohibitions of theft, idolatry, and various other forms of moral corruption can be "abolished from the human heart" in fitting historical and cultural settings. Moreover, as regards moral knowledge at least, Scotus's assessment of the power of natural reason is even more bleak than Aquinas's.[8]

With this point fixed firmly in mind, we can now move on to investigate the differences between Ockham and his predecessors.

II. THE COGNITIVE STATUS
OF CHRISTIAN THEOLOGY

As noted earlier, if the medieval Catholic thinkers concur in seeing themselves as the heirs of the classical philosophers, it is because they view Christian theology as the successor, broadly speaking, to the best of classical philosophical inquiry, both speculative (metaphysics) and practical (ethics). The disagreement between Ockham and his predecessors is most fruitfully understood as a dispute about the exact way in which this "successor" relation should be spelled out.[9]

According to Aquinas, Christian theology is a successor to classical metaphysics and ethics not merely because it replaces them or merely because it brings them to fulfillment in the sense of providing otherwise hidden answers to the questions they pose, but precisely because it perfects them according to standards of intellectual perfection that the best classical philosophers themselves subscribe to.[10] In an effort to show this clearly, Aquinas himself finally abandoned the standard theological practice of commenting on Peter Lombard's *Sentences* in order to reconfigure Christian theology in a systematic and nonrepetitious way that was expressly intended to satisfy the criteria for a science laid down by Aristotle in the *Posterior Analytics*. This effort explains the origins of *ST*.[11]

Ockham, for his part, denies that Christian theology can be thought of as a successor to classical philosophy in this strong sense. But in order to put his disagreement with Aquinas into proper relief, we must begin by drawing some pertinent distinctions. The first is laid out by Aquinas in *SCG* I.3:

Among the things we profess about God there are two types of truths. There are some truths about God that altogether exceed the capability of human reason, for example, that God is [both] three and one. But there are other truths that natural reason is also capable of arriving at, for example, that God exists, that there is one God, and others of this sort. Indeed, the philosophers, led by the light of natural reason, have proved these truths about God demonstratively.

Aquinas thus divides divinely revealed truths into what he else-where calls the "mysteries" [or "articles"] of the faith, which "al-together exceed the capability of human reason," and the "pream-bles" of the faith, which can at least in principle be established by the light of natural reason. Ockham draws a similar distinction between theological truths we are naturally able to have evident cognition of and theological truths we can have cognition of only supernaturally.[12]

Aquinas and Ockham agree that if we are to assent to the myster-ies in this life, then we must accept them on faith and thus cannot have evident cognition of them.[13] This leads us directly to the dis-tinction between faith and other intellectual acts (or habits) with propositional objects. Aquinas defines Christian faith in its most proper sense as an intellectual act (or corresponding habit) by which a person, desirous of everlasting human fulfillment and moved by di-vine grace, gives firm intellectual assent voluntarily to propositions that are not evident by the light of natural reason but are taken to be revealed as truths by an unfailingly trustworthy God. Christian faith so defined is distinguished from intellectual acts like vacilla-tion, tentative preference, and probable opinion by the fact that it involves firm assent to its objects; on the other hand, faith is distin-guished from the grasp of evident first principles and the knowledge of conclusions seen clearly to follow from such principles by its ob-jects' not being evident by the light of natural reason and hence not commanding "automatic" assent but instead being freely assented to.[14] Ockham's own remarks about the supernaturally infused habit of faith fully cohere with this account.[15]

We can now begin to appreciate the quite astonishing strength of Aquinas's claim that Christian theology counts as a science and in-deed as the highest science possible for us in this life. According to Aristotle, inquiry in a given domain has as its goal wisdom with re-spect to that domain. Starting with an indistinct and tentative grasp of an initial set of pertinent first principles, and making full use of available logical, conceptual, and experiential resources, one con-ducts the inquiry by reasoning from effects back to causes, aiming ultimately to perfect one's cognitive grasp of the domain in such a way as to be able to exhibit it as a series of evident conclusions validly derived from a fully specified set of what have now become evident first principles. To have wisdom with respect to a domain is just to have a solid grasp of a full set of evident first principles of that domain along with firm knowledge of the conclusions that are seen clearly to flow from those first principles (*scientia*). And to have absolute or unqualified wisdom is just to have wisdom with respect to the first principles of all being; alternatively, as Aquinas and Ockham would put it, to have absolute wisdom is to have a share in God's own knowledge of himself and in God's own knowledge of all other beings insofar as they originate from him as their efficient cause and are ordered to him as their final end.[16]

Yet, as we have seen, Aquinas not only admits but insists that in this life we can never have an evident grasp of the mysteries of the faith, which are included among the first principles of Christian theology. Rather, we must accept these mysteries on faith not only at the beginning of theological inquiry but for as long as that inquiry continues in this life. It seems to follow straightforwardly that theological inquirers cannot have *scientia* with respect to the conclusions of theology. This is a point Ockham emphasizes repeatedly in his critique of the claim that "our theology" counts as a science:

An [intellectual] habit with respect to the principles is better known and more evident than [the corresponding] habit with respect to the conclusions; therefore, it is impossible for the principles to be taken merely on faith and the conclusions to be known scientifically.[17]

As Ockham well realizes, Aquinas has a reply to this objection.[18] An evident grasp of the first principles of theology is, to be sure, had only by God himself and by the blessed in heaven, who see God face-to-face and participate to greater and lesser degrees in the "light of glory." Still, one science can be subordinated to a second and higher science in the sense that it includes among its own first principles propositions that are evident only to one who possesses that second science – in the way, for instance, that physicists and chemists take for granted various conclusions of the mathematical sciences. Similarly, Christian theology is a subordinate or subalternate science that includes among its first principles certain propositions – namely, the mysteries of the faith – which are evident only to those who have perfect absolute wisdom, namely, God and the blessed in heaven. And just as it is reasonable to credit physicists and chemists with scientific knowledge of their domains even when they do not have an evident grasp of all the mathematical conclusions they make use of, so too theological inquirers can be credited with scientific knowledge about God and creatures even though they do not have an evident grasp of the mysteries of the faith. Thus, Aquinas concludes, Christian theology augments the first principles available to the classical philosophers with certain propositions which, though they can be grasped evidently only by God and the blessed in heaven, must be firmly assented to by anyone who wishes to attain the highest science, and thus the highest degree of absolute wisdom, possible for us in this life.

To this line of thought Ockham has an unceremonious reply. He is simply unwilling to back away from the strict definition of what it is for someone to have scientific knowledge of a conclusion:

As for the claim that there are two kinds of science, one of which proceeds from principles that are known *per se* by the light of a higher science, I reply that even though this is true of a subordinate science, still, no given individual ever has evident knowledge of the relevant conclusions unless he knows them either through experience or through premises that he has evident cognition of. Hence, it is absurd to claim that *I* have scientific knowledge with respect to this or that conclusion by reason of the fact that *you* know principles which I accept on faith because you tell them to me. And, in the same way, it is silly to claim that *I* have scientific knowledge of the conclusions of theology by reason of the fact that *God* knows principles which I accept on faith because he reveals them.[19]

Once again, though, Aquinas has the resources for an interesting counterargument. Classical philosophical inquirers had aimed for a certitude that perfects the human intellect both in its theoretical function of grasping ultimate metaphysical and moral truths and in its practical function of making good deliberations, judgments, and precepts of action whose purpose is to guide the philosophical wayfarer successfully through day-to-day living. But, says Aquinas, there are two distinct types of certitude, one associated with faith and the other with the natural intellectual virtues of *intellectus* (evident grasp of first principles), *scientia* (evident knowledge of conclusions derived from those principles), and *sapientia* (wisdom that combines *intellectus* and *scientia* so defined):

Certitude can be thought of in two ways. First, in terms of the *cause* of certitude and, accordingly, that which has a more certain cause is said to be more certain. And in this sense faith is more certain than the three intellectual virtues mentioned above [*intellectus*, *scientia*, and *sapientia*], since faith is founded on divine truth, whereas those three virtues are founded on human reason. In a second way, certitude is thought of in terms of the *subject* and, accordingly, that which the human intellect perceives more fully is said to be more certain; and because the things that belong to faith, but not the things that belong to the three virtues in question, lie beyond human understanding, faith is less certain in this sense. Yet since each thing is judged absolutely according to its cause, ... it follows that faith is more certain absolutely speaking.[20]

Thus, even though it is true that the natural intellectual virtues in their perfected states exceed faith in the degree of *evidentness* with which one who has them grasps their objects, it is equally true, Aquinas asserts, that Christian faith in its perfected state exceeds the natural intellectual virtues in the degree of firmness with which one who has it *adheres to* divinely revealed truth – even to the point of voluntarily undergoing martyrdom in order to give witness to that truth.

Here we glimpse unmistakably the wariness about natural reason that characterizes Aquinas no less than Ockham. In other places Aquinas cites approvingly Aristotle's dictum that natural reason is as incapable of comprehending the most intelligible natures as the eye of an owl is of viewing the sun.[21] Even though the mysteries of the faith are not evident to us by the light of natural reason, they are nonetheless more certain for the devout and prayerful believer than are even the simplest self-evident truths. For God himself, who by his grace enables us to recognize certain nonevident propositions as divinely revealed truths and empowers us to adhere to those truths by the gift of faith, is a more reliable source of true cognition than is the relatively dim light of natural reason. In short, our grasp of the first principles of theology by faith is firmer and more certain than any grasp of first principles we might have by the faint light of natural reason, and our consequent grasp of the conclusions validly derived from those principles will share in the certitude we have with respect to the first principles and will thus be more certain, absolutely speaking, than our grasp of the conclusions of any merely human science. If, therefore, like the classical philosophical inquirers, we have as our goal certitude with respect to a full set of ultimate metaphysical and moral truths, then Christian theology, by including the mysteries of the faith among its first principles and by exemplifying the highest available degree of certitude in both its first principles and its conclusions, brings classical philosophical inquiry to perfection and provides us with the surest and most comprehensive philosophical wisdom possible for us in this life. Consequently, it is wholly appropriate to extend to "our theology" the honorific status of a science; it is, after all, a "superscience" that exceeds every human claim to absolute wisdom according to the very same standards – namely, completeness and certitude – appealed to by the classical philosophical inquirers themselves.

In response, Ockham begins by conceding that "the Saints all call [theology] a science by extending the term 'science' to the certain cognition ... of [propositions] that are of themselves fit to be the objects of science and wisdom [in the strict sense]."[22] Yet he resolutely insists that the strict Aristotelian standard of evidentness must govern any proper application of the terms *'intellectus,' 'scientia,'* and *'sapientia.'* And by this standard, Ockham charges, Aquinas is inconsistent in denying that Christian inquirers have *intellectus* with respect to the *principles* of theology, which they firmly adhere to without evidentness, while affirming that they have *scientia* – which by Ockham's lights can only mean *evident* knowledge – with respect to the *conclusions* of theology:

It does not detract from the dignity of our theology that its *conclusions* are not known with evidentness – just as it does not detract from the dignity of our cognition of the *principles* of theology that they are not known with evidentness. And so just as there is no derogation involved in the fact that the principles are not known evidently, so too with the conclusions. And when it is claimed that [our theology] exceeds other [sciences] both in the dignity of its subject matter and in certitude, I reply that this argument proves equally well that the *principles* [of our theology] are known with evidentness; for those principles exceed the others both in certitude (since they are not subject to human reason) and in the dignity of their subject matter just as well as the *conclusions* do. Therefore, I claim that 'certitude' is being taken either for adherence or for evidentness. In the first sense, they do exceed [the conclusions of the other sciences], but not in the second sense.[23]

III. SUBSTANTIVE OR MERELY VERBAL DISAGREEMENT?

At this juncture it might appear that the dispute between Ockham and Aquinas is merely verbal. And to some extent this is surely true. After all, both agree that neither our grasp of the first principles of theology nor our logically subsequent cognition of the conclusions of theology strictly satisfies the definitions of *'intellectus'* and *'scientia'* laid down by Aristotle because those definitions include the stipulation that the objects of these cognitive virtues are evident by the light of natural reason. Further, they agree that theology has, in Ockham's words, "the role of standing in judgment on the other arts because of a greater truth in the things that are cognized and because of a firmer adherence [to them]."[24] For even though the mysteries of the faith are, like the sun, too bright for us to take in directly, they nonetheless illuminate all other things much more brightly than do the deliverances of natural reason. Again, Ockham and Aquinas agree that theological sophistication is not necessary for salvation and that all devout believers, even the theologically unsophisticated, have divinely infused "gifts of the Holy Spirit," habits by which they are able – through supernatural instinct, as it were, rather than through reasoned cognition – (1) to distinguish genuinely revealed doctrines from counterfeits, (2) to view created things in the supernatural light of faith, and (3) to know more intimately the Divine Persons to whom they are joined in the friendship of supernatural charity.[25] Finally, Ockham and Aquinas agree that the systematic study of theology engenders in theological inquirers various intellectual acts and habits that distinguish them from those theologically unsophisticated believers who are ill-equipped to engage in the properly theological activity of articulating and defending Christian doctrine. Yet, although Aquinas confers the honorific title 'science' on this set of intellectual acts and habits, Ockham steadfastly demurs:

From the distinction between the acts [proper to faith and those proper to theology] it cannot be proved that theology is a science. For every [properly theological] act that a believer has can be had by a nonbeliever who is trained in theology. After all, such a nonbeliever could defend and confirm the faith, persuade believers and nonbelievers, and reply to the arguments of heretics and nonbelievers in just the way that any believer could. And yet it is obvious that such a nonbeliever would not have *scientia* properly speaking. Therefore, from such acts it cannot be proved that theology is a science properly speaking.[26]

One could, of course, accept the entire antecedent of this argument and still reject the consequent, noting that it is hardly implausible to restrict the terms *'scientia'* and *'sapientia'* to those who actually assent to the first principles from which the conclusions of theology are derived. But, once again, this terminological point does nothing to dispel the impression that on the issues we have been discussing there is no substantive disagreement between Aquinas and Ockham.[27]

Nevertheless, if we situate the dispute over the cognitive status of theology within the broader context that renders it fully intelligible, we will indeed discover a substantive disagreement. We must begin by fleshing out more explicitly Aquinas's claim that Christian theology perfects classical metaphysics and ethics according to standards of intellectual perfection that the best classical philosophers themselves subscribe to. Once we see clearly the far-reaching implications of this claim, we will be in a better position to understand just why Ockham rejects it.

What Aquinas is suggesting is that those classical philosophical inquirers who are morally and intellectually well-disposed could be led, by standards they themselves have adopted, toward recognizing Christian theology as a plausible candidate for the absolute wisdom they are seeking. This is not to say, however, that such recognition would come immediately or easily; rather, if it came at all, it would likely emerge in three stages, each of which presents a daunting challenge to the Christian apologist.

In the first stage the Christian apologist would try to convince the best classical philosophers that certain first principles of Christian theology – namely, the preambles of the faith – are either conclusions that they themselves have already arrived at by their own standards of successful philosophical inquiry or conclusions that they would have arrived at had they done better by those very same standards. This is precisely the apologetic task that Aquinas undertakes in the first three books of *SCG* and that Anselm and Scotus undertake in their own natural theologies.

Now suppose the Christian apologist accomplishes this first task and in so doing removes one set of intellectual obstacles that might prevent classical philosophical inquirers from seeing Christian theology as a serious candidate for absolute wisdom. At this point the classical philosophers will likely express the worry that even if one part of Christian doctrine can be established by their own standards, there are other elements – including doctrines about the Trinity, the Incarnation, the Atonement, the Sacraments, and so forth – that not only cannot be so established but also have every appearance of directly contravening those standards. At this second stage, then, the Christian apologist, who concedes that the mysteries of the faith cannot be proved by the light of natural reason, has the task of showing that neither can they be shown to be false or impossible by the light of natural reason. This is precisely the task that Aquinas undertakes in Book IV of *SCG*, and the result of which Scotus (as summarized by Ockham) characterizes as follows:

With respect to any [truth] of [Christian] theology it can be known scientifically that nothing impossible follows from it, since either (i) there will be a flaw in the form [of the relevant argument], in which case the argument can be refuted, or else (ii) there will be a flaw in the matter [of the argument], in which case [the relevant premise] can be rejected.[28]

Assume, once again, that the Christian apologist has accomplished this task and in so doing has removed a second set of intellectual obstacles that might prevent the classical philosophers from acknowledging Christian theology as the culmination of their own search for absolute wisdom. Obviously, not just any claim to absolute wisdom will have survived this far and been shown to be consonant with the classical standards of successful intellectual inquiry as measured by the light of natural reason. Indeed, one can plausibly imagine that well-disposed classical inquirers, especially those who have a just sense of the limitations of human reason, might by this point have adopted a cautious openness toward Christian revelation that was not present at the beginning of their dialogue with the Christian apologist. Recall Aristotle's comparison of the light of reason to the eye of an owl, and consider the words that Plato puts into the mouth of Simmias during an interlude in the debate over immortality in the *Phaedo*:

I think, Socrates, as perhaps you do yourself, that it is either impossible or very difficult to acquire clear knowledge about these matters in this life. And yet he is a weakling who does not test in every way what is said about them and persevere until he is worn out by studying them on every side. For he must do one of two things; either he must learn or discover the truth about these matters, or if that is impossible, he must take whatever human doctrine is best and hardest to disprove and, embarking upon it as upon a raft, sail upon it through life in the midst of dangers, unless he can sail upon some stronger vessel, some divine revelation, and make his voyage more safely and securely.[29]

The third stage of the Christian apologist's task consists in pointing out that because some elements of Christian theology have been proved by the light of natural reason (first stage) and all of them have been shown not to be contrary to reason (second stage), the classical philosophical inquirers can now see by their own standards that those who assent to Christian revelation are, from within the framework of faith, entitled to think of Christian theology, which articulates that revelation systematically, as the perfection of classical philosophical inquiry. After all, given the admission that natural reason cannot take us all the way to our preferred destination of certitude with respect to a full set of ultimate metaphysical and moral truths, the classical philosophical inquirers would be foolish by their own standards if they curtly dismissed any claim to divine revelation that passes the first two tests and promises certitude with respect to matters that all sides admit to be crucial for living the sort of life worthy of a human being.

The Christian apologist would presumably go on from this point to produce, as Aquinas does in *SCG* I.7, various further indications of the reliability of the specifically Christian claim to divine revelation over other such claims. However, we have already said enough to establish a context that renders intelligible and perhaps even plausible the Thomistic and Scotistic claim that Christian theology is a science that perfects classical philosophical inquiry.

Yet given this same context, we can now understand more easily why Ockham balks at the suggestion that Christian theology is a science and why he insists on adhering to the strict senses of terms such as 'intellectus,' 'scientia,' and 'sapientia.' The reason is simple and straightforward: he is convinced that the first two stages of the Christian apologist's task, as described in the preceding paragraphs, are doomed to failure. But if this is so, then it is utterly pointless to claim Christian theology is something more than a mere replacement for classical philosophical inquiry. Why, after all, would Christian intellectuals even bother to press such a claim? Whom would they be trying to impress? If little or none of Christian doctrine can be established by natural reason, and if much of what is peculiarly Christian cannot even be shown not to be contrary to the light of natural reason, then no classical philosophical inquirer, no matter how well-disposed, would be so much as tempted to accord any special intellectual merit to the acceptance of Christian revelation.

I will now expound a bit more on Ockham's attitude toward natural theology and on his contention that the mysteries of the faith cannot be shown to be consonant with natural reason.

IV. NATURAL THEOLOGY

As a Catholic thinker of the late thirteenth and early fourteenth centuries, Ockham inherited from Anselm, Aquinas, and Scotus three magnificent, yet quite dissimilar, attempts to establish by the light of natural reason the existence of a being with an array of positive and negative perfections that Christian revelation attributes to the divine nature.

Anselm had formulated a two-step natural theology consisting of (1) an ingenious a priori argument that, if successful, immediately yields the existence of an absolutely perfect being, and (2) a systematic deduction and explanation of various attributes such a being must have.

Aquinas, rejecting Anselm's a priori argument along with the assumption that we begin with a concept of God on a par with our simple natural-kind concepts of material entities, had constructed a three-step natural theology consisting of (1) an a posteriori argument for the existence of a first efficient cause or unmoved mover, that is, a being that acts but is not itself caused or acted upon; (2) the *via remotionis*, in which he argues that a first efficient cause lacks various limitations characteristic of entities that we do have simple natural-kind concepts of, with the result that a first efficient cause must be an absolutely perfect being; and (3) the *via affirmationis*, in which he argues that several pure positive perfections, suitably abstracted from the restrictive conditions under which they occur in other entities, are to be attributed literally, though analogically, to this perfect being.[30]

Scotus's natural theology, in certain respects the most impressive of all, consists of three main stages: (1) a three-pronged proof for (a) the existence of an entity with the relational property of being first in the order of efficient causality, (b) the existence of an entity with the relational property of being first in the order of final causality, and (c) the existence of an entity with the relational property of being first in the order of perfection; (2) an argument showing that exactly one being has all three of these preeminent relational properties; and

(3) a series of arguments showing that the possessor of this "triple primacy" is an infinite being with intensively infinite power, knowledge, goodness, and overall perfection.[31]

Ockham, by contrast, is decidedly less sanguine than his predecessors concerning what natural reason, unaided by divine revelation, can demonstrate about the existence and nature of God. It is demonstrable, he believes, that there is a being such that no being is prior to or more perfect than it, but it is not demonstrable that there is just one such being.[32] Moreover, even though there are "probable" – that is, not implausible – philosophical arguments for the conclusion that one or another infinite absolute perfection is actually possessed by some being,[33] unaided reason cannot demonstrate that any being has any such perfection.

Like many another medieval thinker, Ockham tries his hand at refuting Anselm's a priori argument for the existence of an absolutely perfect being.[34] However, he focuses his attention mainly on Scotus, arguing in effect that each of the three stages of Scotus's natural theology is flawed. In particular, he contends that (1) natural reason cannot prove the existence of a being that has any one of the three types of primacy Scotus argues for; that (2) even if natural reason could prove the existence of a being with one or another of these types of primacy, it would still be unable to prove that just one being has all three of them; and that (3) even if natural reason could prove that there is just one being with all three types of primacy, it would still be unable to prove that this being has any intensively infinite perfections.[35] Without spelling out in detail the many objections that Ockham levels at Scotus's arguments, I will note only that these objections are of uneven quality. Some are quite ingenious and worthy of serious consideration, whereas others amount to little more than the unadorned assertion that a given proposition or inference cannot be proved by natural reason or that it would be rejected by a nonbelieving philosopher.

However, the most important difference between Ockham and his predecessors is more subtle than any standard philosophical disagreement over a particular premise or inference. In perusing the objections Aquinas and Scotus raise against Anselm's natural theology or Scotus raises against Aquinas's natural theology, the reader has the sense that the later thinkers take themselves to be collaborators with their predecessors in the shared project of exhibiting the intellectual merits of Christian doctrine from the perspective of natural reason. Their intent is always either to rectify arguments they see as defective or to suggest alternative ways of proceeding. Moreover, they view their common project both as perfective of the thinkers who engage in it and as useful for carrying on a potentially fruitful conversation with those nonbelieving yet morally and intellectually well-disposed classical philosophers with whom they feel a special kinship. By contrast, Ockham's discussions of natural theology give the clear impression that he has no interest at all in repairing the arguments he finds defective or in trying to reveal new intellectual horizons to the nonbelieving philosophers he so often invokes as witnesses against his predecessors. And even though this negative attitude is undoubtedly as much a symptom as a cause of Ockham's misgivings about Scotus's arguments, it often permeates his discussions of natural theology to such an extent as to give them the appearance of being mere technical exercises.

V. CONFLICTS BETWEEN FAITH AND REASON

Yet even though the disagreements over natural theology are significant, the deepest split between Ockham and his predecessors is reflected in their differing attitudes toward the epistemic tensions generated by certain mysteries of the faith, especially the doctrines of the Trinity and the Incarnation.

I will focus here on Ockham's discussions of the Trinity. According to this doctrine, a unitary divine nature with undivided intellect and will is shared by three distinct divine persons. A tension first arises in Ockham's thought when, after having argued in favor of what he takes to be Aristotle's contention that there are no real relations and hence that relative terms do not signify entities distinct from absolute entities, he concedes that the doctrine of the Trinity entails or at least strongly suggests that the three divine persons are constituted by real relations of knowing and loving that they bear to one another.[36]

Given this apparent conflict between faith and reason, Aquinas and Scotus would maintain that the ontological theory (call it *T*) leading to the strong conclusion that there are and can be no real relations contains a flaw that may at least in principle be detected and rectified by the light of natural reason. In a case like this, revelation guides reason by prompting the reexamination of a philosophical theory that it has exposed as unsound.[37]

Ockham, however, does not see things this way. To be sure, T contains a flaw because it yields the false conclusion that there are and can be no real relations. But it is only through revelation that we can so much as detect T's falsity, and so we should not expect the flaw in T to be one that can be corrected by the light of natural reason. Indeed, the presence of this sort of flaw in T does nothing to alter its status as the best account of the signification of relative terms that can be formulated by unaided natural reason. Thus, although we must reject T, the proper course is to accept a restricted version of T (call it T^*) that applies to all and only those cases about which revelation has nothing contrary to say – even while we admit that T has no flaw detectable by natural reason and hence that by the light of natural reason there is no warrant for preferring T^* to T.

To make this a bit clearer, suppose that a non-Christian philosopher invokes T to pose an objection to the doctrine of the Trinity. This philosopher argues that because, according to T, there are and can be no real relations, the doctrine of the Trinity is false.

As we have seen, Aquinas and Scotus will maintain in response that T can be correctly impugned and rejected by the light of natural reason alone. For, they will argue, natural reason is a gift from God, who cannot be the direct source of error and hence could not create us with cognitive faculties that systematically mislead us regardless of how carefully or skillfully we use them and regardless of the conditions under which we carry out our inquiries. It follows that T is not so highly warranted by the light of natural reason as to rule out its competitors as unacceptable by that same light. Christian thinkers are thus charged with the task of carrying out a careful critique of T by the light of natural reason and constructing an alternative to it. In general, they will try to show (1) that the doctrine of the Trinity, whether or not it generates exceptions to otherwise general truths, cannot be shown to be unacceptable by the light of natural reason, and thus that (2) an adequate ontological account of relations will have within itself the conceptual resources to accommodate this doctrine, as well as any exceptions it might engender, without inconsistency or incoherence. To be sure, there is no guarantee that any particular attempt to carry out this task will be successful, but there is a guarantee that success is at least in principle possible.

Ockham, by contrast, seems fully prepared to hold that T, despite entailing conclusions contrary to the faith, is indeed warranted to such a degree that it renders its ontological competitors unacceptable by the light of natural reason. His response to the nonbelieving philosopher goes like this: "I affirm by faith that T is mistaken, even though you and I share no common ground upon which I can argue my case against T in a way that has some purchase on you. But because T is the only rationally acceptable account of relations, I do not propose to jettison it entirely. Instead, I will substitute T^* for T so that we can agree at least on all those cases that divine revelation does not speak to. You might find this response deficient and even a bit annoying because I have not tried to refute your objection directly. But in this instance such a refutation is impossible."

In short, Ockham seems clearly to countenance the possibility of conflicts between faith and reason that are in principle irresoluble. As he sees it, certain mysteries of the faith are not just *beyond* natural reason but *contrary* to natural reason. And, once again, it is easy to understand why someone who holds this view would not be inclined to value very highly – or, a fortiori, engage in – the sort of apologetic outreach to philosophically sophisticated non-Christians that Aquinas and Scotus take as an integral part of the task of Christian intellectuals.

VI. CONCLUSION: OCKHAM'S IRENIC SEPARATISM

Ockham is not a radical intellectual separatist who disdains natural reason or regards with suspicion any Christian thinker who wishes to study the works of non-Christian philosophers with the same intensity as the books of Sacred Scripture. In fact, anyone familiar with Ockham's thought knows that he has immense respect for Aristotle and that his theology is marked by (what he believes to be) Aristotelian positions on a wide range of issues in ontology and philosophical semantics.[38]

Yet, as we have seen, Ockham rejects the notion that intellectual inquiry as practiced by the classical non-Christian philosophers, even Aristotle himself, is a useful propaedeutic to the Christian faith. Natural reason is sufficiently powerful and trustworthy when it operates within its proper sphere, but it is too weak to provide much illumination in the arena of natural theology, and it is downright unreliable when used to pass judgment on the first principles of revealed theology. To be sure, philosophical inquiry unaided by divine revelation can help foster logical skills and intellectual habits that are required for the articulation of true wisdom within Christian theology; it can even provide Christian thinkers with new and useful conceptual resources. But it cannot on its own make any noteworthy progress toward providing us with the substance of absolute wisdom.

Therefore Ockham's is an irenic separatism that rejects the prototypically Catholic intellectual project of unifying classical philosophy and the Christian faith in such a way as to exhibit the latter as the perfection of the former, and yet that stops short of disdaining the light of natural reason in the manner of radical intellectual separatism. Perhaps this explains why, on the matters we have been discussing here, Ockham will always be viewed as something of an outsider both by the radical separatist, who is bent on isolating faith and reason completely from one another, and by the mainstream Catholic thinker, who seeks a genuine synthesis of faith and reason.

NOTES

1 The most salient piece of evidence for this claim is found in the table of contents and introduction of Kretzmann et al. 1982.
2 *SCG* I.1, I.9.
3 See, for example, *ST* IaIIae.85, on the effects of sin, both original sin and personal sin.
4 For an excellent discussion of the relevant theological and philosophical issues, see Murray 1964, Chap. 2.
5 *ST* IIaIIae.2.4. See also *SCG* I.2.
6 Chesterton 1908, Chap. 3. Chesterton is uncannily prescient in his delineation of the conceptual rhythm of postmodern skeptical movements, especially pragmatism and Nietzscheanism.
7 Surprisingly, even though almost every anthology designed for use in introductory college courses in philosophy either contains or alludes to Aquinas's arguments for God's existence, hardly any of them (I know of only one) sets the context for those arguments by reprinting *SCG* I.4, or *ST* IIaIIae.2.4.
8 A closely reasoned argument for this claim can be found in Williams 1994, especially Chap. 5.
9 I will concentrate here mainly on Aquinas's argument for the claim that Christian theology is a science, for his discussion is somewhat richer

and more easily available than Scotus's. However, Scotus holds basically the same position, and Ockham's arguments are directed against him as well as against Aquinas. I wish to acknowledge here a debt of gratitude to my colleague John Jenkins, C.S.C., whose recent book, Jenkins 1997, has helped me appreciate the centrality of the medieval discussion of whether Christian theology is a science and has shaped my reflections on that question.

10 This is the thrust of the first seven articles of *ST*, which should be read in conjunction with the first nine chapters of *SCG*. In similar fashion, Ockham takes up these questions at the very beginning of his commentary on Peter Lombard's *Sentences*; see *Sent.* I.Prol., especially q. 7.

11 In the prologue to *ST* Aquinas explains: "We have taken into consideration the fact that newcomers to this study are commonly hampered by the writings of different authors – (i) partly because of the proliferation of superfluous questions, articles, and arguments, (ii) partly because the things they need to know are taught not according to the order of learning, but instead as is required by the exposition of given texts or as opportunities arise for disputing given questions, and (iii) partly because frequent repetition has generated both antipathy and confusion in the minds of the listeners. In an effort to avoid these and other such problems, we will try, with trust in God's help, to set forth what pertains to sacred doctrine as briefly and clearly as the subject matter allows."

12 See †*Sent.* I. Prol.1 (7).

13 This claim stands in need of a minor qualification, for, according to Ockham, there are some mysteries of the faith that we could – though only miraculously – have evident cognition of in this life without having attained the beatific vision. See †*Sent.* I.Prol.1 (49–51), and *Quodl.* V.4. However, this qualification does not figure in what follows.

14 See *ST* IIaIIae.2.1 and *De veritate*, 14.1.

15 See, for instance, *Quodl.* III.7–8, IV.6.

16 For an especially penetrating account of inquiry according to the Aristotelian model, see MacIntyre 1990, §§ III–IV. Notice that there is a systematic ambiguity between (1) science (or better, wisdom) conceived of as an abstract propositional structure that is capable of being grasped by an intellect and (2) science conceived of as an ordered set of psychological acts or habits that are present in an intellect. In what follows I will not always take the time to translate claims made in one of these modes into the other mode. However, this should engender no confusion because the relevant translations are easy enough to make.

17 *Sent.* I. Prol.7 (189).

18 What follows is a reconstruction of remarks Aquinas makes in *ST* I.1.2, 5, 6.

19 *Sent.* I.Prol.7 (199).

20 *ST* IIaIIae.4.8.

21 See, for example, *ST* I.1.5, ad 1.

22 *Sent.* I.Prol.7 (200).

23 Ibid. (199–200).

24 Ibid. (200). Aquinas makes precisely the same point in *ST* I.1.6, ad 2.

25 The three functions mentioned here are assigned, respectively, to the gifts of *intellectus*, *scientia*, and *sapientia*, which are similar to the homonymous intellectual virtues in their functions but dissimilar in their mode of operation. Aquinas characterizes this dissimilarity as a difference between judging "by way of inclination" and judging "by way of cognition." (See *ST* I.1.6, IIaIIae.45.2.) Consider the following analogy: One who has acquired the virtue of temperance will judge by way of inclination – that is, instinctively or by second nature – that a certain concrete situation calls for restraint and will act accordingly even without having thought deeply about moral theory; by contrast, a moral theorist who lacks temperance might make the very same judgment by way of cognition even though lacking the capacity to act promptly on that judgment. The same, says Saint Thomas, holds for Christian wisdom. All devout Christians possess the gift of wisdom, which enables them to judge things correctly by way of inclination and to act promptly on those judgments; this is the wisdom that accompanies the supernatural love of God and is especially well-developed in those who lead saintly lives. On the other hand, those versed in theology or sacred doctrine acquire through study the ability to make wise judgments about divine things by way of cognition. As with temperance, it is better, all other things being equal, to have wisdom in both ways than to have it in just one; but given that one has it in only one way, it is better to be wise by way of inclination than merely by way of cognition.

26 *Sent.* I.Prol.7 (190).

27 Aquinas would undoubtedly question Ockham's assertion that every theological act had by a believer could be had by a nonbeliever trained in theology. For, he would claim, certain theological acts can be had only by one who combines intellectual brilliance, the infused gifts of the Holy Spirit, and a deep sanctity nurtured by prayer and the sacraments. However, this issue is too complicated to pursue here.

28 *Sent.* I.Prol.7 (186). Compare Aquinas, *SCG* I.7.

29 *Phaedo*, 85c–d, translated by Howard North Fowler.

30 This triadic structure is clearly evident in *SCG* I.10–102.

31 See *Opus Oxoniense* I.3.1–2 (Scotus 1950– , III.1–68). An English translation of q. 1 (from an original manuscript) is available in Scotus, 1987, 13–33.

32 See *Quodl.* I.1, where Ockham argues for the existence of a being that is unsurpassed in perfection.

33 See, for instance, *Quodl.* VII.18, where Ockham lays out and defends an interesting argument for God's omnipotence.

34 See *Quodl.* VII.15 (especially 759–761).

35 The following questions of the *Quodl.* contain Ockham's most mature thought on these issues: I.1, II.1, III.1, IV.1–2, VII.11–18.

36 "This fourth opinion, [namely, that the divine persons are constituted by absolute properties and not by real relations] could seem plausible to someone. Nonetheless, since the citations from the Saints seem expressly to posit relations in the divine nature – not just in the sense that certain relative concepts are truly predicated of the divine persons, as when we say that Socrates is similar and that Socrates is a father or a son, but rather in the sense that in the divine nature there exists a real paternity and a real filiation and that these are two simple entities neither of which is the other – I affirm in agreement with them that the divine persons are constituted and distinguished by relations of origin." *Sent.* I.26.1 (156–7).

37 I am assuming that in the present context there is no question about what the relevant theological doctrine entails. But this need not always be the case according to Aquinas and Scotus. For they believe that reason can legitimately constrain the interpretation of the sources of revelation, and thus apparent conflicts between philosophical or scientific theories and articles of the faith may in some instances call for careful analysis of doctrinal statements as well as of arguments yielded by the light of natural reason.

38 He is not so taken with Plato and neo-Platonism, but that is a tale for another time.

15 Ockham's Repudiation of Pelagianism

Pelagianism is a heresy first defined in reaction to the views of the monk Pelagius in the fifth century and attacked by Saint Augustine. In the centuries since Pelagius's defeat, theologians have repeatedly stigmatized their opponents as Pelagians. Such disputes typically pit those who emphasize predestination and original sin against those who believe in human free will and human capacity for goodness. But seldom are the arguments in these debates straightforward. Often incredibly refined, they frequently ask us to consider not the human situation as we know it but the situation before the Fall and even the options that obtained (or did not obtain) before humans were created. Not only is Pelagianism a heresy, but so is semi-Pelagianism, and so complicated are the issues involved that advocates of contrary views on relevant issues have both been accused of Pelagianism. So the first question to be addressed here is why anyone should care whether Ockham was a Pelagian (or a semi-Pelagian).

This question is important in evaluating Ockham because, as a Christian theologian, it was an essential part of his philosophical project to describe human relations with God in terms consistent with the teaching of the saints. Like Saint Augustine, Ockham believed that relationship could not be correctly described without exalting divine freedom and stressing human dependence on divine liberality. Some who accuse Ockham of Pelagianism, however, say that he depicted not a generous God but an arbitrary tyrant who fails to provide reasonable guidance for people seeking salvation.[1] Others fault Ockham for departing from Thomas Aquinas's characterization of grace as an effect of the sacraments acting as instrumental causes.[2] Elsewhere I have argued that God's promises are reliable in Ockham's view.[3] Here I will consider the suggestion that

Ockham's views were Pelagian. Dismissing each reasonable form of the accusation in turn, I hope to persuade readers to reject the quite common claim that Ockham was either a Pelagian or a semi-Pelagian.

Because the issues are many and their presentation sometimes confusing, a roadmap may be useful. The most basic issue is whether humans can achieve salvation without divine assistance. Here two secondary issues confront us: (1) For what do we require assistance and what form does it (or can it) take? (2) Who or what controls the offer of assistance? The third and last basic issue is whether (given that unaided salvation is impossible) any role for human initiative remains; here we will consider the doctrines of predestination and semi-Pelagianism.

I. THE NECESSITY FOR GRACE

Pelagius opposed the doctrine of original sin, according to which the whole human race dies as a result of Adam's transgression; he was also incorrectly accused of denying the necessity for infant baptism.[4]

By contrast, Ockham accepts without reservation the doctrine of original sin, which makes the unbaptized newborn detestable to God on account of Adam's sin,[5] and no one has accused Ockham of denying the necessity for infant baptism. Ockham holds that the punishment for original sin is the loss of eternal life, whereas actual sins merit the pains of hell.[6]

Though Pelagius was accused of denying that grace is necessary for salvation, he affirmed its necessity. What made Pelagius's affirmation unacceptable was his definition of grace. Instead of seeing grace as a special form of assistance to individuals, Pelagius argued that creation itself involves grace. As the author of our nature, God graciously created the whole human race with the capacity not to sin. God's grace is generally available, and it serves a purpose; it is necessary for every act, every hour, every minute.[7]

Ockham, too, has been accused of misrepresenting grace (an accusation we will consider in Section I.2), but not by claiming God created us with the capacity not to sin. As noted earlier, Ockham holds that original sin makes us detestable to God. Indeed, for Ockham, no natural act could possibly be meritorious. "For no act [elicited] by natural [causes] or by any created cause whatever can be meritorious.

Rather [merit comes only] from the grace of God voluntarily and freely accepting [some act]."[8]

1.1. For What Is Grace Necessary?

For Ockham, grace is necessary for salvation, merit, and divine acceptance – closely related concepts for him. On the other hand, Ockham does not hold that grace is necessary for virtue. He shares with Pelagius, and more importantly with Aristotle, the view that created human nature functions properly for the most part. Ockham did not hold that without baptism human goodness is impossible. By contrast, Augustine claims that the very capacity to will the good comes from God, not in creation but through grace in baptism.[9]

Like other Christian Aristotelians, Ockham has to find a way to reconcile Augustine's views with a more optimistic view of the capacities of human nature. Ockham's response contains two distinctions: the first is between merit and virtue; the second, between different degrees of virtue. Merit is contrasted with sin; virtue with vice. Merit is the lovable quality that God rewards with eternal life; virtue is the practice of the good life on earth. Merit requires obedience to divine precept and is impossible without grace; virtue is defined by right reason and does not require grace.[10] Cases of unbaptized members of the Christian community and apparently upright pagan moral philosophers make this evident according to Ockham.

Whereas some medieval theologians simply deny that pagans can be virtuous,[11] Ockham considers only pagan merit impossible. According to Ockham, experience teaches that a person raised among Christians but not baptized can believe all the articles of faith. Although she cannot elicit a meritorious act and be saved, since she lacks infused virtues, she can pray and praise God, and she could even love God above all if God had not ordained otherwise.[12] Provided they do not engage in idolatry, pagans can be virtuous.[13] Some pagans, especially pagan philosophers, have been just without divine assistance.[14]

The second distinction restricts the scope of virtue possible without adherence to the Christian faith. In a famous definition from his treatise On Free Will, Augustine describes virtue not only as a quality that enables us to act correctly but as one that does so infallibly so that no one can misuse it.[15] Such perfect virtue is possible only for those who profess Christians views, not pagans. Though he holds that the capacity to will the good is possible for the unbaptized, Ockham denies that the virtue of upright pagan philosophers is like Christian virtue. Christian virtue is specifically different from pagan virtue because Christian virtue has a different object.[16] The ultimate purpose of Christian virtue is love of God and obedience to divine precept. It is the virtue that aims precisely at obedience to divine precept, the will to obey divine commands, which is not susceptible of abuse.[17]

Thus for Ockham, pagans are capable of virtue. Correctly instructed in the divine precepts by Christians, even the unbaptized have access to an infallible guide to virtue. But unaided human reason is not capable of the sort of virtue described by Augustine, for "no act is meritorious or perfectly virtuous without [infused] charity."[18] True but not perfect virtue is possible for pagan moral philosophers.[19] Facing the same difficulty, Aquinas makes similar distinctions. He allows that we can achieve natural ends by natural means, but divine assistance is necessary to achieve supernatural ends[20]; moral certainty is not possible for human virtue.[21] Both Aquinas and Ockham agree with Augustine's claim that virtue, as Augustine understood it, is not possible for unaided human nature. There is no certainty of virtue without divine assistance. As Christian Aristotelians, both Aquinas and Ockham have made the sort of compromises dictated by the Christian doctrine of original sin.

1.2. In What Does Grace Consist?

In defining grace, Ockham distinguishes between grace as an infused habit or form of supernatural origin and God's gratuitous and merciful acceptance of creatures.[22] The second sense of 'grace' he considers primary.

Antecedents of this distinction may be found in patristic and Scholastic theology. Theologians distinguish between what is called "operant grace" and divine acceptance, which is God's decision to bring an individual to salvation, grace as it destines someone for eternal life. By contrast with divine acceptance, which marks us for eternal beatitude in the future, operant (or cooperant grace) is a form or habit that enables us to act correctly in this life.[23] Both elements of Ockham's twofold definition can be found in the magisterial definition presented by Saint Bonaventure: "grace is a form given without merit, making someone who has it lovable and rendering their work good."[24] Ockham differs from Bonaventure in associating the form exclusively with the operant grace that renders a Christian good in this life, not with what destines the Christian for eternal life. In this respect, Ockham's views resemble those of Scotus, who like Ockham, primarily associates salvation with divine acceptance and connects the form or habit of grace with virtuous acts.[25]

If Ockham had denied the necessity for grace in either sense, he might plausibly be accused of Pelagianism. But he did not do so.[26] Ockham affirmed our need for grace under both descriptions. Salvation without being destined by God for eternal life Ockham considered a contradiction in terms; being destined by God for eternal life is logically necessary, for no one can be beloved by God without God's loving him. By contrast, the requirement for operant grace – or, as Ockham describes it, the infused habit of grace – results from divine ordination; supernatural habits are necessary for us by God's ordained power.[27] As a result of divine covenant, the habit infused with the sacrament affects the souls of the baptized so that they can act meritoriously.[28] According to Ockham, infused grace or charity is necessary but not sufficient for meritorious acts. Taken together, however, acquired and infused charity constitute a sufficient cause not just for merit but for any act of virtue.[29] Thus the masters at Avignon who accused Ockham of Pelagianism in the 1320s were mistaken when they claimed that according to Ockham either there was no habit of grace or it served no purpose.[30]

Ockham affirmed the necessity for grace insofar as it is a habit conveyed by the sacrament of baptism as well as for grace insofar as it is simply identical with divine acceptance. He emphasized the second sense of grace because he believed that grace must primarily be understood as an expression of divine mercy and liberality. Divine acceptance must be freely given; it cannot be constrained by any creature. Indeed, Ockham believed that the danger of Pelagianism in the works of his contemporaries was to be found in accounts of the economy of salvation that stressed the first sense of grace. For Ockham, Pelagianism was an issue of who or what controls salvation. And that brings us to Section II of this chapter, which is about Ockham's claim that God alone controls the offer of divine assistance.

II. GOD ALONE CONTROLS THE OFFER OF DIVINE ASSISTANCE

II.1. Ockham Against Auriol: Does Created Grace Necessitate God?

As Ockham understood the heresy, Pelagius's error was to affirm that creatures control salvation, to suggest that an act of our own could merit salvation. Of course, in Ockham's time, no one suggested that the human who was (or was not) saved was in control. But what about the form or habit infused at baptism? Did its presence or absence dictate the outcome? If so, then not God but a creature determines whether we are saved. That is the problem with the views of Peter Auriol, as Ockham understood them. Auriol differed from Pelagius only in that he supposed that a supernatural, not a natural creature, controls the offer of salvation, according to Ockham.[31]

Marilyn Adams has considered Ockham's dispute with Auriol.[32] As she describes it, Auriol emphasizes God's goodness and rationality. He holds that God never loves without justification. For Auriol, God's goodness and justice require that he save the lovable and damn the detestable. What makes creatures lovable is grace (a created form), not God's love. God's general love for creation provides no basis for distinguishing the detestable from the lovable. In the absence of the form of grace, God's love of creatures would be unjustified and so impossible (because God loves only with justification); in its presence God's rationality and goodness dictate the contrary outcome. For God is the most reasonable of lovers.[33]

By contrast, for Ockham, God is the most merciful and generous of lovers, which he would not be if his love were necessitated by the nature of the form of grace. What Ockham reacts against – so strongly, in fact, as to prompt him to reply in the intemperate language that attracted unfavorable attention at the papal court – is Auriol's claim that the nature of this form *"necessarily"* pleases God, that its very existence in the soul makes that soul dear to God. This created form is the immutable object required by God's unchanging love according to Auriol. Auriol assimilates God's love of creatures to God's necessary love of self: God loves the form of grace as he loves himself because of the nature of the thing loved. And he loves that form not freely but immutably, from natural necessity. God's very nature dictates that he love all grace and virtue just as he loves his own justice. Contrary to Scotus, Auriol explicitly denies that the form is infused in us as a result of God's love or acceptance; it is rather the lovability of the form which dictates God's love. If the acceptance were prior, the love would be unreasonable for want of the immutable object it requires.[34]

Against Auriol, Ockham argues that God could, *de potentia abso-luta*, accept a soul for salvation without infusing any form whatever. Ockham is not arguing about what God does but about what God could do, for if God could not help but love us, his love would not be generous. Ockham's aim is to establish that nothing whatsoever could necessitate God's conferral of everlasting life. Indeed, none of God's external acts is necessitated because God cannot be obligated by creatures in any respect[35] – a truth that was generally accepted by medievals[36] though seldom stressed as much as by Ockham. Certainly no accidental form could necessitate God so that it would be logically impossible for God not to award beatitude. Rather we are saved by sheer grace freely granted.[37]

This does not mean that there is no reliable path to salvation; it means rather that the divine laws according to which we are saved by operant grace are freely and contingently ordained. Ockham repeatedly insists that there is no limit to God's power to do otherwise and that there would be nothing contradictory or even unreasonable about God's ordaining salvation without operant grace. But his point is not that God is free from what he in fact ordains; it is rather that God freely ordains the laws he establishes. That is why Ockham says each of us is saved not primarily by the infusion of an acceptable nature but by special acceptance granted by benevolent divine ordination. Ockham employs the phrases 'by sheer free love' and 'by sheer divine ordination' almost synonymously[38]; the ordination is love's manifestation.

II.2. Ockham Against Aquinas: Is Grace an Efficient Cause?

Ockham argued against Aquinas as well as against Auriol; Ockham and Aquinas disagreed about the manner in which operant grace acts.[39] Ockham attacked the claim that the sacraments are efficient causes of grace. Neither are they sufficient causes, for the effect involved – predestination to salvation – cannot be achieved without God. Instead, Ockham sees the efficacy of this and the other sacraments of the New Testament in terms of God's will; the sacraments are causes without which God has ordained that he will not act.[40] Grace is required for merit, not as a natural cause but only because God so ordains.[41] Grace is not superfluous, for God ordains that he will not act without it, but not because he cannot act without it. Not a natural necessity but the order freely willed by a voluntary cause is what makes grace necessary for salvation.

II.3. Ockham in Defense of Lombard: How Is Created Grace Necessary?

Ockham's account of grace got him into trouble for two reasons: First because in showing that the only natural necessity involved is acceptance, he emphasized that operant grace need not have been ordained. Moreover, he provided a defense of Peter Lombard's views that sometimes seems to describe an even more minor role for operant grace. Some may have thought Ockham's favorable interpretation of Lombard meant that he himself considered that grace as an infused habit was unnecessary.

Lombard identifies grace with the Holy Spirit. Because Ockham holds that the only logically necessary condition of salvation is divine acceptance, he suggests that Lombard may endorse a similar account. Perhaps Lombard means that charity or grace principally signifies the Holy Spirit's accepting the soul as worthy of eternal life. Ockham excuses Lombard's failure to mention created grace on the grounds that created grace in the absence of the cooperation of the Holy Spirit would not produce merit. Moreover, as Ockham points out, Lombard never denied that a habit inclining us to love of God was infused. Ockham defends Lombard by saying Lombard understood the primary sense of grace correctly and did not deny its secondary sense. Ockham concludes this defense by affirming the orthodox conclusion that created charity (though not logically necessary) is in fact presumed in every act of merit.[42]

Ockham argued that the necessity of infused grace is *de potentia Dei ordinata*, not *de potentia Dei absoluta*. But he never disputed the necessity for infused grace, and he never espoused the view that salvation is possible without created grace. Infused grace is neces-sary because God has ordained that no one can be saved without the infusion of a supernaturally produced form.[43]

II.4. Ockham and the Saints: Does God Employ Ockham's Razor?

The second reason for suspicion was that Ockham pretty clearly did not believe that the system of operant grace was economical. God could have ordained a system without operant grace. That he did not do so was evident to Ockham not from reason but from the testi-mony of the saints.[44] This might justify the charge of Pelagianism if Ockham believed that the principle of parsimony – Ockham's razor – operated in the economy of salvation. But Ockham certainly did not believe that. On the contrary, Ockham explicitly stated that God frequently achieves by many means what could be achieved with fewer.[45]

Unlike his opponents, Ockham never believed God's acts could be deduced by theologians describing the most reasonable state of affairs. Rather he believed God was unconstrained either by crea-tures or by creaturely considerations. Ockham claimed, plausibly enough, that his denial that creatures could in any way necessitate God maximally distanced him from the error of Pelagius, who be-lieved that natural human acts could merit salvation. Indeed, one of Ockham's most important theological themes is that God and only God controls the offer of assistance; salvation can come only from God's gracious and liberal acceptance of human souls.[46]

III. THE ROLE FOR HUMAN INITIATIVE IN SALVATION

III.1. Merit and Will

Although Adams exonerates Ockham on the charge of Pelagianism because of his emphasis of divine sovereignty, she considers him a semi-Pelagian. She suggests that for Ockham the scope of God's power is restricted by the human will. According to Adams, Ockham's claim that merit must involve an act of will restricts the operation of God's will, leaving Ockham open to the charge of semi-Pelagianism.

Semi-Pelagianism questions predestination; it affirms that human free will has occasionally taken some initiative in faith. Repudiating semi-Pelagianism, the Council of Orange affirmed that the "beginnings of faith are always due to the inspiration of the Holy Spirit."[47] Ockham believes in predestination (a subject about which he wrote a treatise). He does not claim for creatures any initiative in faith.

The issue about merit raised by Adams is closely related to the subject of the beginnings of faith, to human cooperation in salvation, and to predestination. But more basically it is an issue of control, like the issues considered in Section II, so we will deal with it first. The possibility of human initiative will be considered in Section III.2; predestination in Section III.3. The last section of this chapter (III.4) concerns human cooperation in salvation and the question of whether humans can resist grace.

Contrary to Adams, I do not believe Ockham allows any creaturely restriction on divine power. His claim about the activity of the human will addresses issues about the nature of merit and reward, not about the limits of divine power. His views on the role of the human will in eliciting meritorious acts are philosophically sensible and theologically orthodox.

Ockham emphasizes God's freedom to love creatures and to reward them with beatific vision and eternal life on any basis he chooses, or even without a basis. No human act or quality could possibly merit this reward; the reward of beatific vision is entirely incommensurate with any possible human merit. God offers us the reward of beatific vision, but justice does not require that offer; indeed, God could even annihilate us without injury or injustice.[48]

What Adams sees as a restriction on God is Ockham's belief that only a voluntary act can be meritorious.[49] Adams considers this as a restriction on God, for she thinks it eliminates the possibility that God could have chosen to reward an involuntarily acquired quality with eternal life. Adams asks, "Since the worthiness of eternal life is a value dependent solely on God's free and contingent volition, why could God not have legislated that everyone with blue eyes is worthy of eternal life. . . . In maintaining the contrary, are not Ockham's claims about the order of salvation semi-Pelagian?"[50]

The answer to this question, in my opinion, is a resounding no. Justifying my opinion will involve two things. First, I will show that Ockham's insistence on the role of human will in merit is entirely reasonable and in accordance with the views of other great medieval theologians. Second, I will show that, contrary to Adams, Ockham does not maintain the opposite; he does not maintain that God could not have rewarded a certain quality, an eye color, for instance, with eternal life.

Adams presents Ockham's insistence on the voluntary character of meritorious action as if it were a singular opinion. "For in Ockham's opinion, it is a matter of *definition* that 'nothing is meritorious unless because it is elicited or produced freely and voluntarily'."[51] But Ockham is not stating a personal opinion; he is repeating a medieval Aristotelian dictum: "No one is involuntarily good or blessed."[52] Without exception, the great medieval theologians accept this view. To cite three: Bonaventure holds that every meritorious act is voluntary.[53] Ockham is echoing Aquinas[54] when he says that the merit of human acts requires both God's acceptance and human willing.[55] Scotus, too, holds that no act is meritorious unless it is freely elicited.[56]

As Adams correctly points out, this is a question of *definition*. Ockham defines 'merit' nominally; it connotes an act of will.[57] Merit describes a situation in which a reward is earned. We often reward blue-eyed blonds for their looks, but these rewards cannot be correctly described as *merited*. By contrast, heroic acts or acts of obedience sometimes *merit* reward.

When Ockham indicates that what is praiseworthy is both good and within our power,[58] he is making the point that only rewards for things within our control can correctly be described as merited. Though he does not say so explicitly, Ockham would presumably allow that, *de potentia Dei absoluta*, God could reward physical traits with eternal life. Ockham does expressly state the complementary point: God can make us suffer without sin, though no one can be penalized without demerit. When we inflict injury on the innocent, strictly speaking this should not be described as a "penalty" but rather as "suffering" because the pain inflicted is not merited.[59] Moreover, Ockham does explicitly indicate that it is within God's power to confer (or not to confer) eternal life on anyone.[60] Ockham would not, however, describe eternal life conferred on account of an involuntary trait (such as eye color) as a *merited* reward.

Ockham is not committed to the view that a freely elicited act is a logically necessary condition of divine acceptance (and Adams is mistaken to support Chatton's claim that he is).[61]

That God has ordained that he will accept meritorious acts, and hence freely elicited acts of will, is a contingent fact according to Ockham. There is no restriction on God's freedom to confer benefits (or for that matter, inflict suffering) on his creatures.

Ockham is committed to the view that a freely elicited act is a condition for merit. But merit is not a condition for grace.[62] Saint Paul received grace and was destined for eternal life without merit.[63] Paul was probably not blue-eyed, but whatever quality God chose tó reward, it was less remarkable than Paul's disqualifications, as a persecutor of Christians, for mercy and reward. The point of the story, as Ockham cites it, is that Paul was entirely without merit. God could have rewarded meritless blue-eyed bastards, deeming them worthy of eternal life, just as he rewarded Paul. As Ockham was perfectly aware, inferences from what is the case to what can be the case are legitimate (*ab esse ad posse valet consequentia*). That is the point of his citing the case of Paul. God could have ordained otherwise; it would be just as reasonable to doom us all as it is to offer eternal life to everyone. Because God's nature does not restrict God's acts with respect to creatures, we have only the authority of Scripture and of the saints to tell us what God has actually ordained for humanity.

Making a voluntary human contribution necessary for merit is not semi-Pelagianism, as Adams suggests.[64] It is part of any reasonable analysis of the terms 'merit' and 'reward'. In this case, of course, Ockham has denied that human acts could merit the reward of the beatific vision. The divine economy of eternal life differs from ordinary natural circumstances in that we can have no claim on this reward. But the resemblance is not entirely absent, for the acts God chooses to reward are our own – a point to which we will return in Section III.4.

III.2. Can Humans Achieve a Disposition for Grace?

Ockham's closest approach to Pelagianism is a statement he made in course of discussing predestination. Ockham holds that there are generically good works that people in a state of sin should perform so that God might sooner confer on them the grace by which eternal life is merited. Such works dispose sinners for grace, but though they are good works, they are meritorious only in a qualified sense.[65]

Though many Christian theologians today would deny this claim, others still accept the necessity for such dispositions among adults seeking baptism,[66] and this view was common in the medieval period. Ockham claims for this position the support of the saints and the doctors. One such doctor was Matthew of Aquasparta, who cites Augustine, Dionysius, and John Damascene in favor of the view that a disposition for grace is necessary.[67] Aquinas, against whom Ockham is arguing in this passage, also held that a prior disposition is required – namely, free will.[68] Among the many other authors who held this view are Bonaventure[69] and Scotus.[70] As Doucet indicates in his edition of Aquasparta, this was the common view.

Like his contemporaries, Ockham allows a humanly achievable "disposition" to grace. However, neither for Ockham nor for other medieval theologians is this tantamount to maintaining that people can take an initial step toward meriting salvation. As Aquinas says, the first preparation for grace is by divine aid.[71] Ockham himself clearly states that such works can earn only a temporal, not an eternal reward. Because his brief statement comes from a discussion of predestination, presumably the claim is that if someone is predestined for grace, performing generically good acts may prompt God to confer grace sooner in that person's lifetime. Though they are not rewarded by eternal life, adults are supposed to perform such good acts while still in a state of mortal sin in preparation for baptism. Because these generically good acts prepare us for grace, they are in some odd sense causes – though they are neither enabling causes nor causes in any of the four traditional senses. According to Ockham, our knowledge of this requirement for penitents comes from the saints and the doctors. Meeting this requirement, however, cannot earn an eternal reward; only grace suffices for merit.[72]

III.3. Does Grace Cause Predestination?

In his dispute with Thomas, Ockham makes another statement on which the charge of Pelagianism is based, namely that some predestination or reprobation is not without an explanatory cause. Somewhat timidly – without daring to assert it – Ockham suggests that in some sense *foreseen* merit is prior to predestination to eternal life. It is prior in the order of explanation. According to Ockham, when we can infer proposition q on the basis of proposition p, proposition p is in some sense the cause of proposition *q*, using the word 'cause' in an unaccustomed sense. Here modern usage might dictate reference to a "reason" rather than a "cause." Ockham's "explanational causality" would certainly be strange usage today, and he says that cases of "explanational causality" in the absence of formal, final, or efficient causality are rare. However, it was a common medieval usage with good Aristotelian warrant; as Ockham mentions, it is the sense in which an antecedent "causes" the consequent.[73] If Ockham had used the phrase 'explanational priority,' we would not have much difficulty with the concept. Indeed, not all of us would agree with Ockham that cases in which priority in the order of explanation does not correspond to causal priority are rare.

Ockham's example of "explanational priority" is ordinary enough. He says that when we explain why fire does not warm distant objects, we say "it is because the fire is not close enough."[74] The statement has explanatory force, although fire, not proximity, produces heat. 'The fire does not warm me' is true because 'The fire is not near me' is true. By analogy, Ockham wants to claim that 'God foresees Marilyn's merit' in some sense explains why God predestines Marilyn to eternal life, although it is not true that Marilyn's merit causes her predestination. Foreseen merit explains or makes intelligible most cases of predestination[75] without causing predestination efficiently, finally, formally, or materially.

Aquinas condemns as Pelagian the view that *preexisting* merit is the efficient cause of predestination.[76] Ockham clearly avoids this error, denying both that the merit in question preexists and that it is the efficient cause of predestination. Nonetheless, some consider Ockham's position tantamount to semi-Pelagianism, for they believe that it effectively vitiates the doctrine of predestination. This seems mistaken. The position gives too little credence to Ockham's explicit statement that the priority involved is not that of an efficient, final, formal, or material cause.[77] Moreover, the position overstates the difference between Ockham's position and that of Aquinas and neglects an important theological reason for their essential similarity.

The reason Ockham dared to argue against Thomas, maintaining his own view only "without prejudice" to better judgment, was to block the inference that 'the damned sin' can be explained because God reprobates them.[78] In this respect, Ockham's views were not only sensible and ethically attractive but orthodox. Predestination to damnation or reprobation is affirmed by the Church in a more limited way than predestination to salvation. God both intellectually knows and disposes people to salvation; he also wills their salvation. But Roman Catholic theologians teach that God does not destine people to eternal punishment before their sins are foreseen.[79]

When Ockham maintains that foreseen merits are prior to predestination in the order of explanation, he means that in some sense our merits justify our predestination, and one can say 'God reprobates the damned' is in some sense justified because they sin. The converse inference is the problem case theologians were out to avoid; one cannot claim that the damned sin because God reprobates them or that their sin is justified on account of reprobation. On the other hand, though sin may explain damnation, it does not efficiently cause damnation any more than merit efficiently causes eternal life. What Ockham is trying to do here is difficult, and some may consider he has failed, but the attempt is certainly orthodox. Ockham is claiming that, though foreseen merits are not temporally or causally prior to predestination, they may explain predestination by making it intelligible.

Of course, Ockham was not alone in facing the theological dilemmas occasioned by the doctrine of predestination. Other theologians advanced similar solutions to the problem, solutions that allow for some ordering relation between foreseen sins and reprobation. Scotus, who exercised the profoundest influence on Ockham's thinking, held that, although foreseen good works are not the reason for predestination, foreseen sins are the reason for reprobation. Although sins do not effectively cause reprobation, they explain why one person rather than another is destined for damnation.[80]

Aquinas, the target of some of Ockham's sharpest attacks, held that in explaining the reason for predestination, it was necessary to distinguish between the general and the particular cause. In general, the justification for the effect of predestination is God's goodness. In particular, two things can be said: (1) predestination is the final cause of grace, and (2) grace is causally prior to predestination "as a cause of merit which reduces to a material disposition." For this reason, we can say that "God preordained both that he would give someone glory on the basis of their merits and that he would give someone grace in order that they might merit glory."[81] The claim that merit in some sense justifies predestination to glory may weaken the doctrine of predestination too much for some Christian theologians, but like

Aquinas, Scotus, and Ockham, most have held that it is compatible with the doctrine.

III.4. Is Grace Irresistible?

There is a strand of Augustinianism that would claim that the acts for which we are rewarded in the divine economy are not our own but those of God.[82] This ultra-Augustinian view might be based on Paul's words to the Corinthians[83]: "For I am the least of the apostles. ... But by the grace of God I am what I am, and his grace toward me was not in vain. On the contrary, I worked harder than any of them, though it was not I, but the grace of God which is in me." Similarly, at Gal. 2:20 Paul says that "it is no longer I who live, but Christ who lives in me." These passages must be interpreted literally by the ultra-Augustinian, but in fact they cannot be intended literally. If they were intended literally, the phrase "Not Paul but Christ" would mean the same thing in the sentences 'Not Paul but Christ lives' and 'Not Paul but Christ fed the four thousand at the Sea of Galilee'.[84] In Corinthians and Galatians, Paul is not suggesting that only Christ and not Paul is acting. Rather, Paul is asserting that Christ enables *Paul* to preach, that the credit for *Paul's* preaching belongs to Christ, and that without divine assistance, *Paul* would be altogether unable to preach.

The ultra-Augustinian not only asserts that such biblical passages are intended literally but claims that divine grace is irresistible, so that if God offers us grace, then no human agent could pose an obstacle to its operation. The position described here is not attractive. It would suggest that when hardened sinners are redeemed, they do not change for the better; instead, they exchange one identity for another. Not they but Christ lives; not their acts but God's acts are redeemed. Moreover, the change from enslavement to sin to submission to justice would have to be involuntary.[85]

Such an ultra-Augustinian might well accuse Ockham of semi-Pelagianism. For Ockham, like Aquinas,[86] holds that humans can oppose divine grace *de potentia Dei ordinata*; God has ordained that grace is conferred only in cases where there is no obstacle to its reception.[87] Ockham also holds that meritorious acts are human acts freely accepted by God. However, Ockham does not claim that the initiation of such acts must be human; he maintains only that such acts must in some sense be in our power; we can prevent their being elicited though we could not elicit them on our own. It is the claim that we could initiate meritorious acts, not the claim that we cooperate in them, that was condemned in the canons of the Council of Orange that define semi-Pelagianism.

Only an ultra-Augustinian would condemn as semi-Pelagian the view that humans participate in their own salvation. And though Ockham does not uphold the Augustinian dogma of the irresistibility of grace, he affirms that whatever God wills is effected, and if he wills that it be effected by another, it is effected by another.[88] So Ockham is not claiming that God *could not* save us despite ourselves but rather that God *chooses not* to do so.

As Adams would be the first to point out, Ockham's theology is a celebration not only of divine freedom but also of divine mercy and liberality. It would be a poor liberality that allowed no role at all to the sinner in human salvation.

IV. CONCLUSION

In this chapter I have examined the more plausible grounds for suggesting that Ockham was a Pelagian; none of them can bear examination. Ockham's insistence on the role of will in acts of merit (Section III.1) in no sense restricts God's freedom to save or to damn in accordance with plan. It is both doctrinally sound and philosophically defensible to claim that no act can be meritorious unless elicited freely. Neither Ockham's claim that people participate in their salvation (Section III.4) nor his espousal of the common medieval view that adults must prepare for baptism (Section III.2) is tantamount to claiming that people initiate their salvation. Instead of espousing the semi-Pelagian view that people initiate their salvation, Ockham maintained the orthodox view the humans participate in their own salvation. His claim that foreseen sins in some sense explain reprobation does not amount to a denial of predestination (Section III.3). In this, as in many of these cases, Ockham did not depart much from the views of most medieval theologians.

Ockham differed sharply from several medieval theologians in that he did not believe that the operant grace postulated by Augustine and the other saints was entirely reasonable or much in accord with experience. But then he also believed that we could not know with certainty anything that depends on the divine will's acting freely and contingently, since neither reason nor experience can guide us in such cases.[89] Very controversially, Ockham claimed to be able to show that the supernatural form of grace is logically compatible both with divine rejection and with sin. But the conclusion he based on these claims is that the economy of salvation is *freely* ordained, not that the form of grace is *not* ordained for, and hence necessary to, our salvation or that it is ineffective.

Although Ockham argues that infused grace is not logically necessary for salvation, he never claims it is unnecessary. To the contrary, infused grace is necessary because God has so ordained. 'Not logically necessary' is not equivalent to 'unnecessary' or 'superfluous.' God does many things that are not logically necessary; if he did not do so, he would not be free. Ockham's razor was never meant to explain God's providence; God frequently accomplishes with many means what could be accomplished with fewer.[90]

Ockham not only argues that infused grace is necessary, he also maintains it immediately inclines us to every virtue and is presupposed by every meritorious act; that explains its function in unifying the virtues.[91] For Ockham, grace is not merely a conventional sign of divine acceptance; it is rather the means ordained by God for our salvation.

Ockham believed with considerable justification that his position was as far removed as possible from Pelagianism, since he, like Augustine, was committed to accepting every consequence of the thesis that God completely controls the economy of salvation. On the other hand, Ockham also differed from Augustine in many respects. He did not believe grace was necessary for virtue; neither did he believe grace was irresistible. In these respects, however, Ockham's was the common opinion of the medieval Church. Thus, to accuse him of Pelagianism on these grounds would be anachronistic.

In response to the accusation made by his contemporaries, Ockham had a good defense, as Adams showed some years ago. That probably explains why the judgment of the commission appointed to examine his works was quite mild, despite the presence of his enemies at Avignon and the difficulties in which his Order found itself at that time. It explains why when Pope John XXII subsequently tried to hunt Ockham down and threatened to burn down a city if it sheltered him and his companions,[92] Pelagianism was not mentioned. It is anachronistic folly to reinvent and redescribe the error now, based on views his contemporaries would not have questioned. Ockham was a competent and well-trained theologian. Though he occasionally stated them in language disconcerting to the philosophically untutored, the views he stated were consistent with ecclesiastical dogma – or, as he would have put it, with the truths found in Scripture and stated by the saints and the doctors, the authorities he took to be our only guide to what God has actually ordained concerning human salvation.[93]

NOTES

1 Strehle 1988, 1, 47–49, 51, 54–55, 61–63, 80–81.
2 *Sent.* IV.1 (8).
3 Wood 1994.
4 Pelikan 1971, 315–318. See Pope Innocent I, epistle *"Inter ceteras Ecclesiae Romanae,"* Denzinger 1976, 81 (§ 219); Acts of the Council of Carthage (A.D. 418), Denzinger 1976, 82–84 (§§ 222–230); (Pseudo-) Pope Celestine I, *"Capitula pseudo-Caelestina seu 'Indiculus,'"* Denzinger 1976, 88–90 (§§ 238–245); Acts of the Council of Ephesus (Ecumenical Council III, A.D. 431), *Actio* VII, Denzinger 1976, 97 (§ 267).
5 *Sent.* I.17.1 (447): "Someone born in original sin . . . is detestable to God."
6 *Sent.* IV.3–5 (54): "The absence of eternal life is owing to original sin; the pains of Gehenna to actual sin."
7 Pelikan 1971, 313–6.
8 *Sent.* I.17.2 (471–2).
9 Pelikan 1971, 313–316.
10 *Quodl.* II.14 (176–8).
11 See Aquasparta 1957, 96 (q. 3, §14).
12 *Sent.* III.9 (279, 281, 312). There are passages in which Ockham is supposed to have said not that such a person could love God *de potentia absoluta*, but that she actually can do so – most importantly *Sent.* I.17.1 (451–5). In the *Reportatio*, in close conjunction with such a statement, Ockham states explicitly that God has ordained that such acts cannot exist without infused grace (*Sent.* III.9 [279, 312]). So it is difficult to know to what extent Ockham believed unassisted natural love of God was possible. This is not altogether surprising since the point is still disputed. See Tanquerey 1959, 158. In any case, such passages support only the conclusion that, *de potentia absoluta*, a supernatural habit is not necessary for *merit*; at *Sent.* I.17, as elsewhere, Ockham affirms at the same time that supernaturally infused grace is *actually* necessary for merit *de potentia ordinata*. (*Sent.* I.17.1 [451–5]).

13 *Dial.* I.vi.77.

14 *Sent.* I.17.1 (447).

15 Augustine, *De libero arbitrio* II.19.192 (Augustine 1970, 271.8–9; PL 32.1268). It is also a quality by which God acts on us and without us. The problems raised by this part of the definition will be considered in Sec. III.4.

16 *Sent.* IV.3–5 (58).

17 *Connex.* 1.124–30.

18 *Sent.* IV.3–5 (58).

19 *Dial.* I.vi.77. Though the basic distinction is found in *Connex.*, there is some terminological imprecision. See Wood 1997, commentary on *Connex.* 2.137.

20 *ST* IaIIae. 65.2 resp.

21 *ST* IIaIIae.51.1 ad 2.

22 *Sent.* I.17.1 (466), IV.10–11 (213).

23 Burns 1980, 7.

24 Bonaventure, *Sent.* II.27.dub. 2 (Bonaventure 1882–1902, II.648–9).

25 Scotus, *Ordinatio*, I.17.pars 1, qq.1–2 (Scotus 1950– , V.211).

26 Perler 1988, 285–8, like a number of earlier authors, takes Ockham to affirm that grace in the second sense is unnecessary, incorrectly inferring this conclusion from the assertion that it is unnecessary *de potentia Dei absoluta*.

Perler mistakenly suggests that considerations of God's power in the abstract (*potentia absoluta*) are intended to describe God's ability to intervene directly in the world, setting aside its ordinary functioning (*potentia ordinata*). In SL III–4.6 (779–80), Ockham considers a fallacy that is relevant here. He says the proposition 'God can accept someone without grace by his absolute power but not by his ordained power' has more than one sense. If interpreted to mean that God cannot save without grace by ordained power, but can by absolute power, it is false. It is true only if understood to mean that it does "not include a contradiction" to save someone without grace, "although God has ordained that he would never do so." God's actual exercise of power is always ordinate – that is, *potentia ordinata*. "The sentence 'God can do *x* de potentia absoluta but not *de potentia ordinata*' is true only if interpreted as follows: God can do *x*, though he has ordained that he will never do *x*; nevertheless if God were to do *x*, it would be done *de potentia ordinata*, since if he were to do *x*, he would have ordained that he would do *x*" (*OND* 95.420–30). Absolute power arguments refer to the scope of God's powers – to God's powers without considering whether he wills their exercise.

Ockham argues that God's power, considered simply as such, is unaffected by whether he chooses to exercise or not to exercise it. Theologians refer to God's undiminished capacity when they say he could save without the habit of grace *de potentia absoluta* (*Sent.* I.17.1 [452–63], I.17.2 [469], IV.3–5 [58]) and to the restriction implied by God's exercised or ordained power when they say that perhaps *de potentia ordinata* God could not fail to save once grace is posited (*Sent.* IV.10–11 [233]). God could have ordained otherwise. But had he ordained the contrary, it would have been foreseen. Nothing actual has ever transpired or will ever transpire that is not preordained by God; everything actual is ordinate.

27 *Sent.* I.17.1 (466), III.9 (281, 312).
28 *Sent.* IV.10–11 (214–5).
29 *Sent.* IV.3–5 (51, 57–8).
30 Koch 1935–36, 84–5.
31 *Sent.* I.17.1 (455).
32 Adams 1987a, 1186–1207, 1257–1297.
33 *Sent.* I.17.1 (443).
34 Ibid. (441–5).
35 *Sent.* II.15 (343, 353), IV.3–5 (45, 55); *Connex.* 4.321.
36 Lombard, *Sent.* I.43, §3, (Lombard 1971–81, I.300); Scotus, *Ordinatio* I.44, §§ 8–10 (Scotus 1950– , VI.366–7); Scotus, *Opus Oxon.* IV.46.1, § 1.11 (Scotus, 1891–5, XX.399, 428).
37 *Sent.* I.17.1 (454–5).
38 Ibid. (462–4).
39 *Sent.* IV.1 (4–19).
40 *Sent.* IV.3–5 (60).
41 *Dubitationes addititiae* (289).
42 *Sent.* I.17.2 (475), I.17.3 (478).
43 *Sent.* III.9 (281).
44 *Sent.* I.17.3 (476–8); *Dubitationes addititiae* (221).
45 *Sent.* I.17.3 (478).
46 *Sent.* I.17.1 (455–6).
47 Pelikan 1971, 318–31; Acts of the Council of Orange (A.D. 529), Denzinger 1976, 132–3 (§§371–8).
48 *Sent.* IV.3–5 (55).
49 *Sent.* I.17.1 (450), I.17.2 (470).
50 Adams 1987a, 1295.
51 Ibid., 1272. (Italics added.)
52 Hamesse 1974, 236. Hamesse cites *Nicomachean Ethics* III.5.1113^b 15–16. But see rather "the excellences are voluntary" at 1114^{b}23.
53 Bonaventure *Sent.* II.26.6 (Bonaventure 1882–1902, II.646): "Grace never elicits a work of merit unless the will cooperates with it."
54 *ST* IaIIae.114.4 resp.: "A human act has the character of merit from two things: first and indeed principally from divine ordination. . . but second from the part played by the free will." See also ibid., IaIIae.114.6.

55 *Sent.* I.17.2 (473): "Because the will itself moves actively, the act will be ours (*in nobis*). And because it is effectively [caused] by the will and accepted by God, it will be meritorious."

56 Scotus, *Quodlibet* XVII.2, §8 (Scotus 1891–5, XXVI.205): "Nothing is accepted as meritorious unless it is freely in the power of the person acting.... Nothing is imputed to someone, neither is it rewardable or punishable unless it is in his power."

57 *Sent.* III.11 (389): "But 'goodness' is only a connotative word or concept, signifying principally that neutral act itself, connoting a perfectly virtuous act of will and [the act of] right reason in conformity with which it is elicited." On connotative acts, see Boler 1985 and Spade 1975.

58 *Sent.* I.17.1 (449): "Since it is good, it is the more praiseworthy, the more it is in our power."

59 *Sent.* IV.3–5 (45).

60 *Sent.* I.40 (593).

61 For a brief summary of the grace–merit debate and an edition of Chatton's *Lectura in I Sent.* 17.1, see Etzkorn 1977.

62 We should note, however, that Ockham does say that no adult receives eternal life without a work of merit (*Sent.* I.40 [593]). Presumably then, though one could receive grace without merit, once grace is awarded, adults who receive eternal life also elicit a work of merit – they might, for example, hope for beatitude.

63 *Sent.* III.9 (280–1).

64 Adams 1987a, 1297.

65 *Sent.* I.41.1 (600).

66 Tanquerey 1959, 126.

67 Aquasparta 1935, q. 3, 71–2.

68 *ST* IaIIae.113.3 ad 1.

69 Bonaventure, *Sent.* IV.14. pars 1, q. 2, a. 3 (Bonaventure 1882–1902, IV.327).

70 Scotus, *Ordinatio* III.19, §8 (Scotus 1639, VII.418).

71 *ST* I.23.5.

72 *Sent.* I.41.1 (600).

73 *Posterior Analytics* I.1.71[b]19–22. See Wood and Andrews 1996.

74 *Sent.* I.41 (605–6). See also *Praedest.* 1 (519) (= Adams and Kretzmann 1983, 53).

75 The case of the Blessed Virgin is the exception. In her case, unlike most of the predestined, grace was irresistible, and thus she did not voluntarily merit eternal life.

76 *ST* I.23.5.

77 *Sent.* I.41 (606).

78 Ibid. (605).

79 Tanquerey 1959, 300.

80 Scotus, *Ordinatio* I.41, § 40 (Scotus 1950– , VI.332).

81 *ST* I.23.5 resp.

82 Many of the texts from Augustine's writing cited in support of ultra-Augustinianism were well known to the medievals. For example, Peter Lombard quotes Augustine's letter to Sixtus: "Since he crowns our merits, he crowns his [own] gift ... even the merits which are rewarded are not ours." *Epistula* 194, 5.19 (Augustine 1911, 190–1; PL 33.880–1); compare Lombard, *Sent.* I.43, § 3 (Lombard 1971–81, I.300).

83 1 Cor. 15:9–10.

84 See Mark 8:1–9.

85 See Rom. 6. What some call "hyper-Calvinism" does espouse a similar doctrine. It holds both that grace is irresistible and that reprobation cannot be annulled. Accordingly, the view is that Christ does not offer salvation to everyone. On the one hand such Calvinists combat what is called the heresy of the "well-meant offer" but nonetheless defend the "promiscuous preaching of the Gospel." This is true even though, according to this view, grace is "for the elect alone ... others who come under preaching, God hates...." See Engelsma 1980, 30–31, 128, 197.

86 *ST* IaIIae.55.4 ad 2.

87 *Sent.* I.17.1 (458, 461).

88 *Sent.* I.46.2 (677), II.5 (74).

89 *Sent.* II.14 (319).

90 *Sent.* I.17.3 (478).

91 *Sent.* IV.3–5 (57).

92 See the introduction to Wood 1997 for an account of Ockham's life that describes these events.

93 In general the accusation of semi-Pelagianism is easy to make and difficult to refute. It is difficult to refute, not because any individual argument for the view that Ockham (or some other theologian) is a semi-Pelagian cannot be examined and rejected. But once such an accusation has gained currency in the secondary literature, people ask themselves not whether it is true, but what justifies it. Despite every argument to the contrary, even this chapter, by linking 'Ockham' and 'Pelagianism' in its title, may contribute to the currency of the common opinion that condemns Ockham as a Pelagian or semi-Pelagian. (On this issue, not only is there no presumption of innocence, but even the attempt to show someone's innocence is taken as evidence of guilt.) Perhaps, then, it would be appropriate to ask if, apart from Augustine himself, and perhaps Jansenius and John Calvin, there ever was a theologian who could not be accused of Pelagianism. Indeed, even Calvin has been condemned for excess liberality. Hyper-Calvinists condemn him for holding that grace is offered to all

and not only to the elect (Engelsma 1980, 132). Medieval scholastics, like their modern counterparts, were all too ready to suggest that their contemporaries were heretics. The Franciscans Matthew of Aquasparta and Roger Marston, for example, accused Aquinas of Pelagianism because of his views on the necessary preparation for the infusion of grace. See Aquasparta 1935, 94; Marston 1932, 195. Surely this regrettable history shows that repeating the charge of Pelagianism, in its many guises, serves to hinder and not to promote serious discussion of theological views.

BIBLIOGRAPHY

Ockham has been well served by bibliographers. Very full bibliographies can be found in Heynick 1950, Reilly 1968, and especially Beckmann 1992. The present list is selective. It includes (a) the primary texts and best translations of Ockham, (b) the most important items in the secondary literature since 1990, and (c) all items cited in this volume. (The last ensures that the most important items from the earlier literature are included as well.)

I have adopted the common custom of listing pre-1500 authors by their given name rather than surname. Thus, 'William of Ockham,' not 'Ockham, William of.' This avoids the problem of deciding, for example, whether John Duns Scotus should be listed under 'Scotus' (= the Scot), which is really a place name, or under 'Duns,' which is a place name but may also be a family name. Cross-references will direct the reader to the right entries. (But observe that in the notes to this volume, pre-1500 authors are cited in their most familiar form. Thus, 'Ockham,' 'Scotus,' but 'Giles of Rome.')

Abelard, Peter. *See* Peter Abelard.
Adams, Marilyn McCord. 1970. "Intuitive Cognition, Certainty, and Scepticism in William Ockham." *Traditio* 26, 389–98.
———. 1976. "What Does Ockham Mean by 'Supposition'?" *Notre Dame Journal of Formal Logic* 17, 375–91.
———. 1977. "Ockham's Nominalism and Unreal Entities." *The Philosophical Review* 86, 144–76.
———. 1978. "Ockham's Theory of Natural Signification." *The Monist* 61, 444–59.
———. 1982. "Universals in the Early Fourteenth Century." In Kretzmann et al. 1982, 411–39.
———. 1985. "Things Versus 'Hows,' or Ockham on Predication and Ontology." In Bogen and McGuire 1985, 175–88.
———. 1986. "The Structure of Ockham's Moral Theory." *Franciscan Studies* 29, 1–35.

————. 1987a. *William Ockham*. 2 vols. Notre Dame, IN.: University of Notre Dame Press. 2d rev. ed. 1989.

————. 1987b. "William Ockham: Voluntarist or Naturalist?" In Wippel 1987, 219–47.

————. 1989. "Ockham on Truth."*Medioevo* 15, 143–72.

————. 1995a. "Duns Scotus on the Will as Rational Potency." In *Via Scoti: Methodologica ad mentem Joannis Duns Scoti*, edited by Leonardo Sileo, 839–54. Rome: PAA-Edizioni Antonianum.

————. 1995b. "Ockham's Razor." In Audi 1995, 183.

————. 1996. "Scotus and Ockham on the Connection of the Virtues." In *John Duns Scotus: Metaphysics and Ethics*, edited by Ludger Honnefelder, Rega Wood, and Mechthild Dreyer, 499–522. Leiden: E. J. Brill.

————. 1998. "Ockham on Final Causality: Muddying the Waters." *Franciscan Studies* 56, 1–46.

Adams, Marilyn McCord, with Norman Kretzmann, trans. 1983. *William Ockham: Predestination, God's Foreknowledge, and Future Contingents*. 2d ed. Indianapolis, IN.: Hackett.

Aegidius Romanus. *See* Giles of Rome.

Andrews, Robert. 1994–97. "The *Defensorium Ockham.*" *Franciscan Studies* 54, 99–122.

————, ed. 1997. *Franciscan Philosophy and Theology: Essays in Honor of Father Gedeon Gál, O.F.M. on his Eightieth Birthday*. St. Bonaventure, NY: The Franciscan Institute. (= *Franciscan Studies* 53–54 [1993–97, 1994–97]).

Anselm. *Opera omnia*. 1946–61. Edited by F. S. Schmitt. 6 vols. Edinburgh: Thomas Nelson & Sons.

Aquasparta, Matthew of. *See* Matthew of Aquasparta.

Aquinas, Thomas. *See* Thomas Aquinas.

Audi, Robert, ed. 1995. *The Cambridge Dictionary of Philosophy*. New York: Cambridge University Press.

Augustine. 1911. *Epistulae. Pars IV: Ep. CLXXXV–CCLXX*. Edited by Alois Goldbacher. Vol. 57, "Corpus scriptorum ecclesiasticorum latinorum." Vienna: F. Tempsky.

————. 1970. *De libero arbitrio*. Edited by William M. Green. Vol. 29, "Corpus Christianorum: Series Latina," 207–321. Turnhout: Brepols.

Augustinus (Triumphus) de Ancona. 1584. *Summa de potestate ecclesiastica*. Rome: G. Ferrarii.

Auxerre, Lambert of. *See* Lambert of Auxerre.

Balić, Charles. 1956. "Adnotationes ad nonnullas quaestiones circa *Ordinationem* I Duns Scoti." In Scotus 1950– , IV.1*–39*.

_____. 1959. "Henricus de Harcley et Ioannes Duns Scotus." In *Mélanges offerts à Étienne Gilson*. Paris: Vrin, 93–121.

Baudry, Léon. 1950. *Guillaume d'Occam. Sa vie, ses oeuvres, ses idées sociales et politiques*. Vol. 1, *L'homme et les oeuvres*. Paris: Vrin.

_____. 1958. *Lexique Philosophique de Guillaume d'Ockham*. Paris: Lethielleux.

Bayley, C. C. 1949. "Pivotal Concepts in the Political Philosophy of William of Ockham." *Journal of the History of Ideas* 10, 199–218.

Beckmann, Jan P. 1992. *Ockham – Bibliographie: 1900–1990*. Hamburg: Felix Meiner.

_____. 1998. "Ockham, Ockhamismus und Nominalismus: Spuren der Wirkungsgeschichte des Venerabilis Inceptors." *Franciscan Studies* 56, 77–95.

Benedict (St.). 1982. *The Rule of St. Benedict: The Abingdon Copy*. Edited by John Chamberlin. Toronto: Pontifical Institute of Mediaeval Studies.

Bianchi, Luca, with Eugenio Randi. 1990. *Le verità dissonanti: Aristotele alla fine del medioevo*. Rome: Laterza.

Birch, T. Bruce, ed. and trans. 1930. *The De sacramento altaris of William of Ockham*. Burlington, IA: Lutheran Literary Board.

Bocheński, I. M. 1961. *A History of Formal Logic*. Translated by Ivo Thomas. Notre Dame, IN.: University of Notre Dame Press. Originally published as *Formale Logik*. Freiburg: Karl Alber, 1956.

Boehner, Philotheus. 1943. "The Notitia Intuitiva of Non-Existents according to William Ockham." *Traditio* 1, 223–75. Reprinted (omitting a textual edition and its introduction, 240–75) in Boehner 1958, 268–300. References are given according to the later pagination.

_____, ed. 1944. *The Tractatus de successivis Attributed to William Ockham*. St. Bonaventure, NY: The Franciscan Institute.

_____. 1945. "In propria causa." *Franciscan Studies* 5, 37–54. Reprinted in Boehner 1958, 300–19.

_____. 1946a. "Ockham's Theory of Signification." *Franciscan Studies* 6, 143–70. Reprinted in Boehner 1958, 201–32.

_____. 1946b. "Ockham's Theory of Supposition and the Notion of Truth." *Franciscan Studies* 6, 261–92. Reprinted in Boehner 1958, 232–67.

_____. 1946c. "The Realistic Conceptualism of William Ockham." *Traditio* 4, 307–35. Reprinted (omitting a textual edition and its introduction, 319–35) in Boehner 1958, 156–74.

_____. 1952. *Medieval Logic: An Outline of Its Development from 1250 to c. 1400*. Manchester: Manchester University Press.

————. 1958. *Collected Articles on Ockham*. Edited by Eligius M. Buytaert. St. Bonaventure, NY: The Franciscan Institute.

————, ed. and trans. 1990. *William of Ockham: Philosophical Writings*. rev. ed. Indianapolis, IN.: Hackett. Original edition, London: Thomas Nelson, 1957.

Boethius. 1906. *Anicii Manlii Severini Boethii In Isagogen Porphyrii commenta*. Edited by Samuel Brandt. Vol. 48, "Corpus Scriptorum Ecclesiasticorum Latinorum." Vienna: F. Tempsky.

Bogen, James, with James E. McGuire, ed. 1985. *How Things Are: Studies in Predication and the History of Philosophy and Science*. Dordrecht: D. Reidel.

Boh, Ivan. 1966. "Conception of Nature and the Logical Structure of Medieval Law Statements." *La filosofia della natura nel medioevo: Atti del 3. Congresso internazionale di filosofia medioevale*. Milan: Vita e pensiero, 135–47.

Boler, John. 1973. "Ockham on Intuitive Cognition." *Journal of the History of Philosophy* 2, 95–106.

————. 1985. "Connotative Terms in Ockham." *History of Philosophy Quarterly* 22, 21–37.

————. 1990. "The Moral Psychology of Duns Scotus: Some Preliminary Questions." *Franciscan Studies* 28, 31–56.

————. 1993. "Transcending the Natural: Duns Scotus on the Two Affections of the Will." *American Catholic Philosophical Quarterly* 67, 109–126.

————. 1994–97. "Accidents in Ockham's Ontological Project." *Franciscan Studies* 54, 79–97.

————. 1998. "Ockham on Difference in Category." *Franciscan Studies* 56, 97–113.

Bonaventure. 1882–1902. *Opera omnia*. 10 vols. Quaracchi: Collegium S. Bonaventurae.

————. 1966. *The Works of Bonaventure: Cardinal, Seraphic Doctor, and Saint*. Vol. 4. Paterson, NJ: St. Anthony Guild Press.

Bosley, Richard N., with Martin Tweedale, ed. 1997. *Basic Issues in Medieval Philosophy: Selected Readings Presenting the Interactive Discourse among the Major Figures*. Peterborough (Canada): Broadview.

Bourke, Vernon J. 1968. *History of Ethics*. Garden City, NY: Doubleday.

Brampton, C. Kenneth 1963. "The Probable Order of Ockham's Nonpolemical Works." *Traditio* 19, 469–83.

————. 1964. "Nominalism and the Law of Parsimony." *The Modern Schoolman* 41, 273–81.

————. 1964. "Personalities in the Process Against Ockham at Avignon, 1324–1326." *Franciscan Studies* 26, 4–25.

Brett, Annabel S. 1997. *Liberty, Right and Nature: Individual Rights in Later Scholastic Thought*. Cambridge: Cambridge University Press.

Brooke, Rosalind B., ed. and trans. 1970. *The Writings of Leo, Rufino and Angelo, Companions of St. Francis*. Oxford: Clarendon Press.

Brown, Stephen F. 1966. "Richard of Conington and the Analogy of the Concept of Being."*Franziskanische Studien* 48, 297–307.

————. 1981. "A Modern Prologue to Ockham's Natural Philosophy." In *Sprache und Erkenntnis im Mittelalter: Akten des VI. internationalen Kongresses für mittelalterliche Philosophie der Societé internationale pour l'étude de la philosophie médiévale*. 2 vols. Berlin: Walter de Gruyter, vol. 1, 107–29.

————. 1985. "Walter Chatton's *Lectura* and William of Ockham's *Quaestiones in Libros Physicorum Aristotelis*." In *Essays Honoring Allan B. Wolter*, edited by William A. Frank and Girard J. Etzkorn, 81–115. St. Bonaventure, NY: The Franciscan Institute.

Burley (= Burleigh), Walter. *See* Walter Burley.

Burns, J. Patout. 1980. *The Development of Augustine's Doctrine of Operative Grace*. Paris: Études Augustiniennes.

Cajetan, Thomas de Vio. *See* Thomas de Vio (Cajetan).

Campsall, Richard of. *See* Richard of Campsall.

Chatton, Walter. *See* Walter Chatton.

Chesterton, G. K. 1908. *Orthodoxy*. San Francisco, CA: Ignatius Press.

Condillac, Étienne Bonnot de. 1788. *Essai sur l'origine des connaissances humaines*. rev. ed. 2 vols. Amsterdam: Changuion.

Conti, Alessandro D. 1990. "Ontology in Walter Burley's Last Commentary on the *Ars Vetus*." *Franciscan Studies* 50, 121–76.

Copleston, Frederick Charles. 1947–75. *A History of Philosophy*. 9 vols. Westminster, MD: The Newman Press.

Corvino, Francesco. 1966. "Il significato del termine natura nelle opere filosofiche di Occam." In *La filosofia della natura nel medioevo: Atti del 3. Congresso internazionale di filosofia medioevale*. Milan: Vita e pensiero, 605–15.

Courtenay, William J. 1978. *Adam Wodeham: An Introduction to His Life and Writings*. Leiden: E. J. Brill.

————. 1984. "The Reception of Ockham's Thought at the University of Paris." In *Preuve et raisons à l'Université de Paris: Logique, ontologie et théologie au XIVᵉ siècle*, edited by Zénon Kałuża and Paul Vignaux, 43–64. Paris: Vrin.

————. 1987a. "The Reception of Ockham's Thought in Fourteenth-Century England." In Hudson and Wilks 1987, 89–107.

————. 1987b. *Schools and Scholars in Fourteenth-Century England*. Princeton, NJ: Princeton University Press.

_____. 1990. "Ockham, Chatton, and the London *Studium:* Observations on Recent Changes in Ockham's Biography." In *Die Gegenwart Ockhams*, edited by Wilhelm Vossenkuhl and Rolf Schönberger, 327–37. Weinheim: VCH-Verlagsgesellschaft.

_____. 1991a. "The Articles Condemned at Oxford Austin Friars in 1315." In *Via Augustini: Augustine in the Later Middle Ages, Renaissance, and Reformation: Essays in Honor of Damasus Trapp*, edited by Heiko A. Oberman and Frank A. James III, 5–18. Leiden: E. J. Brill.

_____. 1991b. "*Nominales* and Nominalism in the Twelfth Century." In Jolivet et al. 1991, 11–48.

_____, ed. 1992. *Vivarium* 30.1 (May 1992). Special issue devoted to the origins and meaning of medieval nominalism.

_____. 1997. "The Debate over Ockham's Physical Theories at Paris." In *La nouvelle physique du 14. siècle*, edited by Stefano Caroti and P. Souffrin, 45–63. Firenze: L. S. Olschki.

Cova, Luciano. 1993. "La polemica contro la distinzione formale tra le perfezioni divine nelle *Questioni disputate di Riccardo di Conington*." In *Parva mediaevalia: Studi per Maria Elena Reina*, edited by Barbara Faes de Mottoni, 43–86. Trieste: Università degli studi di Trieste.

Cross, Richard. 1997. Review of McGrade and Kilcullen 1995. *Journal of Ecclesiastical History* 48, 164.

Davies, Julian, trans. 1989. *Ockham on Aristotle's Physics, A Translation of Ockham's Brevis Summa Libri Physicorum*. St. Bonaventure, NY: The Franciscan Institute.

Day, Sebastian. 1947. *Intuitive Cognition: A Key to the Significance of the Later Scholastics*. St. Bonaventure, NY: The Franciscan Institute.

Denifle, Heinrich, with Émile Chatelain, ed. 1889–97. *Chartularium Universitatis Parisiensis*. 4 vols. Paris: Delalain.

Denzinger, Heinrich, with Adolf Schönmetzer. 1976. *Enchiridion symbolorum definitionum et declarationum de rebus fidei et morum*. 36th ed. Barcelona: Herder.

Desharnais, R. Paul. 1966. "The History of the Distinction between God's Absolute and Ordained Power and Its Influence on Martin Luther." Ph.D. diss., Catholic University of America.

Dijksterhuis, Eduard Jan. 1961. *The Mechanization of the World Picture*. Translated by C. Dikshoorn. Oxford: Clarendon Press.

Dolcini, Carlo. 1977. *Il Pensiero politico di Michele da Cesena 1328–1338*. Faenza: Fratelli Lega Editori.

Dolnikowski, Edith Wilks. 1995. *Thomas Bradwardine: A View of Time and a Vision of Eternity in Fourteenth-Century Thought*. Leiden: E. J. Brill.

Domingo Soto. 1554. *Summulae*. 2d ed. Salamanca: Andreas a Portonariis. Reprint, Hildesheim: Georg Olms, 1980.

————. 1587. *In Porphyrii Isagogen, Aristotelis Categorias, librosque de demonstratione, Commentaria.* Venice: Dominicus Guarraei et Io. Baptista. Reprint, Frankfurt/Main: Minerva, 1967.

Doucet, Victorin. 1937. "L'Oeuvre scholastique de Richard de Conington." *Archivum Franciscanum Historicum* 29, 396–442.

Douie, Decima. 1932. *The Nature and the Effect of the Heresy of the Fraticelli.* Manchester: Manchester University Press.

Dretske, Fred. 1995. "Perception." In Audi 1995, 568–72.

Dumont, Stephen. 1989. "Theology as a Science and Duns Scotus's Distinction between Intuitive and Abstractive Cognition," *Speculum* 64, 579–99.

Dunne, John. 1969. *The Political Thought of John Locke.* Cambridge: Cambridge University Press.

————. 1979. *Western Political Theory in the Face of the Future.* Cambridge: Cambridge University Press.

Duns Scotus. *See* John Duns Scotus.

Dutton, Blake D. 1996. "Nicholas of Autrecourt and William of Ockham on Atomism, Nominalism, and the Ontology of Motion." *Medieval Philosophy and Theology* 5, 63–85.

Emden, Alfred Brotherston. 1957–59. *A Biographical Register of the University of Oxford to A.D. 1500.* 3 vols. Oxford: Clarendon Press.

Engelsma, David. 1980. *Hyper-Calvinism and the Call of the Gospel.* Grand Rapids, MI: Reformed Free Press Publishing Association.

Etzkorn, Girard J. 1977. "Walter Chatton and the Controversy on the Absolute Necessity of Grace." *Franciscan Studies* 37, 32–65.

————. 1987. "Codex Merton 284: Evidence of Ockham's Early Influence in Oxford." In Hudson and Wilks 1987, 31–42.

————. 1990. "Ockham at a Provincial Chapter: 1323. A Prelude to Avignon." *Archivum Franciscanum Historicum* 83, 557–67.

Eubel, Conrad, ed. 1898. *Bullarum Franciscanum.* Vol. 5. Rome: Typis Vaticanis.

Fairweather, Eugene R. 1956. *A Scholastic Miscellany: Anselm to Ockham.* London: SCM Press.

Farah, Martha J. 1990. *Visual Agnosia: Disorders of Object Recognition and What They Tell Us about Normal Vision.* Cambridge, MA: MIT Press.

Freddoso, Alfred J., with Francis E. Kelly, trans. 1991. *Quodlibetal Question.* 2 vols. New Haven, CT: Yale University Press.

Freddoso, Alfred J., with Henry Schuurman, trans. 1980. *Ockham's Theory of Propositions: Part II of the Summa Logicae.* Notre Dame, IN.: University of Notre Dame Press. Reprinted South Bend, IN.: St. Augustine's Press, 1997.

Freppert, Lucan. 1988. *The Basis of Morality according to William Ockham*. Chicago: Franciscan Herald Press.

Friedberg, Emil, ed. 1879–81. *Corpus iuris canonii*. 2 vols. Leipzig: B. Tauchnitz. Reprint, Graz: Akademische Druck- u. Verlagsanstalt, 1955.

Gál, Gedeon. 1971. "Henricus de Harclay: Quaestio de significato conceptus universalis." *Franciscan Studies* 31, 178–234.

————. 1982. "William of Ockham Died Impenitent in April 1347." *Franciscan Studies* 42, 90–5.

Gál, Gedeon, with Rega Wood. 1991. "The Ockham Edition: William of Ockham's *Opera philosophica et theologica*." *Franciscan Studies* 51, 83–101.

Geach, Peter Thomas. 1972. "Nominalism." In *Logic Matters*. Oxford: Basil Blackwell, 289–301.

Genest, Jean-François. 1979. "Le '*De futuris contingentibus*' de Thomas Bradwardine." *Recherches Augustiniennes* 14, 249–336.

————. 1992. *Prédétermination et liberté créée à Oxford au XIVe siècle: Buckingham contre Bradwardine, avec le texte latin de la "Determinatio de contingentia futurorum" de Thomas Buckingham*. Paris: Vrin.

Gewirth, Alan. 1951. *Marsilius of Padua and Medieval Political Philosophy*. New York: Columbia University Press.

Gibson, Arthur. "Ockham's World and Future." In Marenbon 1998, Chap. 14, 329–67.

Giles of Rome. (= Aegidius Romanus). 1521. *In Primum Librum Sententiarum*. Venice: [N.P.]. Reprint, Frankfurt/Main: Minerva, 1968.

————. 1986. *On Ecclesiastical Power*. Translated by R. W. Dyson. Woodbridge, Suffolk: The Boydell Press.

Glassberger, Nicholas. *See* Nicholas Glassberger.

Goddu, André. 1984a. *The Physics of William of Ockham*. Leiden: E. J. Brill.

————. 1984b. "William of Ockham's Arguments for Action at a Distance." *Franciscan Studies* 44, 227–44.

————. 1993. "Connotative Concepts and Mathematics in Ockham's Natural Philosophy." *Vivarium* 31, 106–39.

————. 1994. "Music as Art and Science in the Fourteenth Century." In *Scientia und ars im Hoch- und Spätmittelalter*, edited by Ingrid Craemer-Rügenberg and Andreas Speer, vol. 2, 1023–45. Berlin: Walter de Gruyter.

Goldast, Melchior. 1614. *Monarchia S. Romani imperii*. Vol. 2. Frankfurt: Conrad Biermann. Reprint, Graz: Akademische Druck- u. Verlagsanstalt, 1960.

Graham, Rose, ed. 1952. *Registrum Roberti Winchelsey Cantuariensis Archiepiscopi A. D. 1294–1313*. 2 vols. Oxford: Oxford University Press.

Grant, Edward, ed. 1974. *A Source Book in Medieval Science*. Cambridge, MA: Harvard University Press.

Grice, H. Paul. 1990. "Meaning." In *The Philosophy of Language*. 2d ed., edited by Aloysius Patrick Martinich, 72–8. New York: Oxford University Press. Originally published in *The Philosophical Review* 66 (1957), 377–88.

Habig, Marion, ed. 1983. *St. Francis of Assisi: Writings and Early Biographies*. Chicago: Franciscan Herald Press.

Hamesse, Jacqueline. 1974. *Les Auctoritates Aristotelis: un florilège médiéval: étude historique et édition critique*. Louvain: Publications univeritaires.

Hamilton, Sir William. 1853. *Discussions in Philosophy and Literature, Education and University Reform*. 2d ed. London: Longman, Brown, Green and Longman's.

Henninger, Mark G. 1989. *Relations: Medieval Theories 1250–1325*. Oxford: Clarendon Press.

Henry, Desmond Paul. 1972. *Medieval Logic and Metaphysics*. London: Routledge & Kegan Paul.

Heynick, Valens. 1950. "Ockham-Literatur 1919–1949." *Franziskanische Studien* 32, 164–83.

Hoenen, M. J. F. M. 1993. "Albertistae, Thomistae und Nominales: Die philosophisch-historischen Hintergrunde der Intellektlehre des Wessel Gansfort († 1489)." In *Wessel Gansfort (1419–1489) and Northern Humanism*, edited by Fokke Akkerman, Gerda C. Huisman, and Arie Johan Vanderjagt, 71–96. Leiden: E. J. Brill.

Hoffmann, Fritz. 1959. *Die Schriften des Oxforder Kanzlers Johannes Lutterell: Texte zur Theologie des vierzehnten Jahrhunderts*. Leipzig: St. Benno-Verlag.

————. 1994–97. "Die Bedeutung der Disputation für die Entwicklung der Theologie an der Universität Oxford zwischen 1322 und 1332." *Franciscan Studies* 54, 69–78.

Holopainen, Taina M. 1991. *William Ockham's Theory of the Foundations of Ethics*. Helsinki: [Luther-Agricola Society].

Hudson, Anne, with Michael Wilks, ed. 1987. *From Ockham to Wyclif*. Oxford: Basil Blackwell, for the Ecclesiastical History Society.

Hyman, Arthur, with James J. Walsh, ed. 1983. *Philosophy in the Middle Ages: The Christian, Islamic, and Jewish Traditions*. 2d ed. Indianapolis, IN: Hackett.

James of Viterbo. 1995. *On Christian Government*. Translated by R. W. Dyson. Woodbridge, Suffolk: The Boydell Press.

Jenkins, John. 1997. *Knowledge and Faith in Thomas Aquinas*. Cambridge: Cambridge University Press.

John Duns Scotus. 1639. *Opera omnia*. 12 vols. Edited by Luke Wadding. Lyon: Laurentius Durand. Photoreprint, Hildesheim: Georg Olms, 1968.

————. 1891–95. *Opera omnia*. 25 vols. Paris: L. Vivès.

————. 1950– . *Opera omnia*. Vatican: Ex Typis Polyglottis Vaticanis.

————. 1975. *God and Creatures: The Quodlibetal Questions*. Translated by Felix Alluntis and Allan B. Wolter. Princeton, NJ: Princeton University Press. Reprint, Washington, DC: The Catholic University of America Press, 1981.

————. 1986. *Duns Scotus on the Will and Morality*. Edited and translated by Allan B. Wolter. Washington, DC: The Catholic University of America Press.

————. 1987. *Philosophical Writings: A Selection*. Translated by Alan Wolter. Indianapolis, IN: Hackett Publishing Co. Reprint, with new foreword, introduction and bibliography. Originally published, Edinburgh: Nelson, 1963.

John of Paris. 1971. *On Royal and Papal Power*. Translated by J. A. Watt. Toronto: Pontifical Institute of Mediaeval Studies.

John Wyclif. 1985. *Tractatus de Universalibus*. Edited by Ivan J. Mueller. Oxford: Clarendon Press.

Jolivet, Jean, with Zénon Kałuża and Alain de Libera, eds. 1991. *Lectionum varietates: Hommage à Paul Vignaux (1904–1987)*. Paris: E. J. Vrin.

Kałuża, Zénon. 1988. *Lesquerelles doctrinales à Paris. Nominalistes et réalistes aux confins du XIVe et du XVe siècles*. Bergamo: P. Lubrina.

Kane, Robert. 1996. *The Significance of Free Will*. New York: Oxford University Press.

Kant, Immanuel. 1960. *Religion Within the Limits of Reason Alone*. Translated by Theodore M. Greene and Hoyt H. Hudson. New York: Harper & Row.

Karger, Elizabeth. 1980. "Would Ockham Have Shaved Wyman's Beard?" *Franciscan Studies* 40, 244–64.

————. 1984. "Modes of Personal Supposition: The Purpose and Usefulness of the Doctrine Within Ockham's Logic." *Franciscan Studies* 44, 87–106.

————. 1991. "Référence et non-existence dans la sémantique de Guillaume d'Ockham." In Jolivet et al. 1991, 163–76.

————. 1996. "Mental Sentences According to Burley and to the Early Ockham." *Vivarium* 34, 192–230.

Kaufmann, Matthias. 1994. *Begriffe, Sätze, Dinge: Referenz und Wahrheit bei Wilhelm von Ockham*. Leiden: E. J. Brill.

Kaye, Sharon Marie 1997. "William of Ockham's Theory of Conscience." Ph.D. diss., University of Toronto.

Kilcullen, John. 1993. "Natural Law and Will in Ockham." *History of Philosophy Yearbook* (The Australasian Society for the History of Philosophy) Vol. 1, 1–25. Also available under the title "Natural Law and Will" as an appendix to Kilcullen and Scott 1998.

Kilcullen, John, with John Scott, trans. 1998. *The Work of Ninety Days.* Charlottesville, VA: InteLex.

Kingsford, Charles Lethbridge. 1915. *The Grey Friars of London: Their History, with the Register of Their Convent and an Appendix of Documents.* Aberdeen: The University Press.

Klima, Gyula. 1991. "Ontological Alternatives vs. Alternative Semantics in Medieval Philosophy," *S: European Journal for Semiotic Studies* 3, 587–618.

―――. 1993a. "'Socrates est species': Logic, Metaphysics and Psychology in St. Thomas Aquinas' Treatment of a Paralogism." In *Argumentationstheorie: Scholastische Forschungen zu den logischen und semantischen Regeln korrekten Folgerns*, edited by Klaus Jacobi, 489–504. Leiden: E. J. Brill.

―――. 1993b. "The Changing Role of Entia Rationis in Medieval Philosophy: A Comparative Study with a Reconstruction," *Synthese* 96, 25–59.

―――. 1996. "The Semantic Principles Underlying Saint Thomas Aquinas's Metaphysics of Being." *Medieval Philosophy and Theology* 5, 87–141.

―――. Forthcoming a. "Contemporary 'Essentialism' vs. Aristotelian Essentialism." *Thomistic Papers* 7.

―――. Forthcoming b. "Old Directions in Free Logic: Existence and Reference in Medieval Logic." In *New Directions in Free Logic*, edited by Karel Lambert. Sankt Augustin bei Bonn: Akademia Verlag.

Kluge, Eike-Henner W., trans. 1973–74. "William of Ockham's Commentary on Porphyry: Introduction and English Translation." *Franciscan Studies* 33 (1973), 171–254; 34 (1974), 306–82.

Kneale, William and Martha. 1962. *The Development of Logic.* Oxford: Clarendon Press.

Knowles, David. 1962. *The Evolution of Medieval Thought.* New York: Random House.

Knysh, George. 1986. "Biographical Rectifications concerning Ockham's Avignon Period." *Franciscan Studies* 46, 61–92.

―――. 1994. *Ockham Perspectives.* Winnipeg: The Ukrainian Academy of Arts and Sciences in Canada (UVAN).

―――. 1996. *Political Ockhamism.* Winnipeg: WCU Council of Learned Societies.

Koch, J. 1935–36. "Neue Aktenstücke zu dem gegen Wilhelm Ockham in Avignon geführten Prozess." *Recherches de théologie ancienne et médiévale* 7 (1935), 353–80; 8 (1936), 79–93, 158–97.

Kretzmann, Norman, trans. 1966. *William of Sherwood's Introduction to Logic*. Minneapolis: University of Minnesota Press.

————, trans. 1968. *William of Sherwood's Treatise on Syncategorematic Words*. Minneapolis: University of Minnesota Press.

————, ed. 1982. *Infinity and Continuity in Ancient and Medieval Thought*. Ithaca, NY: Cornell University Press.

————. 1991. "Infallibility, Error, and Ignorance." In Tweedale and Bosley 1991, 159–194.

Kretzmann, Norman, with Anthony Kenny and Jan Pinborg, ed. 1982. *The Cambridge History of Later Medieval Philosophy*. New York: Cambridge University Press.

Kretzmann, Norman, with Eleonore Stump, ed. and trans. 1988. *The Cambridge Translations of Medieval Philosophical Texts*. Vol. 1: *Logic and the Philosophy of Language*. Cambridge: Cambridge University Press.

————, ed. 1993. *The Cambridge Companion to Aquinas*. New York: Cambridge University Press.

Lahey, Stephen. 1998. "William of Ockham and Trope Nominalism." *Franciscan Studies* 55, 105–20.

Lambert of Auxerre. 1971. *Logica (Summa Lamberti)*. Edited by Franco Alessio. Firenze: La nuova Italia editrice.

Lambert, Malcolm. 1961. *Franciscan Poverty: The Doctrine of the Absolute Poverty of Christ and the Apostles in the Franciscan Order, 1210–1323*. London: S. P. C. K.

————. 1977. *Medieval Heresy: Popular Movements from Bogomil to Hus*. New York: Holmes & Meier.

Lambertini, Roberto. 1994–97. "*Usus* and *usuria*: Poverty and Usury in Franciscans' Responses to John XXII's *Quia vir reprobus*." *Franciscan Studies* 54, 185–210.

Lang, Helen S. 1992. *Aristotle's Physics and Its Medieval Varieties*. Albany, NY: State University of New York Press.

Leff, Gordon. 1957. *Bradwardine and the Pelagians: A Study of his "De causa dei" and Its Opponents*. Cambridge: Cambridge University Press.

————. 1967. *Heresy in the Later Middle Ages: The Relation of Heterodoxy to Dissent, c. 1250–c. 1450*. Manchester: Manchester University Press.

Leppin, Volker. 1995. *Geglaubte Wahrheit: Das Theologieverstandnis Wilhelms von Ockham*. Göttingen: Vandenhoeck & Ruprecht.

————. 1998. "Does Ockham's Concept of Divine Power Threaten Man's Certainty in His Knowledge of the World?" *Franciscan Studies* 55, 169–80.

Lerner, Ralph, with Muhsin Mahdi, ed. 1963. *Medieval Political Philosophy: A Sourcebook*. New York: The Free Press.

Lewis, David. 1986. *On the Plurality of Worlds*. Oxford: Blackwell, 145–46.

Lewis, Ewart. 1954. *Medieval Political Ideas*. 2 vols. New York: Knopf.

Lindberg, David C. 1992. *The Beginnings of Western Science: The European Scientific Tradition in Philosophical, Religious, and Institutional Context, 600 B.C. to A.D. 1450*. Chicago: University of Chicago Press.

Livesey, Steven J. 1985. "William of Ockham, the Subalternate Sciences, and Aristotle's Theory of *Metabasis.*" *British Journal for the History of Science* 18, 127–45.

Lombard, Peter. *See* Peter Lombard.

Longpré, Ephrem. 1924. "Jean de Reading et le B. Jean Duns Scot." *La France Franciscaine* 7, 99–109.

Loux, Michael J., trans. 1974. *Ockham's Theory of Terms: Part I of the Summa Logicae*. Notre Dame, IN: University of Notre Dame Press. Reprinted, South Bend, IN.: St. Augustine's Press, 1997.

MacDonald, Scott, with Robert Pasnau, ed. and trans. Forthcoming. *The Cambridge Translations of Medieval Philosophical Texts: Epistemology and Philosophical Psychology*. Cambridge: Cambridge University Press.

MacIntosh, J. J. 1998. "Aquinas and Ockham on Time, Predestination, and the Unexpected Examination." *Franciscan Studies* 55, 181–220.

MacIntyre, Alisdair. 1990. *First Principles, Final Ends and Contemporary Philosophical Issues*. Milwaukee, WI: Marquette University Press.

Maier, Anneliese. 1958. *Zwischen Philosophie und Mechanik*. Rome: Edizioni di Storia e Letteratura.

————. 1963. "Das Problem der Evidenz in der Philosophie des 14. Jahrhunderts." *Scholastik* 38, 183–225. Reprinted in Maier 1964–77, II.366–419. References are given according to the later pagination.

————. 1964–77 *Ausgehendes Mittelalter: Gesammelte Aufsätze zur Geistesgeschichte des 14. Jahrhunderts*. 3 vols. Rome: Edizioni di Storia e Letteratura.

Mann, William E. 1991. "The Best of All Possible Worlds." In *Being and Goodness: The Concept of the Good in Metaphysics and Philosophical Theology*, edited by Scott MacDonald, 250–77. Ithaca: Cornell University Press.

Marenbon, John, 1998, ed. *Routledge History of Philosophy, Volume III: Medieval Philosophy*. London: Routledge.

Markosian, Ned. 1988. "On Ockham's Supposition and Karger's Rule of Inference." *Franciscan Studies* 48, 40–52.

Marsilius of Padua. 1980. *Defensor pacis*. Translated by Alan Gewirth. Toronto: University of Toronto Press.

Marston, Roger. *See* Roger Marston.

Matthew of Aquasparta. 1935. *Quaestiones disputatae de gratia*. Quaracchi: Collegium. S. Bonaventurae.

————. 1957. *Quaestiones disputatae selectae: Quaestiones de fide et de cognitione*. 2d ed. Quaracchi: Collegium S. Bonaventurae. (1st ed. 1903.)

Maurer, Armand A. 1962. *Medieval Philosophy*. New York: Random House.

————. 1978. "Method in Ockham's Nominalism." *The Monist* 61, 426–43.

————. 1984. "Ockham's Razor and Chatton's Anti-Razor." *Mediaeval Studies* 46, 463–75.

McGrade, A. S. 1974a. Abstract of "Natural Law as Tacit Divine Command: A Supplement to Ockham." *The Journal of Philosophy* 71, 750.

————. 1974b. *The Political Thought of William of Ockham*. Cambridge: Cambridge University Press.

————. 1980. "Ockham and the Birth of Individual Rights." In *Authority and Power: Studies on Medieval Law and Government Presented to Walter Ullmann on his Seventieth Birthday*, edited by Brian Tierney and Peter Linehan, 149–65. Cambridge: Cambridge University Press.

————. 1981. "Ockham on Enjoyment: Towards an Understanding of Fourteenth-Century Philosophy and Psychology." *The Review of Metaphysics* 34, 706–28.

————. 1985. "Plenty of Nothing: Ockham's Commitment to Real Possibles." *Franciscan Studies* 45, 145–56.

————. 1987. "Enjoyment at Oxford after Ockham: Philosophy, Psychology, and the Love of God." In Hudson and Wilks 1987, 63–88.

————. 1996. "Aristotle's Place in the History of Natural Rights." *The Review of Metaphysics* 49, 803–29.

————. 1994–97. "William of Ockham and Augustinus de Ancona on the Righteousness of Dissent." *Franciscan Studies* 54, 143–65.

McGrade, A. S., ed., with John Kilcullen, ed. and trans. 1992. *A Short Discourse on the Tyrannical Government Over Things Divine and Human, but Especially Over the Empire and Those Subject to the Empire, Usurped by Some Who Are Called Highest Pontiffs*. Cambridge: Cambridge University Press.

————. 1995. *William of Ockham: A Letter to the Friars Minor and Other Writings*. Cambridge: Cambridge University Press.

McMullin, Ernan. 1965. "Medieval and Modern Science: Continuity or Discontinuity?" *International Philosophical Quarterly* 5, 103–28.

Michon, Cyrille. 1994. *Nominalisme: La théorie de la signification d'Occam*. Paris: Vrin.

Miethke, Jürgen. 1969. *Ockhams Weg zur Sozialphilosophie*. Berlin: Walter de Gruyter.

————, trans. 1992. *Wilhelm von Ockham: Dialogus: Auszüge zur politischen Theorie*. Darmstadt: Wissenschaftliche Buchgesellschaft. Selections in German translation.

————. 1994. "Ockham-Perspektiven oder Entführung in eine falsche Richtung? Eine Polemik gegen eine neuere Publikation zu Ockhams Biographie." *Mittellateinisches Jahrbuch* 29, 61–82.

————. 1994–97. "Herrschaft und Freiheit in der politischen Theorie des 14. Jahrhunderts." *Franciscan Studies* 54, 123–41.

————, ed. and trans. 1995. *Wilhelm von Ockham: Texte zur politischen Theorie: Exzerpte aus dem Dialogus*. Stuttgart: Reclam. Latin and German.

————. 1998. "Die 'Octo Quaestiones' Wilhelms von Ockham in zwei unbeachteten Handschriften in Lissabon und Tübingen." *Franciscan Studies* 56, 279–305.

Miethke, Jürgen, with Arnold Buhler, ed. 1992. *Das Publikum politischer Theorie im 14 Jahrhundert*. Munich: Oldenbourg.

Migne, Jacques-Paul. 1844–64. *Patrologiae cursus completus ... series latina*. 221 vols. Paris: J.-P. Migne.

Moody, Ernest A. 1935. *The Logic of William of Ockham*. New York: Sheed and Ward. Reprinted, 1965 New York: Russell & Russell.

————. 1953. *Truth and Consequence in Mediaeval Logic*. Amsterdam: North-Holland.

————. 1975. "Ockham and Aegidius of Rome." In his *Studies in Medieval Philosophy, Science, and Logic*. Berkeley: University of California Press, 161–88.

Moore, Walter L. 1989. "Via Moderna." In *Dictionary of the Middle Ages*. 13 vols., edited by Joseph Reece Strayer, XII. 406–9. New York: Scribner's.

Murdoch, John E. 1981. "*Scientia mediantibus vocibus*: Metalinguistic Analysis in Late Medieval Natural Philosophy." *Sprache und Erkenntnis im Mittelalter: Akten des VI. internationalen Kongresses für mittelalterliche Philosophie der Societé internationale pour l'étude de la philosophie médiévale*. 2 vols. Berlin: Walter de Gruyter, Vol. 1, 73–106.

Murray, John Courtney. 1964. *The Problem of God*. New Haven, CT.: Yale University Press.

Nicholas Glassberger. 1887–97. *Chronica fratris Nicolai Glassberger*. In *Analecta Franciscana*. Quaracchi: Collegium S. Bonaventurae, 1887 (vol. 2), 1897 (vol. 3).

Normore, Calvin G. 1985. "Buridan's Ontology." In Bogen and McGuire 1985, 189–203.

————. 1987. "The Tradition of Mediaeval Nominalism." In Wippel 1987, 201–17.

————. 1990. "Ockham on Mental Language." In *Historical Foundations of Cognitive Science*, edited by J.-C. Smith, 53–70. Dordrecht: Kluwer.

————. 1997. "Material Supposition and the Mental Language of Ockham's *Summa logicae*." *Topoi* 16, 27–33.

————, ed. Forthcoming. *The Language of Thought: The Medieval Perspective*. Toronto: University of Toronto Press.

Oakley, Francis. 1961. "Medieval Theories of Natural Law: William of Ockham and the Significance of the Voluntarist Tradition." *Natural Law Forum* 6, 65–83.

Oberman, Heiko Augustinus. 1957. *Archbishop Thomas Bradwardine, a Fourteenth Century Augustinian: A Study of His Theology in Its Historical Context*. Utrecht: Kemink.

Ockham, William of. *See* William of Ockham.

Panaccio, Claude. 1983. "Guillaume d'Occam: Signification et supposition." In *Archéologie du signe*, edited by Lucie Brind'Amour and Eugene Vance, 265–86. Toronto: Pontifical Institute of Mediaeval Studies, 1983.

————. 1990. "Connotative Terms in Ockham's Mental Language." *Cahiers d'épistémologie*, No. 9016. Montréal: Université du Québec à Montréal. To be reprinted in Normore forthcoming.

————. 1992. *Les Mots, Les Concepts et Les Choses. Le sémantique de Guillaume d'Occam et le nominalisme d'aujourdhui*. Montréal: Bellarmin.

Pasnau, Robert. 1997. *Theories of Cognition in the Later Middle Ages*. New York: Cambridge University Press.

Pelikan, Jaroslav. 1971. *The Emergence of the Catholic Tradition (100–600)*. Chicago: University of Chicago Press.

Pelster, Franz. 1924. "Heinrich von Harclay, Kanzler von Oxford und seine Quästionen." In *Miscallanea Francesco Ehrle: Scritti di storia e paleografia*. 5 vols. Roma: Biblioteca apostolica vaticana, I.307–56.

Perler, Dominik. 1988. *Prädestination, Zeit und Kontingenz: Philosophisch-historische Untersuchungen zu Wilhelm von Ockhams Tractatus de praedestinatione et de praescientia dei respectu futurorum contingentium*. Amsterdam: B. R. Grüner.

Peter Abelard. 1970. *Dialectica*. Rev. ed. Edited by Lambert M. De Rijk. Assen: Van Gorcum.

Peter Lombard. 1971–81. *Sententiae in IV libris distinctae*. 2 vols. in 3. 3d ed. Quaracchi: Collegium S. Bonaventurae.

Peter of Spain. 1972. *Tractatus, Called Afterwards Summule Logicales*. Edited by Lambert M. De Rijk. Assen: Van Gorcum.

Priest, Graham, with Stephen Read. 1981. "Ockham's Rejection of Ampliation." *Mind* 90, 274–9.

(Pseudo-) Campsall. *See* Richard of Campsall (Pseudo-).

Reilly, James P. 1968. "Ockham-Bibliography, 1950–1967." *Franciscan Studies* 28, 197–214.

Richard of Campsall. 1982. *The Works of Richard Campsall*. Vol. 2. Edited by Edward A. Synan. Toronto: Pontifical Institute of Mediaeval Studies.

Richard of Campsall (Pseudo-). 1982. *Logica Campsale Angicj ualde utilis et realis contra Ocham*. In Campsall 1982, 51–420.

Roensch, Frederick J. 1964. *Early Thomist School*. Dubuque, IA: Priory Press.

Roger Marston. 1932. *Quaestiones disputatae: De emanatione aeterna, De statu naturae lapsae et De anima*. Quaracchi: Collegium S. Bonaventurae.

Rome, Giles of. *See* Giles of Rome.

Salter, Herbert Edward, ed. 1924. *Snappe's Formulary and Other Records*. Oxford: Clarendon Press.

Santidrian, Pedro Rodríguez, trans. 1992. *Guillermo de Ockham. Sobre el gobierno tiránico del papa*. Madrid: Tecnos, 1992. Spanish translation of *Brev*.

Schoedinger, Andrew B., ed. 1996. *Readings in Medieval Philosophy*. New York: Oxford University Press.

Scholz, Richard. 1911–14. *Unbekannte kirchenpolitische Stretschriften aus der Zeit Ludwigs des Bayern (1327–1354)*. 2 vols. Rome: Loescher.

————. 1944. *Wilhelm von Ockham als politischer Denker und sein Breviloquium de Principatu Tyrannico*. "Monumenta Germaniae Historica," Schriften, VIII. Stuttgart: Anton Hiersemann.

Scott, T. K., trans. 1966. *John Buridan: Sophisms on Meaning and Truth*. New York: Appleton-Century-Crofts.

————. 1969. "Ockham on Evidence, Necessity and Intuition." *Journal of the History of Philosophy* 7, 27–49.

Scotus, John Duns. *See* John Duns Scotus.

Searle, John R. 1969. *Speech Acts: An Essay in the Philosophy of Language*. Cambridge: Cambridge University Press. Reprinted 1974.

Sellars, Wilfrid. 1970. "Toward a Theory of the Categories." In *Experience & Theory*, edited by J. W. Swanson, 55–78. London: Duckworth.

Soto, Domingo. *See* Domingo Soto.

Spade, Paul Vincent. 1974. "Ockham's Rule of Supposition: Two Conflicts in His Theory." *Vivarium* 12, 63–73. Reprinted in Spade 1988.

————. 1975 "Ockham's Distinctions between Absolute and Connotative Terms." *Vivarium* 13, 55–76. Reprinted in Spade 1988.

————. 1980. "Synonymy and Equivocation in Ockham's Mental Language." *Journal of the History of Philosophy* 18, 9–22. Reprinted in Spade 1988.

_____. 1988. *Lies, Language and Logic in the Late Middle Ages.* London: Variorum Reprints.

_____. 1990. "Ockham, Adams and Connotation: A Critical Notice of Marilyn Adams, *William Ockham.*" *The Philosophical Review* 99, 593–612.

_____. 1994–97. "The Logic of *Sit verum* in Richard Brinkley and William of Ockham." *Franciscan Studies* 54, 227–50.

_____, trans. 1994. *Five Texts on the Mediaeval Problem of Universals: Porphyry, Boethius, Abelard, Duns Scotus, Ockham.* Indianapolis, IN: Hackett.

_____, trans. 1995. *William of Ockham: From His Summa of Logic, Part I: Adam (of Wodeham's) Prologue, Ockham's Prefatory Letter and Chs. 1–5, 6, 8–13, 26–28, 30–31, 33, 63–66, 70, 72, with Summaries of Chs. 7, 29, 32.* Available in Adobe PDF format at http://pvspade.com/Logic.

_____. 1996. *Thoughts, Words and Things: An Introduction to Late Mediaeval Logic and Semantic Theory.* Version 1.0. Available in Adobe PDF format at http://pvspade.com/Logic.

_____. 1998a. "Late Medieval Logic." In Marenbon 1998, Chap. 17, 402–25.

_____. 1998b. "Three Versions of Ockham's Reductionist Program." *Franciscan Studies* 56, 335–46.

Spain, Peter of. *See* Peter of Spain.

Spruit, Leen. 1994. *Species intelligibilis: From Perception to Knowledge.* Vol. 1: *Classical Roots and Medieval Discussions.* Leiden: E. J. Brill.

Strawson, Peter Frederick. 1991. "Intention and Convention in Speech Acts." In *Pragmatics: A Reader*, edited by Steven Davis, 290–301. New York: Oxford University Press. Originally published in *The Philosophical Review* 73 (1974), 439–60.

Strehle, Stephen. 1988. *Calvinism, Federalism, and Scholasticism: A Study of the Reformed Doctrine of Covenant.* New York: Peter Lang.

Streveler, Paul. 1975. "Ockham and His Critics on Intuitive Cognition." *Franciscan Studies* 35, 223–36.

Stump, Eleonore. 1982. "Theology and Physics in *De sacramento altaris*: Ockham's Theory of Indivisibles." In Kretzmann 1982, 207–30.

_____. 1991. "Aquinas on the Foundations of Knowledge." In Tweedale and Bosley, 1991, 125–58.

_____. 1993. "Intellect, Will, and the Principle of Alternate Possibilities." In *Moral Responsibility*, edited by John Martin Fischer and Mark Ravizza, 237–62. Ithaca, New York: Cornell University Press.

_____. 1996a. "Libertarianism and the Principle of Alternative Possibilities." In *Faith, Freedom, and Rationality*, edited by Jeff Jordan and Dan Howard-Snyder, 73–88. Englewood Cliffs, NJ: Rowman and Littlefield.

_____. 1996b. "Persons: Identification and Freedom." *Philosophical Topics* 24, 183–214.

_____. 1997 "Aquinas's Account of Freedom: Intellect and Will." *The Monist* 80,576–97.

_____. 1998. "Aquinas's Account of the Mechanisms of Intellective Cognition." *Revue internationale de philosophie* 25, 287–307.

_____. Forthcoming. "Aquinas on Sensory Cognition." In *The Copenhagen School of Medieval Philosophy*, edited by Sten Ebbesen.

Suarez, Francisco. 1960. *Disputaciones metafísicas*. 2 vols. Madrid: Editorial Gredos.

Suk Othmar. 1950. "The Connection of the Virtues According to Ockham." *Franciscan Studies* 10, 9–32 and 91–113.

Swiniarski, John J. 1970. "A New Presentation of Ockham's Theory of Supposition with an Evaluation of Some Contemporary Criticisms." *Franciscan Studies* 30, 181–217.

Sykes, Norman. 1956. *Old Priest and New Presbyter*. Cambridge: Cambridge University Press.

Tachau, Katherine H. 1988. *Vision and Certitude in the Age of Ockham: Optics, Epistemology and the Foundations of Semantics, 1250–1345*. Leiden: E. J. Brill.

Tanquerey, A. 1959. *A Manual of Dogmatic Theology*. Edited by J. Brynes. New York: Desclée.

Thomas Aquinas. 1882– . *Opera omnia*. Vatican: Vatican Polyglot Press.

_____. 1949. *On Kingship, to the King of Cyprus*. Translated by Gerald B. Phelan. Toronto: Pontifical Institute of Mediaeval Studies.

Thomas de Vio (Cajetan). 1939. *Scripta Philosophica: Commentaria in Praedicamenta Aristotelis*. Edited by Marie-Hyacinthe Laurent. Rome: Angelicum.

_____. 1964. *Commentary on Being and Essence*. Translated by Lottie H. Kendzierski and Francis C. Wade. Milwaukee, WI: Marquette University Press.

Thomas, Laurence. 1990. "Trust, Affirmation, and Moral Character: A Critique of Kantian Morality." In *Identity, Character and Morality: Essays in Moral Psychology*, edited by Owen Flanagan and Amelie Oksenberg Rorty, 235–57. Cambridge, MA: MIT Press.

Tierney, Brian. 1954. "Ockham, the Conciliar Theory, and the Canonists." *Journal of the History of Ideas* 15, 40–70.

_____.1955. *Foundations of the Conciliar Theory: The Contribution of the Medieval Canonists from Gratian to the Great Schism*. London: Cambridge University Press.

_____. 1980. *The Crisis of Church and State, 1050–1300*. Englewood Cliffs, NJ: Prentice Hall.

————. 1988. *Origins of Papal Infallibility, 1150–1350: A Study on the Concepts of Infallibility, Sovereignty and Tradition in the Middle Ages.* 2d impression with postscript. Leiden: E. J. Brill. Originally published 1972.

————. 1997. *The Idea of Natural Rights: Studies on Natural Rights, Natural Law and Church Law* 1150–1625. Atlanta: Scholars Press.

Trentman, John. 1970. "Ockham on Mental."*Mind* 79, 586–90.

Tweedale, Martin M. 1992. "Ockham's Supposed Elimination of Connotative Terms and His Ontological Parsimony." *Dialogue* 31, 431–44.

Tweedale, Martin, and Bosley, Richard, ed. 1991. *Aristotle and His Medieval Interpreters.* Calgary: University of Calgary Press (= *Canadian Journal of Philosophy*, Supplementary Volume 17).

Urban, Linwood. 1973. "William of Ockham's Theological Ethics." *Franciscan Studies* 33, 310–50.

Vignaux, Paul. 1930–50. "Nominalisme." In *Dictionnaire de Théologie Catholique*, Vol. XI, cols. 717–84.

Walter Burley. 1955. *De puritate artis logicae tractatus longior, with a Revised Edition of the Tractatus brevior.* Edited by Philotheus Boehner. St. Bonaventure, NY: The Franciscan Institute.

Walter Chatton. 1989. *Reportatio et Lectura super Sententias: Collatio ad Librum Primum et Prologus.* Edited by Joseph C. Wey. Toronto: Pontifical Institute of Mediaeval Studies.

Weisheipl, James A. 1974. *Friar Thomas D'Aquino: His Life, Thought, and Work.* Garden City, NY: Doubleday.

Weiskrantz, Lawrence. 1997. *Consciousness Lost and Found: A Neuropsychological Exploration.* Oxford: Oxford University Press.

William of Ockham. 1496. *Opera plurima.* Bologna: Benedict Hector of Bologna.

————. 1956–97. *Opera politica.* Edited by H. S. Offler et al. 4 vols. Vols. 1–3, Manchester: Manchester University Press, 1956–74. (Vol. 1 first published 1940, revised 1974.) Vol. 4, Oxford: Oxford University Press, 1997.

————. 1967–88. *Opera philosophica et theologica.* Edited by Gedeon Gál et al. 17 vols. St. Bonaventure, NY: The Franciscan Institute.

————. Forthcoming. *Dialogus.* John Kilcullen and John Scott, ed. and trans. "Auctores Britannici Medii Aevi." This is a work in progress, being published on the Internet at http://britac3.britac.ac.uk/ockdial.html.

Williams, W. Thomas. 1994. *The Moral Philosophy of John Duns Scotus.* Ph.D. diss., University of Notre Dame.

Wippel, John F., ed. 1987. *Studies in Medieval Philosophy.* Washington, DC: The Catholic University of America Press.

Wippel, John F., with Allan B. Wolter, ed. 1969. *Medieval Philosophy From St. Augustine to Nicholas of Cusa.* New York: The Free Press.

Wöhler, Hans-Ulrich. 1994. "Die Naturphilosophie als *"scientia realis"* bei Wilhelm von Ockham." In *Scientia und ars im Hoch- und Spätmittelalter,* edited by Ingrid Craemer-Rügenberg and Andreas Speer, Vol. 1, 440–5. Berlin: Walter de Gruyter.

Wolter, Allan B. 1972. "Native Freedom of the Will as a Key to the Ethics of Scotus." In *Deus et homo ad mentem I. Duns Scoti: Acta tertii Congressus scotistici internationalis.* Rome: Societas internationalis scotistica, 1972, 360–70. Reprinted in Wolter 1990b, 148–62.

————. 1990a. "Duns Scotus on the Will as Rational Power." In Wolter 1990b, 163–80.

————. 1990b. *The Philosophical Theology of John Duns Scotus.* Edited by Marilyn McCord Adams. Ithaca, NY: Cornell University Press.

Wolter, Allan B., with Marilyn McCord Adams. 1994–97. "Memory and Intuition: A Focal Debate in Fourteenth Century Cognitive Psychology." *Franciscan Studies* 54, 175–230.

Wood, Rega. 1994. "Göttliches Gebot und Gutheit nach Wilhelm von Ockham." *Philosophisches Jahrbuch* 101, 38–54.

————, trans. 1997. *Ockham on the Virtues.* West Lafayette, IN.: Purdue University Press.

Wood, Rega, with Robert Andrews. 1996. "Causality and Demonstration: An Early Scholastic 'Posterior Analytics' Commentary." *The Monist* 79, 325–56.

Wyclif, John. *See* John Wyclif.

Yrjönsuuri, Mikko. 1997. "Supposition and Truth in Ockham's Mental Language." *Topoi* 16, 15–25.

Zeki, Semir. 1993. *A Vision of the Brain.* Oxford: Blackwell Scientific Publications. Reprinted with corrections 1994.

Zheng, Yiwei. 1998. "Metaphysical Simplicity and Semantical Complexity of Connotative Terms in Ockham's Mental Language." *The Modern Schoolman* 75, 253–64.

INDEX

Names in the Bibliography are not indexed here unless they do not appear in the articles or notes of this volume.

403

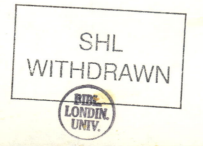